The church in British archaeology

Frontispiece   Hadstock (Essex): detail of double-splayed window showing Anglo-Saxon wooden window-frame. (Photo: W J Rodwell)

The church

in British

archaeology

Richard Morris

In this report 'church archaeology' is taken to be the
complete historical study of the material remains of a
church, above and below ground, in relation to its site,
contents, historic setting, and to the community it has
served. The objectives of such study are explained
within.

1983

Research Report 47   The Council for British Archaeology

Copyright © 1983 Richard Morris and the Council for
British Archaeology

ISBN 0 906780 17 9

Designed by Allan Cooper FSIA and Henry Cleere

Published by the Council for British Archaeology
112 Kennington Road
London SE11 6RE

Printed and bound at The Camelot Press Ltd, Southampton

British Library Cataloguing in Publication Data

Morris, Richard
   The church in British archaeology. – (CBA research reports,
   ISSN 0589-9036; 47)
   1. Christian antiquities – Great Britain
   2. Churches – Great Britain – History
   3. Great Britain – Antiquities
   I. Title   II. Series
   941   BR133.G6

   ISBN 0-906780–17–9

Contents

Illustrations

Tables

Preface and acknowledgements

Professor Martin Biddle prophesied the appearance of this report nearly ten years ago, in his preface to *The erosion of history* (Heighway 1972). At that time the report was conceived as a lineal successor to *The erosion of history*, being intended to do for ecclesiastical sites what had then just been done for towns.

In embryo the report did resemble the prototype. Emphasis was placed upon the problems and trends of church redundancy, inadequacies of archaeological provision, shortcomings in legislation, and the analysis and quantification of archaeological threats to churches in use.

Almost before the report was begun, however, the changes that it was intended to bring about were beginning to occur. Mainly as a result of evangelization by the CBA, many Anglican dioceses and most of the national ecclesiastical statutory bodies were quick to appreciate the importance and vulnerability of archaeological evidence in and around churches. The extent of this awakening can now be seen in the fact that diocesan archaeological consultants exist in nearly all dioceses, and that a number of cathedrals and several greater churches have made similar appointments. In promoting its policies for the integration of archaeology with the processes of caring for churches, therefore, the CBA Churches Committee has found itself pushing against an open door, and although much remains to be done the cause can be forwarded as well through diplomacy as by formal public statement. The Committee has, in addition, been active in promoting publications of various kinds which, when taken together, have already covered much of the ground which might have been occupied by an '*Erosion of churches*'.

As a result of these developments, the design of this report has undergone a process of progressive modification, shedding its graphs of demolitions and tales of archaeological damage and moving towards an expansion of what was originally envisaged merely as one part of one chapter: namely, a discussion of the academic purpose of the archaeological study of churches. It must be confessed here at the outset that the discussion which has emerged is by turn overdetailed, superficial, spe-culative, argumentative, and repetitive. Themes that deserve theses are given fleeting treatment, while some others are tackled in ways that might seem unduly tedious. There is a certain amount of clumsy trespassing into areas that it might have been safer, if less interesting, to leave unentered. The field of church archaeology is so large, adjoins so many others, and spans so great a period of time that consistency in approach would have been impossible to achieve. Hence there are no 'last words' here on anything. The report aims simply to draw together, to use a broad perspective for the presentation of issues which are more usually viewed through a microscope, and to offer a few ideas.

With the exception of the last chapter, which is the work of Dr Lawrence Butler, the drafting of the text has been done by myself. However, this fact conceals the very considerable direct and indirect contributions which have been made by members of the CBA Churches Committee who have read, criticized, and improved parts of the various drafts as work proceeded: Mr P V Addyman (Chairman of the Churches Committee at the time the report was begun), Professor R N Bailey, Dr L A S Butler, Professor Rosemary Cramp (Chairman), Mr Ian Fisher, Mr D. J. Fowler, Dr R Gem, DR D J Keene, and Dr W J Rodwell. In a real sense, therefore, the preparation of this report has been a team effort, although responsibility for its shortcomings must rest with me.

Separate acknowledgement must be made to colleagues who have assisted with particular sections of the volume: Dr C J Arnold, Dr Margaret Faull, Dr R Lamb, Professor P H Sawyer, and Dr I Wood; to Miss Julia Roxan for her help with Appendix I; to Dr D J Keene and the CBA Urban Churches Working Party for Appendix II; to Miss Nancy Foster and Mr A Wood for their help with the drawings; and to Professor Rosemary Cramp, Mr P V Addyman, and Dr L A S Butler who not only read the complete text at several stages, but also had the difficult task of making sure that I finished it.

Illustrations and data supplied by others are acknowledged separately, but warm thanks are due here to all those who have assisted in this way.

Richard Morris
Leeds, February 1981

Introduction

During the last thirty years there have been radical changes in the techniques that are used to maintain, repair, and conserve historic buildings. The invention of new materials has led to a sharp reduction in the numbers of craftsmen who are accustomed to practise traditional methods of construction and repair. At the same time, while major repairs of the Victorian era are nearing the end of their life, the architectural training of the 'modern movement' has provided no sound foundation upon which to base a philosophy for the care of ancient buildings.

Recently these problems have been thrown into stark relief with the provision by central government of Historic Building Grants for the repair of listed churches in use for worship. For more than a century it has been realized by some that works necessary to maintain churches in good order may be fatal to the evidence they contain unless they are carried on in a manner which blends the best practices of several disciplines, including materials science, art and architectural history, and archaeology. What seems to have been less well apprehended is that techniques of investigation also advance, and in so doing enlarge our perceptions of the volume and variety of evidence it is feasible or desirable to record, and increase the ways in which it is possible for this evidence to be used. Such developments, however, must not be judged only from the standpoint of technical efficiency. Whereas today we are better technically equipped than ever before to take advantage of opportunities for investigation, we have lost something of the sense of urgent curiosity which lay behind, and indeed provided a moral justification for, the practice of church archaeology by antiquaries in the 19th century.

A paradox lies here, because the 19th century has bequeathed a legacy of attitudes towards the aims and methods of church archaeology which threatens to blinker the modern investigator. There is a persisting tendency to pursue the study of churches in isolation from other lines of historical inquiry. Investigations continue to be directed in the main to the solution of architectural problems posed by individual buildings, rather than the exploration of themes and patterns. Most insidious of all is the belief that almost everything worth knowing about churches is already known. The study of churches has been in progress for more than a century and a half, and an idea exists that little remains to be done apart from dotting i's and crossing t's. In fact, past study has usually concentrated on the visible and most easily accessible parts of the standing fabric, with the result that questions of origins have been ignored, the development of the church in its earlier phases has been oversimplified, and its liturgical history has been neglected.

Previous publications which have appeared under the auspices of the Churches Committee have dealt mainly with threats, methods, and administration (Jesson 1973; Addyman & Morris 1976; J Jones 1976; Rodwell & Rodwell 1977; R K Morris (I) 1978). This Report explores more deeply those topics previously considered in superficial terms. It is intended to examine the nature of the evidence which is available for study, to outline the extent and achievement of past work, and to suggest what there is to be gained from the investigation of churches in the future.

Over the last few years scholars have turned increasingly to archaeology as a means of extending knowledge of ecclesiastical history and geography. Archaeology is of particular relevance to the study of the pre- and early medieval phases in the evolution of the Church. Professor Biddle, for example, has pointed out that discussion of the development of the parochial system requires 'a chronological framework provided by the date of the foundation of . . . churches established as a result of archaeological excavation' (1976a, 69). Professor Brooke has observed how 'archaeologists have become rapidly and increasingly aware how vital churches are to them, if only because they provide so high a proportion of the solid material still available to the investigator' (1977, 460). Writing of the emergence of the town as an ecclesiastical centre, Brooke concluded that 'the chief foundation on which this subject can be enlarged is archaeological' (1977, 471).

Limitations of written records

Written records, where they survive, may be used to assist in the selection, investigation, and interpretation of church sites, but until *c* 1250 it is unusual to find records which duplicate the information which archaeology can provide. Mrs Dorothy Owen has pointed out that it is 'very rare indeed to discover a precise, or even an approximate, date, for the foundation of any parish church or chapel known to have been in existence before 1100' (1976a, 22). Dr H M Taylor has found that out of 267 church fabrics which can be shown to date in part or whole from before the Norman Conquest there are only seven 'for which close ranges or precise dates are fixed within the Anglo-Saxon period by the historical method alone' (1978, 737). Hence archaeology could be regarded first as an alternative to, and later, additionally, as a control upon and supplement to the evidence contained in written records. However, it should be stressed that archaeology is an unsatisfactory alternative to the study of documents, since it cannot be made to probe many of the issues with which writers were concerned (cf Atkinson 1960, 8).

Cases sometimes occur in which information about a particular church is provided in a written source which nevertheless cannot be related with certainty to any part of the building as it now stands. Taylor explains that the application of archaeological methods may provide evidence which will permit the association of the historical record with a specific phase in the development of the structure (1978, 736). This applies equally to churches of pre- and post-Conquest date.

Dedications

Church dedications are notoriously unreliable as indicators of date, since, like place-names, they have often been subject to change (Forster 1899; Bond 1914). While it is true that in England certain dedications achieved greater popularity in particular periods than in others (eg St Nicholas in the late 11th and 12th centuries), or could be regarded as being appropriate to certain quarters of a town (eg St Olave) or an establishment of specialized nature (eg St Barbara and military chapels), it would be unsafe to assume that the churches which bear them must or are even likely to date from the periods at which they were preferred. Dedications have been used with some success in the context of broader historical studies (eg Phythian-Adams 1977), but the extent of their value to the church archaeologist usually depends upon the availability of corroborative evidence. Such evidence is seldom to be found. Pre-Conquest tastes in parish church dedications are largely obscure. A small amount of information about dedications in some areas is provided by Domesday, but even in these instances it is hardly ever possible to show that a given dedication was original. Many exotic dedications were applied to churches in the 19th century, and there are numerous instances of churches being rededicated in earlier centuries. Outside towns, evidence for the dedications of churches is usually no earlier than post-medieval.

In Wales and parts of south-west England many dedications are thought to be proprietary in origin. A considerable literature devoted to the analysis of these dedications has accumulated during recent years (eg O Chadwick 1959; Bowen 1969; Yates 1973a; 1973b). Nevertheless, uncertainties as to the origin and subsequent stability of dedications are even greater in Wales than they are in England.

Archaeological evidence

Archaeology involves the investigation and evaluation of physical deposits and structures. In view of the expectations which have been raised regarding the contribution of church archaeology (eg Rodwell & Rodwell 1977, 4, 72, 93) it would seem to be worthwhile to consider the nature and limitations of the evidence which is available.

It is necessary to begin by insisting that there is no intrinsic *archaeological* difference between a church and any other type of site. For discussions and classifications of archaeological evidence the reader should thus turn to consult the works of authors who have approached the subject in general terms (eg Binford 1972; Hirst 1976; P A Barker 1977). However, there are classes of artefact, portable find, and material which are typical of or virtually particular to ecclesiastical sites, and these are presented in a diagrammatic fashion here (Fig 1).

Physical evidence will be introduced as it relates to the (a) fabric of the church, (b) use of the church, (c) churchyard, (d) site of the church, and (e) historic setting of the church.

The fabric of the church

In the past, antiquaries were usually selective in the evidence they chose to examine or ignore. Attention centred mainly on diagnostic features such as mouldings, tracery, types of masonry, window forms, plans, and the broad relationship of one part of a church to another. Recent years have seen the emergence of a

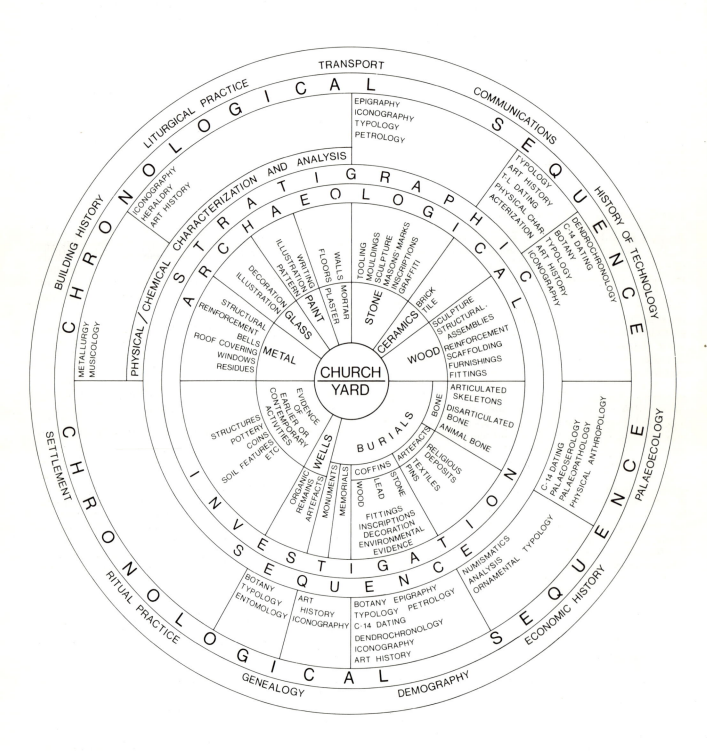

Fig 1   Diagram displaying types of evidence to be encountered at ecclesiastical sites. (Drawing: Dick Raines)

more inclusive approach, which seeks to scrutinize and record the fabric in greater detail than hitherto. Mortars, timber joints, the petrology of building stone, medieval construction methods, and the precise dimensions of buildings now claim expert attention. The need to identify and assess the impact of post-Reformation repairs and contributions is increasingly recognized.

The special advantage of this modern approach lies in its capacity to enlarge understanding of the development of a building in ways which go beyond the information provided by surface features. This process is not simply a matter of disclosing features and structural remains which were previously hidden. It should clarify the sequence in which the various parts of a church were erected and provide a comparable account of the order of events on the site which the church occupies. This *relative chronology*, if properly established, is unassailable, although even with relative chronologies there may be alternative interpretations (eg Rahtz 1976a, 22).

The provision of an *absolute chronology* for different parts of the building, on the other hand, except for example where there are radiocarbon determinations, dendrochronological dates from structural timbers, or dated epigraphs, almost always depends on *secondary evidence*. That is to say, it hinges on conclusions drawn from the typological assessment of such things as architectural sculpture, mouldings, pottery, and other artefacts. Objects which are closely datable in themselves, like coins, usually provide no more than *termini post quos*. Inscriptions may furnish important information (eg in the case of the rededicatory tablet at Kirkdale (N Yorks): Okasha 1971, 63–4), but their full value will depend upon proof that they are contemporary with the fabrics in which they occur. For most purposes of dating, therefore, the chief use of archaeology is as a means of enhancing traditional methods of assessment by increasing the range of material which is available for examination and by extending the time-scale within which the material may occur.

Scientific dating methods are often applied to finds rather than fabrics, and hence may be subject to the same limitations as, say, coins, while not being of the same order of precision. Nevertheless, the radiocarbon assay of burials which lie in close stratigraphic relation with structures is one useful way in which a framework of dates can sometimes be obtained for the structures concerned (eg in the early phases of the church at Rivenhall (Essex) and the otherwise undatable church excavated at Barrow (S Humberside) (Fig 2)). Structural mortars, too, are increasingly the subject of experiments in scientific methods of dating. Dendrochronology is a technique of particular relevance to churches which contain woodwork, pre-Victorian roofs, structural reinforcement, or vestiges of scaffolding, and where doors and panelling may provide long sequences of rings.

It has been claimed that the 'fabric of a church is the essential basis for research into its past' (Biddle 1976a, 69). The truth of this statement must be measured against the extent to which the archaeologist has access to the church in its entirety, above and below ground, and to the surrounding site. For example, the absence of an earlier church within the area occupied by an existing church building cannot be regarded as proof that no predecessor existed. Several recent excavations have produced evidence suggestive of early timber buildings alongside later churches (eg Rivenhall and Asheldham, both in Essex), apparently at variance with the more

familiar technique of reconstituting a timber church with masonry. The recovery of the total structural history of a church may thus require investigation which extends beyond the limits of the present fabric.

Use of the church

The potentials for study here have been outlined by Biddle, who points out that the liturgical arrangements of a church over a succession of periods will consist of a series of different layouts, each 'composed of an amalgam of features which originated at different earlier stages' (1976a, 70). The physical materials for the archaeological study of church functions are chiefly:

i specialized structures (eg crypts, chapels, *porticus*)
ii furnishings and fittings
iii features in the fabric or site which indicate the former presence of furnishings or fittings, or which are suggestive of former patterns of use
iv evidence of secular functions.

The recording and analysis of specialized structures like burial vaults and chapels are normally quite straightforward, although difficulties can arise (eg over the interpretation of the relationship between the 'south *porticus*' and the nave at Ledsham (W Yorks)). There are, too, classes of feature, like the channels round the interior of the church at Ormesby (Cleveland) (M Brown 1976, 10–11), the mysterious tank-like structure at St Nicholas, Colchester (Rodwell & Rodwell 1977, 31), the vertical-sided pits at Burnham (S Humberside) (Coppack 1978, 5), or the pot buried in the middle of the first church at Raunds, for which no definite explanations exist at present (cf Binding 1975).

Where medieval furnishings and fittings survive *in situ* they may tell their own story. Where they do not, there may be clues to their former presence or purpose which will respond to archaeological investigation. The location(s) of the medieval font can sometimes be detected by an area of floor which has remained undisturbed by burials, or by a foundation or soakaway (eg at Barton-on-Humber (Rodwell & Rodwell 1980); Fig 3). Medieval altars seem sometimes to have been physically rooted in the floor and may thus have left traces in the below ground record, as at Reculver (Peers 1927) and St Mark's, Lincoln (Colyer 1976). At Winchester Old Minster the site of the principal altar was suggested by post-holes interpreted as having held supports for a ciborium (Biddle 1970). Vanished screens may be commemorated by post-holes, beam-slots, or chases in the standing fabric concealed by plaster. The development of the seating plan may be echoed by periodic alterations in the distribution of burials. Patterns of wear on floors may suggest the positions of focal points such as venerated graves or altars which have since lost their importance. Above ground the survival of upper doorways, eccentrically positioned windows, or redundant corbels may point to the former presence of galleries, and may, in addition, shed light upon the dispositions of earlier roofs (Parsons 1979a).

However, archaeological indications of former use and internal arrangement are typically negative: items such as fonts, screens, and galleries are reinstated on the basis of zones that have not received burials, holes that do not contain posts, or doors that lead nowhere. A firm distinction must be kept, therefore, between the raw evidence and any interpretation which is offered. Cases have occurred in which internal arrangements that have

Fig 2 Barrow-on-Humber (Humberside): plan of church revealed by excavation. (Drawing made available by courtesy of Humberside Archaeological Unit)

4

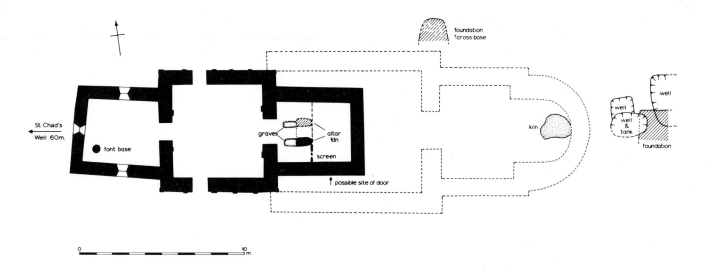

Fig 3   Barton-on-Humber (Humberside): liturgical layout of 10th century church. (Drawing: W J Rodwell, Crown Copyright Reserved)

been reconstructed by analogy with those of other churches have come to be accorded the status of fact. The spurious 'triple arcades' of the early Kentish churches of St Mary, Lyminge, and St Andrew, Rochester, are examples (H M Taylor 1978, 1082–3).

The secular use of churches and churchyards is a subject to which archaeologists have not devoted much attention. Churches were used for a wide variety of non-ecclesiastical purposes during the Middle Ages: fairs, festivities, markets, ordeals. We know about some of these activities only because bishops went out of their way to try to put a stop to them. Schools might leave traces in the archaeological record (eg graffiti and slates), so, too, might Sunday trading or markets (Sawyer 1981). Ovens, perhaps for the baking of Eucharistic bread, are occasionally encountered (eg at Pontefract (W Yorks) or St Paul-in-the-Bail, Lincoln), but they might equally well be connected with the use of parts of churches by gilds and fraternities. The imprints left on churches by such bodies would form a valuable topic for research.

The churchyard

Evidence under this head is presented in Fig 1 and has been discussed by Rahtz (1976b). Monuments, monumental inscriptions, and the recording of churchyards have been discussed by Burgess (1963), White (1977), and J Jones (1976).

The site

Every church and churchyard occupy a part of what was previously a different landscape. Elements of this earlier landscape, or evidence of its nature, may be preserved. Boundary banks sometimes stand over ridge and furrow or other traces of cultivation, and may in themselves contain remnants of earlier types of enclosure. In some cases, as perhaps at Wharram Percy, these features may have exerted an influence upon the layout of the churchyard. Alternatively, where earlier features are not in agreement with the present boundary a combination of modern agriculture or development and persistent burial may have removed all other traces of them. A few churchyards appear to be centred on barrows (eg

High Wycombe (Bucks)), and a number might be regarded as the medieval successors of earlier cemeteries, pagan and Christian (see below, Chapter 4). Excavation sometimes shows that the church site was previously the scene of domestic occupation (Drury & Rodwell 1978). The apparently pre-ecclesiastical phases of urban church sites are often of special interest (eg St Mary, Tanner Street, Winchester; St Paul-in-the-Bail, Lincoln; St Mary Bishophill Senior, York). Sometimes the sequence of secular occupation of a site giving way to ecclesiastical use is reversed; most commonly this is a post-Reformation process, but it can be seen also in the medieval period (eg Raunds (Northants); Denny (Cambs)).

Setting of the church

Just as the excavation of a site involves the removal of each layer or feature in the reverse order to that of its deposition or creation, so the relationship between a church and other elements in the landscape may sometimes be susceptible to archaeological investigation. At the sites of deserted settlements it may be feasible to correlate the time-sequence of the church with the time-sequences of neighbouring structures (eg manor site, motte, earthworks, dwellings, roadway) using stratigraphic methods. Where a church has been fitted into or superimposed upon a portion of an earlier settlement plan, investigation may clarify the relationship or help to explain aspects of settlement topography in the vicinity. This technique has been discussed briefly by Rodwell & Rodwell (1977) and in greater detail by Drury & Rodwell (1978). A good illustration of the method in practice is being provided at Raunds (Northants), where the investigation of a medieval manorial complex went on to disclose the remains of a pre-Conquest church. The boundaries of the late Saxon churchyard are under investigation, and in due course it may be possible to relate these to a surrounding network of middle Saxon land divisions and associated structures (A Boddington, *pers comm*; see Fig 21).

A brief account of the various types of evidence to be found in, under, and around churches has been given. It is now necessary to consider the ways in which these different classes of evidence have been regarded and recorded by antiquaries and archaeologists in the past.

A short history of church archaeology in Britain

Beginnings

The systematic investigation of churches in Britain dates mainly from the 19th century. However, ecclesiastical sites had attracted the sporadic attention of individuals long before this. The 13th century Chronicle of St Edmunds Abbey records how when the site was being prepared for a new Lady Chapel in 1275 the builders came upon the ambulatory of the 11th century rotunda. In the last quarter of the 15th century, William Worcestre 'was pacing out the dimensions of churches, recording inscriptions, and sifting, as critically as he could, the local traditions' (L A S Butler 1976, 20; J H Harvey 1969; Gransden 1980). John Leland, active in the 1530s and 1540s, reported on the condition of a number of monastic sites (L T Smith 1907). Later came Sir William Dugdale with his epic *Monasticon Anglicanum*. Camden and Stukeley concentrated more on field antiquities, but some compensation for this bias was provided by men who worked within particular counties or regions: eg William Lambarde (Kent), Gervase Holles (Lincolnshire), Plot (Staffordshire), Drake (York), Morant (Essex).

The British tradition of church archaeology might be said to have had its clearest beginning with Sir Christopher Wren, who discussed the origins of pointed architecture and observed excavations on a number of church sites in London during the campaign of urban reconstruction which followed the Great Fire of 1666. Wren was an exceptional figure, however, and broadly speaking the local antiquaries of the 16th century had concerned themselves with large monuments and relics, while those of the 17th century specialized in heraldry. In the 18th century a feeling for historical perspective began to emerge, but until *c* 1780 remarks about churches were generally restricted to descriptions of the condition of the fabric, and to comments about monuments and fittings.

The first attempts at an objective assessment of medieval architecture were made during the concluding decades of the 18th century. Today the efforts of men like John Carter and Francis Grose may seem naive, sometimes even comical, but it must be remembered that those concerned at the outset lacked a framework of facts within which to conduct their inquiries. 'There is no Stile or Architecture so little observed and less understood than that which we call Gothic' wrote the 18th century architect James Essex. The first architectural historians also had to rid themselves of the 17th century prejudice which insisted that Gothic was 'barbarous and inelegant'.

Development

Early in the 19th century logic began to prevail over opinion, and the study of churches entered a new phase. Now, for the first time, men began to analyse the constructional histories of church buildings. Much of the credit for this more objective approach belongs to the architect Thomas Rickman, who in 1817 published the first version of his *Attempt to Discriminate the Styles of English Architecture*, and in so doing originated the evergreen nomenclature of Early English, Decorated, and Perpendicular. By scrutinizing large numbers of medieval buildings, and by recording and comparing the features within them, Rickman was able to show that certain styles were typical of particular periods. As time went on it became possible to correlate the results of some such studies with information contained in written records, and the methods pioneered by Rickman came to be applied with increasing precision. Rickman used the law of stratification to show that some churches, or parts of them, dated from before the advent of the Normans (cf H M Taylor 1976).

The speed with which architectural history developed during the 19th century may be appreciated not only from the avalanche of publications which appeared before 1850, but also from the rapidity with which a strong reaction developed against the works of ecclesiastical architects who had been active only a few decades previously. 'All that is vile, cunning, and rascally is included in the term *Wyatt*' wrote A W Pugin, reeling from a visit to Hereford Cathedral. Appalled by Wyatt's west front at Hereford, Pugin could 'hardly summon sufficient fortitude to enter and examine the interior' (letter cited in *Assoc Architect Socs Rep Pap*, **8** (1865), xli).

Criticisms of the kind expressed by Pugin were directed against stylistic impropriety, and until about 1860 scholars concentrated upon formal aspects of medieval architecture. This is evident from the academic ring of keywords in the titles of some of the important publications of the period: *Specimens*, *Remarks*, *Parallels*, *Manual*, etc. This pedantic approach was taken for a practical reason. The adoption of Gothic as Christian architecture demanded source-books for the construction of new churches and for the restoration of old ones. Root-and-branch restorations designed to return churches to their 'original' state required dictionaries of detail and ground rules, and it was these that the antiquaries and architects of the first half of the century set out to supply. Interest in the building history of churches took second place to a concern for stylistic purity. Indeed, it was the evidence for the evolution of a church which the most ardent restorers tried hardest to eradicate, since the aim of returning a church to its 'original' form was incompatible with the preservation of features which were stylistically extraneous to it.

The output of Paley, Freeman, Parker, and others can thus be seen as part of a larger, essentially theological phenomenon. It was another facet of the growth of interest in medieval liturgy, vestments, and Catholicism which was promoted by the Oxford Movement and which found its most extreme expression in the doctrines of the Cambridge Camden Society. This latter organization reached the peak of its influence during the 1840s, and remained a force to be reckoned with for several decades more.

As early as 1849 John Ruskin was insisting that restoration 'means the most total destruction which a building can suffer', but it was not until the 1870s that an approach which balanced together the treatment, repair, and investigation of churches began to win popular acceptance. Historical studies had been undertaken well before this, of course, notably by Professor Willis in his monographs on cathedrals between the 1840s and 1860s, but the last quarter of the 19th century saw the emergence of a more specifically archaeological approach to the study of churches, witnessed in the works of such men as Irvine, Micklethwaite, Bilson, and St John Hope.

Just as the studies made by antiquaries earlier in the century had often been wedded to the ecclesiological movement, so those towards its end were accompanied by a counter-revolution. In 1877 Sir Henry Dryden delivered a lecture in which he argued that whereas medieval architects had styles of their own, 'We have confessedly no *style*, and with us a restored church is generally speaking a building which cannot be appealed to as an example. We cannot be certain how much is original and how much new invention . . .' (1878, 246). This was in flat contradiction to the doctrine of the ecclesiologists in the 1840s which defined restoration as the recovery of the 'original appearance, which has been lost by decay, accident, or ill-judged alteration' (*Ecclesiologist* (1842), **1**, 70). Opinion as to what was deemed to be 'ill-judged' was now shifting rapidly. In the same year as Dryden reviewed the implications of the word 'restoration', the founders of the newly formed Society for the Protection of Ancient Buildings deplored the extent of the damage that had been wrought by what they described sarcastically as the previous fifty years of 'knowledge and attention'. In 1886 *Archaeologia Cambrensis* began to run a series of articles on *unrestored* churches in Wales.

Methods of investigation, c 1820–1914

Nineteenth century scholars deserve their reputation as expert analysts of historic buildings. However, it is necessary to qualify this general assessment by pointing out that even by the standards of the age investigations were not always satisfactory. Victorian archaeologists were highly selective in their work, and hence missed or ignored much evidence. Since successful excavation was thought to depend upon finds of masonry by which to ascertain the layout of a building, the actual process of digging could be delegated to workmen, it being left to the antiquary to appear only when something solid was encountered which demanded interpretation. Sometimes the antiquary managed to interpret a site without leaving his study. Even Willis was not above writing an excavation report largely on the basis of information sent to him (Willis 1861b; Gould 1976, 9–10). However, instances of this kind were heavily outnumbered by cases in which no record was kept at all. At the start of Victoria's reign many churches were in poor repair. Operations to drain, stabilize, refloor, heat, and reorder them were seldom accompanied by even perfunctory recording. Cheerful reminiscences of the following kind were not untypical:

> 'Owing to the great accumulation of soil . . . the walls were much injured, and they were rendered still more insecure by the numerous interments close to their foundations. To prevent further damage the church was literally dug out of the ground, a barrel drain was constructed and the foundations underpinned. In the course of excavation we met with many fragments of sculptured stone of the eleventh and twelfth centuries' (Brereton 1865, 95–6).

The church was St Mary, Beverley. Some of the discoveries made in this period were extremely important. In 1867, for instance, workmen at Brompton (N Yorks) unearthed a collection of memorial slabs, hogbacks, and crosses in the foundations of the chancel. Many of the points which (one would like to think) would merit careful recording today went unremarked. Did any of the stones bear traces of paint or colour? How had they been reused? Were any other fragments present, some of which, perhaps, were too small, fragmentary, or inscrutable to merit attention at the time? The frequency with which items of pre- and post-Conquest sculpture are now being rediscovered in private gardens, rockeries, and walls provides us with some inkling of the very large quantities of such material that must have been encountered and casually discarded in the course of 19th century repairs.

Romanticism, too, coloured the thinking of some antiquaries. In June 1888 the Rev J T Fowler led a visit to the church at Winterton (Lincs: now S Humberside). Musing on the origins of English Christianity in that area, Fowler said: 'We all know how Coifi, the heathen priest, was . . . converted, and how he set fire to the heathen temple . . . The glow of that fire would be seen in the sky from "Winterington" as we now see the glow from the Scunthorpe Iron Works' (1888). Alas and alack, the stringent requirements of Level IV publication would preclude such atmospheric embellishments today.

Where excavations were made for reasons of research they were often strictly limited in extent. The normal technique of tactical excavation was considered to be perfectly adequate for the task of recovering the outline of a vanished building. John Bilson used the method when he came to reconsider the plan of the 11th century cathedral at Lincoln. A plan of this building, 'in some degree conjectural', had already been published by G A Poole in 1857. Under Bilson's direction small excavations were made in places likely to provide 'fixed points for a definite plan'. However, these excavations were made *only* 'in places likely to furnish data for the principal lines of the plan . . .' (1911, 546). The risk of this method of using small trenches to intercept expected walls lies in its tendency to be self-confirmatory. Assumptions are made about the nature of the evidence – eg that a plan is of a certain type – before the evidence is actually examined.

Other limitations of method which were common, though not universal, at this time included a failure to indicate the boundaries of excavations on plans, a belief that it was only necessary to bare the tops of walls in order to understand their significance or to date them, and a habit of merging fact with conjecture in the preparation of written reports and drawings. The consequences of these limitations can be judged at Hexham, where investigations carried on over a period of nearly thirty years by the architect C C Hodges involved no systematic study and led to no proper publication (Bailey 1976).

Antiquaries were less exclusive in their approach to evidence above ground, although important facts were sometimes missed, especially at high level (eg at Canterbury: Tatton-Brown 1978), and attempts to correlate the building histories of some of the greater churches, particularly the cathedral priories, with information contained in fabric rolls and accounts kept by sacrists met with considerable success. Here again, however, a policy of selectivity was usually exercised by those who prepared editions of such records for publication. Material was rarely published in full, and much of it still awaits modern critical examination (Dobson 1976).

Despite the limitations of Victorian methodology an immense amount of valuable information about churches and their contents was collected during the 19th century. Around the end of the century antiquaries began to condense these data into general works. Baldwin Brown's volume on Anglo-Saxon architecture in his series *The Arts in Early England* (1903; rev ed 1925) is the exemplar. Other, more hesitant studies had preceded it, but Brown's work stands out, and remains to this day a key work of reference, because he was in command of sufficient detail to enable him to generalize. More surveys followed, including a notable series of books on bells, dedications, screens, fonts, and architecture which flowed from the pen of Francis Bond in rapid succession, mostly during the reign of Edward VII. Other authors, like Lethaby and Prior, though less prolific than Bond, made important contributions. At the time, however, Bond was unconvinced that the majority of his contemporaries were much interested in medieval architecture, believing rather that the period of supreme achievement in architectural history belonged to the middle years of the 19th century (Bond 1905, xvii). This opinion seems to foreshadow the period of stagnation in church archaeology which was about to begin.

The years of complacency

William St John Hope's excavation of the hilltop cathedral site at Old Sarum on the eve of World War I was to be the last great episode in British church archaeology for many years. Churches, and especially their furnishings, fittings, and monuments, were by no means neglected during the decades which followed, but the spirit of exploratory zeal which had characterized the best work of the Victorians had now largely evaporated.

Improvements in site technique pioneered by Bersu and Wheeler were largely ignored by ecclesiologists, who continued to excavate, if they excavated at all, with the limited aim of ascertaining where walls once stood. The stratified deposits which lay between walls were generally either shovelled out or left where they lay, and hence were not utilized for interpretation. (In the latter case, however, they would be available for reinterpretation.)

So, to take examples, the excavations which were carried out on the site of Abingdon Abbey in 1922 under the nominal superintendence of Peers and Clapham have since been judged as being ill-recorded 'even by comparison with other amateur excavations' of the day (Biddle et al 1968, 61). Although Reculver was 'fully explored' by Peers in 1927, important evidence seems to have been missed (Medieval Archaeol, 14 (1970), 161), and doubts have been expressed about the accuracy of some aspects of Peers's recording (H M Taylor 1978, 1082). The persistence of Victorian attitudes towards recording is exemplified by Fairweather's excavation at Blyth, which concentrated on the recovery of 'the plan' by selective trenching (Fairweather 1926), although few examples of methodology between the wars seem quite as extreme as the extraordinary episode at Merton Priory (Surrey), in the 1920s, where observations were made between the sleepers of a railway track (Bidder & Westlake 1930, 56).

Buildings and their plans were not the only objects of scholarly interest during this period. From time to time finds of portable objects were made, some of which attracted attention. For example, a stone 'chair' was dug up in the north-west corner of the cathedral close at Lichfield in 1932. Hamilton Thompson diagnosed this, from photographs, as an Anglo-Saxon cathedra. Despite the apparent importance of the find the cathedral authorities managed to lose it. A fresh look at the 'cathedra' after its rediscovery in the masons' yard at Lichfield in 1976 led to the suggestion that it was in fact the hoodstone of a 17th century housing for a statue of Charles II on the west front (Gould 1977, 69–72).

Incidents of this kind bespeak a casual attitude towards archaeological affairs by antiquaries and churchmen alike.

Although it is now easy to criticize the work of Victorian antiquaries, it is important to stress that the 19th century approach, at its best, was a total approach, in which excavation, analysis of the fabric, and the study of written records were combined with sound architectural practice. During the first half of the 20th century this approach underwent some disintegration. The principles of structural criticism became blurred or were forgotten, while the term 'archaeology' was gradually and unnaturally narrowed in sense and practice until it became synonymous with 'excavation'. For their part, many of the excavators were no longer much concerned with ecclesiastical sites. The Ancient Monuments Acts of 1913 and 1931 ensured that they had no direct access to churches that were in use, while the creation of the Royal Commissions on Ancient and Historical Monuments in 1908 and the reorganization of guardianship and scheduling by the Office of Works in 1920 had placed emphasis on inspection and recording rather than systematic investigation by excavation.

World War II proved to be a great stimulus to church archaeology on the Continent, but in Britain archaeologists were on the whole slow to apply the methods developed by their German, Dutch, and Danish colleagues. Grimes's work in London stands out all the more because it was exceptional (Grimes 1968). Many other church sites were summarily cleared during the 1950s and 1960s, and where perfunctory examinations did take place the results have not always been published. Moreover, as Addyman has pointed out (1973, 21), while the initial impetus for German church archaeology came from reconstruction schemes following war damage, many subsequent investigations were undertaken for more positive reasons.

Continental church archaeology has become more a matter of well-funded research projects and systematic rescue work in conjunction with schemes of restoration and repair (eg Fehring et al 1970; 1972; Hugot 1968; Kreusch 1963; 1967; Blomqvist & Mårtensson 1963).

In Britain cooperation has not been so close nor interest so great, and the phase of stagnation outlasted World War II by several decades. At least three factors explain this. First, the fact that most operations in and around churches are regulated by ecclesiastical committees and courts helped to foster an idea that churches were outside the purview of archaeology and that there was some inherent difference between churches in use and other types of site. The Inspection of Churches Measure 1955 reinforced this belief, since its far-sighted provisions for the regular scrutiny of church fabrics went beyond the statutory requirements which then existed in the secular sphere. The fact that these requirements took little or no account of the archaeological implications of caring for churches seems to have been overlooked. Redundant churches were victims of a similar oversight. The Report of the Bridges Commission, of which Sir Mortimer Wheeler was a member, issued in 1960, offered no indication that archaeological evidence was likely to be at risk in churches which were no longer needed for worship. Evidence was submitted to the Commission by the Society of Antiquaries and the then Ministry of Works, though not by the CBA (Bridges 1960, 70–1). Secondly, the growth after the war of a broadened interest in medieval archaeology and particularly in the history of settlement was accompanied by a reaction against the somewhat restricted and architecturally orientated outlook of the ecclesiologists. In part this reaction was conditioned by the third factor, namely the inability of traditional methods of excavation to respond to the problems and complexities of church sites (Rodwell & Rodwell 1976, 45). Hence, even where controlled excavations were undertaken, the results did not always appear to justify the effort. The excavation of the site of the Victorian church of St Michael, Gloucester, in 1956, provides an example. There is written evidence to show that a church existed on this site at least as early as the 11th century, but the application of a box grid system of digging was defeated by the foundations of the 19th century church, while mechanical excavation of the churchyard made by 'running five trenches across it' proved 'uninformative' (Cra'ster 1961, 59–74).

Solutions to some of the technical problems were evolved during the 1960s (eg Biddle & Kjølbye-Biddle 1969), but it was not until the 1970s that an attempt was made to confront the administrative issues. The energy for this task derived from the rescue movement and was canalized by the Churches Committee of the CBA, which pointed out that operations prescribed to cure the structural maladies of churches were not always good for their archaeology (Jesson 1973; H M Taylor 1973a; 1974; Rodwell 1975; Wade-Martins & Morris 1976; Rodwell & Rodwell 1977; R K Morris (I) 1978).

Nevertheless, as a final comment on the era of complacency it is salutary to recall that as late as 1967 it was possible for an extensive programme of repair to begin at an important cathedral with provision for no more than a watching brief. The collaborative exercise which followed, and the technical virtuosity displayed at York Minster between 1969 and 1973 under the leadership of Mr A D Phillips have distracted attention from the circumstances in which the work began. Writing of events in 1967–8 Phillips recalled that: 'It was soon clear that an archaeological watch kept upon an excavation carried out by contractor's men was not only, in archaeological terms, hopelessly outdated but also unworkable' (1975, 21).

Church archaeology in Britain 1955–80

Some recent developments in church archaeology will emerge in the course of the chapters that follow. However, it will be useful to conclude this brief sketch of the history of church archaeology in Britain with an analysis of the nature and emphasis of the work which has taken place during the last twenty-five years.

A list of archaeological investigations that have been undertaken on ecclesiastical sites in Britain since 1955 is given in Appendix I. Archaeological work has been carried out at about 500 separate sites. The exact number is impossible to ascertain, since where detailed regional studies have been made they reveal significant numbers of small or private projects, often unpublished and not always executed with permission from the appropriate authority (see, for example, the list in Rodwell & Rodwell 1977, 22–3). The true number of sites will be well above 500. Information has been drawn mainly from printed sources: chiefly, annual reviews in *Medieval Archaeology*, national and county journals, supplemented by personal knowledge and data supplied by individual investigators.

For the purposes of this summary 'investigation' has been taken to mean:

   I an excavation carried out under controlled conditions
   II a critical survey of the fabric carried out according to archaeological principles
   III a disturbance of the fabric or site which has been monitored by an archaeologist
   IV an archaeological survey of the site.

If we look at the relative emphasis of activity under these four heads it emerges that 75% of the sites have seen excavations, 10% have undergone fabric studies, observations have been made at 11%, and that 4% have been the object of surveys. It should be added that some sites have been dealt with under more than one category of approach, as for example at Repton and Rivenhall, where excavations and fabric studies have gone hand in hand, or have been visited by archaeologists on more than one occasion. Hence there is some overlap between the percentages for work under the different categories.

The total of investigations thus includes:

   a total investigations of sites of vanished churches: eg Raunds (Northants) (I)
   b partial investigations and selective trenching on church sites: eg St Peter, Frocester (I)
   c the investigation of sites of demolished redundant churches, pre- and post-Pastoral Measure: eg St Mary Bishophill Senior, York; St Mark, Lincoln (I)
   d investigations, above and below ground, carried out in conjunction with the repair of churches, whether in use (eg Rivenhall) or redundant (eg Little Somborne (Hants)) (I, II)
   e 'pure' fabric studies: eg Bradford-on-Avon (II)
   f the observation of summary clearances of church sites: eg St Nicholas Acon, London (III)
   g observations of restoration works in churches in use (eg St Mary-le-Bow, London), or repairs of ruined churches (III)
   h investigations of monastic sites (I, II, III, IV)
   i projects of research: eg Deerhurst (I, II, III, IV)

Geographical distribution of sites

England	86%	Wales	6%
Scotland	7%	Isle of Man	1%

It should be noted that the same factors which threaten the archaeology of churches in England have prompted rescue investigations in Wales and Scotland: the repair of churches in use (eg Crail (Fife)), disturbance of churchyards (eg Barry (Glam)), and redundancy (eg Llangar (Merioneth)). However, in Scotland, because of the abandonment of many churches at the Reformation, most investigations seem to have taken place on the sites of isolated ruined churches or chapels. Overall, the counties which have seen the greatest number of projects include Norfolk, Kent, Yorkshire, Gloucestershire, Sussex, Greater London, Hampshire, and Suffolk. At the other extreme, nineteen pre-reorganization counties have seen only single investigations during the last two decades, these being predominantly in Wales and Scotland.

Condition of site

Church or chapel in use for worship	26%
Ruin	12%
Redundant	5%
Structure surviving in other use	2%
Site only	55%

Status

Parish church	40%
Chapel	13%
Cathedral	5%
Monastic	42%

These figures have been rationalized, since some of them conceal circumstances which are not readily reducible to simple statements. Many churches have not kept within the same category of status for the full length of their history. A number of parish churches originated as chapels, for example, and at least 12% of the sites which would now be classified as parochial have a monastic or collegiate background.

Cathedrals (including former sees and precincts)

Investigations have taken place at Bath, Bristol, Canterbury, Chichester, Durham, Coventry, Exeter, Glasgow, Gloucester, Hexham, Lichfield, North Elmham, Norwich, Oxford, Peel, Peterborough, Ripon, Rochester, St Albans, St Andrews, St Germans, Sherborne, Wakefield, Wells, Winchester, Worcester, and York (27).

Monastic sites

Projects at sites of the later Middle Ages (c 1050–1540) can be classified according to the orders which used them, as follows:

Order	Approximate % of total of later medieval monastic sites investigated
Benedictine	27
Augustinian	22
Cistercian	12
Dominican	8
Franciscan	6
Cluniac	5
Carmelite	3
Premonstratensian	2
Carthusian	2
Military orders	2
Austin / Gilbertine / Observantine / Tironian / Trinitarian	4
Others (incl seculars)	7

From this it would appear that projects have been *very* roughly in proportion to the original relative strengths of the respective orders, although this leads one to suspect that there may have been unnecessary repetition in studies of sites belonging to the stronger orders (Benedictine and Augustinian sites account for 49% of all monastic investigations), at the expense of houses of the smaller reformed orders. Sites of the mendicant orders have attracted much attention, though accidentally so.

Urban churches (including buildings of religious communities; one investigation only unless a figure is given)

Aberdeen (2), Abingdon, Arundel (2), Aylesbury, Bangor, Bath (2), Bedford (2), Beverley (2), Bicester, Boston, Bristol (6), Burton-on-Trent, Bury St Edmunds, Cambridge (2), Canterbury (10), Chelmsford, Chepstow, Chester (2), Chichester (3), Christchurch (2), Cirencester (2), Colchester (3), Coventry (3), Derby, Dover (3), Dunstable, Durham, Edinburgh, Exeter (3), Glasgow (2), Gloucester (7), Guildford (3), Hereford (2), Ipswich (2), Kingston upon Hull, Leicester (2), Leominster, Lichfield, Lincoln (2), London (14), Monmouth, Newark, Newcastle upon Tyne (3), Northampton (5), Norwich (6), Oxford (5), Peel (2), Penrith, Peterborough, Pontefract (2), Reading, Rhuddlan, Ripon (2), Rochester, Salisbury, Sandwich (2), St Albans (2), St Andrew's (2), St David's, St Neots, Scarborough (2), Silchester, Southampton (3), Southwark, Stafford (2), Stamford (2), Tamworth (2), Thetford (6), Wakefield, Warwick (2), Wells, Westminster, Winchester (12), Worcester, York (9).

The figures in this list represent sites, not numbers of campaigns. When taken together they account for approaching 40% of the sites investigated during the last twenty-five years.

Discussion

A minimum total of 500 investigations of ecclesiastical sites spread over the last twenty-five years seems impressive. It might prompt some readers to call for an immediate moratorium on church archaeology. However, it should be pointed out that the figures do not differentiate between the scale or quality of the various investigations. For purposes of counting, a watching brief of one afternoon at a redundant chapel and five years of continuous excavation and recording at York Minster are of equal value. The overall total is indeed inflated by many Category III investigations, often conducted in unfavourable conditions, and it has been swollen further by a large number of minor projects, often on monastic sites and, arguably, leading to much repetition in terms of the kind and quality of data recovered. In most cases, moreover, investigation has involved excavation alone. It is not feasible to classify the investigations according to their standard, but it would seem reasonable to suggest that appropriate techniques have not been applied with sufficient regularity and that the total of intensive, high-quality investigations is very low.

Many recent investigations fall into one of two categories: (1) projects intended to solve problems pertaining to the building histories of individual churches, and (2) investigations occasioned by threats. As a result there is some uncertainty as to the wider relevance of church archaeology, which in some circles is still looked upon as an introverted pursuit, concerned only with the resolution of arcane problems particular to itself. It has even been suggested that churches are not particularly edifying as archaeological sites (Carver 1978, 11).

It is true that secular churches often yield little in the way of conventional archaeological data (pottery, coins, small finds, etc), and at present pre-Conquest churches are notoriously difficult to date by archaeological methods alone. On the other hand, the importance of the church in relation to the history of settlement and society at large is not seriously disputed, and it may be argued that refinements of the archaeological method itself need to be developed in order to maximize classes of data which have hitherto been ignored or have received only perfunctory attention. Here it is necessary to stress that the selection and the counterpart, the rejection, of sites for investigation should be placed upon a more positive basis. Despite the hundreds of investigations and observations that have been made in recent years, only a handful have been undertaken with the kind of technical and intellectual precision which could assist in the formulation of a secure framework for future research. Probably even fewer have taken place at sites which would be appropriate to the issues which such a framework might accommodate. Hence the first need is for reliable data, and for access to it.

Nevertheless, new work requires a point of departure. The next six chapters, therefore, comprise a survey of what might be called promising areas of inquiry. This survey is not exhaustive – many areas are left quite untouched, especially those which would demand unacceptably large amounts of explanatory material in order to introduce them – but it is presented as an attempt to relate the archaeological study of churches to the world beyond the churchyard boundary.

Until Christians began to build and worship in architecturally distinctive buildings the scope of their activities is largely proof against archaeological methods of investigation. Abroad, the concept of the church as an architectural type seems to have emerged only gradually, during the latter half of the 4th century, and it is not yet possible to argue with absolute confidence that churches were ever built in Roman Britain at all. Such archaeological evidence for Christianity in later Roman Britain as there is appears to be either unusually impenetrable, or else susceptible to a broad range of interpretation and emphasis. Items such as chi-rho monograms, scratchings on stones and portable objects, word puzzles, lead tanks, and mosaics which embody Christian motifs communicate little about the extent of Christian belief and the basis upon which it was practised. Thus it is not clear from the Hinton St Mary mosaic whether the Christ figure was thought of as dominating the surrounding pagan elements or as being one of them, or indeed whether the pagan figures had been conscripted to do allegorical duty on Christ's behalf.

Hitherto the case for the existence of an organized Church in late Roman Britain has rested mainly upon a small body of written references: to British bishops and their sees, to the sites of martyrdoms, to the travels of ecclesiastical persons, and to theological controversies. Not all these accounts were contemporary with the events they describe, and there are no incontrovertibly explicit references to Romano-British church *buildings* in 4th or 5th century writings. The finite and often retrospective nature of the written evidence means that archaeology is the only source of fresh information which remains available. Confirmation of the considerable value of archaeology in this respect is provided by discoveries made both abroad and in England during recent years which have helped to clarify what may be expected at Romano-British Christian sites, and hence may assist in the recognition of new sites and the reinterpretation of old ones.

Summary of past research

Much of the material evidence has been discussed by Toynbee (1953) and mapped by Frend (1955) and Thomas (1971, 12). More recent surveys have been provided by Frend (1968) and Radford (1971). Pagan motifs in Christian art have been considered by Toynbee (1968). Aspects of Romano-British ecclesiastical organization have been reviewed by Mann (1961). Christian cemeteries have been discussed by Green (1977), while Rahtz (1977; 1978) has explored problems of interpretation posed by Romano-British and later cemeteries composed of oriented burials unaccompanied by grave-goods. The subject of churches in late Roman Britain has come in for a very full examination from Thomas (1980), and a large-scale survey of the whole subject by the same author appeared the following year (1981).

Churches

No building which can be unequivocally identified as a Romano-British church has yet been found. However, there are three sites where excavations made at various times have revealed structures which are generally accepted as churches, while investigations at four more have disclosed buildings for which an ecclesiastical identity has been alleged, not always with much conviction. The smallness of this body of evidence means that it is possible to look at each site in turn.

Silchester (Fig 4)
Main reference: Frere 1975
Site: in eastern section of small *insula* south-east of forum; site previously occupied by a large timber building, possibly in association with a well, until late in the 3rd century.
Oriented: west–east
Description: rectangular nave termination in a semicircular western apse, flanked by narrow aisles, each leading to a squarish western chamber of slightly greater width. To the east, a rectangular porch embracing the full width of the three main divisions. The walls were formed of flint rubble with tile quoins; paving of coarse red tesserae, apart from a square chequered mosaic panel preceding the apse.
Entrances and internal arrangements: a door central to the east wall of the porch; perhaps one door apiece into the nave and aisles. The north aisle was divided from its western chamber by a timber-framed partition containing a doorway. Traces of pink cement were found to be adhering to the mosaic panel in front of the apse, and a flint ledge projected from the north wall adjacent to the panel.
Associated structures: 3·35m to the east of the 'church' lay a square foundation formed of tiles set on a rough pavement of flints. A small square pit lined with flints was encountered just to the west of the tiled base.
Suggested date: c 360 or later

Icklingham (Suffolk) (Fig 5)
Main reference: West & Plouviez 1976
Site: at south-western edge of unwalled Roman settlement, within cemetery. Building(s) of uncertain nature and purpose nearby. The construction level of the 'church' sealed a nearby pit containing six human skulls and a stone pillar.

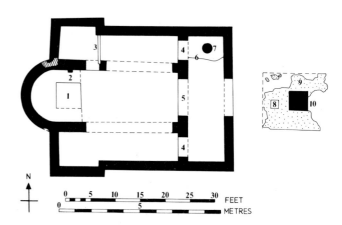

Fig 4 Silchester (Hants): simplified interpretative plan of probable church (after Richmond in Frere 1975). The function of the strip-footings to north and south of the nave (shown by broken lines) is not certain.
Key: *1: mosaic panel (site of altar?); 2: support for (?) shelf-table; 3: door (first phase); 4: door (?); 5: foundation of threshold; 6: limit of surviving paving; 7: base; 8: soakaway; 9: platform built of flints; 10: tiled base.*

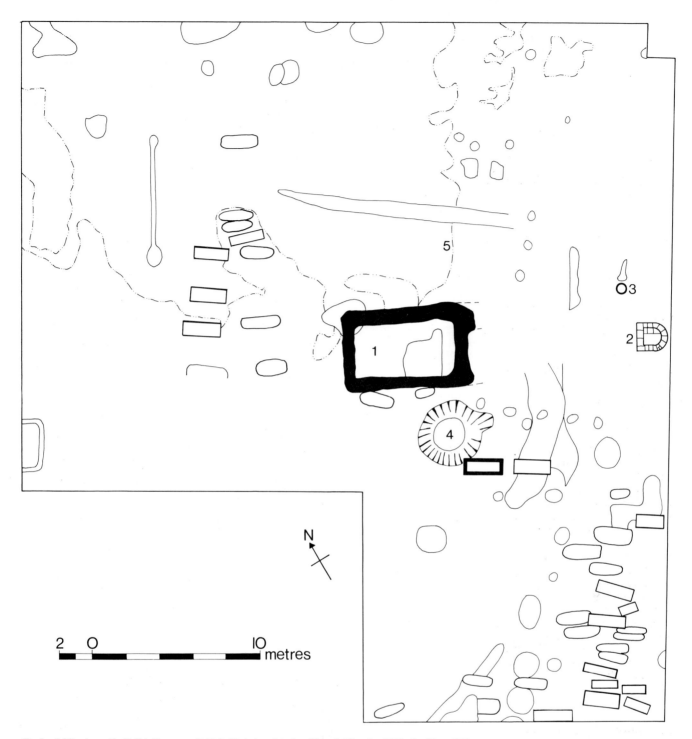

Fig 5   Icklingham (Suffolk): Romano-British Christian site after West & Plouviez 1976, figs 32 and 33).
Key: *1: remnants of foundations of (?) church; 2: baptistery; 3: lead tank; 4: pit (pre-church), contents including six human skulls, a child, limestone pillar, and decorated roof tiles; 5: edge of chalk spread which postdated (4) but preceded (1). Graves indicated by rectangular outlines contained coffin burials.*

Oriented: east–west
Description: rectangular building with walls of mortared flint. 'Slight protuberances ... noted near the corners of the east wall ... may indicate buttressing of a gable end or a projection of the building to the east' (1976, 71).
Entrances and internal arrangements: no evidence survived
Associated structures: c 10m east of the main building lay an apsidal structure, formed of coursed tiles and set into the ground. 'Internally, about one-third of the area ... was occupied by a "step" ... The damaged tile floor, the inner surfaces of the apse wall and the step, showed traces of a white plaster lining' (1976, 71). Fragmentary remains of a wall between the apsidal structure and the 'church' may indicate that the former was originally enclosed within a larger building.

Cemetery: the 'church' lay in a cemetery comprising at least 41 inhumations, all oriented with heads to the west, and all but one devoid of grave-goods. Seventeen graves yielded evidence of wooden coffins; one burial was made in a stone coffin. Discoveries at the site in the 19th century included a group of four burials surrounded by the traces of a building which had been robbed away. Two of these burials were in stone coffins, and the third was in a wooden coffin which had been lined with lead. One of the sarcophagus burials had been packed in plaster (Prigg 1901, 65–71; Green 1977, 51).
Finds: three lead tanks have been found at Icklingham. The first was found in about 1726 and has been lost. The second was found in the same field as the 'church' in 1939 and bears chi-rhos on opposing panels. The third was found in 1971 and was subsequently shown to be in the immediate vicinity of the detached apsidal structure. This tank

also bears chi-rho symbols (*Britannia*, **8** (1977), 444–5). A hoard of Romano-British pewter objects is also known from the site (Liversedge 1959).
Suggested date: second half of 4th century

Richborough
Main reference: P D C Brown 1971
Site: within north-west corner of Saxon-shore fort
Oriented: east–west, but with slight deflection towards south
Description: two lines of stone blocks, at right-angles, exposed by clearance in the 1920s and later reconstructed as a church by analogy with continental examples. Construction probably of timber on stone bases.
Entrances and internal arrangements: no evidence recorded
Associated structures: hexagonal structure formed of tiles and mortar a little to the north-east of 'church'. The six outer faces were fashioned as concave niches and coated with pink plaster. Two of the niches (those to the north and south) had been blocked, forming steps up to the rim of the internal basin. The basin bore plaster on its sides and floor.
Suggested date: late 4th to early 5th century

Possible churches

Caerwent (i)
Main references: Nash-Williams 1930, 235–7; 1953, 165–7
Site: in north-west angle of hall/peristyle north of baths, south of forum
Oriented: east–west
Description: small rectangular 'nave' with apsidal blister central (and secondary? cf 1930, pl 78) to east wall. The form of the western part of the 'church' could not be ascertained, but a fragment of forebuilding survived which, although not in bond with the nave, was thought by Nash-Williams to be 'evidently contemporary with it' (1930, 235). If reconstructed symmetrically this forebuilding would appear as a long transverse chamber, giving the whole structure a T-shaped plan. Nash-Williams regarded the forebuilding as a narthex.
Entrances and internal arrangements: no external doorway was found, but a possible door, almost the full width of the 'nave', communicated with the 'narthex'. A bench ran along the south wall of the narthex.
Cemetery: 'early' burials were found to the west of the 'church' (1930, 230). The early medieval church of St Tathan, Caerwent, stands just to the west of the site, and is said to be 'close enough . . . to suggest the possibility that the one may in a sense be the lineal successor to the other' (1930, 235).
Suggested date: 5th to 6th century
Doubts: Alcock (1963, 63) has argued that 'there is no cogent evidence, from stratification or structure, to demand a date later than 400 for this building'. Alcock has also challenged the identification of the building as a church (1963, 63, n 2).

Caerwent (ii)
Attention is drawn to Boon's hope 'to show that House XXII North embodied a church (cf *Archaeologia*, **62** (1911), 411–2, pl 57)' (Boon 1976, 175, n 28).

Verulamium
Main reference: Wheeler & Wheeler 1936, 122–3
Site: in south quarter of Roman city
Orientation: north-east to south-west
Description: small basilica with rectangular rooms projecting from each end of 'nave'. The north-eastern room was slightly smaller than its companion, although its foundations were the more substantial and incorporated a square projection on the north-west side.
Entrances and internal arrangements: no evidence
Suggested date: no evidence, but 'the character of the masonry' suggested a late Roman date to the excavator.
Doubts: the plan bears a slight resemblance to a church, but conforms more closely to a medieval than to any known Roman model. The excavator himself laid no stress upon the suggestion.

Several other sites may be mentioned as being of possible relevance: the Roman building recently excavated at Flaxengate, Lincoln, and the first phase of the church of St Pancras, just outside the Roman city at Canterbury.

The Flaxengate structure was situated in the lower *colonia*. Only a portion of it has been examined, but it seems to have been a large and unusually well-appointed building (note in *Britannia*, **8** (1977), 390). Excavation revealed part of an apse and two lateral rooms. The larger room, to the south, was floored with tesserae. The apse projected eastwards beyond the east side of this room, and may have been flanked by engaged columns. Finds included small pieces of Italian marble, a limestone Tuscan capital, and painted wall-plaster. Thomas has observed that the building occupied a 'prime site in the middle of the settlement' and concludes that 'a public building of some significance late in the Roman period might be indicated' (1980, 142). It is of interest that the part of the structure which was examined may have stood until the 9th century, when the area was given over to industrial and commercial activity (note in *Medieval Archaeol*, **21** (1977), 210). The suggestion that the building may have been a church is extremely tentative, and rests mainly on the incompletely revealed plan and an absence of contemporary finds which point to any other function (M J Jones, *pers comm*).

The church of St Pancras, Canterbury, still stands as a ruin, *c* 100m east of the important monastic complex of St Augustine's abbey. St Pancras was partly excavated in 1900, with results which led Clapham to affirm that as the design conformed so exactly to the pattern of other 7th century churches then known in Kent 'there can be no doubt as to its date' (1930, 19). In recent years there have been fresh excavations at the site under the superintendence of Dr Frank Jenkins. In short notes on this work Jenkins has indicated that the early building history of the church was not completely understood by all previous commentators, and in particular that some of the 'Kentish' features were additions made over a period to a simpler pre-existing structure (*Medieval Archaeol*, **17** (1973), 144; **20** (1976), 163; Jenkins 1976). The original building consisted of a rectangular nave, opening through an arch into a polygonal eastern apse. It is possible that this building was an extra-mural church of late Roman date (Thomas 1980, 145). If this is so, then the church might be regarded as an alternative candidate (cf Jenkins 1965) for the 'old church . . . on the east side of the city' which Bede tells us was used by Æthelberht's Christian queen, Bertha, and where Augustine and his entourage were accustomed to worship, evangelize, and baptize until the king's own conversion made it feasible for the mission to build and recondition churches elsewhere (*HE*, i.26). This possibility and its ramifications have been reviewed in some detail by Thomas (1980, 143–5).

Discussion

Considered individually these sites might not appear to be too promising as a basis for further research. Icklingham, the site with the widest array of evidence, was found to be in a poor state of preservation. Conclusions about Silchester and Caerwent have been drawn mainly on the strength of their plans, and are not supported by other facts. The case for the church at Richborough depends mainly upon the identification of the nearby baptistery.

Nevertheless, if the most doubtful cases – ie Caerwent, Lincoln, and Verulamium – are set aside, those forming the residue present several common characteristics. First, they are all of approximately the same date: the latter part of the 4th century. Secondly, they are all consistent in their orientation, although at Silchester the orientation was reversed, and both there and at Richborough the axis could be explained simply as conforming to the surrounding layout. Thirdly, at least three of the sites included detached ancillary structures. Two of these, at Icklingham and Richborough, can be interpreted with confidence as baptisteries, on the basis of continental and Mediterranean analogies (for these, see

P D C Brown 1971 and J G Davies 1962). The third, the square foundation of tiles east of the main building at Silchester, might once again be regarded as a baptistery. This identification has been opposed by Radford on account of the structure's 'open and exposed position' (1971, 3), and it is true that the rite of initiation was normally screened from the outside world, partly so that it should not be witnessed by the uninitiated and partly out of concern for modesty (J G Davies 1964, 4). However, no well-preserved Christian complex has yet been excavated under favourable conditions in Britain, and it is possible that timber structures were used to enclose baptisteries and that these have left little trace. (In 627 Edwin, king of Northumbria, was baptized by Paulinus within a small wooden oratory (*HE*, ii.14). It is not inconceivable that some late Roman baptismal enclosure(s) survived to suggest the type.)

Another baptistery, an octagonal tile-built structure, has recently come to light at Witham (Essex), where excavation is still in progress at the time of writing (preliminary notice in *Rescue News*, **18** (1979), 2). As at Icklingham, the site seems to have been operated first as a pagan religious focus and then converted to Christian use in the 4th century. It is interesting to notice that the Icklingham baptistery stood within a cemetery. J G Davies (1964, 4–6) points out that in Western Europe many early baptisteries had definite funerary associations, sometimes being made to resemble mausolea both in form and decoration. 'St Paul provides the clue to the interpretation of this architectural ideology when he tells the Colossians (2.12) that they have been buried with Christ in baptism'. This also provides a theological *raison d'être* for the polygonal layouts which were often adopted. The hexagon (cf Richborough) is said to recall Christ's crucifixion on a Friday, the sixth day of the week; the octagon expresses the co-resurrection of the baptismal candidate with Christ 'who was raised from the dead on what the Fathers call the eighth day, the first day of the new week' (1964, 5). Ideas of death and resurrection also permeated much of the art used to decorate baptisteries.

The villas

The most impressive evidence for a Christian outlook on the part of some villa owners comes from representations and motifs in mosaic pavements. The best known of these, the bust of Christ against a chi-rho monogram found at Hinton St Mary (Dorset) in 1963 (Toynbee 1964), occurs at the centre of a square pavement, with a subsidiary figure at each of the four angles. At Frampton, also in Dorset, a chi-rho featured at the centre of the diameter of an apsidal projection from a square room. Beyond it, within the curve of the apse, lay a cantharus: a motif of Dionysus, but one also capable of representing the eucharistic cup. A third Dorset mosaic which may have embodied chi-rho symbols was found at Halstock (D J Smith 1969, 88, n 2).

Toynbee has explained that by the 4th century 'the representation in *pagan* art of the traditional Graeco-Roman myths, gods, and personifications and of many motifs from daily life (such as hunting-scenes) had increasingly tended to shed their literal meaning and assume an allegorical, symbolic and quasi-spiritual significance' (1968, 182). As they did so, some of them became available, or acceptable, as vehicles for the expression of Christian ideas. Depictions of Oceanus and sea-beasts, Bellerophon slaying the Chimaera, and Orpheus taming wild creatures may on occasion be

Table I Christian or potentially crypto-Christian art at Roman villas

after D J Smith 1969, 82–6

Villa name	County	Motif(s)
Barton Farm	Glos	Orpheus, panther, peacocks
Brading	Isle of Wight	Abraxas, Orpheus
Chedworth	Glos	Doves
Fifehead Neville	Dorset	Cantharus ringed by fish and dolphins
Frampton	Dorset	Chi-rho, cantharus
Halstock	Dorset	Chi-rho, evangelists
Hinton St Mary	Dorset	Christ, chi-rho
Horkstow	Lincs	Peacocks, Orpheus
Keynsham	Somerset	Doves
Littlecote Park	Wilts	Orpheus, panther, cantharus
Lullingstone	Kent	Chi-rho, *orantes*
Newton St Loe	Somerset	Orpheus
Northchurch	Herts	(?) Chi-rho (wallplaster)
Stonesfield	Oxon	Peacocks
Wellow	Somerset	Dolphins, fish, panthers, peacocks
Withington	Glos	Dolphins, doves, cantharus between peacocks, fish
Woodchester	Glos	Orpheus, birds and twigs, peacocks

examples of this allusive technique of presenting Christian concepts. (Later on, in the 5th and 6th centuries, the Church on the continent was to become one of the main forces for the maintenance and preservation of classical values and culture in the face of change and uncertainty.) Seen in this way, the art of late Roman Britain includes a considerable body of material which *could* reflect Christianization among villa proprietors (Table I).

Alongside questions arising from the imagery of the mosaics is the matter of the architectural forms they imply. Little is known about the sites at Hinton St Mary and Frampton, but in a recent paper D J Smith has observed that these villas, and also at Pitney (Somerset) and Littlecote Park (Wiltshire) 'a continuous mosaic of two different designs was planned to fit two rooms intercommunicating by means of a wide opening in the wall between them . . .' (1978, 128). The liturgical implications of this arrangement at Hinton St Mary have been discussed by Toynbee (1968, 185). Of this mosaic it has been said that from any angle 'the subject of almost every element of the pavement is placed precisely the wrong way round to be viewed easily' (Painter 1976, 50). Following Toynbee (1964), Painter suggests that the pavement was designed as a kind of orthographic reflection of the three-dimensional scheme by which it was overspread, which would appear to have included a dome set on a square (1976, 50–1, figs 1 & 2). At Littlecote Park, now re-excavated (Walters & Phillips 1979), a rectangular pavement preceded a square mosaic enclosing a circular design, with apsidal projections on three sides giving a trefoiled plan. Smith argues that such a room 'demands to be crowned by a dome', and has reconstructed the two rooms on the model of a 4th century church (1978, 129, 135–5; cf Thomas 1980, 148–9). Previously unrecorded iconographic details disclosed by the recent excavation have led to suggestions that the Littlecote building served as an Orphic temple. However, the imagery common to the cults of both Orpheus and Christ merely serves to emphasize the modern difficulty in differentiating between pagan and Christian cult buildings of the 4th century.

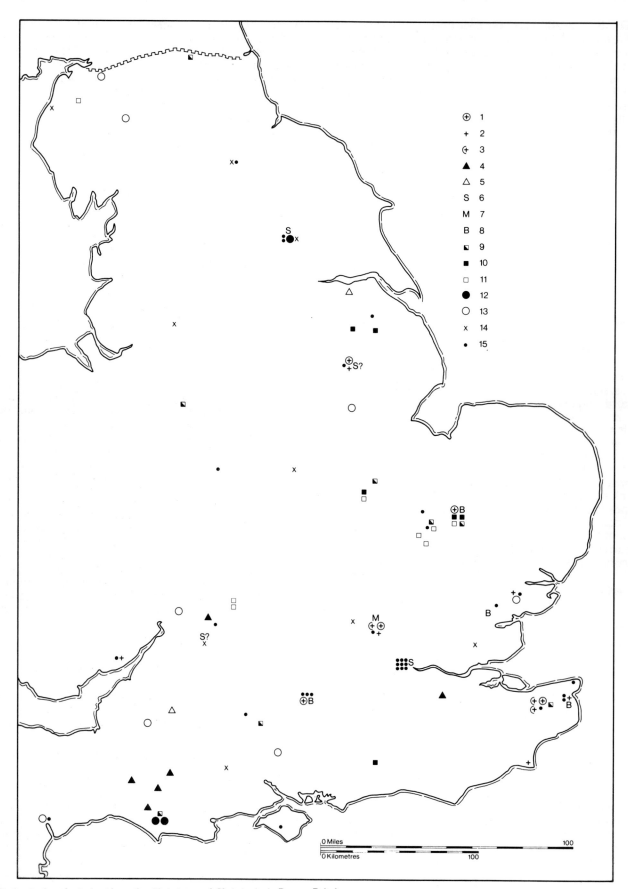

Fig 6   Archaeological evidence for Christians and Christianity in Roman Britain.
Key to symbols: *1: church; 2: possible church; 3: church, suggested from literary source; 4: villa with integral Christian iconography; 5: villa with possible Christian evidence; 6: see; 7: site of martyrdom; 8: baptistery; 9: hoard; 10: lead tank bearing Christian symbols; 11: lead tank, plain; 12: Christian cemetery or burial; 13: possible Christian cemetery or burial; 14: Christian symbol on building material; 15: portable find. (Drawing: Dick Raines)*

Other problems of recognition are illustrated by the villa at Lullingstone (Kent) where the main dwelling had a history which spanned the greater part of the Romano-British era (Meates 1955). Around 350 the walls of two rooms on the north side of the house were decorated with paintings which included three chi-rho symbols, an alpha and omega, and a series of six figures, of which at least three were depicted as being in an attitude of prayer (Painter 1969). The larger room, that containing these *orantes*, was not completely excavated, but the suite as far as it is known comprised two rooms and a vestibule, the latter having been formed by the conversion of a corridor in such a way as to prevent direct entry from the living quarters. It seems that this Christian suite continued to be frequented after the domestic sector of the villa had passed out of use.

The Lullingstone suite is not easy to classify. Toynbee inclined to the view that it was a house-church (1953; 1968, 186). Radford conjectured that it also served as a *memoria* (1971, 5–6), a possibility which has received support from Green (1977, 51). Thomas maintains that the two rooms 'correspond functionally to the narthex and sanctuary of a free-standing church', and visualizes the suite as an estate church rather than as a private chapel (1980, 137, 147). Whatever the function(s), it is salutary to reflect that but for the recovery and reassembly of fallen painted wall-plaster, the Christian context of the complex would never have been recognized. The plan alone is not enough.

Before leaving Lullingstone it is interesting to notice that it possessed two medieval churches: St Botolph's, which survives, and a former church of St John which served a settlement that is now deserted. St John's stood upon a Roman mausoleum (which resembled a temple) overlooking the villa (Taylor & Taylor 1965, 401–2). Both churches were in existence in the 11th century when they were recorded in the *Textus Roffensis* (Ward 1932, 47). St John's was probably a chapelry of Eynsford (Douglas 1944, 108). The subordinate status of the church does not, however, necessarily mean that it was of late foundation. The emplacement of certain medieval Kentish churches on the sites of Roman masonry buildings (often, apparently, mausolea) has been noted by Rigold (1972, 38–41), but the cult history of the estate at Lullingstone, although frequently mentioned, has received surprisingly little discussion.

The evidence for Christianity provided by the villas is substantial, though far from overwhelming. Just how extensive it may be depends upon what criteria are adopted for the admission of pagan scenes as crypto-Christian art (Table I). The evidence as we perceive it today is concentrated chiefly in southern and south-western England. Whether this bias arises from a particular set of factors pertaining to the background of the proprietors of the villas in question, from a centre within the region where Christianity was well established (Cirencester has been mentioned as a possibility: Thomas 1980, 155–6), or for other reasons, is not yet clear. However, it should be noted that the immediate cause for the apparent weighting towards the south-west arises from the comparatively durable works of mosaicists. Where other media were preferred for Christian art, such as textile or painted wall-plaster, the chances of discovering it must be reduced. To some extent, therefore, it is arguable that the fixed remains left by Christians in villas may be less reliable as a guide to the *overall* pattern of Christian activity than the distribution of small portable objects of Christian character or

bearing Christian symbols (Fig 6). It is true that the find-spots of the latter will be affected by factors operating haphazardly, like loss or theft (Thomas 1971, 10–11), but this only renders them unreliable as indicators of precise sites. The volume of such material and its general spread may be less susceptible to the differential survival of evidence which is likely to be influencing, and perhaps distorting, our view of the extent to which Christianity appealed to the proprietors of villas in the lowland zone as a whole.

Cemeteries

Christian cemeteries of any period are not easy to recognize unless they are accompanied by structures or inscriptions which disclose their character. The archaeologist who encounters a Christian cemetery of the 4th century thus faces problems which are akin to those that surround the identification of cemeteries containing the remains of English Christians in the 7th and 8th centuries: the characteristics of such cemeteries – the rite of inhumation, burials oriented east–west (Rahtz 1978), an absence or sparseness of grave-goods – are not in themselves fully diagnostic. Some of the features of Christian cemeteries in Roman Britain were anticipated by, and almost certainly derived from, pagan modes of burial. Conversely, some of the burials which can be accepted with reasonable confidence as Christian, such as the Sycamore Terrace coffin burial from York (RCHM *Eburacum*, 73, 135, pl 65 [150]), would be classified as pagan but for the presence of an inscription of Christian type or of some object of exclusively Christian character. There is evidence from several quarters which goes to show that the custom of placing objects in secular graves was not always discontinued after the adoption of Christianity (Toynbee 1968, 191; James 1979). Nor is orientation always a secure guide: the pre-Conquest (?) cathedral cemetery at York, for example, contained graves aligned south-west to north-east, and there are several instances of Christian graves aligned north–south. It has been observed that 'The danger of defining as Christian only those cemeteries in which the bodies are extended west–east without grave-goods, is that Christian burials in areas with strong local traditions which do not fully conform to this rule, are liable to be excluded' (Faull 1977, 7). By the same token, non-Christian cemeteries which do conform to the rule may be wrongfully included.

These difficulties are reflected in the very small number of authenticated Romano-British Christian cemeteries. This does not necessarily mean that such cemeteries were scarce, or even that they have seldom been found; more probably it reflects the limitations of the archaeological method.

Christian burial practices in Roman Britain and the Empire at large have been considered by Toynbee (1971), and more recently by Green (1977) in a short but valuable essay which concentrates on the significance of burials packed in lime or gypsum. Plaster burials are not exclusively Christian, but there is firm evidence to show that this technique came to be favoured by those who subscribed to the faith. Plaster burials occur at a wide variety of Romano-British sites, with notable concentrations at the Christian cemetery at Poundbury, outside Dorchester (Dorset) (Green 1979), and at York (Ramm 1971). Examples in Yorkshire have been listed by Faull (1977, 26–30), and an intriguing though unconfirmed instance has been noted at Lichfield, from an old excavation made in the nave of the cathedral (Gould 1976).

The Poundbury cemetery and its extension contained a number of mausolea. Some of these structures may have been of more than purely family importance, since they attracted dense clusters of graves. The significance of specially marked graves as the foci of cemeteries, and in some places as stimuli for the founding of contemporary or later churches, has often been remarked (eg Biddle 1976a), and in the case of Poundbury the suggestion has been made that some of the mausolea served as small churches (Green 1979). Similar circumstances seem to have existed, although on a much reduced scale, at Icklingham (West & Plouviez 1976). Green stresses the requirement that cemeteries should be investigated as entities rather than as mere collections of individual graves, with due regard for the 'burial types in a cemetery, their relative frequency, the layout and development of the graveyard, the character of any monuments, and the cemetery's relationship to the surrounding pattern of rural and/or suburban settlement' (1977, 52).

In the long run, it may be that this more inclusive approach will prove to be at least as sensitive to contrasts between Christian and non-Christian sites as methods which concentrate on the supposedly cultural or ritual attributes of individual burials.

Conclusion

Romano-British Christianity has been depicted as an essentially urban and aristocratic phenomenon (Radford 1967, 105–6), and as a religion which may have been 'largely confined to the poorer classes' (Clapham 1930, 10). The former view seems to rise from the establishment background to a site such as Silchester, and more particularly from the impressive, if numerically limited, fixed remains from country houses, some of which may have been in the hands of urban aristocrats, in southern and eastern England; the latter derives from the meagre tally of churches – small churches at that – so far delivered by archaeology, and a suggestion of ecclesiastical poverty contained in a literary source (Frend 1968, 39).

The contradiction between these two views may be more apparent than real. A faith which held appeal at different social levels is likely to be reflected in a broad spectrum of material remains, with the proviso that remains left by aristocrats and civic authorities are likely to be more durable than those of the poor. Even this distinction, however, may have to be reconsidered in the light of recent results from several sites. Lead tanks bearing chi-rho symbols, for example, once regarded as costly items reflecting the outlook of wealthy villa proprietors, are now known to occur near rural settlements as well. Icklingham alone has yielded three (*Britannia*, **8** (1977), 444–5). The tank from Wiggonholt (Sussex) was once thought to belong to a villa, but excavations have now shown that Wiggonholt was a single complex settlement, an 'area of Romano-British occupation the great extent of which was hitherto unsuspected' (Evans 1974, 97). Another tank which would seem to derive from a settlement rather than a villa has been recovered from a well at Ashton, by Oundle (Northants) (*Britannia*, **8** (1977), 399).

The 4th century Christian silver treasure found at Water Newton points to a Christian focus which presumably was associated with the town of Durobrivae (Painter 1975, 333–45; 1977). Unfortunately it is not known whether this focus consisted of a single wealthy house-hold, an important shrine, or a congregational church. Thomas (1980, 133) has suggested that the choice of the word *altare* in the inscription on the silver bowl of the treasure could signify the presence of a church building, 'the use of the part for the whole'. However this may be, the Durobrivae assemblage raises new and fascinating questions about the status of Christianity in 4th century Britain.

At this point it is appropriate to raise a matter that has not often been discussed in connection with the archaeology of Romano-British Christianity, that is the various and sometimes conflicting attitudes to Christian art which were held within different sections of the early Church. Opinion was divided as to whether the artistic embellishment of Christian buildings was permissible at all. By the 4th century much of this hesitation had been overcome, but in Britain it is interesting to notice that the plainest of the probable Christian buildings so far encountered occur in urban or suburban settings, whereas the more ostentatious and eclectic manifestations have appeared at sites which were presumably in private hands. The contrast has usually been explained in terms of differences in patronage and taste, but it might conceivably reflect a deeper division, as between those who interpreted the instructions of the Decalogue in a strict and literal way, and those who were more liberal. The ascetic outlook was represented at an earlier date by the refusal of men like Tertullian (*c* 170–220) to come to any kind of 'cultural accommodation with the secular world' (Markus 1974, 50), and indeed by certain churchmen in the 4th century (Toynbee 1968, 178). It would be rash to regard Romano-British Christianity as a homogeneous phenomenon.

The general picture to emerge from archaeological work and chance finds during the 1960s and 1970s is of slowly growing evidence for diversity. This, coupled with the (albeit thin) cross-section of sites which have probably produced churches (cantonal town, small town, villa, fort) conforming with the categories in which they might be expected to occur (congregational, extra-mural, and estate churches: Thomas 1980, 134–8), suggests that the diffusion of Christianity in the 4th century may have been more geographically and socially extensive than was once supposed.

For the immediate future there is a need to suspend the conventional site classifications of medieval church archaeology, and to look instead at ways in which different liturgical and ritual functions may have been combined or juxtaposed. Cemeteries, for instance, may have served other purposes apart from burial or commemoration (Green 1977, 52). The ambiguous character of the estate church at Lullingstone may reflect a possibility that it was intended for use in a variety of ways. Finally, it is not inconceivable that some Romano-British ecclesiastical sites may lie below or close to churches which were founded in later centuries, or that particular aspects of late Roman Christianity were to have repercussions for what was to follow. The prospects for research in this direction, which may in turn throw extra light upon the Christian archaeology of Roman Britain, are examined in the chapter which follows.

'... *the Christianity of the British Isles is a continuing whole, and the absorption of the English appears as a new starting point only if its earlier history is disregarded*' (J Morris 1973, 389).

It is difficult to formulate any corresponding generalization about the archaeology of this 'continuing whole'. Indeed, if we were to be deprived of the literary sources which fitfully illuminate the ecclesiastical history of Britain from the 5th to the 7th centuries it is salutary to reflect how little of the story they tell could be pieced together from the study of material evidence alone. There is no archaeology that is yet recognizable for the Patrician phase of Irish Christianity, for example (Thomas 1976, 251), and not much which can be definitely connected with the Church from which it sprang. What evidence there is is mostly of a peculiarly arcane nature, being difficult to identify or associate and even harder to date, without constant appeal to external sources. The external sources, the texts, present considerable difficulties themselves. All but a handful are later in date than the period under review. Where there is a likelihood that a text was based upon an earlier source it is not always easy for archaeologists to evaluate or choose between the different views of historians who have attempted to distinguish between original material, speculation, and interpolated fiction. Even comparatively well known works, like Gildas's *De Excidio Britonnum* (Winterbottom 1978) and the *Life of St Sampson* (Fawtier 1912), offer little in the way of internal corroboration. The insecurity of both written and archaeological evidence is increased when one is used to cross-brace an argument suggested by the other.

To the foregoing difficulties may be added some others of scholarly making. First, the use by archaeologists of defeatist or vague terminology, like 'Dark Ages' and 'Celtic Church', has not assisted study and may possibly have done something to retard it. Secondly, Bede's determination to emphasize the importance of the Augustinian mission, and hence to affirm the Roman authority of which it was an extension (Pepperdene 1958), has perhaps led to an undervaluation of the part played by Irish evangelists in the affairs of the English Church in the 7th century, and has certainly distracted archaeological attention away from whatever ecclesiastical structure – however we choose to label it – that existed, whether continuously or not, in parts of west and north Britain in the 5th and 6th centuries.

Here we meet a third problem, which has been identified as follows: 'All aspects of British archaeology tend at the moment, certainly in the post-Roman period, to be highly particularistic, to be concerned with a particular object or class of objects, an individual building, or a single site, rather than with trying to see the broader patterns within which these fit' (Biddle 1976a, 65). The problem lies in the fact that particularistic inquiries require, but do not always receive, careful co-ordination and knowledgeable oversight, since the boundaries which multiply between them have an inherent tendency to influence and ultimately dominate discussion by causing important judgements to be founded more upon contrasts (or 'turning points') than upon correspond-ences (or 'continuity'). Bias of this kind is unwelcome at any time, and never more so than in the immediately post-Roman centuries, when the pivotal issues can now be seen to centre not so much upon the identities of different ethnic, dynastic, or political groups as upon the nature and quality of the relations which existed between them. So, to take a banal example, the rewards of intensive studies of objects contained in the graves of pagan English (or, at least, of those who are customarily considered to have been both pagan and English on the basis of the objects), or of the early Christian cemeteries of west and north Britain, might also be assessed in relation to each other. We may notice that while there are no early Christian monuments in south-east Britain and no pagan English burials in Wales, there are features which are common to the structure of cemeteries in both regions, such as the specially marked grave and graveyards composed of findless, oriented burials, and even that, apparently (*HE*, i.15), it was not unknown for an important Englishman to be commemorated by a lettered memorial. Nevertheless, the *modus operandi* of modern archaeology ensures that the cemeteries of the two regions (and, frequently, of pagans and Christians in the *same* region) are regarded as falling within the provinces of separate groups of investigators, each of whom may be proceeding with only a limited awareness of the preoccupations and insights of the other. The task of synthesis and reconciliation of data, if it is undertaken at all, is left to third parties.

This chapter is written with two aims: first, to review the archaeological evidence which pertains to Christianity in Britain during the post-Roman centuries and, secondly, to identify some lines of inquiry which show promise as means of elucidating this evidence, or of acquiring more of it, or of opening up areas which hitherto have not been explored. In compiling the review an attempt has been made to avoid the problems outlined in the previous paragraph: that is, to adopt, where possible, a thematic rather than a particularistic approach. It is also important to stress that the Christianity of the post-Roman age, as of other ages, was not a phenomenon divorced from worldly life. The Church was closely engaged with political organization, technology, trade, lines of communication (internal and international), and the pattern of settlement; it cannot be considered apart from them. Evidence about Christianity in these centuries is thus worth seeking not only as an aid to the writing of more enlightened religious history, but also for the insights it affords into other aspects of the *milieu* within which it existed.

The evidence and its presentation

It is convenient to arrange the archaeological evidence for Christian organization and activity in the post-Roman centuries under two main heads: cemeteries and churches. The former embrace not merely burial grounds but also their adjuncts: forms of enclosure, shrines, memorials, and inscriptions. Under the latter can be taken not just the church building but also the previous history of the site, which will frequently be found to have to do with a cemetery, and its setting, eg as part of a royal complex, or a religious community. Both must be discussed in relation to the settlement history of which they were products. Evidence which is not archaeological, such as place-names, linguistic evidence, and the dedications of churches, is introduced where this has been or could be directly related to the archaeology. The review that follows is prefaced by a short survey of some of the opinions that have exerted influence on discussion of the ecclesiastical history of the period.

Continuity or discontinuity? Minutes of a debate

The visit of Germanus of Auxerre to Britain in 428–9, possibly that of Palladius to Ireland in the next decade (cf J Morris 1973, 345), and the ministry of Patrick testify that a Church in Britain was alive, if not flourishing, in the second quarter of the 5th century. After Germanus's second visit, conventionally held to have occurred in c 448, but very possibly earlier, in the mid 430s (Wood, forthcoming), we hear little. British clergy are occasionally glimpsed abroad, but it is seldom stated from what parts of the island they came, or where they had received their training. Hence an opinion has arisen that organized Christianity in south-east Britain was extinguished during the 5th century. How, why, and when the Church failed in this part of the former province is not, however, explained.

It has been argued that Christianity in late Roman Britain was essentially urban and that its organization was in the hands of an aristocratic minority. As urban life seems to have declined both in quality and extent in the 5th century, quite possibly to vanishing point, it is imagined that the Church would have withered, since it is claimed that the clergy of the 4th century had made little, if any, progress towards the conversion of folk residing in the countryside who might have provided the popular base which could have prolonged the survival of the faith through the vicissitudes which followed (Radford 1962, 1–2; cf Alcock 1971, 133–4).

This view, which archaeology is ill-equipped to reinforce or contest, remains in fashion, although attention has been drawn in the previous chapter to some scattered signs that the extent of archaeological evidence for Christianity in the 4th century may have been underestimated. Whatever it was that brought about such a rapid shift in the balance of power in south-east Britain around 440–450 is outside the scope of this discussion. Decisive military action on the part of the English, some of whom were already present (but in what numbers? (Arnold 1980)), allegedly in a military capacity, is an obvious possibility. But the political change seems to have been so abrupt that we may wonder if parts of Britain were formally ceded to the English, an arrangement that can certainly be paralleled in other regions of the west, and to which there is a faint pointer in the Gallic Chronicle of 452.

In areas outside the south-eastern zone it is possible that elements of Christian organization did survive. Three regions in particular – Wales, south-west England, and an arc of country reaching north-eastwards from the Solway to the Tweed basin (Fig 7) – contain archaeological indications of Christian activity in the 6th and, to a lesser extent, in the 5th century (Thomas 1971, 10–47).

However, the interpretation of this evidence is no easy task. Many scholars incline to the view that it does not reflect any continuation of Romano-British Christianity, but was the outcome of an evangelical ministry deriving from monasticism in 5th century Gaul. According to Frend, the age of the 'Celtic saints' opened 'an entirely new chapter' (1968, 46).

Two lines of argument, one negative and one positive, have been used to support the case for a re-entry of Christianity into Britain. The negative argument centres on the paucity of archaeological evidence for Christianity during the 4th century in south-west England and in Wales: that is, in two of the three regions which contain concentrations of evidence for a Christian presence in the 5th and 6th centuries. On this view the case for discontinuity rests not only on the likelihood that the Romano-British Church failed to maintain itself in western areas through the 5th century, but also, and perhaps more particularly, on the proposition that there was little, if anything, to maintain.

The second, positive, argument complements the first: there was a 'complete cultural break' with the past in 5th century Wales, and we must reckon 'with a new cultural movement involving the spread of Christian immigrants into Wales from Gaul by way of our western approaches' (Bowen 1954, 17). The archaeological case for this 'complete cultural break' hangs mainly upon the interpretation of inscribed memorial stones. Wales has so far yielded over 150 stones bearing inscriptions, not all explicitly Christian, which are thought to date from the 5th, 6th, and 7th centuries (Nash-Williams 1950). Some of these inscriptions contain exotic elements, consisting 'principally of Christian formulae in use in Gaul and around the shores of the Mediterranean' (J M Lewis 1976a, 179; cf Nash-Williams 1950; RCAHMW Anglesey, xciv–xcv, civ–cxvii; Jackson 1953, 149–93). It is claimed that these formulae, taken in conjunction with the predominantly western distribution of the stones which bear them, point unmistakably to an extraneous origin for the Christianity of post-Roman Wales. If this case is accepted, it ought also to apply to south-west England, for according to Radford 'Topographical and hagiographical research has shewn that Somerset, like Devon and Cornwall, was evangelized by missionaries based on Wales and directed ultimately to Brittany' (1961–2, 33).

It is interesting to compare the foregoing arguments with the analysis of evidence, chiefly archaeological, from north Britain which has been put forward by Professor Thomas (1968; 1971). In this region there are distinct, though limited, archaeological traces of 4th century Christian activity in the Carlisle–Solway area, evidence of Christians in the army within the Hadrian's Wall zone, together with signs of a Christian community centred on Whithorn in the 5th century (Thomas 1980). Thomas has argued that the pattern and date of early Christian antiquities in other northern regions (Galloway, the Tweed basin, the lands around the Forth, and Strathclyde) are consistent with a gradual expansion of Christianity from the Carlisle zone into these other areas during the 5th and especially the 6th century. The apparent coincidence of these areas with individual kingdoms of the North British leads Thomas to propose that 'we are dealing with territorial, tribal, bishoprics' (1968, 111–12). Part of the importance of this hypothesis lies in the sequence of dates which is envisaged. A diocese of Whithorn/Galloway seen as an offshoot of a diocese of Carlisle is considered to have been in being 'by the middle of, if not by the beginning of, the fifth century . . .' (1968, 111). This time-sequence offers little

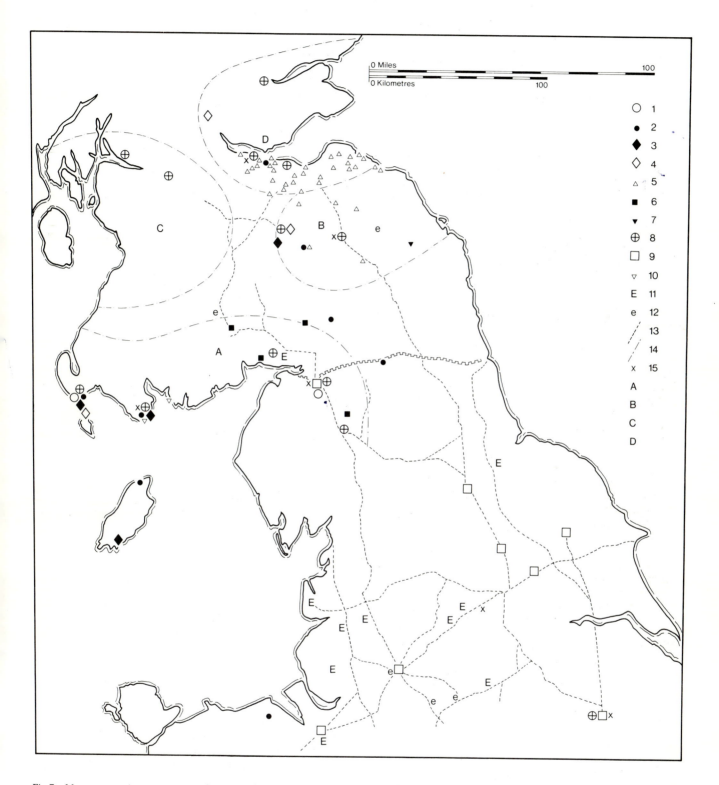

Fig 7   *Map representing an attempt to bring together the various strands of evidence pertaining to the existence and spread of Christianity in north Britain during the period 400–650. The source, unless otherwise stated, is Thomas 1968.*
Key to symbols: *1: memorial stone, −450; 2: memorial stone, 450–550; 3: memorial stone, 550–; 4: memorial stone, date uncertain; 5: long-cist cemetery; 6: cross slab; 7: royal centre; 8: ecclesiastical centre; 9: former Roman centre; 10: sub-Roman cemetery; 11: place-name,* Eccles- *(source: Cameron 1968); 12: place-name,* Eccles *(source: Cameron 1968); 13: course of Roman road; 14: approximate boundary of sub-Roman territorial diocese envisaged by Thomas (1968, 114–15); 15: non-Anglian place-name applied to place of ecclesiastical importance; A: diocesan zone, Rheged; B: diocesan zone, Tweed basin; C: diocesan zone, Strathclyde; D: diocesan zone, Gododdin. (Drawing: Dick Raines)*

Table II The career of St Patrick: alternative chronologies

	Bury 1905	Thomas 1979
Birth of grandfather		360×65
Birth of father		390
Birth	389	415
Capture	405	430
Escape	411	436
Ordination	−418	Diaconate 445
Episcopal return	432	450
Church at Armagh	444	*Epistola* 470–1
Death	461	493

scope for the prising open of any 'cultural break', especially as the main indications of an infusion of Gaulish Christianity come later in the 5th century and in the 6th.

This view of a loosely articulated diocesan pattern, ultimately rooted in the organization of the late Roman Church, is reinforced by what we know of St Patrick. Whether, as Thomas has proposed, Patrick originated in a north British *milieu* or emerged from somewhere further south does not really affect our understanding of the outline of his career (Table II), nor should controversy over the placing of the termini of this career be permitted to obscure the essential fact that 'all save the most eccentric views would see him as working, and dying, in the 5th century' (Thomas 1979, 82). From the two short writings which are generally attributed to Patrick, the *Confessio* and *Epistola* (for versions of the texts see list in Thomas 1979, 98), we gather that Patrick's grandfather had been a priest (*presbyter*), and his father a decurion. Patrick's knowledge of Latin points to a period of formal schooling. While still a teenager Patrick was abducted and spent a period of captivity in Ireland. Subsequently he escaped, possibly to Gaul, and underwent training for the priesthood. Patrick later returned to Ireland as bishop, where his episcopal career was subject to controversy, largely on account of the opposition from churchmen on the British mainland. It has been said that the importance of Patrick's texts lies in the conclusion that among 'the few facts that may be inferred is the continued existence in Britain of a diocesan church with a hierarchical structure and occasional synods. It would seem too that Patrick regarded his compatriots in Britain as still *cives* and *Romani* and to that extent nominal Christians at least' (W H Davies 1968, 136–7). Patrick's use of formal Roman titles, which are both echoed (in the case of *cives*) and supplemented by others on inscribed stones from north Wales (eg Nash-Williams 1950, nos 92, 103) later on, invites a reconsideration of the objection to continuity raised by Bowen, Radford, and others: namely, that such details occur in areas that had never been extensively Romanized, and where there is no archaeological evidence to suggest that the late Roman Church had made progress in enlarging its membership beyond aristocratic circles before the end of the 4th century.

There are really two points here: (1) that the Church in Britain, like its counterpart in Gaul up to the time of St Martin, had made little impression upon the *pagani*; and (2) that the eventual collapse of urban society, and hence of the Christian aristocracy that it sustained (or vice versa), would have deprived the Church of even that slender base of support that it had previously enjoyed. Both points carry extra force when it is remembered that urban life was not extensive in south-west England, and virtually non-existent in Wales.

The first half of this argument we might accept, though always keeping in mind the visit of the evangelical Victricius to Britain in the 390s, the growing evidence for late Roman Christianity, witnessed in both rural and urban surroundings, as at Icklingham and Poundbury, and possibly now for its sub-Roman continuation in places like Exeter (Bidwell *et al* 1979). But the second part of the argument does not flow inevitably from the first. Wilson has argued that '. . . the case for continuity does not . . . turn on the question of whether the peasantry of Roman Britain had already been converted. It is very doubtful whether the peasantry of early sub-Roman Wales had been converted; the evidence of the early saints' lives . . . not to mention that of the genealogies, strongly suggests that Christianity was still an aristocratic way of life, but it was aristocratic and monastic instead of aristocratic and urban' (P A Wilson 1966, 9–10).

If this can be argued for Wales, where urban life had hardly existed, the 'late chronology' proposed by Thomas for Patrick and his dealings with the British Church hardly seems out of place, even though this would imply the continuation of Romanized institutions, including 'an urban-controlled hierarchical Church', in north-west England at least until late in the 5th century. Thomas has observed that the archaeology appropriate to such a scene has not yet emerged (1979, 93). It is tempting to argue that the archaeology has not yet been recognized, for Barker's summary of the latest occupation of the baths basilica at Wroxeter reaches the provisional conclusion that 'the final period can now be subdivided and consequently shown to last a good deal longer than was first thought, so that it is likely to stretch well into the 5th century, if not to its end' (P A Barker 1979, 181). The first of Barker's options would match the 'orthodox' chronology for Patrick's career. The second would provide fitting accompaniment to the 'late chronology'. There is, of course, nothing at all to connect Wroxeter the place with Patrick, but one is bound to doubt whether the monumental wooden buildings at Wroxeter were unusual or particular to that site. Could it be that excavators elsewhere, as previously at Wroxeter, have excavated with a kind of 5th century night-blindness following the cessation of pottery, the coin-list, and masonry building, the traditional sources of illumination?

Wilson's argument about the aristocratic/monastic *milieu* of post-Roman Welsh Christianity, which differs from the more staunchly sub-Roman model proffered by Thomas, may also be considered in relation to the predominantly westerly distribution of the inscribed memorial stones of Wales, and the influx of missionary elements that this is held to represent. The general absence of these stones from south-east Wales and the Welsh borderlands – 'the very areas where Roman life and culture struck its deepest roots (Bowen 1954, 17) – is mirrored in other aspects of the history of the region. Alcock, for instance, has noticed in his discussion of the early Christian phase of Dinas Powys that in 'the relatively unromanized areas of Gwynedd, Dyfed and much of Powys, we find in the post-Roman centuries relatively stable dynasties ultimately of Roman establishment. In the Romanized south-east, by contrast, we have difficulty in discerning either a stable dynasty or an underlying Roman authority' (1963, 72). According to

Davies we *may*, in fact, be able to discern an underlying Roman authority in south-east Wales (W Davies 1979b), but in the light of Alcock's point it seems desirable to discriminate, at least initially, between arguments founded on the distribution of the stones and those which centre on the intrusive formulae that are sometimes found upon them. The former could have to do with the pattern of Roman-derived authority, the latter, possibly, with the ways in which external contributions were being assimilated by that authority.

The subject of external contributions leads us to consider the use in Britain and Ireland, and ultimate abandonment, of an 84-year Easter cycle. An old, though still quite widespread misconception argues that the 'Celtic' method of computing Easter arose out of some deviant insular evolution, following the supposed isolation of churches in Atlantic Britain by the pagan English. This is wrong. The idea that churchmen in 6th century Wales or Ireland were unaware of significant ecclesiastical developments in Gaul is out of the question. Alternative views include the proposition that Paschal reforms adopted in Gaul during the 6th century were resisted in Wales, not out of ignorance but as a matter of policy (Miller 1979, 116–21, n 65), or that the Welsh preference for a traditional method of reckoning can be seen as a pointer in the direction of continuity (P A Wilson 1966). The subject can best be introduced in a suggestion that the controversies which did occur are traceable less to a clash between distinctively rival methods of calculation and more to a confusion, a confusion, moreover, which was by no means confined to the churches of the British Isles.

From the early days of the Church there had been some regional variation in methods used for the determination of Easter (C W Jones 1934). The bishops who attended the Council of Nicaea in 325 were conscious of this problem, and expressed the hope that uniformity could be achieved. No decision upon a particular system was actually taken at Nicaea, however, and for the next century Rome seems to have relied upon the already antique 84-year cycle which was then in use (Harrison 1976, 32–3). Meanwhile, a superior 19-year cycle had been developed by the skilled computists of Alexandria, to whom the papacy often deferred in the interests of concord (C W Jones 1934). Nevertheless, there were sporadic divergences between the Latin and Greek usages, and clashes which occurred in 444 and 455 prompted Pope Leo I to refer the whole problem to his archdeacon, Hilarius, who in turn commissioned one Victorius of Aquitaine to review the issue.

In 457 Victorius published a set of Easter tables. In essence this was a modified version of the Alexandrian system, although certain Latin elements were retained. Unfortunately Victorius also introduced several strands of error into his reckoning, with the result that alternative dates were available for Easter in certain years between which the papacy had to choose. Beyond this, errors sometimes cancelled each other out, leading to a coincidence between Greek and Latin Easters which spawned confusion as to which was really which. The Victorian tables circulated widely in the west, and were officially adopted in Gaul at the Second Council of Orleans in 541. It seems certain that they were known, if not actually used, in Ireland before the end of the 6th century (O'Connell 1936; Harrison 1976).

In 525 a canonist by the name of Dionysius produced an Easter cycle which was soundly based upon Alexandrian principles and overcame the deficiencies of the Victorian tables. The Dionysiac system was not adopted immediately, but it did begin to win favour early in the 7th century. It was a Dionysiac system which was adopted at Whitby in 664 (Poole 1934, 32; Harrison 1973, 108–9) and which, indeed, has remained the basis of reckoning down to the present.

The traditional method of reckoning employed in Ireland, Gwynedd, and presumably elsewhere in the Christian zones of Britain during the 6th century was an 84-year cycle. When and how this system entered Britain is not known, nor has the ultimate source of the cycle been identified, although an origin in Asia Minor is possible. It is conceivable that the Irish/British 84-year cycle was inherited from the Church in late Roman Britain. But this is not certain, and the usage could have been derived from Gaul or even somewhere more exotic. However, if a link with late Roman Britain is to be ruled out, the failure of the Victorian tables to win acceptance in Ireland during the latter part of the 6th century would seem to argue that the missionaries from Gaul (or elsewhere) had earlier been operating a conservative usage, and that they introduced it into Britain at a date which gave time for the system to become firmly bedded in Irish/British tradition before the official promulgation of the Victorian tables after the decision of 541. There is, however, a further problem in that when Irish churchmen looked into the Victorian tables they judged them to be unsatisfactory – which, of course, they were. Around the year 600 the Irishman Columbanus, then Abbot of Luxeuil, wrote to Pope Gregory with complaints about the Victorian system, and stressing the advantages of the traditional Irish 84-year cycle (Harrison 1976, 57–9; C W Jones 1943, 91). Hence it would be wrong to attribute a reactionary mood to the British and Irish churches simply on the basis of their resistance to Victorian practice.

What can be said is that evidence exists to show that all three usages – Irish/British-84, Victorian, and Dionysiac – were under discussion in parts of Britain and Ireland during the first half of the 7th century. We also know that Irish and, probably, Welsh acquaintance with the tables of Victorius can be traced to the second half of the 6th century. Conformity was achieved gradually during the 7th century, although Gwynedd obstinately continued to employ the ancient 84-year cycle until the reform of Archbishop Elfoddw in 768.

In summary:

(1) In most years the various usages would yield a common date for Easter. Discord was occasional, and was normally forestalled by a papal circular giving details of the forthcoming Easter. Such messages did not always arrive, particularly in outlying provinces (Spain was also sometimes out of step), and hence clashes could occur.

(2) The persistence in Britain of an 84-year cycle, in existence in Wales and Ireland during the 6th century, and transmitted to Northumbria via Iona in the 7th, could be regarded as a link with the Church of late- or sub-Roman Britain. If not, then we must infer the presence of missionaries, themselves operating a conservative usage, acting in ignorance of Victorius, or both.

Gildas

This brief sketch can best be rounded off with some discussion of Gildas and his *De excidio et conquestu Britanniae*, the text of which is now conveniently accessible in translation (Winterbottom 1978).

Opinions about Gildas are diverse and full of conflict. Thus it has been claimed that Gildas never existed; that the *De excidio* is a forgery; that it consists of two separate texts. There are, however, solid grounds for believing the *De excidio* to be authentic and one integral work, and if these be accepted then we may look to the text for indications of the environment in which it was written. Further, because Gildas was setting the moral problems of his own day within an historical perspective, we might hope to acquire some insight into the course of events leading up to the composition of the text. Publication of the *De excidio* is usually regarded as having taken place in the second half of the 540s, although earlier dates have been proposed and could perhaps be argued for from the high standard of Gildas's education. If parts of Gildas's account are factually wrong or chronologically garbled (eg c. 15, 18) this may not matter; what counts for more is Gildas's attitude towards those events.

The picture that emerges is of the greatest interest. We are told that the 5th century had been a period of intermittent conflict, first with the Picts and Scots, later with the English. We hear that 'the cities of our land are not populated even now as they once were; right to the present they are deserted, in ruins and unkempt' (c. 26). Gildas suggests that he lives in an age of contradictions. The prevailing condition is one of *serenitas*, but the 'controls of truth and justice' have been 'overthrown' (c. 26).

The decline, however, has involved a progressive attenuation of those things that are held to represent *romanitas* rather than a severance from them. The vocabulary of Roman tradition is still there, as it had been in the writings of Patrick. The question of a 'cultural break' does not arise. Formal graduations of society are remembered with the use of terms like *reges*, *publici*, *privati* (c. 26). Britain has her *sacerdotes*, *ministros*, and *clericos* who minister in churches (*ecclesiae domus*) (c. 66). There is no shortage of clerical manpower; the problem lies in its inferiority, for the grades of clergy are *insipientes*, *impudentes*, and *raptores*. There is a *mater ecclesia*, but its authority is being subverted by *sacerdotes* whose teaching is being 'darkened by bad deeds' (c. 96).

W H Davies suggests that this 'is a scene evocative in some ways of the declining *romanitas* of fifth-century Gaul rather than the somewhat restricted and austere background usually associated with the tendentious accounts of early British monasticism and the Age of the Saints . . . it is an altogether unexpected picture and one never to be inferred without Gildas's contemporary testimony' (1968, 141; cf Miller 1979, 12).

Missing from Gildas's Britain are references to a permanent episcopal framework, although it is stated that bishops sought consecration by travelling overseas (c. 67). This point deserves some discussion.

In the 5th and 6th centuries the world of the western Roman Empire was broken by the barbarians, but it was not destroyed. The emergence of a number of autonomous Romano-Germanic kingdoms was accomplished partly through the maintenance and exploitation of existing administrative arrangements, but partly too as a result of cultural defensiveness on the part of Gallo-Roman aristocrats, who for nearly two centuries resisted the dilution of what was now seen as a Romano-Christian heritage, and thereby caused a political, or tribal reaction against it. During this time, therefore, the Gallo-Roman Church was not a missionary Church. Barbarians could be assimilated to it, but only on Roman terms.

Bishops in the 5th century were at the centre of public affairs. Hailing as they did from the aristocratic elite, they organized urban life, acted as administrators, and might even superintend the making of defences and fund-raising for military operations. Instruction manuals on how to be a political bishop were prepared. In the 5th, 6th, and 7th centuries the town often re-formed around the church, both in a political and, sometimes, in a physical sense. No metamorphosis of this kind could be imagined in Wales, save possibly in the south-east or Severnside (W Davies 1979b), as the prerequisite Roman urban geography did not exist. Instead, the ecclesiastical structure was wedded to tribal dynasties which appear to have wielded authority of Roman derivation. Gildas certainly *believed* that the authority was of Roman derivation. In north-west England, on the other hand, it is conceivable that some development roughly cognate with what was going on in Gaul did occur. Initially, this may have been focused on Carlisle (Thomas 1968; 1979). If that seems to be unduly speculative it is worth remembering that the most striking exceptions to 5th/6th century trends were the towns of south-east Britain, the leaders of which, whether they included bishops or not, after *c* 450, were unequal to the task of reaching a working accommodation with the English. By that yardstick, the development in Wales and the north was comparatively orthodox.

Cemeteries

Cemeteries tend to be studied, and often selected for investigation, according to their yield of artefacts. This has led to a heavy investment of effort in regions containing object-laden, and therefore usually English, cemeteries, and a corresponding reluctance to tackle sites, not only in western Britain, which are largely devoid of objects. Until fairly recently (see now Hope-Taylor 1977, 262; Rahtz 1978) the narrow equation of objects with data has involved a strange indifference to other potential sources of information: patterns of orientation, boundaries, internal pathways, groupings, structures. Moreover, there has been a tendency to investigate cemeteries without due regard for the history of the communities which supplied their occupants.

All this is now changing, but as an illustration of the complications which may be engendered by divisive or exclusive scholarship we may consider the circumstances which appear to have existed in a number of English cemeteries between *c* 600 and *c* 750. Commonly, we find a progressive though by no means universal or steady reduction of grave-goods during this period, followed by closure of the burial ground. It has been argued that these closed graveyards, which in the nature of things are the only ones to have been consciously investigated, were replaced by Christian graveyards on different and usually distant sites. This argument has been formulated chiefly by those who specialize in the investigation of pagan English cemeteries, with the result that issues connected with the establishment of churchyards have sometimes been either oversimplified or ignored. These issues are discussed in more detail in the next chapter. The point to be registered here is that in the present state of knowledge it would be equally valid to regard some of the late-pagan 'closed graveyards' as churchyards in an arrested state of development. In other words the hiatus, at present widely looked upon as the norm, could be providing a commentary upon a more general tendency towards continuity. This possibility – it is only that – assumes a special relevance in connection with our failure to detect even a handful of post-Roman cemeteries in some of the areas which did not fall under English dominion until late in the 6th century or early in the 7th century, such as the countries of the western Midlands or Elmet. Could this failure be explicable in terms of the *absence* of contrasting (ie find-laden English) cemeteries with which we have become accustomed to calibrate developments elsewhere? In the absence of a hiatus, we are obliged to begin by thinking of continuity.

With the foregoing points in mind we may turn again to the writings of Gildas. Near the start of the *De excidio* Gildas refers to the *sanctorum martyrum* of Roman Britain. Those mentioned by name are *sanctum Albanum Verolamiensem* and Aaron and Julian *Legionum urbis cives*, the first of the latter pair possibly reflecting the importance of Jewish colonies in the early transmission of Christianity through the Empire. (Curiously, relics of Aaron and Julian, linked with those of another martyr named Salvius, were listed as being held by the church at Leominster in 1286 (Capes 1909, 124).) Gildas mentions no other early martyrs by name, but says he knows of others *in diversis locis*, stating that it is a matter for serious regret that many *corporum sepulturae* and *passionum loca* are now no longer accessible to citizens who would wish to visit them, apparently because of the intervention of enemies. Gildas, then, is quite explicit about the importance of martyrial graves and allied *loca*. We are left in no doubt that such sites held a fundamental appeal to the Christian British public.

Gildas's statement may be paralleled in the archaeological record. But just as some of his terms (eg *sacerdos*) are duplicated but not precisely explained in the wording of inscriptions upon monuments in Wales and north Britain, so the significance of the archaeological parallels is not fully understood. Focal graves, for example, are often met with in British, Irish, and later English cemeteries of the period which is under consideration (Thomas 1971, 58–64, with examples). Far from all such graves are Christian. It is possible that some may have an ancestral, family, or status significance rather than any purely religious *raison d'être*. Moreover, in origin the specially marked grave is unmistakably pagan. This presents no conceptual problem – the physical characteristics of Christian burial were in the main acquired through a sieving out of pagan mortuary practices – but it poses a definite archaeological difficulty in that it is often impossible to discriminate between pagan cemeteries and genuine Christian burial grounds which may resemble them. This in itself points to a kind of continuity, or conservatism, a process which might be underlined by J M Lewis's observation that some isolated memorials in Wales which stand or once stood 'within small circular earthworks, assumed to be disc barrows of the Bronze Age' could in fact be the surviving foci or sub-foci of early Christian cemeteries (1976b, 15). The suggestion that pagan English places of worship were situated within cemeteries (Hope-Taylor 1977, 263) raises further questions (cf Rahtz & Watts 1979). Would such arrangements arise in imitation or parody of Roman Christian practice, or are we to see them in terms of independent development? If pagan cemeteries were furnished with shrines, to what extent, if at all, could these be regarded as forerunners of the later *Eigenkirchen* and their graveyards (see below: 75)?

These and related issues are now well to the fore in discussion, thanks particularly to the pioneering efforts of Professors Thomas and Rahtz, and it is not necessary to reproduce the large amount of case material that has been marshalled elsewhere (eg Thomas 1971; Rahtz 1977; 1978; Rahtz & Watts 1979; Hope-Taylor 1977). Thanks, too, to the publication of regional surveys which assimilate the fragmentary researches of many individuals (eg Pearce 1978), we are approaching the stage where it is becoming possible to contemplate the shape of patterns. Thus in south-west England the development of graveyards before the arrival of the English is tolerably clear in principle, although there is still much 'play' in the scheme of dates. To a body of investigated late-to-sub-Roman cemeteries such as Camerton (Rahtz & Fowler 1972), Henley Wood (Greenfield 1970), and Exeter (Bidwell 1978; 1979) may be added 'a large group of potentially pre-Saxon sites' (Pearce 1978, 67). Characteristically these graveyards contain inhumation burials oriented east–west, they tend towards the circular or oval in plan, they are girdled by an embanked enclosure, and they were designated by the topographically descriptive Old Cornish word *lann*, which may be perpetuated in a medieval or modern place-name element (1978, 67–8). A number of graveyards with *lann* names contain inscribed memorial stones, either displaced (eg Lanivet (Cornwall)) or *in situ*. The *lan* prefix occurs in place-names extending into Dorset and Somerset (1978, 73), and there seem to be some outliers in Gloucestershire. Not all such graveyards continued in use. Some, of which that at Beacon Hill, Lundy, is a good example, were closed down (Thomas *et al* 1969). Alternatively, a graveyard might attain 'maturity' with the later emplacement of a church within it.

It is worthwhile attempting a comparison of the pattern that is now crystallizing in parts of western Britain with the archaeology of certain types of cemetery in the east. These cemeteries include some which have been listed and described by Rahtz as being 'neither obviously Roman nor clearly related to the English settlement'. As with the graveyards discussed above, most 'seem to be late or immediately post-Roman, but there is some evidence that the class begins in earlier Roman or even in prehistoric times' (1977, 53). In distribution they can occur virtually anywhere in England. Few, if any, of these cemeteries, including some of those that later attracted churches, are demonstrably Christian. However, a view seems to have arisen that a cemetery must either be fully Christian, or contain a distinct enclave of Christian burials, if it is not to be pagan. Other possibilities might be considered.

The demise of the Church in eastern Britain after *c* 450 does not oblige us to assume that all *corporum sepulturae* were promptly forgotten, still less that all late Roman cemeteries which contained them immediately passed out of use. Important Christian graves may still have been places of pilgrimage, local devotion, or simply superstitious interest after the collapse of the institutional framework of the Church. At St Albans we may well have an example of the progression *locus sanctus*/ *memoria*/medieval church which is exemplified on the continent at such places as Xanten and Bonn (Levison 1941; J Morris 1968; Radford 1971; Biddle 1976b, 110–11). According to Gildas, as we have seen, Verulamium was still regarded as a premier cult site in his own day. Bede wrote of its continuation in the 8th century, and mentioned a church which had been built there by, he thought, the Romans (*HE*, i.7). If this could happen at St Albans, in south-east England, there would seem to be no inherent reason why interest in what might be provisionally termed 'neighbourhood cults' should not have been maintained or subsequently deliberately stimulated elsewhere. The embers of some cults, particularly in the north and west, may still have been glowing at the end of the 6th century, to be kindled back into flame with the advent of the Roman mission and Irish evangelists in the decades that followed. It would not be necessary to invoke a Christian impulse to explain the survival of cults during the 6th century. Other mechanisms can be observed in Gaul. Gregory of Tours tells an instructive tale of the *rustici* of Dijon, who for several generations had been accustomed to deposit *ex voto* offerings at a certain sarcophagus. Ecclesiastical attempts to suppress this habit met with no success, and it seems that the practice was eventually rationalized by the fabrication of a martyrial cult to render it respectable (Wood 1979a, 103). At any rate, the necessary *passio* of Benignus, the saint in question, was not discovered until rather later. Wood suggests that it is possible 'that there was a martyr, Benignus, but just as likely that the story of Benignus was created to christianise a pagan cult which the bishop had failed to destroy'. Gregory of Tours records a similar tradition about Patroclus of Troyes, and other parallels can be found in various parts of Gaul (1979a, 103). In some of these cases it is possible that Gallic bishops had strategic motives, since from the 4th to the 6th centuries they took a strong interest in early Christian martyrs 'to provide their congregations with some historical origins for their dioceses ... because martyrdom in Gaul had not been common, this led to the fabrication of *passiones* or even, as in the case of the Tergemini of Langres, to a reworking of a Greek text, with the names of places changed when the translator remembered' (Wood 1979a, 109).

At present the case for such a mechanism in Britain would be entirely speculative, and it could be objected that the pattern of later medieval cults and church dedications is wholly against it. On the other hand, the pattern of dedications before the 12th century is virtually unknown, and there seems to be little doubt that many of the later Old English dedications were altered after the Conquest, even if they had remained unchanged during the preceding centuries (Parsons 1980a, 179). But here and there freakish dedications do occur. St Ricarius, an early 7th century Gallic saint, occurs at Aberford (West Yorks) on a Roman roadside site. The general prevalence of dedications to St Helen in the north-east, Yorkshire and Lincolnshire is also worth notice (L A S Butler 1980); does this reflect something akin to the 'search for roots' which exercised the Gallic bishops in the 4th, 5th, and 6th centuries? Near Guildford (Surrey) there is a church dedicated to St Martha. This stands in isolation on a hilltop within a semicircle of earthworks which have seen prehistoric, Roman, and Anglo-Saxon activity, including at least one 6th century burial. John Morris believed this dedication to be unique in England, and suggested that it may derive from martyrium (cf Welsh *merthyr*) (1959, 142–3). Dedications favoured by Merovingian royalty – Martin, Vedast, Vincent, Radegund, Maurice – are all to be found in Lincolnshire, although whether some could represent foundations of the pre-Danish era or all must be regarded as importations by foreign proprietors after the Norman Conquest is not known. Studies of the kind undertaken for London by Professor Brooke and Mrs

Keir (1975, 139–46) are of special value (eg their observations on the likely correlation between churches with dedications to St Bride and areas of Hiberno-Norse settlement), but could be taken even further if ideas about dedications were to be compared with a definite framework of dates, established as a result of archaeological investigation, for the origins of a proportion of the churches concerned.

If the evidence of dedications is dubious or, more usually, simply unavailable, we might expect to derive something more definite from a study of the sites of parish churches. At Ilchester, for example, the Anglo-Saxon mother church of St Andrew was located outside the Roman town at Northover, in the vicinity of a Roman cemetery (Dunning 1975; Leech 1980, 357). In Essex the mother church of St Mary, Great Dunmow, lies a mile to the north-east of the modern town but on a Roman site with at least one Roman grave nearby. It has been suggested that the churches of St Bride, Fleet Street, St Andrew, Holborn, and St Martin-in-the-Fields may mark a return to abandoned or 'latent' Christian sites in the suburbs of early London (Biddle & Hudson 1973; Biddle 1976a). The Rodwells' survey of churches in the Archdeaconry of Colchester has yielded other possible candidates, including Kelvedon, Great Chesterford, and Braintree (1977). Attention has also been drawn to the previously unknown church which was found by excavation in the monastic cemetery of St John's Abbey, Colchester, in 1972 (Thomas 1980, 145). This church, of purely Anglo-Saxon structural origin, was built within a former Roman cemetery, centred on a large Roman grave, and demolished in the early medieval period (Crummy 1980, 276, n 10). Still in Colchester, Crummy has suggested that a martyrium may have existed on the site of the 12th century priory church of St Botolph, itself likely to be the successor to a pre-Conquest minster (Crummy 1980, 274). Excavations in the church of St Mary-de-Lode, Gloucester, have disclosed a Roman building beneath the church, followed by a sub- or post-Roman structure which may have acted as a mausoleum (Bryant 1980). The Anglo-Saxon ecclesiastical afterlife of the mausoleum-cum-shrine at Stone-by-Faversham (Kent), which was not necessarily Christian, is now well known (Fletcher & Meates 1969; 1977); the (possibly similar?) story of the so-called 'temple mausoleum' at Lullingstone is less familiar (cf Rigold 1972, 40). Deerhurst has yielded burials which precede the earliest church that has so far been recognized (Rahtz 1976a, 6–7), and the traces of a structure built in a Roman idiom have been found outside the west end. The church at Wells is normally considered to be one of the rural, non-Roman pre-Conquest ecclesiastical sites. Recent excavations have shown that the wells in question were much frequented in the Roman period, and that a late- or sub-Roman building, almost certainly a mausoleum, stood beside the site of the first Anglo-Saxon church (Dr W J Rodwell, *pers comm*) (Figs 8 and 9). Lastly, for what it is worth, a Roman building with a mosaic pavement and a nearby single Roman burial lay beneath and beside the first, probably 10th century, stone church of St Helen-on-the-Walls, York (Magilton 1980, 17). No stress has been laid upon this point in the report, however, and discussion of local traditions which appear to prefigure the archaeological facts (the identity of the Roman aside) is understandably diffident (Palliser in Magilton 1980, 6).

One objection to the ideas advanced above, which in essence amount to no more than the suggestion that

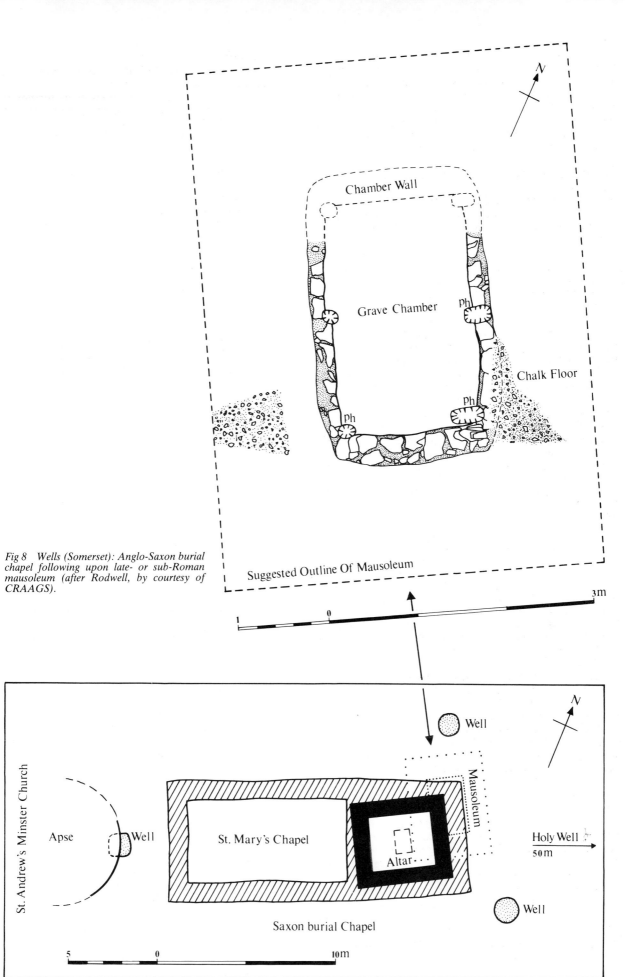

N

Chamber Wall

Grave Chamber

ph

ph

ph

Chalk Floor

Fig 8 Wells (Somerset): Anglo-Saxon burial chapel following upon late- or sub-Roman mausoleum (after Rodwell, by courtesy of CRAAGS).

Suggested Outline Of Mausoleum

0   3m

N

Well

St. Andrew's Minster Church

Apse

Well

St. Mary's Chapel

Mausoleum

Altar

Holy Well

50m

Well

Saxon burial Chapel

5   0   10m

Fig 9   Wells (Somerset): late- or sub-Roman mausoleum. (Photo: W J Rodwell, by courtesy of CRAAGS)

there is unweighed evidence for a measure of homogeneity in early cemetery history between 'English' and 'British' areas, would be based upon the contrasting forms of many cemeteries in these areas. West of a line from Chester to Exeter the form is sometimes oval or circular (O'Sullivan 1980a). To the east, rectangular forms predominate. 'Alien' forms can, of course, be found in both zones (eg the remarkable large oval churchyard at Bramham (W Yorks)), and in the north-east it is not inconceivable that some originally circular yards have been squared off. The circular form, as Thomas has pointed out (1971, 51–3) had enjoyed a venerable history before it was adopted by Christians. However, there is something to be said for a rather different line of argument, which would see graveyard forms not previously as products of religious tradition but as aspects of the prevailing pattern of land-use in a given area. There are now several cases on record where the excavation of a churchyard has shown that its boundaries, or some of them, were predetermined by earlier land divisions. This seems to have been so at Wharram Percy, and it was certainly the case at Nazeingbury, in Essex, where a Middle Saxon graveyard was found to be arranged within the bounds of a Romano-British field. In the west of England it has been suggested that the circular form 'may owe something to the example of the enclosed homesteads or "rounds" which cluster thickly in the same broad area' (Pearce 1978, 68). One is tempted to push this further: individual graves, markers, and containers have frequently been made to resemble dwellings (eg Roman tile-tombs;

structures on Anglo-Saxon graves (Hogarth 1973); house-shaped reliquary chests; the shingled hogback; the feretory (a room apart) in the cathedral or monastic church). Would it be far-fetched to wonder if this principle could have been applied at a larger scale, with the graveyard evolving as a ritualized counterpart of its settlement – the community of the dead disposed as an image of the community of the living? However this may be, we may now pass on from cemeteries as sites to the commemoration of individuals within them.

Early Christian memorials

There are in Britain more than 200 stones which are classified as Early Christian memorials. Roughly speaking, the phrase 'Early Christian' denotes the period of the 5th to the 7th centuries.

Distribution

With very few exceptions the stones are distributed between three main regions: south-west England (Dumnonia), Wales, and a tract of north Britain (Fig 10). Approximate figures for the totals of stones which have so far been recognized in these areas are as follows:

Dumnonia	50
South Wales	90
North Wales	55
North Britain	12

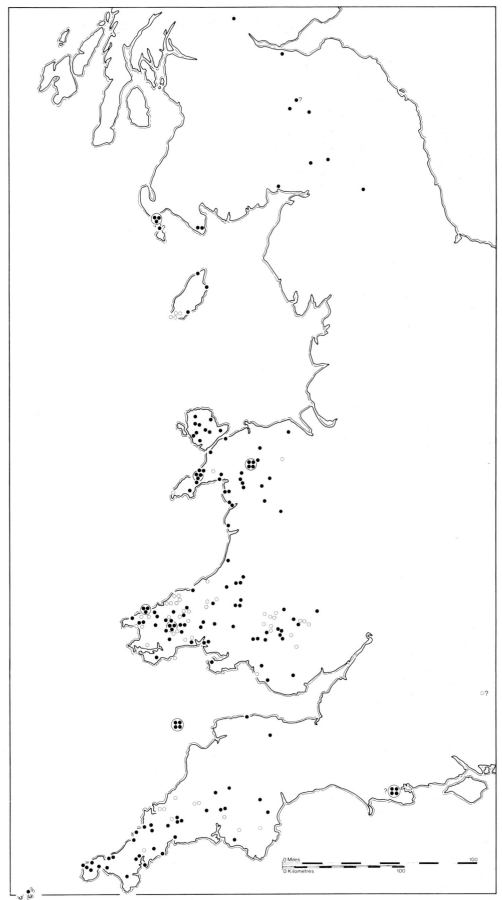

Fig 10   Map showing general distribution of memorial stones of the 5th–early 7th centuries. Solid dots represent stones bearing inscriptions in Latin. Open dots represent stones with ogams. Dots within a circle represent stones at one place. For reasons explained in the text, the dating of early Christian memorials is full of difficulty; hence no attempt has been made here to differentiate between the stones on grounds of date. (Drawing: Dick Raines)

New specimens continue to come to light, and what fraction of the original totals these figures may represent cannot be guessed at. Nevertheless, it is noticeable that recent discoveries have not greatly altered the ratios between figures for the various regions.

Within Wales, which contains nearly 75% of the known memorials, the bulk of the stones are concentrated in the north-west and south-west of the region, although there is a notable cluster in central southern Wales, between Brecon and Aberdare, and other examples are known from the coastal districts of the south-east (RCAHMW, *Glamorgan*, I.iii, 18, fig I). The Welsh stones have been described and discussed by Nash-Williams (1950), who concluded that the westerly emphasis in their distribution reflected a cultural origin outside Britain.

Virtually all the stones bear inscriptions in Latin, but a significant minority (over sixty) are bilingual and employ the Ogam script in addition to Latin. Ogam is a script based on the Latin alphabet which employs notches cut across a vertical stem line. Ogam was used above all in Ireland, where over 300 inscriptions survive, especially from the later 5th and 6th centuries. Bilingually inscribed stones occur chiefly in west Wales, where over 30 have been identified (J M Lewis 1976a). They are rare in north Wales, but a handful is known in the Isle of Man, and up to seven have been recorded in Devon and Cornwall (Pearce 1978). The concentration of stones inscribed in Ogam, complemented by others in Latin alone but which imitate Irish forms or Ogam mannerisms (eg a vertical rather than a horizontal layout), in west Wales, may reflect the presence of Irish immigrants who were settled in that area as an act of policy around 400 for purposes of defence (Alcock 1970, 58). A monolingual Ogam outlier is recorded from Silchester (Macalister 1945–9, 203), about which reservations have recently been expressed (Fulford & Sellwood 1980), but some kind of Irish presence seems to be indicated at Wroxeter, perhaps in the 5th century, by the Cunorix stone which employs the Latin alphabet in an Irish manner (Wright & Jackson 1968).

Function

As a group the Early Christian inscribed stones are generally looked upon as funerary monuments. Often this is made explicit by the use of the formula HIC IACIT (*sic*) within the inscription, together with occasional descriptive expansions such as HIC IN TUMULO/LOCO. Elsewhere a religious, if not sepulchral, intention is sometimes indicated by a chi-rho or cross. By no means all of the stones were so inscribed, however, and it has been suggested that some of them were deployed for other purposes, such as dedicatory functions or the definition of boundaries (RCAHMW, *Glamorgan* I.iii, 19; cf L A S Butler 1980). Nor is it certain that all the stones originated within a Christian *milieu*: there is a large group where the inscription is of purely genealogical character, in which X is designated the *filius/filia* of Y. This form, and its contracted variants, occurs predominantly in areas which were subject to Irish influence, although it is more extensive in distribution than Ogam.

A good number of stones now stand in churchyards but it is not clear what proportion of these are actually *in situ*. Many, to be sure, have been collected from their original positions, some of which, to judge from surviving examples, were remote, and taken into churches and churchyards for display and safer keeping. Others have been rescued from secondary locations, such as stone walls and gateways.

Surprisingly, hardly any burials associated with stones have been scientifically excavated (Alcock 1971, 247–8), and in most cases it is not even clear whether the stones represent undiscovered cemeteries or isolated wayside graves. Bu'lock (1956, 134–5) has noticed that the distribution of the monuments coincides with areas where there was a strong survival of pre-Roman culture, and suggests that the inscribed memorial may represent a fusion of the megalithic custom of raising standing stones with a contemporary concern for inscriptions. The consideration of function, therefore, requires a long perspective, further fieldwork, and excavation.

Origin

Several strands of evidence may be examined. First, as has just been mentioned, there is a possibility that archaic precedent may have played some part in the establishment of a genre of Christian memorial stones. Secondly, arguments have been advanced to the effect that the contents of some of the inscriptions offer firm pointers to the sources from which they were derived. Thirdly, it is necessary to consider what effects, if any, the monumental forms and epigraphic practices of Roman Britain may have had on the memorial-raisers of the following centuries. The issue of origin is said to be of fundamental importance to the debate about continuity. For example, it has been said that 'Historically, the stones are noteworthy as contemporary records of the *conversion* of Wales to Christianity' (Nash-Williams 1950, 1; italics mine). Less prominence seems to have been given to the possibility that the stones may represent an amalgamation of traditions, part native and part exotic, although this less dogmatic attitude appears to be reflected in the recent work of the Royal Commission: 'The process of evangelisation in the area [ie Glamorgan] is unavoidably obscure, perhaps owing as much to the survival of the faith from the late Roman period as to missionary efforts from outside the area and derived ultimately from monasteries in Gaul' (RCAHMW, *Glamorgan*, I.iii, 12).

A prehistoric contribution?

This has been discussed by Bu'lock (1956) and Thomas (1971). The extent to which prehistoric custom, itself a matter of uncertainty, may have lingered is usually beyond estimation unless facts about the circumstances of particular cases are available. In some cases these facts show that there has been unwarranted romantic speculation about the pagan ritual background to a churchyard, as in the case of the four upright stones at Ysbyty Cynfyn (Briggs 1979). However, the example of Yeavering suggests that a prehistoric monolith or timber upright could play some dynamic part in the later development of a graveyard. Hope-Taylor has drawn attention to a large 'wooden orthostat that had served as the primary datum-point for two successive halls', that had a 'ritual' grave attached to it, and subsequently 'became the centre of attraction for other burials, before finally being taken into the bounds of a Christian churchyard' (1977, 258). One possibility to be mentioned here is whether some of the Early Christian memorials really *are* prehistoric menhirs which were put to Christian use by the addition of an inscription and the making of a grave nearby. If this did happen it might explain the extreme solitude of some of the memorials; it would also require new reflections on the question of distribution. Secondary, sometimes potentially Christian burials are not uncommon in prehistoric barrows outside Wales.

The inscriptions

The formulae have been discussed by Nash-Williams (1950), Jackson (1953, 149–93), Radford (1971, 8–10; 1975), Thomas (1971), and Pearce (1978); see also RCAHMW, *Anglesey* (xciv and Appendix V). Many commentators are agreed that the early group of Latin inscriptions does not represent 'a corrupt continuation of the monumental tradition of the Roman province' but derived rather from the formulae of tombstones in 5th and 6th century Gaul, and possibly also the Rhineland (Jackson 1953, 162–4). Bowen maintained that there is 'abundant evidence in the style of writing adopted, in the type of formula employed, and sometimes in the actual allusions made, not only to date the memorials with some precision, but also to trace back their cultural origin to the Lyon and Vienne areas of Gaul' (1954, 16). Radford has argued that the content of the inscriptions – 'generally no more than a name, often accompanied by a patronymic and a very simple formula, such as HIC IACET – represents a reduction of the memorial to the barest essentials, which can only be paralleled on the contemporary Christian memorials of the continent' (1971, 9).

Perhaps some of these views merit further discussion. The claim that there is 'abundant evidence' with which to date the memorials with 'some precision' is unduly sanguine. In fact there are very few stones which can be dated with any real accuracy (eg Nash-Williams 1950, nos 104, 138, 13). The theory that the others fit into a typological sequence depends on the proposition that the change from Roman capitals to uncial letter forms took place at a measurable pace, within a definite framework of epigraphic development. This is doubtful. Moreover, as Alcock points out: 'even if a typological series of inscriptions could be established, there are not enough fixed points to calibrate the series and so use it for close dating' (1971, 244). In most cases, therefore, the order of precision which may be allowed in the dating of an individual inscription will be very low. Few, if any, monuments (some of which might be earlier than their inscriptions) have been dated by excavation, and it is not uncommon to find phases of excavated sites being dated with reference *to* monuments (eg the beginning of the burial sequence at Lundy and the O/P/TIMI stone: Thomas *et al* 1969). And were there wooden memorials, of which we are now ignorant?

The claim that the basic concept of the Early Christian memorial was imported from abroad also bears re-examination. The case for a continental, Gaulish derivation for the Early Christian memorials turns on three main assertions:

1 the inscriptions can only be paralleled abroad;
2 the distribution of the monuments reflects a western, maritime orientation; and
3 there are no intermediate monuments which bridge the gap between Romano-British memorial types and the crude, tersely worded formulae of the later insular British series.

These points are now considered in turn.

(1) There is a resemblance between some elements of some of the British inscriptions and contemporary continental forms. There are, moreover, several inscriptions which testify directly to links between Wales and Gaul (eg Nash-Williams 1950, nos 33, 104), as it seems do one or two others to intercourse between regions at home (eg the ALIORTVS stone: Nash-Williams 1950, no 87). Overseas contacts are reflected in other aspects of the archaeological record, notably in the distribution of pottery which appears to have been imported from the Mediterranean area and the French Atlantic coast (Thomas 1976). There is, too, the exotic term MEMORIA, which appears on a small number of (probably) 6th century monuments, and may be of North African derivation (Nash-Williams 1950, nos 10, 107, 191, 205; Macalister 1945–9, no 466), while attention has been drawn to international parallelisms in the development of the chi-rho (Thomas 1971, 106–10). However, the fact that there was cultural and commercial exchange between Atlantic Britain, Gaul, and beyond is hardly proof of a religious vacuum in 5th century Britain. And not all missionaries originated abroad. British churchmen journeyed to Gaul, to attend meetings or to receive instruction (cf *De excidio*, c. 97). For a number it was a round trip, and this in itself could be seen as a mechanism for the spread of epigraphic habits. Moreover, the stones themselves bear terms such as PRESBYTER (Nash-Williams 1950, nos 77, 78), SACERDOS (nos 33, 83), MAGISTRATUS (no 103), and MEDICUS (no 92), which harmonize with the sense of nostalgic romanity that is communicated by Gildas. It is difficult to regard them as importations or self-conscious attempts to ape a more sophisticated society known only by report. It is simpler to accept that they 'hint at real continuity in the form of a settled civil existence' (Thomas 1971, 102; cf Nash-Williams 1950, 14). It may be that the memorials hint at links with Gaul only because there were no nearer memorials to link them with.

There is no reason to suppose that the Church in the 5th century had made any deep impression on those outside the ranks of the aristocracy, but the contribution from overseas could be seen as having been in the nature of a reinforcement and extension of the indigenous Church rather than evangelism begun *de novo*. The evidence of influence from the Church on the continent is thus not necessarily to be seen as being in contradiction with the case for continuity, and may rather be providing a commentary upon it.

(2) The western, maritime distribution of Christian memorials has been held to confirm arguments for an external cultural origin. Support for this view might be claimed from the fact that there is an absence of such monuments in other British, but conceivably Christian zones in the 6th century (such as Severnside, Herefordshire, and Shropshire, possibly Elmet). It is, on the other hand, of interest that the western pattern is replicated in other respects (particularly in the political sphere (above: 22), and in the prehistoric background (above: 30) which cannnot be explained directly in terms of external influence. Moreover, while the regions which are poorly endowed with, or devoid of, Early Christian memorials do lie, in the main, inland, they harbour other types of evidence which point to a Christian presence within them. Names in *Eccles*, for example, occur chiefly in western Yorkshire, the north-west, and western Midlands. This distribution can hardly be fortuitous, and may, as Faull (1979) has suggested, reflect the presence of British ecclesiastical communities in the 6th century rather than the whereabouts of defunct Romano-British churches (see below: 46).

Probably the strongest reason for taking guard against a simplistic view of the distribution of early Christian monuments lies in the evidence of written records, notably the Llandaff charters which 'provide a corpus of records about property in south-east Wales, stretching from the late 6th to the 11th centuries' (W Davies 1979b, 156; 1973; 1979a). Although the earlier charters exist only in later copies, Davies has pointed out that the terminology and objects of these land grants change through time, the earlier transactions tending to deal with larger estates on better land in a manner suggesting that 'the language and conceptual apparatus . . . derives from a late Roman tradition' (1979b, 158). These records are of particular relevance to our grasp of developments in the agriculturally productive south-eastern zone of Wales, including the Archenfield area where Bowen, for different reasons, visualized the possibility of the active influence of Romano-British Christianity (1954, 36–8). Davies has argued persuasively for a 'high probability that the early medieval estates were the successors of late Roman ones' (1979b, 160). Yet this is an area poor in lithic inscriptions of the 5th–7th centuries. So – this point is P A Wilson's – 'if there was continuity in the south-east [of Wales] without the supporting evidence of monumental inscriptions, how much is left of the argument that in the south-west (and north-west) a continental origin is to be inferred from the distribution of the monuments?' (1966, 8).

(3) Opinion remains divided on the question of whether there was a complete break in monumental tradition between the 4th and 6th centuries. Explicit classical echoes, such as DIS MANIBVS (Nash-Williams 1950, no 285) on the stone from Maentwrog, are so exceptional as not to signify in general arguments. Unfortunately, no consensus has been reached on the dating of stones which might be relevant. Alcock has described the RVSTICA stone from Llanerfyl (Montgomeryshire), for example (Nash-Williams 1950, no 294) as carrying 'a very Romanized inscription . . . In terms of its style and epigraphy there is no reason why this monument should not have been erected in the fourth century, but a more cautious date would be early fifth' (1971, 240–1). Nash-Williams dated the stone to the late 5th century or early 6th, and Radford considers the stone to 'have little in common with the architectural layout and the formal monumental character of the normal Romano-British tombstone' (1971, 8), and extends this reservation to the LATINVS stone from Whithorn (for which Alcock nevertheless postulates a Roman ancestry: 1971, 242) and the CVNAIDE stone from Hayle (Cornwall).

Hitherto, views on whether or not there are some stones which provide linkage between Roman and post-Roman monumental traditions have tended to depend upon criteria to which it is *expected* that such stones should conform. This tendency to measure evidence against a theoretical typology can be seen in Radford's demand for at least a trace of the 'architectural layout' and 'formal monumental character' of the ordinary Romano-British tombstone. The argument is also double-edged, since the *differences* between the British stones and some Gaulish parallels are perhaps more striking than the similarities. There is little in Wales which compares with the expansive, literate, detailed stones from, say, Vienne, where dates and ages were recorded as a matter of routine, and extensive embellishments were not unusual (eg Wuilleumier *et al* 1947). One line of approach would be to compare the controversial memorials with proven Romano-British

Christian tombstones of the 4th century, since it might be with these, if any, that the later memorials would display some affinity. But such a comparison merely serves to remind us that there are virtually no authenticated Romano-British Christian tombstones of the 4th century. There is a handful of memorials which have been suggested as Christian (eg *RIB* nos 787, 955, both on the basis of the use of the phrase *plus minus*), but even in these cases the identifications are regarded as being not quite conclusive (Toynbee 1953, 14). In the absence of a corpus of such stones, therefore, it is a modern assumption that the makers of later Christian memorials would have selected Romano-British pagan tombstones as prototypes for their own products. This has added force when we remember that Romano-British memorials were produced by commercial workshops. Such concerns are unlikely to have outlived the collapse of a money economy, the withdrawal of urban and military patronage, and the disruptions of internal trade which are reflected in the disintegration of other craft organizations. There is, too, some evidence to suggest that by the later 4th century old ideas about the disposal of the dead were coming to be superseded by a new, possibly Christian attitude which set comparatively little store by parades of elaborate masonry monuments. The absence of such monuments may lie behind the modern failure to recognize more than one or two Romano-British Christian cemeteries. That there was no revival of earlier tombstone forms in the 5th century is thus hardly admissible as a sign of an interruption in the tradition of Christian burial. The small number, and hybrid character, of such candidates for 5th century stones as there are (eg BRIGOMAGLOS: Macalister 1945–9, no 498; LATINVS: Radford 1957, 170–5; CVNAIDE: Beckerlegge 1953) may have attracted attention at the expense of potentially Christian burial *sites*, which are rather more numerous. This suggestion must be qualified with the point that other forms of 'permanence' or display were being sought in the funerary customs of late Roman Britain. Burials packed in gypsum, some Christian, seem to have been made with fair frequency in the 4th century (Ramm 1971, 188–96; Green 1977). These burials were usually made in lead or stone coffins, and late Roman sarcophagi are quite numerous in certain parts of England, often occurring as singletons which may be the remnants of small ploughed-out cemeteries. Putative gypsum burials have been reported from the sites of a number of later churches, including Lichfield Cathedral (Gould 1976), Westminster Abbey, where the interment is said to have been English in a re-used Roman coffin (Stanley 1870), and Brixworth (*Northants Herald*, 16/12/1865). Mausolea, too, feature at a number of sites excavated recently, including Poundbury (Green 1977), Wells, and probably Icklingham (West & Plouviez 1976; Thomas 1980). The importance of these structures, which can seldom be discerned as Christian without the evidence of painted wall-plaster or inscriptions, both in the 4th century and as religious foci in later centuries, may have been underestimated.

Returning to memorials proper, a different line of descent for the Early Christian memorial has been suggested, with reservations, by Radford himself. In 1971 Radford compared the memorials with Romano-British milestones, and noted a similarity 'both in form and in the roughness of the lettering'. The similarities are indeed suggestive. Milestones were sometimes taken and reinscribed as memorials (eg *RIB* 2254, from the outskirts of Port Talbot), and the resemblances are so close as to have led to occasional scholarly confusion (eg as between *RIB* 2261 and Nash-Williams 1950, no 268). However, while conceding that milestones might offer a clue to some small Romano-British 'technical contribution', Radford went on to reassert the view that the whole early Christian series was subject to continuous influence by contemporary continental practice (1971, 8, 10). As a final comment on the matter of the inscriptions, it may be argued that the choice of the pillar-stone – whether this was suggested by the example of the milestone, derived from prehistoric tradition, influenced by Gallo-Roman idiom, or simply came about as a result of improvisation – would have set its own formal requirements.

In summary it may be said that the potential of Early Christian memorials is very far from being exhausted. Not only do new examples continue to come to light, but there are several avenues of research which still await exploration. One of these would involve the study of regional groups, looking at materials, site types, and related characteristics as well as distribution. Prospects for work in this direction have been outlined by J M Lewis in his survey of memorials in Dyfed (1976a). Equally urgent, if not more so, is the need to devote attention to the actual sites and surroundings of individual stones. Which stones have been brought into churchyards, and which churchyards have developed around stones? The sites of memorials which stand *in situ* outside churchyards might repay careful study; the point has already been made that hardly any of these sites have been subjected to scientific excavation, and in the overwhelming number of instances it is far from clear what the basic characteristics of the site actually were (eg solitary grave, marked grave in cemetery, Christian burial(s) superimposed on prehistoric site, oratory and graveyard, etc). J M Lewis (1976b, 15) has stressed the need to single out those sites where development was arrested at different stages (cf Thomas 1971, 48–90), since these may respond more easily to excavation than the sites which have continued in use down to the present.

Summary and suggestions

The arguments, observations, and hypotheses which have been made in the foregoing pages may now be recapitulated:

1 Romano-British Christianity survived in many areas until the second quarter of the 5th century.
2 There is no evidence to suggest that after this time the Church survived in any institutional sense in south-east Britain.
3 Despite this fact (2), it is possible either that interest in some cult sites was maintained through the 6th century on a local basis, or that a proportion of such sites provided ready-made foci for later churches.
4 British churches existed at the time of Augustine's arrival in 597.
5 Although arguments have been advanced to the contrary, it is conceivable that the roots of some of these churches lay in Romano-British Christianity. In character and organization, however, the ecclesiastical presence in Britain had been much modified by the assimilation of Gallo-Roman and especially monastic influences.
6 In the 5th and 6th centuries conversion proceeded downwards and outwards from the aristocracy. The local cemetery appears to have been the ritual focus of a neighbourhood, and may have fulfilled some of the functions that eventually came to be housed by

churches. Significantly, churches were often added to the cemeteries. But there is a possibility that spiritual life centred as much upon houses as upon churches; sacramental vessels and consecrated elements required shelter and safe-keeping, and these needs could have been combined with facilities for family worship.
7 The institutional character of the churches in Britain is not clear, but it seems to have embraced a loose network of monastic establishments. These served not only as centres of retreat, scholarship, and contemplation, but also provided bases for evangelical activity and pastoral care.
8 The 'plant', cemeteries, and resources of the British were gradually absorbed by the English in south-west and north Britain. Some later monastic, minster, and parochial sites may retain evidence of this pre-Augustinian background.
9 The differences between British and English society were not as extensive as the similarities.

Churches

It remains to consider the churches. This will be attempted under three heads: first, structural evidence for the churches themselves; second, the sites and settings of churches; and third, the political, social, and economic background to the construction of churches.

Structural evidence

1 British churches   The state of present archaeological knowledge can be summarized rapidly: there are no British church sites of this period which have been excavated in recent times and the evidence for which has been fully published. The long list of putative monastic centres in Wales has not yielded a single church which can be dated within the period under consideration. In Glamorgan it is reported that there are no known structural remains earlier than the Norman period, and in most instances it is supposed that 'the continuous use over the centuries of both a church and a churchyard precludes any expectation that such structural remains will be recovered' (RCAHMW, *Glamorgan*, I.3, 12–14). In north Wales, likewise, no structural evidence pertaining to any of the monastic centres known from literary sources has yet to come to light (RCAHMW, *Caernarvonshire*, III, cx). The picture in south-west England is marginally better, but here too definite evidence is lacking and problems remain. The pre-war excavations at Tintagel elucidated elements of what has been interpreted as a monastic settlement (Radford 1935a/b; 1942; 1962; 1968), but the curious character of some of the buildings and the absence of a contemporary church has prompted doubts (Burrow 1973). Excavations at Glastonbury (references conveniently collected in Radford & Swanton 1975, 61) have shed a little light on the monastic complex which is presumed to have existed there before the site was developed by Ine (688–726). In particular, traces were found of what may have been an enclosing ditch, a cemetery containing some stone-lined graves, two mausolea, and several oratories of wattle construction. On the other hand, nothing was found which would assist in dating these early features, and imported wares of the kind recovered at Tintagel were absent. Glastonbury Tor, however, has yielded a variety of finds centred on the 6th century, including imported Mediterranean pottery, together with traces of timber buildings, facilities for metal working, and two graves (Rahtz 1971, 11, 15, fig 6). It is conceivable that this was a small monastic site, but proof is wanting; the eating habits of the residents gave reason to doubt it, and other explanations are possible (Rahtz 1971, 20–1). Likewise, no verdict is yet admissible on the identity of the hilltop site at Congresbury (Rahtz & Watts 1979; Burrow 1979). This has produced imported pottery and evidence of internal structures and industrial activity, but as yet nothing which points incontrovertibly to a monastic settlement.

The inaccessibility of early monastic remains on sites which have remained in ecclesiastical use down to the present, and the curiously inscrutable character of the few unencumbered sites that have been excavated, make it impossible to engage in any discussion of the structural characteristics of churches in this period (but cf Thomas 1980, 138–40). This is not to say that all hope of acquiring such evidence in the future should be abandoned. Three lines of inquiry are suggested. First, it may be that too much has been made of the tendency for later parish churches and churchyards to blot out traces of their early site histories. From recent excavations in and around churches in England it has now been shown that where it is practicable to arrange for total excavation the large area available for inspection may, to some extent, compensate for disruptions of stratification within it, since islands of stratified material often survive. Such islands are seldom recognizable or fully intelligible in small trenches. Survival of early evidence is particularly likely on sloping sites, where primary deposits may be fossilized beneath later levels of make-up which have been introduced to create and maintain a level platform. Opportunities for work on this kind of scale in favourable conditions will be rare, but every effort should be made to grasp them when they occur. Second, the fact that a surviving church is of Early Christian origin does not always mean that it occupies the exact site of its ancestor. Churchyards may alter in shape, and on occasion an early nucleus may be left to one side, protruding beyond the modern churchyard. In circumstances of this kind it may be that a portion of an early ecclesiastical site remains undisturbed by later gravedigging, and may be more accessible for purposes of excavation. Thirdly, other, unencumbered, sites do survive; fieldwork, aerial reconnaissance, and excavation on an appropriate scale may do something to elucidate them. The putative monastic settlement at Merthyr Mawr (Glam) is a case in point.

2 English churches   There is written, architectural, and archaeological evidence for the construction of over 90 churches in England during the 7th century. The particulars of these cases are set out in Table III. From this it will be seen that our knowledge is mostly derived from written records, especially the writings of Bede. In comparatively few instances are there extant architectural remains, although future investigations may well bring more structural evidence to light.

The surviving fabrics are, on the whole, familiar, as will be clear from the references provided in Table III. It remains a fact, however, that, with the important exception of Yeavering, no complete plan of a 7th century church has yet been recorded in England. Moreover, much modern discussion turns on the accuracy of reports made by 19th century antiquaries. In some cases early reports have been embellished by later commentators. The triple chancel-arch attributed to Rochester, for example, appears to have been derived from conjecture rather than observed evidence (H M Taylor 1978, 753), while at Lyminge the 'urgent need for

a re-investigation of the site with modern methods of excavation is shown clearly by the discrepancy between the plan of walls published by Jenkins in 1876 and the plan of the church now commonly accepted as having been determined by his work' (H M Taylor 1969b, 258; cf Fig 26). Little attention seems to have been given to the implications of results obtained by Philp in his re-excavation of Reculver in 1969 (*Medieval Archaeol*, **14** (1970), 161). Interest in plans has distracted attention from elevations. The fabric of St Martin's, Canterbury, for example, was not comprehensively recorded until recently (cf *Antiq J*, **59** (1979), 411), and the elevations at Bradwell were only drawn in the previous year. The north side of Minster in Sheppey awaits a detailed survey, and no detailed drawings of the standing structure of St Pancras have yet been published.

The characteristics of the churches which are or have been available for examination have been described and analysed elsewhere (H M Taylor 1969a; 1978; Cramp 1973; 1976a; Cherry 1976; Rigold 1977), and it is not necessary to duplicate these studies here. However, it will be worthwhile to review some old conclusions and summarize trends in thinking.

The architectural remains of the 7th century are commonly divided into two broad groups: the churches in the south-east, notably Kent, 'the architectural first-fruits of the mission of St Augustine' (H M Taylor 1969a, 192), and those of Northumbria. The Kentish or Kentish-derived churches are said to differ from their northern counterparts, notably in matters of proportion, and, to some extent, in their respective technologies. Clapham thought the two groups were 'sharply divided' in these respects, and explained this as an outcome of the separate cultural environments in which the churches were constructed: the Kentish churches 'were either the work of, or inspired by, the Italian mission of St Augustine, reinforced at a later date by the Greco-Italian influence of St Theodore', whereas the 'general effect of the Northumbrian group of churches is far more barbaric than that of the southern group, and there is little doubt that in this it reflects the contemporary work of Merovingian Gaul' (1930, 41, 42). Clapham took care to stress that the number of individual examples available for comparison in Northumbria was considerably lower than that for Kent, although this did not inhibit his speculating on the para-Northumbrian (= 'Gaulish') affinities of his realization of the assumed plan of St Martin's, Canterbury, and the tendency towards elongation he found in the proportions of the nave at Bradwell led him to suspect that 'here . . . is to be found a blend of the Northumbrian school represented by Bishop Cedd and the southern method of building' (1930, 42). Cedd was operating some twenty years before Benedict Bishop recruited stonemasons from Gaul to assist in the construction of his monastery at Monkwearmouth, so it would seem that Clapham believed that a Gallo-North-umbrian school of design was already in existence by the 650s. On the other hand, Rigold has suggested that St Peter-on-the-Wall at Bradwell is not the church of Cedd's community, but would be better explained as 'a second church, added after Archbishop Theodore had vindicated conformity and Roman obedience, c 669' (1977, 72–3).

However this may be, recent research suggests that distinctions between churches of the north and the south have been over-simplified. It is now clear, for example, that the use of lateral *porticus* was not confined to churches in the Kentish group. A north *porticus* which

Table III Church building in 7th century England

This is an attempt to tabulate information about the first recorded appearances of churches and monasteries in English kingdoms during the 7th century. Details are set out as follows:

I   *Number*
Most of the references concern churches which were evidently already in being by the dates that are mentioned. It follows that the numbering used here should *not* be regarded as a guide to the chronological sequence in which the churches were built.

II   *Place-name*
The modern form is used, unless the location is lost or in dispute.

III   *County*

IV   *Date at or by which the church is said to have been in existence*
All dates should be treated with caution. A single date may be that of a foundation, a point in a building campaign, or a dedication. A dash before the date (eg −680) indicates a likelihood that the church was in existence before the year in which it is first heard of. A plus after a date (eg 680+) indicates a likelihood that the church came into existence at or more probably after the date that is specified. Where two dates are used (eg 696×716) they signify a period of time before, during, or after which (depending upon other symbols) the church is thought to have been founded.

V   *Written source*
References to charters do not indicate acceptance of their authenticity.

VI   *Date of written source*
The *Anglo-Saxon Chronicle* apart, a cut-off date of 750 has generally been used for the sources cited. This is arbitrary, however, and some cases with a good traditional claim to early foundation have been included. Virtually all the references to churches are retrospective.

VII   *Dedication*
As a rule, dedications known only from later sources have been excluded.

VIII   *Status or type*
This is a crude attempt to differentiate between the various terms used in the sources. Some of these (eg basilica, No 11) may have had no special technical meaning, while some others (eg *clymiterium*, No 92) have not been satisfactorily explained. Sites known from references to abbesses, companies of virgins, etc have usually been classed as 'Double monasteries' (cf Rigold 1968), but this is tentative. Reconditioned Romano-British churches deserve special treatment and have, in the main, been excluded. It should be noted that references to the establishment of bishops' sees were not invariably accompanied by reference to churches (eg Nos 44, 56, 59), although it would seem reasonable to assume that churches were provided.

IX   *Modern knowledge of site*

X   *Nature of site or location*

XI   *Archaeology*
The aim here is to register the presence of fabric or archaeological information pertaining to the building referred to in IV, V, VII, VIII. Details of later structures on the same site, finds, sculpture, etc are not normally included, although there may be a general reference in XII. Fabrics which have been correlated with descriptions in VI (eg No 55) have usually been so identified on grounds of probability; such identifications should not be regarded as definite unless there is clear archaeological evidence.

XII   *Modern reference(s)*
In the main these concern the results of investigations; some arise from discussions about dates, identifications, and sites.

Key to abbreviations used in Table III

AC	*Anonymous Life of St Cuthbert* (Colgrave 1940)
ASC	*Anglo-Saxon Chronicle*
bapt	baptistery
bas	basilica
BCS	*Cartularium Saxonicum* (Birch 1885–99)
Bk	Berkshire
BPLC	*Bede's Prose Life of St Cuthbert* (Colgrave 1940)
C	Century
Ca	Cambridgeshire
(d)	doubtful
Db	Derbyshire
Disc	Discussion
Du	County Durham
Cu	Cumbria
eccl	*ecclesia*
Eddi	*Life of Bishop Wilfred by Eddius Stephanus* (Colgrave 1927)
Ess	Essex
Felix	*Life of St Guthlac*, ed & trans B Colgrave (1956)
Finberg	Finberg 1961
Flor	*Florence of Worcester's Chronicle*
Gen	General
Gl	Gloucestershire
GR	Malmesbury: *de Gestis Regum Anglorum*, ed W Stubbs, Rolls Ser **90** (1887–9)
Ha	Hampshire
HA	*Historia Abbatum auctore anonymo* (see Plummer 1896 under Bede)
He	Herefordshire
HE	Bede's *Ecclesiastical history of the English people* (see under Bede)
herm	hermitage
Hu	Humberside
int	intermittent
K	Kent
Le	Leicestershire
Li	Lincolnshire
mart	*martyrium*
mon	monastery
Nb	Northumberland
Nf	Norfolk
Np	Northamptonshire
NY	North Yorkshire
O	Oxfordshire
orat	*oratorium*
Rox	Roxburghshire
S	Sawyer 1968
Sa	Shropshire
sa	*sub anno*
Sf	Suffolk
So	Somerset
St	Staffordshire
Strs	structures
Su	Surrey
Sx	Sussex
Uncer	Uncertain
Unkn	Unknown
W	Wiltshire
Wo	Worcestershire
Y	Yorkshire

No	Place-name					Dedication	Status or type		Nature of site or location	Archaeology			Modern reference(s)
										i Plan	ii Fabric XI	iii Excavation	
I	II	III	IV	V	VI	VII	VIII	IX	X	i	ii	iii	XII
1	Canterbury	K	600× 604	HE i.33	731	Peter & Paul	mon	Exact	Extra-mural	Part	Remains	1904–24 int	St John Hope 1914–15; Peers & Clapham 1927; Saunders 1978
2	Canterbury	K	600	HE i.33	731	Ieshu Christi	see (601)	Gen	in regia civitate	–	–	–	
3	Rochester	K	604	HE ii.3	731	Andrew	see	Exact?	in civitate Dorubrevi	Part?	–	1889; or another?	Livett 1889; Taylor 1978, 1083
4	London		604	HE ii.3	731	Paul	see	Gen	in civitate Lundonia	–	–	–	
5	Canterbury	K	619+	HE ii.6	731	Mary	eccl	Gen	in monasterio beatissimi apostolorum principis (see 1)	–	–	–	
6	Canterbury	K	−624	HE ii.7	731	Four Crowned Martyrs	mart	Uncer	Intra-mural?	–	–	–	
7	York	Y	627+	HE ii.14	731	Peter	orat bapt see	Gen?	Within legionary fortress	–	–	of (later) cemetery 1967–72 int	Phillips 1975
8	Lincoln	Li	c 628	HE ii.16	731	?	?	Uncer	Intra-mural?	–	–	–	See No 9
9	Lincoln	Li	C5 (?)	–	–	?	?	Exact	In forum of upper colonia	Part	–	1978	Gilmour 1979; see now Lincoln Archaeol Trust Annu Rep, 9 (1980–1)
10	Folkestone	K	c 630	S 22	696× 716	?	double mon	Gen	In 'bayle', with (?) Roman background	–	–	–	Rigold 1968, 35; 1972
11	Campodunum	Y?	−632	HE ii.15	731	?	bas	Uncer	villa regia	–	–	–	Gilbert 1964; Taylor 1978, 742; Rigold 1968, 35
12	Lyminge	K	633+	S 15, 19	689 697	Mary	double mon	Exact	(villa regia) beside later church	Part	Remains	1861	
13	Dommoc	Sf	c 630× 635	HE ii.15	731	?	see	Uncer	in civitate Dommoc (Dommocceast-re in OE Bede c 890)	–	–	–	Rigold 1961; 1977; Whitelock 1972
14	Cnobheresburg	Sf?	c 631× 635	HE iii.19	731	?	mon	Uncer	Alleged to be Burgh Castle	Part?	?	1960–1?	Disc in Cramp 1976a, 212–13; Rigold 1977, 72
15	Dorchester	O	c 634	HE iii.7	731	Peter & Paul (?)	see	Gen?	civitas	–	–	–	
16	Lindisfarne	Nb	c 634	AC HE iii.3	699× 705 731	Peter	mon see	Gen	Tidal island	–	–	?	
17	Yeavering	Nb	−641	(HE ii.14) (No reference to church)	(731)	–	?	Exact	villa regia	Part	–	1956	Hope-Taylor 1977
18	?		−646	HE iv.23	731	–	mon	Unkn	On N side of R Wear?	–	–	–	Temporary site? No church specified
19	Hartlepool (?)	Du	c 646+	HE iv.23	731	–	double mon	Gen	Peninsula	?	–	1968	Disc in Cramp 1976a, 220
20	Winchester	Ha	c 648	HE iii.7 ASC (F) sa 648	731	Peter	eccl (see 662)	Exact	in civitate Venta	Part	–	1963–9	Biddle 1964–75
21	Kaelcacaestir (=Tadcaster?)	NY	c 650	HE iv.23	731	–	No church mention-ed	–	In vicinity of Tadcaster?	–	–	–	Rigold 1968
22	St Bees	Cu	c 650										
23	Melrose	Rox	−651	AC	699× 705	–	mon	Gen		–	–	–	
24	Tynemouth	Nb	−651?	BPLC	721	–	mon	Gen	Headland	Strs	–	1963	Jobey 1967
25	Farne Is	Nb	c 651	AC	699× 705	–	herm	Gen	Offshore island	–	–	–	
26	Tilbury	Ess	c 653	HE iii.22	731	–	mon? (No church specified)	?	Riverside?	–	–	–	
27	Ythancaestir (Bradwell)	Ess	c 653+	HE iii.22	731	?	mon	Gen	in civitate (Shore fort)	?	?	?	Rigold 1977
28	Bradwell	Ess			May equal 27		?	Exact	Across wall of Shore fort	Part	Stands	1864	Taylor & Taylor 1965, 93; Rigold 1977, 72–3
29	Icanho	?	653/4	ASC A/E sa 654		?	mon	Uncer	'desert spot' (Folcard's Life of St Botolph: C11)	?	?	?	Rodwell 1976; Martin 1978; see also under Iken in gazetteer
30	Ad Caprae Caput (Gateshead)	Du	−654	HE iii.21	731	?	mon	Uncer	Riverside?	–	–	–	
31	Gilling	NY	−655	HA HE iii.14, 24	c 720 731	–	mon	Uncer	Site of parish church?	–	–	–	
32	?	Nb	−655	HE iii.17	731	–	eccl	Uncer	in villa regia	–	–	–	
33	Streanaeshalch (Whitby)	NY	657±	HE iii.24	731	Peter	double mon	Exact	Coastal, overlooking estuary	Part	–	1924–5	Peers & Radford 1943; Disc and new plan in Cramp 1976a
34	Lastingham	NY	659	HE iii.21	731	?	mon	Gen	Hillside (in montibus arduis ac remotibus)	–	–	–	
35	Medeshamstede	Ca	654× 662	ASC (E) sa 654 (insertion) HE iv.6	731	Peter	mon	Gen	nr river at fen edge	?	?		Taylor & Taylor 1965, 491
36	Paegnalaech	?	−664	HE iii.27	731	–	mon	Unkn		–	–	–	
37	Lichfield	St	c 664	HE iv.3	731	Mary	eccl	Gen	Waterside?	–	–	–	Gould 1973
38	Minster in Sheppey	K	c 664	S 22	696× 716	Mary	double mon	Exact	High ground, overlooking estuary	Part	Part	–	Rigold 1968, 36; Taylor & Taylor 1965, 429–30

I	II	III	IV	V	VI	VII	VIII	IX	X	XI i	XI ii	XI iii	XII
39	Barking	Ess	c 666	S 1171 / HE iv.6	685× 694 731	Mary	double mon	Uncer	Estate bordering R Thames	–	–	–	
40	Chertsey	Su	c 666	S 1165 / HE iv.6	672× 674 731	Peter	mon	Uncer	Riverside	–	–	–	
41	*Colodesburg* (St Abbs Head)	Nb	c 666	AC / Eddi	699× 705 / 710× 720	?	double mon	Gen	Peninsula (*in loco quam Coludi urbem nominant*)	–	–	Fieldwork	Thomas 1971, 35
42	Louth	Li	667 (alleged)	ASC (F) sa 790		–	mon	Uncer	?	–	–	–	
43	Reculver	K	669+	S 8, 22 / ASC (E) sa 669	679	?	mon	Exact	In Shore fort	Part	Part (demol 1809)	1926–7	Taylor 1978 for disc and further references
44	Hereford	He	669			?	see	Gen?	By river bend	–	–	–	Disc in Shoesmith 1980, 1–4
45	Barrow-on-Humber	Hu	669× 672	HE iv.3	731	?	mon	Gen	Inland from estuary	–	–	?	
46	Castor	Np	670			?	double mon?	Gen	Within Roman palace complex	–	–	Surroundings:	Disc in Rigold 1968; 1977; *Britannia* **2** (1971), 264; **3** (1972), 320; Wild 1978
47	Minster in Thanet	K	c 670	S 10, 13–15, 17	c 690× 696	Peter	double mon	Uncer	Site near parish church?	–	–	–	Rigold 1968
48	Ripon	NY	(−)671 −678	Eddi / HE iv.3; v.19	710× 720 731	Peter	mon (see 678)	Exact ?	On slope beside river	Crypt	Crypt	1931 1974	Peers 1931; Hall 1977
49	Ely	Ca	c 673	HE iv.19	731	?	double mon	Gen?	Island in fen	–	–	–	
50	Wearmouth	Du	674	HA / BLPC	c 720 721	Peter	mon	Exact	*ostium Wiri fluminis*	Part	Part	1959–67	Cramp 1969; 1976a; Taylor & Taylor 1965, 433–46
51	Malmesbury	W	−675	S 1169 / HE v.18	731	Peter & Paul	mon	Gen	Hilltop	–	–	–	
52	Threckingham	Li	675	*Flor*	1118	–	double mon	Uncer					
53	Abingdon	Bk	c 675	S 252(d)	688× 690	Mary	mon	Gen	Near river, on site of Roman settlement	?	?	1922–3	Disc and review of evidence in Biddle *et al* 1968
54	Bath	So	c 676	S 51			double mon	Uncer	In Roman town	–	–	–	Foundation date: J A Robinson, *The Times of St Dunstan* (1923)
55	Hexham	Nb	678	Eddi / HE v.20	710× 720 731	Andrew	see	Exact	On hill, overlooking river	Part	Crypt	1880–1908 int 1978	Disc in Bailey 1976 Bailey & O'Sullivan 1979
56	?	Li	c 678	HE iv.12	731	?	see: no church or site specified						
57	*Tunnacaestir*	?	−679	HE iv.22	731	?	mon	Unkn	*civitas*	–	–	–	
58	Gloucester	Gl	−680	S 70	674× 679	Peter	double mon	Gen	In N angle of Roman city	–	–	–	
59	Elmham	Nf	c 680	HE iv.5 (see) / Clofesho (Elmham specified)	731 / 803		see	Gen?	Set back from river crossing	?	?		Rigold 1962–3 (later church) Disc of see in Wade-Martins 1980b
60	Leicester	Le	c 680			?	see	Uncer	Within Roman city (St Nicholas?)	–	–	–	Disc in R Bailey: *Early Christian Church in Leicester and its region* (1980)
61	Worcester	Wo	c 680	S 64, 77	691× 699	Peter	mon see	Gen	Within enceinte of Roman town	–	–	–	Disc of site in Carver 1980
62	Hackness	NY	c 680	HE iv.23	731	?	double mon	Gen	Valley bottom: site of parish church?	–	–	–	Taylor & Taylor 1965
63	Breedon	Le	c 680	S 1804 / HE v.23	675× 692 731		mon	Gen	Hilltop, within prehistoric enceinte	–	–	1975	Dornier 1977b
64	Wenlock	Sa	c 680	Finberg 197–216	−680?		double mon	Gen		?		1901 1962	D Cranage in *Archaeologia*, **72** (1922), 105–32 E Jackson & Fletcher in *J Brit Archaeol Ass*, **28** (1965), 16–38
65	Leominster	He	c 680	Goscelin	C11		double mon	Uncer	Assoc with C12 monastic site?				
66	Selsey	Sx	680	HE iv.23	731	Peter	mon (see 709)	Uncer	Peninsula/tidal island	–	–	–	Disc of site by F Aldsworth in *Sussex Archaeol Collect*, **117** (1979), 103–7
67	Bardney	Li	c 680	HE iii.11	731		mon	Gen	Fen edge	–	–	–	
68	Bosham	Sx	−681	HE iv.13	731		*monasteriolum*	Gen?	*silvis et mari circumdatum*	–	–	–	
69	Coquet Isle	Nb	−684	BPLC c24 / AC	c 721 / 699× 705		herm	Gen	Offshore island	–	–	–	
70	Jarrow	Du	−684	HE v.21 / HA	731 / c 720	Paul	mon	Exact	Set back from river	Part	Part	1963–9	Cramp 1969; 1976a; 1976b
71	Crayke	NY	(−) 684	S 66(d)			double mon?	Gen	Hilltop, now occupied by parish church	–	–	–	
72	Hanbury	Wo	c 685	S 190	836		double mon?						
73	? nr Ovington	Nb	−686	AC	699× 705		*eccl*	Unkn	–	–	–	–	
74	?	Nb	−686	AC	699× 705		*eccl*	Unkn	–	–	–	–	
75	Redbridge	Ha	686	HE iv.16	731		mon	?	–	–	–	–	
76	Hoo	K	−687	S 22	696× 716		double mon?	Uncer	–	–	–	–	Rigold 1968
77	nr Carlisle	Cu	−686	BPLC	c 721		nuns	Unkn	–	–	–	–	
78	Carlisle	Cu	−686	AC	699× 705		*eccl*	Unkn	–	–	–	–	
79	Watton	Hu	−687× 718	HE v.3	731		nuns	Unkn	–	–	–	–	

I	II	III	IV	V	VI	VII	VIII	IX	X	XI			XII
										i	ii	iii	
80	Glastonbury	So	−688	*GR* 23–9 (interpol) *ASC* (A) *sa* 688 (interpol)	C12	Peter (Mary, Patrick)	mon	Exact	Island within marsh	–		1908–64 int	C A R Radford: interim report on excavations in *Medieval art & architecture at Wells and Glastonbury,* 1981, 110–34
81	Pershore	Wo	*c* 689					Gen?					
82	Woking	Su	−690	S 144	757×796		mon?	Uncer		–	–	–	
83	Fladbury	Wo	−691×699	S 76	691×699		mon	Uncer		–	–	–	
84	Muchelney	So	−693	S 240	757×796		mon	Gen	Beside river	?	–		Taylor & Taylor 1965, 451–3, 482
85	Upminster	K	−696×716	S 22	696×716		mon	Uncer		–	–	–	
86	Dover	K	−696	S 22	696×716	Martin	mon	Gen	In Shore fort, possibly relocated from earlier site on hill				Disc of site and recent archaeology in Rigold 1977, 73
87	Partney	Li	−697	*HE* iii.11	731		mon	Uncer		–	–	–	
88	?	Li	−697	*HE* iii.11	731		mon?	Unkn	–	–	–	–	
89	Bradfield	Bk	−699	S 252			mon	Unkn	–				
90	Repton	Db	−700	*Felix*	*c* 745		double mon?	Gen	On river bluff	?	?	1975–	Summary in Taylor 1978, 742–3
91	Crowland	Li	*c* 700	*Felix*	*c* 745		herm	Gen	Island in fen	–	–	–	
92	nr Warden?	Nb	−705	*HE* v.2	731	Michael	clymiterium	Uncer	*vallo circumdato* 1·5 m from Hexham nr No 55	–	?	–	Taylor & Taylor 1965
93	Hexham	Nb	−708	*Eddi*	710×720	Mary	eccl	Gen	nr No 55				See No 55
94	Oundle	Np	−708	*Eddi* *HE* v.19	710×720 731		mon	Uncer	Site of parish church?	–	–	–	
95	Ferring	Sx	−710?	S 1178	711? for 791	Andrew	mon	Unkn	Parish church?	–	–	–	
96	*In Silua Derorum* (Beverley)	Hu	−710	*HE* v.2	731	Peter (?) (later John)	mon	Gen	Dry area in marsh	–	–	1980–81	Excavation in precinct
97	nr Beverley	Hu	−719	*HE* v.4	731	–	eccl	Unkn	2 miles from Beverley	–	–	–	
98	?	Hu/Y	−719	*HE* v.5	731	–	eccl	Unkn	–	–	–	–	
99	Lichfield	St	−731	*HE* iv.3	731	Peter	see	Gen	On or close to site of cathedral?	–	–	–	Gould 1973

overlapped the junction between the nave and chancel was identified at Escomb during excavation in 1968 (Pocock & Wheeler 1971), and it appears that there was a *porticus* in a similar position in the first phase of the monastic church at Monkwearmouth (Cramp 1976a, 231–2). The apsidal east end, it is true, is found mainly in the south-east (H M Taylor 1978, 1029), but the form was not altogether shunned further north, for it appears in one of the churches at Hexham (Bailey 1976, 66) and a likely example is now known from Lincoln (Gilmour 1979). Moreover, in only two cases (Jarrow and Escomb) is the form of the eastern termination of a Northumbrian church of this date definitely known. The liturgical arrangements within the east ends appear to have resembled those of churches in the south. Drawing upon architectural and literary evidence, H M Taylor (1973b) has argued that in the early churches at Reculver, Canterbury, Winchester, and Monkwearmouth and in a cell of Lindisfarne, the principal altar stood at some distance from the east wall.

The argument based on differences in proportion retains some force, but H M Taylor's recent analysis of the relative size and proportions of pre-Conquest churches reveals considerable diversity (1978, 1031–3), and the preliminary results now available from Heysham, where excavation in 1977 revealed an earlier chapel with sides in the ratio of 3:2 as against 3:1 in the *later* building (Andrews 1978), provide a salutary warning against judgements based on the proportions of buildings which have not been fully explored. Lastly, it is far from certain that the Northumbrian churches form a homogeneous group in themselves. The monastic layouts at Jarrow and Wearmouth differed considerably (Cramp 1976a, 241), and neither resembled the complex at Whitby. Hexham seems to fall into a class of its own, but must have been in utter contrast to the original church of the Ionan mission at Lindisfarne, which we are told was altogether lacking in architectural pretension (*HE*, iii.25). Most of the

other key sites in the north remain unexplored, if not unlocated. The problems involved in discriminating between early monastic and secular buildings have been discussed by Professor Cramp (1976a, 220) in connection with the timber buildings excavated at Tynemouth by Jobey (1967). To Professor Cramp's well-justified complaint that of the hundreds of early monastic sites which are known to have existed in Europe 'only a handful have received any consideration save in the analysis, and sometimes excavation, of the church' (1976a, 203), one might add that in the 7th century it may only be through the excavation of the church that the monastic identity of the rest of the site will be confirmed. The variations that have so far been discerned are as likely to have arisen as expressions of different strains of monastic obedience or levels of discipline as from assertive architects.

A possible addition to the corpus of explored 7th century sites has recently been made at Lincoln, where excavations on the site of St Paul-in-the-Bail undertaken in 1978 disclosed a complicated sequence of churches which originated with a substantial structure consisting of an aisleless nave and an elliptical eastern apse separated by a quadruple chancel arch (Gilmour 1979) (Fig 11). On strictly archaeological grounds it cannot yet be shown that this church was built in the 7th century, since no dating evidence was encountered which was stratified in relation to the church. All that is known for certain is that the church was built before the Conquest, and that it was followed by several further pre-Norman ecclesiastical phases. Bede records that a church of wonderful workmanship was built in Lincoln under the auspices of Paulinus during his mission to Northumbria (625–32). In Bede's own day the church was in ruins, although still a place of some renown: this might accord with the evidence of the church having been rebuilt on a smaller scale and on a slightly different alignment later in the pre-Conquest period. The layout

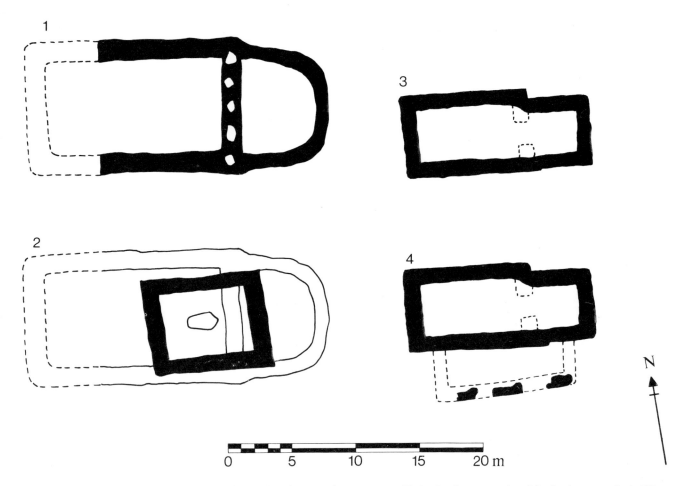

Fig 11   St Paul-in-the-Bail, Lincoln: plan of early church and its immediate successors. Notice that the construction of the simple rectangular building of phase 2 would demand the prior disappearance of the apsidal church with its cancellus-like screen intervening between apse and nave. The first church occupied a site close to the heart of the forum in the upper colonia. It is possible that the grave-like feature which contained the hanging bowl (see Fig 17, below) was associated with phase 2 rather than phase 1. If so, phase 2 could be seen as a mausoleum for an individual of high status, constructed on a site with a religious past. Later still, the site would be redeveloped as a straightforward people's church (phases 3 and 4). Source: Gilmour 1979 (revised interpretation deriving from new information given in the 1980–81 Annual Report of the Lincoln Archaeological Trust).

of the church can only be paralleled, and even so not exactly, by other designs of the 7th century in Kent and Essex. The church at Lincoln was simpler than these, though nearly comparable in scale. The lack of elaboration (eg *porticus*) might be explicable by the fact that Paulinus was operating at long range from the missionary bridgehead in Kent; what perhaps is more surprising is that the church was so elaborate, maybe reflecting the presence of a technical advisor in Paulinus's entourage.

The Lincoln church goes some way to fill a blank area in our knowledge of the architecture of the Conversion period: the character of the Roman mission in the north. However, it might be guessed that the church has little more than a curiosity value as a Kentish transplant, for after Edwin's defeat at Hatfield in 632 Paulinus fled to the south and his mission collapsed. Nevertheless, James the Deacon worked on, living to attend the Synod of Whitby. Moreover, the stone church which had been begun by Edwin in York before his death was completed by Oswald; one wonders whether the Ionan mission could or would have assisted in this. We are told by Bede that the York church possessed *porticus*.

A very different picture to that at Lincoln and implied for York is provided by the Christian church at Yeavering (Northumberland) (Hope-Taylor 1977). This was a timber structure, an elementary rectangle in plan, with entrances to the north, south, and east and an added annexe to the west (Fig 12). The building stood within a cemetery, close to the site of a prehistoric barrow, and the north fence of the Christian graveyard respected earlier alignments of buildings and burials (Hope-Taylor 1977, 73, 278–9, figs 26–8, 33).

Hope-Taylor visualizes this building not as a product of the mission of Paulinus, but as an enterprise of Oswald's days. In its simplicity the church could reflect the Irish orientation of Oswald's Christianity, although the architecture of the building belongs to the contemporary idiom of Yeavering itself. Hope-Taylor does, however, muse about Paulinus's influence in connection with traces of events at another building in the settlement: Building D2. This too was associated with a cemetery, together with signs of periodic feasting, and latterly it was '"rebuilt" by a strange procedure of encasement' that could be taken to represent the Christianization of a pagan building (1977, 278). The observation that these two buildings – one (D2) 'which was presumably a temple', and the other 'which was certainly a church' (1977, 168) – should resemble 'essentially normal minor halls of their respective phases' has repercussions for our thinking about the earliest stages of Christian building in other settlements of the 7th and 8th centuries. In particular, it is worth asking when it is that the church on sites in *secular* hands emerges as an architectural type.

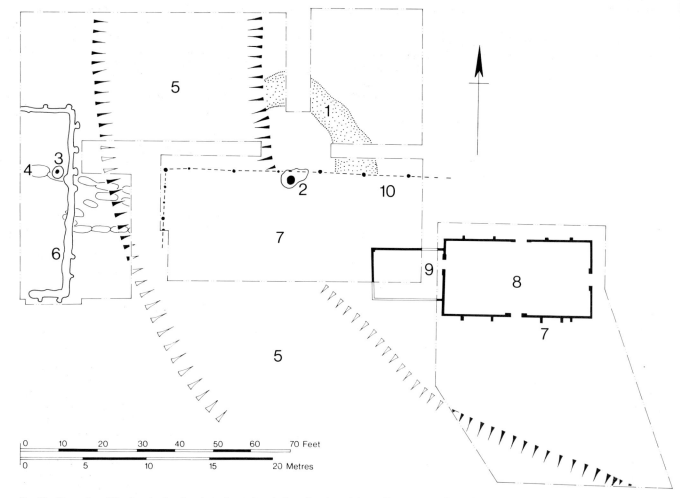

Fig 12   *Yeavering (Northumberland): plan of putative timber church and immediate surroundings.* Key to numbers: *1: ring-ditch, encircling presumed mound of prehistoric barrow; 2: setting for wooden orthostat, focus for earliest graves; 3: setting for wooden orthostat; 4: early grave; 5: course of Great Enclosure, of several phases (here simplified); 6: timber hall; 7: graveyard (detail omitted); 8: 'church'; 9: annex, added to church; 10: churchyard fence. Source: Hope-Taylor 1977, esp 70–85, and, for convenient summary and chronology, 244–5. (Drawing: Dick Raines)*

Do the comparatively numerous simple one- and two-cell stone-built local churches of the 9th, 10th, and 11th centuries represent the first happenings in the growth of neighbourhood ecclesiastical provision, or were they on occasion preceded by essentially vernacular buildings *on separate sites*? The presence of early hall-related churches might have a bearing upon the apparent lack of correspondence between the sites of late pagan cemeteries and their settlements and Late Saxon ecclesiastical geography. Could it be that the hiatus, if there was one in any general sense, fell not between the periods of paganism and Christianity, but between the first and later stages of Christian development?

These suggestions are wholly speculative, and it is important to notice that in strictly archaeological terms they rest upon a narrow platform of data provided by a single building and its immediate context. Moreover, the identification of the Yeavering church is perhaps not wholly assured; despite confident assertions in the body of the text (1977, 168), there is a worm of doubt in the index, in the form of a question mark (1977, 389). Nevertheless, the possible existence of churches constructed in the style of secular buildings at settlements of this period should be kept in mind.

Location and setting

Many of the more important English churches of the pre-Scandinavian age fall into one or more of several quite well-defined categories. Thus churches may occur

1 in a Roman environment, including churches
   a within fortifications (Rigold 1977)
   b in former Roman towns (Biddle 1976b)
   c within the zones of earlier cemeteries
   d on villas or analogous sites (Morris & Roxan 1980)
2 at centres of royal authority (eg Yeavering)
3 at ecclesiastical foci which were counterparts of royal centres (eg Lichfield/Tamworth)
4 on sites with distinctive topographical characteristics, notably peninsulas, tidal islands, river terraces, and at river mouths

Quite frequently sites were selected which combined two or more of the characteristics outlined above. Lindisfarne appears to have been an ecclesiastical counterpart of Bamburgh (3 and 4); the same may have been true of the relationship between Selsey and Chichester (Welch 1978, 29). The Saxon Shore forts of Bradwell and Walton were both situated on peninsulas, Burgh Castle lies close to the mouth of the Yare, Barrow had easy access to the Humber estuary (1a and 4). These and other examples suggest that convenience of communication was an important consideration. Bede regarded Canterbury as a royal civitas (1b and 2). Lyminge seems to have had a Roman background and was a royal vill (1?d and 2). The see at Hereford was fixed on a typical riverside site; was this twinned with some secular power centred nearby?

An enclosure which constituted 'a spiritual and legal, though hardly a militarily defensible, boundary between the monastic establishment and the world outside it' (Thomas 1971, 29) seems to have been regarded as highly desirable in the 7th century. The various forms which such enclosures might take have been discussed by Thomas (1971) and Cramp (1976a, 203–4). Natural features like headlands, peninsulas, islands in marshes, and hill-tops provided sites which were often readily adaptable for monastic use, as well as affording a measure of seclusion. To this extent Roman stone enceintes could be regarded as 'natural' sites, although there may have been other considerations (see below).

From the very first it was usual to establish churches at royal centres, a practice which was to grow through the 7th century and into the 8th, and led to the primary pattern of minsters at royal *tūn*. The early onset of this trend can be seen at Canterbury, *Campodonum*, Bamburgh, and possibly in the tribal sees of the Hwicce and Magonsæte at Worcester and Hereford. Royal power in the 7th century was often spread between relatives within a ruling family who acted as sub-kings responsible to an overlord. Where such delegation was extensive, as it seems to have been in Mercia, it is possible that there was considerable scope for the proliferation of churches. Kings also exercised jurisdiction through *prefecti* or high-ranking agents: one such, called Blæcca, was instrumental in the founding of the church at Lincoln late in the 620s. The concept of twinning an ecclesiastical centre with a royal focus (eg Lichfield and Tamworth) is less easy to grasp. It is paralleled in the British sphere, especially in Wales, and might best be approached as a manifestation of the 'multiple estate,' wherein, it is supposed, the resources and functions of an area were administered from a number of discrete but complementary centres (G R J Jones 1976a; 1976b).

Early churches in Roman surroundings have attracted a good deal of attention in recent years, although with the exception of Rigold's examination of the ecclesiastical afterlives of Saxon Shore forts (1977) there has been no systematic study of any particular aspect of the subject. This deficiency will not be remedied here, although some lines of inquiry are suggested. The topic is complicated by the probability that some churches with Roman backgrounds were so situated for reasons which may have been other than the fact that the site was of a particular type, or of Roman origin. It must also be kept in mind that a church which is located well away from a Roman site may be just as relevant to the consideration of themes which arise from churches that do stand on Roman buildings. Continuity of population does not necessarily mean continuity of place, while continuity of place does not necessarily mean continuity of population or uninterrupted settlement (Janssen 1976, 41). The categories of site already outlined above (40) will provide a convenient framework within which to examine the subject.

Churches and fortified sites   The occurrence of churches inside walled Roman towns is paralleled by the location of churches, often in isolation, inside Roman forts. These have been discussed by Biddle (1976a; 1976b, n 100) and Rigold (1977). It will be seen (Fig 13) that examples are widespread, but that the majority are distributed in north Wales, north-west England, parts of Yorkshire, and along the Saxon Shore. With the exception of the Saxon Shore group (Rigold 1977) the main

concentrations thus lie in areas which remained in British hands until late in the 6th century, or beyond. Possible reasons for the emplacement of churches within earlier defences have been put forward by Biddle (1976a, 67–8), Rigold (1977), and Thomas (1971, 32–5). They may be summarized as follows:

1   the church was built to serve an existing community, or marks a focus of a British tribal authority;
2   the fort was handed over to ecclesiastical use by the authority into whose hands it had passed (eg Caer Gybi, Ebchester, Reculver);
3   the fort fitted into a ready-made route system which would have assisted ecclesiastical communications and pastoral work;
4   the fort was favoured for monastic use because of its seclusion or the existence of an existing enclosure. The Saxon Shore forts may have offered special advantages, since their original internal buildings were mainly of wood and large spaces were probably available. The Shore forts were also well-placed for sea-borne travel.

All such sites are likely to be of high interest. Few have been archaeologically investigated. As with extra-mural, villa and cemetery sites, there is an urgent need for basic fieldwork and the classification of examples.

Churches in former Roman towns   At least ten out of the sixteen primary English sees were centred on Roman towns. It has been pointed out that, with the exception of Worcester, all these former Roman places 'were at the centre of or adjacent to notable concentrations of Anglo-Saxon cemeteries of the fifth to seventh centuries', suggesting that 'pastoral and political factors . . . led bishops to work from these centres, not antiquarian lore' (Biddle 1976b, 119). The actual dioceses, however, reflected kingdoms and kingship: authority vested in a peripatetic aristocracy, which included bishops, governing peoples who were to some extent peripatetic in their exploitation of agricultural resources but static in worship. The ten 'Roman' sees are perhaps to be seen as bases for pastoral effort rather than as symptoms of lingering or reviving urbanism, although later on some of them could well have stimulated urban development (below: 76).

In considering medieval churches on Roman urban sites in general it is necessary to discriminate between Roman structures which were reconditioned and used for worship by the English and churches where the correspondence is coincidental. In former Roman towns a carpet of Roman structures will underlie most later buildings, and some physical contact or agreement of alignment will often be inevitable, as in the case of St Mary Bishophill Senior, York (Ramm 1976). No archaeological evidence has yet been produced to indicate that Romano-British Christian buildings were deliberately re-used in towns. However, there are signs that secular buildings were re-used, as for example at St Nicholas and St Helen, Colchester (Crummy 1980) and possibly St Mary-at-Stalls, Bath. In Canterbury the church of St Mary, Northgate, incorporates a length of the Roman city wall which stands to its full height within the fabric of the north wall. No catalogue of cases of this kind has ever been compiled.

Churches with dedications consistent with an early origin (eg St Peter, SS Peter and Paul, St Mary, St Andrew (a favourite with St Wilfrid)) occur inside the defences of a number of Roman towns (Fig 14). It may be that some of these are of 7th or 8th century origin.

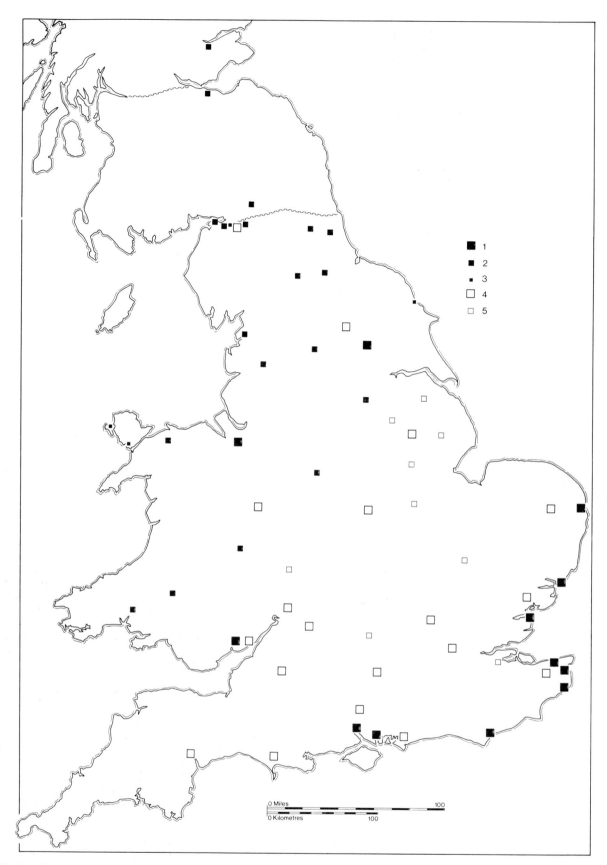

Fig 13   Distribution of churches situated within Roman enceintes. Unless otherwise indicated, all the sites shown on this map are thought to contain at least one church of pre-Conquest origin. It is of interest that a majority of the churches which occur in towns that underwent revival seem to occupy a central or otherwise prominent position in relation to the former layout (eg St Paul and St Martin, Lincoln; St Nicholas, Leicester; St Andrew, Aldborough; St Peter (Old Minster), Winchester) whereas the churches which stand in the failed towns tend to occupy a 'retired' position, often in a corner (eg St Mary, Silchester; St Andrew, Wroxeter; St Edmund, Caistor-by-Norwich). There are exceptions, of which St Michael at Verulamium is perhaps one of the most intriguing. The pattern on military sites and in the small towns appears to be more haphazard.
Key to symbols: *1: legionary fortress, large fort; 2: fort; 3: fortlet, milecastle, signal station; 4:* colonia, civitas *capital, large town; 5: small town.*
(Drawing: Dick Raines)

Horncastle, Great Casterton, Caistor-by-Norwich, and Ancaster all lie close to pagan English cemeteries (Myres 1969, 65–81). The church at Horncastle enjoyed almost cathedral-like rights over the outlying churches of its district (Owen 1978, 11–12), suggesting a pre-Danish maternal status. At Ancaster, Caistor, and Great Casterton the churches stand near the perimeter of the walled area. The church at Great Casterton appears to overlie the bath-house of a *mansio*, parts of which were not removed until the 11th century (Corder 1961; cf Rigold 1977, 74). The church at Ancaster occupies the site of a Roman temple (Ambrose 1979); so, too, may the church of St Mary at Silchester (Wacher 1975, 267) (Fig 15). St Andrew, Aldborough, is located more or less centrally within the Roman town, at the junction between two principal roads. The wall of the medieval north aisle stands upon a stylobate wall (or at least a footing built of re-used stylobate blocks) of differing alignment.

The significance of these churches is uncertain (cf Rodwell 1980, 238–9). Some persisting importance attaching to the settlements seems to be a possibility, particularly in the case of the Ancaster–Caistor–Casterton–Horncastle group, where the churches all lie on a fairly short radius from Lincoln and might be regarded as the successors of subsidiary mission stations established from that city in the 7th or 8th centuries. Aldborough, likewise, might lie on a missionary axis, standing as it does midway between York and Catterick, the latter being close to a Christian centre of some renown after Edwin's defeat at Hatfield. It may, indeed, be necessary to think in terms of lines of communication, as well as of centres and territories.

Churches within the zones of Roman cemeteries have been discussed in an earlier part of this section (above: 26) and are not considered further here.

Churches on villas and analogous sites   The incidence of medieval churches situated in close relation with Roman buildings has often been noted (eg Toynbee 1953), but there has been no systematic attempt to collect all known examples. Cases are known from most parts of England, especially in the south-east and in Dorset and Gloucestershire, but so far it is only from Essex that approximate figures are available. The Rodwells' preliminary survey (1977, 90) suggests that *c* 13% of medieval Essex churches have yielded Roman finds from the churchyard or its immediate vicinity, *c* 35% contain re-used Roman building material, and at least 7% lie directly upon Roman masonry buildings. In all 48% of rural Essex medieval churches display some connection with Romanity, through either re-use of material or location, or both. Figures of this kind may do no more than reflect the ubiquity of Romano-British occupation and a shortage of convenient natural building material. Hence in some instances the association between medieval church and Roman site could be explained either as the result of coincidence or expediency. The residue of cases, however, deserves careful examination. In a number (eg Alphamstone, East Mersea, and Brightlingsea, where a large Roman building underlies the chancel) the church is now quite isolated and its location can scarcely be regarded as fortuitous. SS Peter and Paul, West Mersea, on the other hand, overlies a large villa complex but stands in a village. Other examples of churches situated on Roman buildings include Frocester and Woodchester (Glos), Widford (Oxon), Flawford and Southwell (Notts), Wimborne (Farrar 1962, 106–9) and Tarrant Crawford

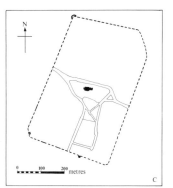

Fig 14   Churches within Roman enceintes. A: SS Peter and Paul, Caistor, Lincs; B: St Mary, Horncastle, Lincs (A and B after Whitwell 1970); C: St Andrew, Aldborough, Yorks (after Charlesworth); D: SS Peter and Paul, Great Casterton, Rutland (after Corder); E: St Martin, Ancaster, Lincs (after Todd).

(Dorset), and Lullingstone, Stone-by-Faversham, and Stone-in-Oxney (Kent) (Taylor & Taylor 1965, 401–2; Fletcher & Meates 1969; 1977; Rigold 1972). Most of these cases involve villa sites, although several, notably those mentioned in Kent, may concern mausolea. At Flawford excavation has shown that the first church followed the precise alignment of walls below, and that the east end of the nave extended over a tessellated floor. A coin of Burgred (852–74) 'at the level of the disturbed tessarae implies the possible use of the floor into Saxon times', and an 8th century date for the first church has been postulated (*Medieval Archaeol*, **20** (1976), 212). Tessellated floors are known beneath the pavements of several Lincolnshire churches (Morris & Roxan 1980).

Mention must be made of what appears to have been a fairly widespread post-Roman practice of using part of a villa or Roman building as a place of burial. Examples include burials at the villas of Scampton (Lincs), Llantwit Major (Glam), Wint Hill and Keynsham (Somerset), and Eccles (Kent). At Scampton the burial area subsequently acquired a chapel dedicated to St Pancras (Owen 1971, 1); a chapel was added to burials on a small villa at Huntingdon (*Medieval Archaeol*, **12** (1968), 175), and a timber building of possibly religious function was associated with the cemetery at Eccles (Detsicas 1976). The triple coincidence of villa/burials/church is extremely common in parts of Gaul. The evidence there has been reviewed by Percival (1976, 178–9, 183–99) who distinguishes between cases where the villa itself went out of use but its religious sector continued and prospered (eg at Arnesp, Haute-Garonne, where a

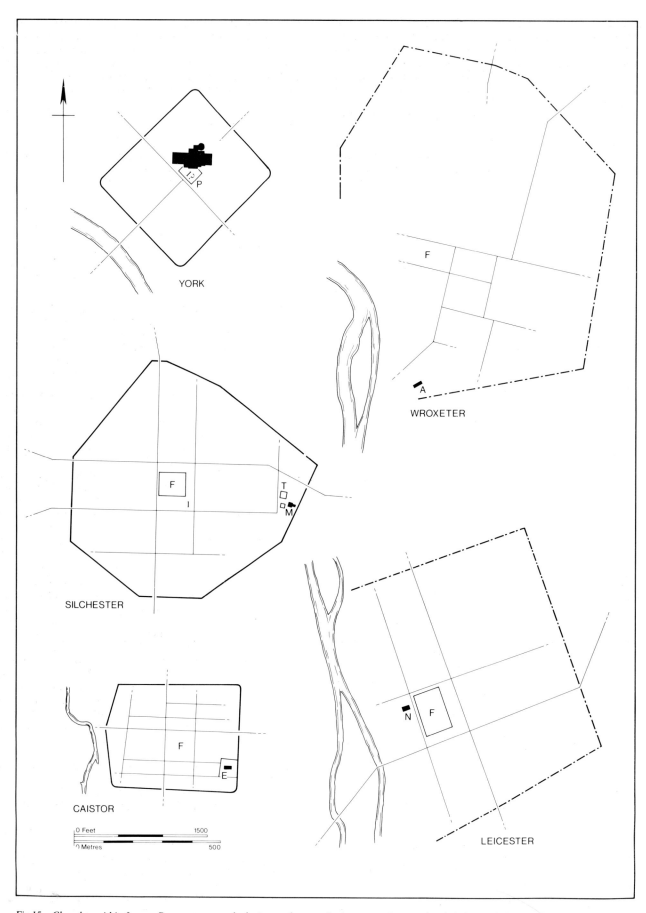

Fig 15   *Churches within former Roman towns and a legionary fortress. In three cases the town has failed entirely but a church persists. Key to symbols: F: forum; P: principia; T: temples; A: St Andrews; E: St Edmund; M: St Mary; N: St Nicholas; 1: site of former church. (Drawing: Dick Raines)*

progression from pagan temple through Christian mausoleum to Frankish chapel and 6th century priory can be traced in four superimposed buildings), and cases where the villa survived as a functioning centre and acquired a church as part of the process of its gradual transformation into a nucleated settlement. There seems to be *prima facie* evidence for both progressions in England, and while the prospect of villa estate churches remaining in use for worship through the 5th and 6th centuries in eastern England appears to be remote, the chance that these or, more probably, secular structures were occasionally reconditioned in the 7th and 8th centuries is stronger. Possible occasions or mechanisms for this kind of translation might include:

a a mausoleum selected for redevelopment as a church either on account of its structural suitability, or because of a presumed or artificially attributed sanctity of an occupant;

b an early monastic centre, established amid or adjacent to a Roman site, possibly in order to exploit its potential as a ready-made settlement (cf Cramp 1976a, 250, n 9). Stone enceintes were generally preferred for this purpose, but it was not unknown for a villa to be selected, perhaps because of its quadrilateral layout (eg Castor), or the presence of an enclosing earthwork. The development of villas as burial/monastic sites seems to be a recurring feature of the British ecclesiastical pattern in south-west England (Pearce 1978). In this area there was contact with south-west Gaul: did the habit spread from there?

c the recovery of a villa or a site in its vicinity as a centre of lordship, which could in due course be provided with a proprietary church in the normal way.

Place-names

Names in *Eccles*, *Eccles-* have long held an interest for scholars (eg Moorman 1910; Ekwall 1922; Jackson 1953; Cameron 1968; Barrow 1973; Gelling 1977), who are generally agreed that in a majority of cases the word has been derived indirectly from Vulgar Latin *eclesia* through Primitive Welsh **egles* (Cameron 1968, 87; for qualifications and exceptions see 88, 90). Most of the names in *Eccles-* occur in the western half of England, with a strong bias towards the north-west Midlands and western Yorkshire. The place-name is absent from the eastern Midlands, the central south and south-west, and Cumbria. There are, however, three instances of *Eccles* in eastern England: two in Norfolk and one in Kent. Gelling (1977) suggests that this apparent hiatus in the distribution may be the result of early borrowing direct from Latin 'which was used in a few place-names in the south-east, but which dropped out of the language after a short period of use'.

Cameron (1968) has observed that many names in *Eccles-* lie close to Roman sites or roads, and it is often said that these names denoted Romano-British churches. However, the general absence of *Eccles-* from those regions which were colonized by the English in the 5th and first half of the 6th century would appear to rule against the word having been used in this way. If this had been the sense in which the word was employed, it is odd not to find it in those areas where, on archaeological grounds at least, Romano-British Christianity left its clearest traces. By the same token, if Gelling's argument is accepted, the three instances of *Eccles* in the south-

east show that the term, or name, was available to be borrowed in the 5th century, but that it was either seldom used or else was used more widely and later superseded. In the other cases, however, it would seem that there is some further dimension to the significance of *Eccles* names which remains to be identified.

There are eight names in *Eccles* in West Yorkshire, and evidence pertaining to them has recently been reviewed in detail by Dr M Faull (1979). Faull observed that:

1 they all occur within the probable bounds of the British kingdom of Elmet;

2 no names are closely related to Roman roads or known major Roman sites;

3 with the exception of one name (Eccleshall) none of the places are located at the centres of parishes. Instead, they lie either on or close to the boundaries of parishes or townships. This phenomenon is pronounced because the upland parishes of West Yorkshire are very large.

Three of the Yorkshire *Eccles-* names refer to fields. Fieldwork and aerial reconnaissance suggest that at least one of these fields contains traces of a settlement. The exact form of this settlement is not clear, but Faull has described it as being 'a complicated pattern of huts within enclosures and a major enclosure containing at least one large rectangular building' (1979, 251; 1980).

At this point is is necessary to digress, for as a kind of reflex to the questions posed by the distribution of place-names in *Eccles-*, there is also the matter of the English use, apparently from an early date, of the word *cirice*. ἐκκλησία was the ordinary Greek word for church, which passed into Latin and into all Romanic languages, and also into all the Celtic languages: thus, OIr *eclais*, Ir and Gaelic *eglais*, Manx *egglish*, OWelsh *ecluis*, W *eglwys*, Cornish *eglos*, *-es*, *-is*, Breton *iliz* (*OED*, 403). The origin of 'church' probably lies with another Greek word, κυριακόν, meaning 'of the lord' or 'dominical'. This occurs, from the 3rd century at least, used substantively as a name for the Christian house of worship. It was this term which gave rise to various representations in Teutonic languages, including *cirice*. It was once supposed that the continental forms were derived from the Old English word, exported by missionaries in the 8th century. However, this is now considered to be 'philologically untenable', and modern opinion sees the origin of both English and continental forms at an early date, presumably in the 4th century. The existence of two source words, ἐκκλησία and κυριακόν, each capable of denoting a church building as well as the concept of the body of believers (Thomas 1980), has led to a hypothesis that the first encounters with churches by German invaders happened to be with those already designated *kirika*, and that as a result of this early familiarity the English 'had seen and sacked Roman and British churches in Gaul and Britain for centuries before they had them of their own, and, we have reason to believe, had known and spoken of them as *cirican* during the whole of that period' (*OED*, 403).

However the English actually treated Romano-British churches, the conclusion that they had their own term for them is hard to avoid. If this was not the case, the failure of either the Roman or the Ionan mission to introduce its own terminology in the 7th century becomes inexplicable. This could even have been a concession to English custom (the term Easter may be another) which was made on the recommendation of Gregory. A likely corollary to this is that there were recognizable Romano-British churches, or buildings which looked like churches, still standing in the 6th century, for if there were not it is difficult to see how the word could have survived something like a century of redundancy and yet still retain sufficient force to be the obvious term to take its place in the English ecclesiastical vocabulary of the 7th century.

This point is pursued by Faull (1979) with the interesting suggestion that it was 'church' rather than *Eccles* which may have been used to designate Romano-British churches in some English place-names. Unfortunately, she produces no examples, and no early form of a pre-Conquest place-name compounded with 'church' has yet been recognized at a site which would lend support to the idea. Nevertheless, the currency of *cirice* in England before the Augustinian mission seems inescapable, and could be finding a negative reflection in the distribution of *Eccles* names, which lie beyond the zones of primary English colonization and for the most part do not seem to occur in the regions where Romano-British Christianity has left most of its tangible traces.

This brings us back to the question of whether *Eccles*- may have some specialized significance beyond the simple sense of church (cf Thomas 1980). Faull's study of the *Eccles*- names in West Yorkshire leads her to the conclusion that, in one case at least, the name was transmitted as a loanword rather than as a simple place-name borrowing (1979, 253). That is to say, *Eccles* denoted a site or concept of a particular kind which had no ready equivalent in Old English at the time when the name was adopted. Faull speculates that this was a Christian settlement, possibly of monastic character (Faull 1979; Faull & Smith 1980). Nothing is yet known of the precise locations of other *Eccles* sites, with the possible exceptions of Eccleston, near Heronbridge (Cheshire), where excavation revealed a cemetery of oriented male inhumations near a Roman building (Rahtz 1977, 61), and Eaglesfield (Cumbria) (P A Wilson 1978).

Politics and patronage

Churches and their sites are usually analysed either individually or in comparison with each other. Progress in the conversion of peoples is attributed to the inspiration provided by individual ecclesiastical leaders, some of whom, like Theodore, are also credited with having fashioned parts of the institutional structure of the Church. An extension of this approach has been to associate particular schools of church design with influences exerted by individual churchmen.

It is, of course, well understood that missionaries and bishops worked with the support of secular leaders. It was kings who were receptive to the Christian message who made the conversion possible. Where this sympathy was lacking the scope for evangelism was small. Missionaries seem to have made little impression in Mercia before the death of Penda in 655, although it seems that towards the end of his reign 'King Penda did not forbid the preaching of the Word, even in his own Mercian kingdom, if any wished to hear it' (*HE*, iii.21). Typically, when Peada, Penda's son, went to Oswiu to ask for the hand of his daughter Alhflæd, 'his request was granted only on condition that he and his nation accepted the Christian faith and baptism' (iii.21). Even in Kent, which is occasionally depicted as a bastion of Christianity from the moment of Augustine's arrival, the Roman mission faced expulsion when Eadbald, Æthel-

berht's son and successor, reverted to paganism (*HE*, ii.5, 6).

It was kings and lords, too, who provided the estates and resources which were essential for the establishment and sustenance of monasteries and churches. Thus Oswiu of Northumbria 'gave twelve small estates on which, as they were freed from any concern about earthly military service, a site and means might be provided for the monks to wage heavenly warfare and to pray with unceasing devotion that the race might win eternal peace' (*HE*, iii.24). Wulfhere of Mercia gave Chad 'fifty hides of land to build a monastery, in a place called *Adbaruae* . . . in the province of Lindsey' (*HE*, iv.3). Donations of this sort were common, and reflect practical concerns which lay behind royal patronage. The reference to 'heavenly warfare' suggests that religious communities were regarded as sources of spiritual power; early English kings looked to them for support, not only after death, but also in their conduct of secular affairs, government and war. The relationship between patron and community was thus close and one of mutual interest. Kinship, too, played a part, for members of rulers' families could be directly involved in ecclesiastical affairs. Many of the 7th century double minsters were ruled by abbesses who were members of royal families. Trumhere, the third bishop of Mercia, Lindsey, and the Middle Angles, was a close relative of King Oswine (*HE*, iii.24). The Church could be used as an instrument for political reconciliation: when Oswine was murdered at the instigation of King Oswiu, Queen Eanflæd, Oswine's kinswoman, asked Oswiu to 'expiate Oswine's unjust death by granting God's servant Trumhere . . . a site at Gilling to build a monastery; in it prayer was continually to be said for the eternal welfare of both kings, for the one who planned the murder and for his victim' (*HE*, iii.24). But a monastery could be partisan: when Oswiu's daughter attempted to instal some relics of Oswald in the monastery at Bardney, the 'community did not receive them gladly. They knew that Oswald was a saint but, nevertheless, because he belonged to another kingdom and had once conquered them, they pursued him even when dead with their former hatred' (*HE*, iii.11). It could thus be said that the mechanisms which enabled the spread and consolidation of Christianity in the 7th century were basically political. Missionaries accompanied Christian princesses on their bridal journeys to the households of pagan kings. Bishops entered kingdoms at royal invitation, and they could also be ordered to leave. Overlords stood sponsor at the initiation of underkings, as when Oswald acted as godfather to Cynegils in the early 630s. Wulfhere acted in a similar capacity for Æthelwealh, king of the South Saxons. Both occasions had political undertones. The see established at Dorchester under the joint auspices of Oswald and Cynegils could be seen as a manifestation of their alliance against Mercia; Æthelwealh received the kingdoms of Wight and the Meonware from Wulfhere. The intricacies of most arrangements of this kind remain unavoidably obscure. Little is known about the political history of East Anglia in this period, for example. Glimpses of Lindsey remind us of the presence of small sub-kingdoms which were being subsumed by the larger blocs. The identities of these kingdoms are rarely discernible unless, like Lindsey, they lay close to a frontier and were repeatedly fought over, or unless their outlines came to be perpetuated by the boundaries of dioceses (eg Hwicce: Worcester; Magonsæte: Hereford). It would seem, therefore, that a knowledge of ecclesiastical developments, including the pattern of

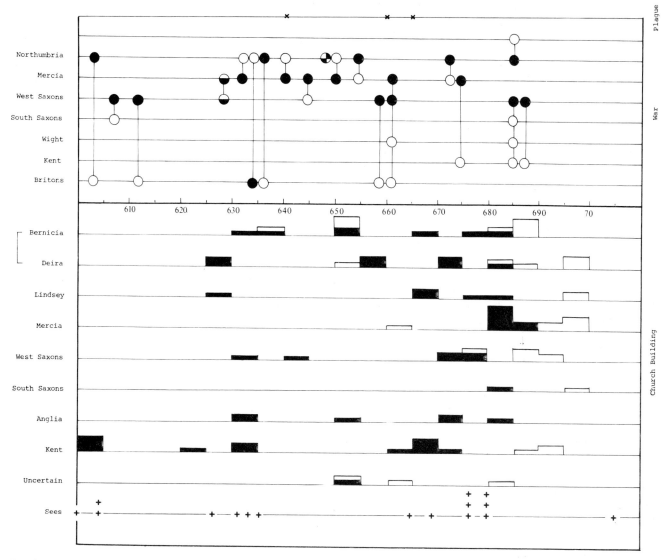

Fig 16   Graph showing progress of recorded churchbuilding in the kingdoms of 7th century England, against recorded warfare and pestilence (after Arnold 1980).
Warfare: *Solid circles represent aggressor, open circles represent victim.* Churchbuilding: *Solid blocks represent foundations of churches. Open blocks represent the first references to the existence of churches (for sources and criteria used, see Table III).*

church building, in the 7th century is likely to throw light on aspects of contemporary political conditions. Conversely, evidence about political affairs may help to illuminate the growth of the Church.

Comparatively little recorded church building was undertaken in England before the second half of the 7th century. Such work as did go on was mainly confined to Kent, with small contributions in East Anglia and the kingdom of the West Saxons. There was a flurry of building in Deira in the later 620s, but this proved to be premature. In Northumbria the pace began to quicken around the middle years of the century. From the accompanying graph (Fig 16) it will be apparent that it was in the later decades, especially in the 670s and 680s, that most recorded church building took place. The preceding years had seen much political turbulence. Between 630 and 665 Northumbria was embroiled in at least seven wars with neighbouring kingdoms, being both a victim of Mercian and British aggression, and also, under Oswald, a successful aggressor in the course of enlarging its territory towards the Forth. Throughout the central decades of the century Mercia appears as a consistently belligerent kingdom, carrying war not only into Northumbria but also to the West and South Saxons, East Anglia, and Kent. It seems likely that one of the factors behind Mercia's taste for conflict was its largely landlocked condition. Apart from Chester and the lower Severn, neither well-placed for purposes of international trade, Mercia lacked an accessible port. It was possibly in order to remedy this problem that the Mercian royal family spent much of its time fighting to assert control over the East Angles, the South Saxons, and Kent; the intermittent wars with Northumbria over Lindsey might also be seen in this light. By the early 8th century Mercia's trading needs seem to have been satisfied by the acquisition of London, and by the 730s Mercian kings were exacting toll from several Kentish ports, including Fordwich. Around the third quarter of the 7th century, however, there had been a lull in conflict, and it was during this relatively settled period that real progress was made in the development of a diocesan structure. No less than nine sees were founded between 660 and 685, compared with only seven during the preceding half-century. This strengthening in the standing of the Church is often attributed to the considerable talents of Archbishop Theodore, but a factor of equal importance might be seen in the favourable conditions in which Theodore was able to work. The approach of Mercian ascendancy might also be reflected in the fact that many of the sees which were founded during Theodore's pontificate were either in Mercia itself (eg Lichfield, Worcester, Hereford), or in areas within the sphere of Mercian political influence (eg Lindsey, Leicester, Selsey). Mercia led the field numerically in the establishment of monasteries at this time. Strangely, no Mercian monastic site of this period has yet been excavated, although there has been limited exploration at Breedon (Dornier 1977b), and work which may prove relevant is still in progress at Repton and Brixworth (Cramp 1977; Everson 1977).

$$* \quad * \quad * \quad * \quad * \quad *$$

These very general observations have been made in order to draw attention to the need for an approach to the archaeology of early Christian sites which takes a more complete account of the social and political environment which brought them into being. In their locations, dates, and forms these sites are likely to contribute not only to our understanding of religious history, but also to knowledge of contemporary developments in a world which the Church reflected and reinforced (Sawyer 1978a, 234). The value of such study is enhanced when it becomes possible to go beyond the consideration of sites as individual entities to the examination and comparison of patterns and regional groups. But this in turn depends upon the availability of evidence of a detail and quality which can only be acquired through the physical investigation of the sites themselves.

Footnote to Chapter 3
Since this chapter was written the danger that the interpretation of archaeological evidence may be 'contaminated' by unjustified reliance upon, or assumptions about the relevance of, a literary source, has been illustrated by a preliminary statement from the Lincoln Archaeological Trust arising from post-excavation work on St Paul-in-the-Bail: 'In the absence of other dating evidence, several samples of human bone from the earliest graves were submitted . . . for radiocarbon analysis. . . . The preliminary results (medial dates between the late 4th and the early 7th centuries) were at the same time unexpected and potentially of considerable national significance' (*Lincoln Archaeological Trust Ninth Annual Report*, 1980–81, 4).

By the time of the Norman Conquest the churchyard was a familiar feature in the British landscape. Not all communities possessed one, but it would be fair to say that over much of the country, and particularly in England, few people would have had to travel very far in order to bury their dead.

This claim can be substantiated in several ways. First, churches with cemeteries were acknowledged in English law-codes of the 10th and 11th centuries (II Edgar, 1 & 2; VIII Ethelred, 5.1; I Cnut, 3.ii). These provide no indication of how numerous churchyards were, but the terminology of other, late 11th century sources suggests that they were widespread. In Suffolk, for example, the Domesday scribes recorded at least 400 churches, while in Kent the names of 365 churches were noted in the *Domesday Monachorum* and the *Textus Roffensis*. If information contained in the White Book of St Augustine is taken into account the figure for Kent would be nearer 400 (Ward 1932; 1933). There are no grounds for believing that the totals of churches in these two counties were outstandingly high; the failure of Domesday scribes to record the existence of churches in comparable numbers elsewhere may be explained by the fact that they interpreted their articles of inquiry differently in different areas (see below: 68). Not all the churches listed for Kent and Suffolk necessarily possessed burial grounds, but it seems likely that the large majority did. When we catch glimpses of the foundation of new proprietary churches in the 11th century it is normal to find that the cemetery was consecrated at the same time. At Peasemore in Berkshire, for instance, where a new church was built between 1084 and 1097 by a certain Richard who was lord of the vill, the sanctification of the *coemeterium* formed part of the rite of dedication (*Chron Abingdon* II, 30–2, 120–1; cf Lennard 1959, 296).

Secondly, stone grave-monuments of pre-Conquest date have been identified at many village churches, especially in northern and parts of eastern England (Lang 1978; L A S Butler 1964). These stones are often the only visible sign that the site was used for purposes of burial before the Conquest. In the Tees valley, for example, a recent survey disclosed the existence of c 300 fragments of pre-Conquest sculpture, mostly grave-monuments, distributed between thirty-seven churches. In all but eleven cases there was no written or architectural evidence for an ecclesiastical use of the site in the pre-Conquest period (C Morris 1976). In west and north Britain there is a substantial body of material evidence: chiefly inscribed memorials, a few of which carry the subject back to the 5th and 6th centuries in explicitly archaeological terms (Nash-Williams 1950; Thomas 1971; see above: 28).

Thirdly, the results of excavations in and around a considerable number of parish churches, rural and urban, demonstrate that their cemeteries were in use before c 1050. Asheldham (Essex), Holton-le-Clay (S Humberside), Rivenhall (Essex), St Helen-on-the-Walls, York, St Mark, Lincoln, St Martin, Thetford, and St Peter, Barton-on-Humber, are examples.

If we may accept that a large number, even a majority, of medieval churchyards were in use before c 1050, it is much less certain when and how these burial grounds originated. Some sites seem to have been used for burial before they acquired churches: frequently long before, and not always by Christians (Thomas 1971, 53ff). At others an oratory, chapel, or church was the first-comer and burial began at a later date. In England during the 'Final Phase' of Anglo-Saxon burial in the 'pagan' manner (Meaney & Hawkes 1970, 50; Hawkes 1973a, 186) it is not always clear if changes of burial custom occurred as a result of the effects of Christian activity, or whether other factors played a part. Findless graves orientated west–east occur before the 7th century (cf Rahtz 1977; 1978), for example, and at some sites the decision to create a burial ground within or close to the settlement seems to have been taken before the arrival of missionaries (see below: 53). There are, too, a number of village churchyards which have yielded artefacts typical of pagan burying places. The impact of Christian opinion upon burial customs in the secular sphere is thus hard to measure in archaeological terms, and it may be that the extension of Christian influence in the 7th and 8th centuries gradually led to the exercise of a preference for those existing burial practices which were felt to be most in accord with the new religion, and to the progressive elimination of those which were not.

Terminology

The evolution and significance of terminology in Atlantic Britain has been discussed by Thomas (1971, 85–9), but very little is known about the vernacular terms which were used to denote the earliest English Christian cemeteries or for that matter the pagan burial grounds which they came to supersede. Bede's use of the word *clymiterium* to describe a site near Hexham is unclear in sense. The site was enclosed by a ditch (*uallo circumdata*) and the *clymiterium* was dedicated to St Michael (*HE*, v. 2). Possibly some kind of oratory or cemetery chapel was meant; at any rate, the Old English version translates it *gebædhus and ciricean* (Colgrave & Mynors 1969, 456, n 2; cf Thomas 1971, 85). Elsewhere Bede uses the word *cymiterium* (eg *HE*, iv.10) and this was the term which was normally employed by ecclesiastical writers throughout the Middle Ages. The word is from the Latin *coemeterium*, in turn from the Greek meaning a 'dormitory' or 'sleeping place'. The Old English word *græf* was sometimes used (eg in a controversial passage in *The Seafarer*, l. 97), but the term 'graveyard' seems not to occur in surviving written works from before the Conquest. What term was used to describe a pagan burial ground we do not know, but one Old English translation of *cymiterium* was *lictun*. The term occurs in pre-Conquest written records, and the element *lic*, which remains today in lych-gate, occasionally appears in place-names (eg Lickpit (Hants), Litchborough (Northants), Litchardon (Dorset)) and was compounded with other words connected with burial (eg *licrest*, gravespace; *licsang*, funeral dirge; cf the common Middle English word for graveyard, *lytton*). In the 11th century the burial of certain classes of criminal in a consecrated graveyard (*gehalgodum lictune*) was prohibited, and this hints at the possibility that there were two kinds of *lictun*: consecrated and unconsecrated. The prohibition is reminiscent of an 8th century instruction contained in a letter of Boniface to Ethelbald that illegitimate children of 'corrupt nuns and others' should be buried in *tumuli* (Haddan & Stubbs 1869–71, III, 354). Presumably these are to be identified with the *tumuli* and judicial 'killing places' which are sometimes specified in Old English charter bounds, although the religious origins of these sites, if any, are not reported.

Another term that occurs fairly frequently, notably in 10th and 11th century law-codes, is *legerstowe*. The element *stowe* gives the word a religious resonance, and both this and *lictun* may have carried the additional sense of an enclosure for the dead.

Evidence provided by written records

The documents of the Old English Church shed little light on the origins of churchyard burial. In view of the intense interest expressed by Bede and other writers in the last hours and funerals of important ecclesiastical figures, the silence of English sources on matters connected with burial in general might seem surprising. All that we learn directly, however, is that a number, and presumably all, of the monastic settlements founded in the 7th century were provided with cemeteries (eg Barking, Ely, Lastingham) and that the *porticus* of certain churches were used for royal or episcopal burials. At Barking, for instance, we are told that the sisters were undecided as to where their cemetery ought to be, until one night a dazzling sheet of light indicated the correct position 'where the bodies were to rest, awaiting the resurrection day' (*HE*, iv.7). The origins of local graveyards were presumably more mundane, but the means whereby such sites were designated are not at all clear. Augustine's requests to Gregory for advice on various doctrinal and procedural points contain no hint that he was perturbed by pagan burial customs. Gregory's advice to Abbot Mellitus about converting *fana idolorum* to Christian use makes no mention of burial (*HE*, i.20). Nearly 150 years later the third canon of the Council of Clofesho enjoined that bishops should tour their dioceses every year in order to oppose superstitious practices – *divinos, auguria, auspicia, fylacteria, incantiones* – but pagan burial was not listed as a practice to be deplored (Haddan & Stubbs 1869–71, III, 363–4). The Clofesho list of 747 presents a problem, however, in that it closely resembles an injunction promulgated by a Frankish synod at about the same time (Levison 1946, 23). It is more than likely that a link between the two is to be sought in the person of Boniface (Parsons 1980a, 182), but we are left in some doubt as to the exact relevance of the Clofesho version. Conversely, although we find in Archbishop Theodore's *Penitential* a statement that *cadavera infidelium* in churches were unwelcome (Haddan & Stubbs 1869–71, III, 190–1), this too may have been derived from a continental source and is not necessarily to be taken at face value. The best-known injunction on this subject occurs in the Paderborn Capitulary (785), which prescribed the death penalty for anyone causing the body of a dead man to be cremated, and ordered that 'the bodies of Christian Saxons shall be taken to the church's cemeteries and not to pagan burial mounds' (Loyn & Percival 1975, 52–3). To what extent conditions in late 8th century Saxony resembled those in England is quite uncertain, however, and it is doubtful if the comparison is particularly helpful. The stringent penalties which were attached to pagan customs in Saxony cannot be seen as an accurate measure of the extent to which the Church opposed them. Failure to accept baptism, for example, was also specified as a capital crime, and the Paderborn Capitulary as a whole is chiefly notable as an expression of the ruthless character of Frankish rule in that region.

Layfolk sometimes sought burial for themselves or their relatives within a monastic cemetery. Bede tells of how Hildmer, King Ecgfrith's *praefectus*, came to see Cuthbert and requested him to send a priest to his wife in order to administer the last rites, and also 'that you will permit her body to be buried here in holy ground' (Colgrave 1940, 204–5). Cuthbert did better than this since he drove out the demon which was at the root of the trouble. It is not clear, however, whether Hildmer made his request because there was no other Christian burial ground in the vicinity, or because the cemetery at Lindisfarne was thought to be a particularly desirable resting-place.

Taken as a whole, the written records of the 7th and 8th centuries suggest that pagan burial was not regarded as a danger by the Church, or that if it did present a threat it was low on the list of priorities for elimination. (This much is suggested by the tradition concerning Cuthbert, Archbishop of Canterbury (740–58), which recalled that it was he who authorized burial inside towns and that he created cemeteries 'everywhere in England' (Allcroft 1928).) Nor is it certain that the Church was implacably hostile to burial with grave goods. Although it is often said that burial with objects was essentially a pagan practice to which the Church had strong objections, there seems to be no contemporary written evidence from any relevant source in which these objections are made explicit. Churchmen themselves were often buried with objects, according to rank: robes, crozier, episcopal ring, comb, chalice, paten. If we are right in supposing that there ever was a pagan rite of burial (as against, say, a customary procedure for the disposal of the dead which was desacralized, or at least distinct from the superstitious practices which we know were energetically opposed), then such evidence as there is suggests that this was not so much abolished by the Church as progressively discontinued, as the Church gained in influence and the attractions of burial within holy ground came to be appreciated. Burial within a churchyard was promoted by the Church as a privilege; it was something to be sought after rather than arbitrarily imposed. Grave goods may have been shed, in churchyards, not because they were prohibited, but because of the realization that there was no need for them. This, at any rate, is the message we receive towards the end of the pre-Conquest era, when to be excluded from a churchyard was a fate worse than death.

Archaeological evidence

Pagan cemeteries often contain burials accompanied by a selection of objects, and hence are regarded by archaeologists as informative sites. Churchyards, by contrast, are distinguished by a general absence of grave goods, and grave goods which do occur, such as mortuary chalices and patens, tend to be stereotyped and of limited historical usefulness. This fact, coupled with the complexity of stratification which may occur within the churchyard, has often acted as a deterrent to detailed excavation. Further, if the removal of burials is judged to be subordinate to some other objective of an investigation it may be difficult to justify the painstaking treatment of graves while excavation is in progress (Kjølbye-Biddle 1975). Ways of excavating churchyard burials with efficiency and rapidity have been proposed (eg Phillips 1976), but site methods usually cling to the extremes of summary clearance on the one hand or laborious cleaning and drawing of burials *in situ* on the other. Constraints placed upon archaeological work in the vicinity of churches in use may add further problems (Rodwell & Rodwell 1976). In England these difficulties have combined to obstruct progress towards an elucidation of the structure of early medieval Christian graveyards. Information about the layout of these sites, internal divisions and buildings, methods of enclosure and the importance of particular graves is, on the whole, lacking. Large numbers of excavations have been undertaken in churchyards, but there have been relatively few excavations *of* churchyards (see below: 89).

The position reached by cemetery studies in Atlantic Britain is more advanced. In south-west England, in Wales and Ireland, and in north Britain there are sites available, in different stages of development, which remain unencumbered by the later parish churches and modern cemeteries which have tended to mask early evidence or to inhibit its investigation over much of lowland England. In his book *The early Christian archaeology of north Britain* Professor Thomas approached the archaeological evidence under two heads: first, the cemetery ('the fixed consecrated area for groups of burials'), and secondly, 'the special treatment accorded to certain individual graves' (1971, 49).

In his discussion of sites in the first category Thomas drew a distinction between large, sprawling open cemeteries (eg Cannington (Somerset)) and the more compact enclosed cemeteries which were defined by some kind of physical boundary. Thomas suggested that these cemeteries, and 'in particular the enclosed ones, antedate any other form of Christian structure in the countryside of post-Roman Britain ...' (1971, 50; cf Rahtz 1977, 56). Thomas divided enclosed cemeteries into two further groups: those which were not subsequently 'elaborated with anything more than the odd cross-incised slab or pillar', and others – a larger class – 'to which oratories and chapels, internal divisions and living-huts, were eventually added, leading in many cases to medieval church sites and, in parts of Cornwall, Wales, and southern Scotland, to parish churches surrounded by their graveyards'. Thomas designated these categories as being *undeveloped* and *developed*, respectively (1971, 50–1). In the course of his analysis of these two 'states' of cemetery Thomas singled out two further matters for discussion: (1) the frequency with which enclosed cemeteries tend to be circular or oval in plan, and (2) the numerous occurrences of cemeteries which are 'imposed upon, and are often spatially coterminous with, pre-Christian burial-grounds' (1971, 51–3; 53–8, with examples).

The second strand of archaeological evidence considered by Thomas concerns what he describes as 'special ... or specially marked' graves (1971, 58). Such graves are known from cemeteries across north-western Europe and occur in Iron Age, Roman, and pagan-Saxon cemeteries as well as in burial-grounds of the early Christian era. Typically, the burial (cremation or inhumation) is surrounded by a circular ditch, wall, or fence, although rectangular enclosures were sometimes preferred. The practice of drawing attention to the graves of individuals thus seems to have been inherited

by converts to Christianity and perpetuated in some of the first cemeteries to be operated under their auspices. The massive open cemetery at Cannington, excavated in 1962–3, contained two 'important nuclei' in the area which was examined: one consisted of a circular enclosure at the summit of the hill, the other was the grave of a young girl, which has been dated by a radiocarbon determination to a period centring upon *c* 620. Her grave was emphasized by a mound, which had been 'much visited' (Rahtz 1977, 58). At Chamberlain's Barn, Leighton Buzzard (Beds) there were two Anglo-Saxon cemeteries. It has been argued that 'Cemetery I is pagan, but cemetery II, for which a starting date of circa 650 is proposed, should be, despite occasional grave-goods, its Christian successor, only a short distance away' (Thomas 1971, 61). Both cemeteries contained specially marked graves. Two of these, one in cemetery I and another on the fringe of cemetery II, were said to be 'clearly non-Christian', but an oriented grave at the centre of cemetery II contained 'a presumably converted male' within a circular ditched enclosure. 'This' reasoned Thomas, 'offers a fairly clear case of pagan-Christian continuity' (1971, 62; Hyslop 1963).

Cemeteries like Leighton Buzzard II and Cannington are often diagnosed as Christian, but it should be stressed that *archaeological* evidence for this view is lacking. Neither oriented burials nor an absence of grave goods amount to 'clear' evidence for the Christian identity of a cemetery.

In summary it may be said that the picture which has been discerned in parts of west and north Britain is essentially that of a sequence. Chapels and churches are typically to be found as developments out of earlier cemeteries, which themselves were transformed from 'mere collections of inhumation graves' through increasingly formal stages. Pagan cemeteries could develop into Christian graveyards, and by the addition of a church evolve into a parish churchyard. The central phases of this sequence are exemplified at Ardwall Isle, off the Kirkcudbright coast: 'unenclosed lay cemetery – timber oratory and hut, with aligned burials – stone chapel and hut, with further aligned burials' (Thomas 1971, 72; 1967, 127–88).

At first sight this progression seems to be in contrast with the pattern which is widely assumed to have existed in those parts of the country that were early colonized by the English. Within the British sphere continuity of site is a leading characteristic of cemeteries, whereas we are told that all over England between *c* 650 and 750 old cemeteries were being abandoned and new ones established (Hyslop 1963). It has been suggested that these secondary, putative Christian cemeteries were in their turn replaced by graveyards, generally remote from former pagan burial-grounds and 'in what was hereafter to be the normal Christian place: right in the village' (Meaney & Hawkes 1970, 51). The contrast is sharpened when we compare Thomas's claim that many British cemeteries are to be regarded as *primary* field monuments of insular Christianity with the argument put forward by Baldwin Brown to the effect that the English graveyard normally came into existence as a 'natural adjunct' of the secular church (1903, 262–3). This opinion has a strong appeal, since it seems unlikely that the essentially proprietary factors which lie behind the origin and siting of so many English village churches could have been foreshadowed in a pattern of pre-existing cemeteries (although see Barlow 1963, 183; Feine 1950, 132–5). However, this must apply equally to the proposition that by the second half of the 8th century a process of transfer from 'Final Phase' cemeteries to graveyards in villages was in full swing (Meaney & Hawkes 1970, 50–1). Quite apart from the question of what is to be understood by the term 'village' at this time, such a process can scarcely be visualized unless it went hand in hand with the establishment of secular churches, or unless significant numbers of unencumbered Middle/Late Saxon settlement-related graveyards await identification. Candidates for what (to borrow Thomas's terminology) might be called English undeveloped cemeteries can be found. Excavations at Sedgeford (Norfolk) in the 1950s, disclosed an extensive burial ground in association with a settlement. All the skeletons were laid east–west, and in several cases sherds of Ipswich ware were found beneath them (*Medieval Archaeol*, **3** (1959), 298). At Kilham (N Humberside) at least six burials in coffins were found during laying of water mains in the eastern part of the village (Eagles 1979). Investigation of the medieval abbey of Elstow (Beds) produced a probable late-Saxon cemetery of over 260 individuals, but no trace of an associated church (*Medieval Archaeol*, **13** (1969), 230). Excavations for the playing-field of a new primary school at Queensway, Thetford, in 1964 yielded a grave-slab carved in an 11th century idiom, apparently upon an inhumation burial (*Medieval Archaeol*, **9** (1965), 173). Other examples can be cited, although in most of these cases it seems probable that the graveyard was originally accompanied by a church which has since been lost.

Such disappearances were fairly common in the 15th and 16th centuries, and it would be a mistake to suppose that the pattern of local churches which existed at the end of the Middle Ages represented either the sum total of previous secular church-building or contained a faithful reflection of their earlier distribution. It is becoming increasingly clear that the ecclesiastical geography of Anglo-Saxon England was more fluid than is sometimes supposed. We are told that the stone church of 'remarkable workmanship' built in Lincoln by Blaecca and Paulinus late in the 620s was in ruins by Bede's day (*HE*, ii.16). Excavation in the former gasworks at Southampton 'revealed a large inhumation cemetery containing the fully or partly articulated remains of seventy-six individuals. The cemetery was divided into two halves by a structure, which may have been a small church' (*Medieval Archaeol*, **19** (1975), 223). Recent excavations at Raunds (Northants) have shown that a manor house which went out of use early in the 14th century overlay the remains of a pre-Conquest church and churchyard. At Nazeingbury (Essex) the excavation of an inhumation cemetery has disclosed traces of two timber buildings, tentatively identified as churches. Radiocarbon determinations upon two of the skeletons have yielded dates of ad 670±80 and ad 830±80 (Huggins 1978, 54). In 1972 excavation in the monastic cemetery of St John's Abbey, Colchester, revealed part of a church which had been demolished early in the medieval period (Crummy 1974, 29; Rodwell & Rodwell 1977, 38–9). Excavations at Barrow-on-Humber in 1978 brought to light traces of an abandoned pre-Conquest church and cemetery (Boden & Whitwell 1979). At present we are unable to tell whether such redundancies are symptomatic of a larger phenomenon. The existing published archaeological evidence is scanty, and while other cases undoubtedly exist they will require methodical analysis before generalizations can be made. Nevertheless, that the pattern of pre-Conquest Christian graveyards underwent modification, perhaps even in ways akin to those changes which affected the pattern of pagan cemeteries during a shorter period, is at least a possibility which deserves attention.

Despite indications that the origins of churchyard burial should be sought in an amalgam of factors, rather than in a straight joint between pagan and Christian customs, two ideas continue to exert a strong influence on discussions of the subject in ways which seem to predetermine conclusions. First, there is an assumption that village churchyards often originated as areas centred on preaching stations marked by free-standing crosses. The second idea arises from the belief – confidently promoted by Baldwin Brown as a 'general rule' – that the church with its graveyard is central to the settlement, while the older pagan cemetery is away at a distance, 'commonly on high ground where the lie of the country allows it, and out of all local connection with the church . . .' (1903, 263). These opinions will now be examined in turn.

Graveyards and crosses

Baldwin Brown was sceptical about the notion that graveyards originated as areas around preaching crosses (1903, 262). Collingwood shared his doubts: 'Generally speaking, in the pre-Norman period we have no indication of the use of carefully carved stones as boundary-crosses or "preaching-crosses" ' (1927, 4). Nevertheless, the idea remains in fashion. Hurst, for example, has speculated that the first church at Wharram Percy was 'perhaps preceded by a free-standing cross' (1976, 39). Elsewhere it has been asserted that 'Before buildings for worship were built in villages . . . it was common practice to mark the Christian presence in a place by erecting a standing cross . . . At the cross the priest from the minster would preach, and assemble his portable altar for the celebration of the mass. Around it too the village dead would thenceforth be buried . . .' (Godfrey 1974, 133).

Contemporary evidence for this 'common practice' is sparse. References to preaching crosses occur in the writings of later medieval commentators, but these nearly always take the form of retrospective explanations for the existence of elaborately carved free-standing crosses. As Collingwood noted, 'a missionary would not wait, even if he had the means, for such a work before delivering his message' (1927, 5, with examples). When crosses which were funeral monuments have been discounted, a high proportion of those which remain occur on sites which either possessed churches by the end of the 7th century (eg Hackness, Hexham, Lastingham, Whitby), or at places where early churches might be suspected (eg Dewsbury, Easby, Bewcastle). The wooden cross hastily set up by Oswald at Heavenfield on the eve of a battle in 634 was planted in supplication rather than for evangelical reasons, so although the site became famous and a church was later built there this can hardly be taken as evidence for routine practice. Accounts of Cuthbert's missionary tours in remote areas do not mention focal preaching crosses: all we are told is that when a clerk or priest came to a village it was customary 'for all to gather together at his command to hear his word' (Colgrave 1940, 187). A significant detail occurs in Bede's relation of Cuthbert's death. The saint requested that he should be buried 'near my oratory towards the south, on the eastern side of the holy cross which I have erected there' (Colgrave 1940, 273). Free-standing crosses, it seems, were conceived as adjuncts to, rather than predecessors of, ecclesiastical sites. When St Oswald preached from a cross in the cathedral cemetery at Worcester he did so because the church of St Peter was too small to contain all those who wanted to hear him. The limited capacity of many early churches might even have been a factor which stimulated the making of crosses, which could have served as foci for large gatherings on special occasions. Bede's description of Paulinus's ministry in Yorkshire implies that there had been an expansion in the provision of ecclesiastical buildings up to his own day: '... *baptizabat in fluuio Suala, qui uicum Cataractam praeterfluit; nondum enim oratoria vel bapistera in ipso exordio nascentis ibi ecclesiae poterant aedificari*' (*HE*, ii.14). This does not prove that crosses were set up as adjuncts to churches, but it does suggest that by *c* 730 there were neighbourhood churches in existence beside which crosses could stand. A passage in the *Vita Willibaldi* is often cited as evidence for the practice of raising crosses in advance of churches: ... *mos est Saxonice gentis quod in nonullius nobilium bonorumque hominum predibus non aecclesia, sed sancte crucis signum ... in alto erectum ad commoda diuini orationis sedulitate habere solent* (*Mon Germ Hist Scriptores*, XV, 88). This seems to be the only reference to such a practice at an early date, however, and, as Lennard points out (1959, 292, n 4), it carries the implication that local lords' churches were not unknown. Brooke (1970, 78) has suggested that small town churches sometimes grew up as the successors of crosses at street corners and crossroads. There are one or two documented instances of such a development, although the example cited by Brooke, of St James, outside Micklegate at York, appears to date from the 12th century (Cronne & Davis 1968, no 987).

Crosses were erected in churchyards, and elsewhere, throughout the Middle Ages. They were particularly important for marking the stations in liturgical processions, which could go some miles from the mother church. The idea that Christian graveyards *originated* as areas around crosses may be questioned, however, particularly as in none of the cases discussed above is the connection between a preaching cross and a churchless burial ground made explicit.

Pagan cemeteries and Christian graveyards

In the introduction to her *Gazetteer* of Anglo-Saxon burial sites Meaney observed that 'the boundary of a territory seems to have been the proper place for them' (1964, 20). Bonney (1966) has shown that some 29% of pagan burial sites in Wiltshire lie on a parish boundary. Boundaries, too, seem to have been appropriate settings for executions and gibbets. In late pagan Ireland burial sites were used to delineate land boundaries and to defend areas within them (Charles-Edwards 1976, 83–7).

Practical factors may have influenced this custom. Arnold has suggested that 'where early Saxon settlements and cemeteries exist, so that there is a dynamic relationship between the two, the cemetery would have been situated on pasture land which would frequently have been on the edges of the land farmed by the users of the cemetery' (1977, 312). Comparison of the results obtained by locational analysis of known settlements and cemeteries with land classification goes some way to support this: in the Isle of Wight, for example, all the known pagan cemeteries occur on the poorest rough pasture (1977, 313–15).

Churchyards, by contrast, appear to be components of settlements rather than boundaries. Baldwin Brown, while accepting a handful of cases in which 'apparently pagan' Saxon interments occurred in churchyards, insisted: 'That the village graveyard was on the same site as the older pagan cemetery of the settlement is contradicted by monumental evidence' (1903, 263). The act of gathering the dead within or close to the living rather than consigning them to the perimeter thus gives the impression of a definite change of practice.

The change of practice has normally been attributed to the impact of ecclesiastical policy, although there are pagan Saxon precedents for a closer relationship between settlement and cemetery. Bishopstone (Sussex), Mucking (Essex), and West Stow (Suffolk) provide examples. However, all three settlements occupied marginal land and hence might equally well be viewed in the light of Arnold's argument.

The phenomenon of a second cemetery, established closer to a settlement than its early pagan predecessor, cannot always be explained in terms of Christian influence. At Sancton (Yorks), for example, a large predominantly cremation cemetery existed on poor, thin soil near what is now the edge of the parish. Burial began at the cemetery late in the 4th century or early in the 5th, and continued until the end of the pagan period. Faull has argued that because of its size and 'location central to the other probable early Anglo-Saxon settlements at Goodmanham, Londesborough, Market Weighton, North Newbald and Nunburnholme ... it may have been a central crematorium serving the surrounding Anglian communities' (1976, 231). In the 6th century a smaller cemetery containing a much higher proportion of inhumations was created on a site close to the present village. Faull speculates that this served 'only the local Sancton settlement'; whereas Sancton I would have been 'just beyond the arable fields ... Sancton II would have been on the edge of the settlement between the village and its cultivated fields' (1976, 231, 232). Sancton II lies adjacent to the medieval churchyard. Faull considers it to be 'very likely that the Christian cemetery was merely a continuation, perhaps with a very slight southward shift, of the pagan cemetery' (1976, 232). If the outline put forward by Faull is correct, then in this case the intimate relationship between settlement and churchyard was anticipated, if not predetermined, in the 6th century.

The task of attempting to ascertain when it was that graveyards were established beside or within communities is complicated by uncertainty over the very nature of Middle Saxon settlement. The tidy sequence proposed for Sancton by Faull, for example, hinges on assumptions about the nature of land-use, the whereabouts and character of settlement, and the absence of other cemeteries in the 6th and 7th centuries. Doubts have been cast on the traditional idea that nucleated villages, now so typical of much of lowland England, originated as a dominant primary form of Saxon settlement. Instead, many scholars now envisage a less formal pattern of villages, hamlets, and farms, in certain areas closely affiliated with the Roman pattern, some of which eventually coalesced or were deliberately regrouped, some of which persisted more or less unchanged, and some of which failed (see, for example, Foard 1978; C C Taylor 1977; 1978). The exponents of these ideas warn of the pitfalls of generalization, and in particular of the risk of thinking in terms of any single predominant settlement type at any one time. This must have repercussions for a consideration of the origins of churchyards in or near villages. These may be assessed first of all in relation to the sequence of burial patterns which is currently suspected. In simplified form this sequence runs as follows:

1 Pagan and (?)Christian inhumation cemeteries near Romano-British centres and settlements (4th–5th centuries)
2 Pagan cemeteries, inhumation or cremation according to local preference (Myres 1969, 16–18), often but not invariably removed from the immediate environment of the settlement(s) (5th–7th centuries)
3 Late cemeteries (7th–8th centuries) displaying:
   a a progressive reduction in grave-goods;
   b consistent orientation;
   c a shift of site, often to a location near or adjacent to the earlier cemetery;
   d a preference for inhumation, followed by:
4 Transfer to a Christian grave- or churchyard and abandonment of grave-goods (?8th–9th centuries).

The sequence sketched above has convinced many scholars that we are now in a position to define 'a kind of burial place which is now broadly regarded as early Christian' (Biddle 1976a, 68–9). Double cemeteries of the kind investigated at Leighton Buzzard, Winnall, and Eastbourne have been held to illustrate the process of transition (see above: 51). At Eastbourne, for instance, an existing pagan cemetery containing a wide variety of grave-goods is alleged to have been replaced by a new burial ground on the ridge of Ocklynge Hill, where inhumation graves were 'laid out in neat orderly rows with the graves orientated west–east ... finds mainly consisted of iron knives with a few iron spearheads and buckles' (Welch 1978, 28). Despite the change of practice it is claimed that the Ocklynge cemetery 'obviously still served the same community'. Another cemetery of similar type has been partially excavated not far away at Crane Down, Jevington, and has been assigned to the 7th or 8th century (Holden et al 1969). The phenomenon of two cemeteries, one early and one late, has also been recognized elsewhere, as at Long Wittenham and Wheatley (Oxon), Desborough (Leics), Polhill (Kent), Dunstable (Beds), and Garton Slack (N Yorks) (see Table IV). At Winchester there seems to have been a number of stages: 'pagan cemeteries (eg Winnall I); cemeteries on new sites, which may be Christian but which belong to a period before the cathedral church obtained control over the right of burial; burial in the cathedral graveyard itself' (Biddle 1976a, 69); and a fourth stage of burial in and around parish churches as well as at the cathedral. At Winnall II the grave-goods are 'unanimous' in testifying that the cemetery came into use in the middle of the 7th century and indicate that the cemetery ceased to be used at some stage in the 8th century (Meaney & Hawkes 1970, 49). It is stated that with the disuse of cemeteries such as Winnall II 'we see an end to the old custom of burying the dead with grave-goods in cemeteries placed on open ground at a distance from the settlement' (Meaney & Hawkes 1970, 50), a view which would seem to involve an assumption that 'the settlement' stayed in the same place. We have already seen that this view of a shifting pattern of cemeteries in the 7th and 8th centuries was shared by Baldwin Brown, who disagreed with Kemble's idea that village graveyards sometimes occurred on pagan burial grounds. Reviewing the evidence for pre-churchyard cemeteries Hyslop concluded: 'Thus we

find that, all over England, more or less at the same period, settled people abandoning their old cemeteries and setting up new ones.' With this change came a 'totally new material culture' (1963, 190–1).

This vision of a general, progressive transformation of the rite and right of burial, culminating in a radical reorganization of cemetery sites in the second half of the 8th century, is open to several comments. The first of these has already been mentioned (above: 51), namely the difficulty of explaining the late Old English sites of proprietary churches in terms of a pattern of 8th century or earlier graveyards. Secondly, our ideas about the strength and significance of the phenomenon of the double cemetery depend upon comparatively few excavated and accurately dated examples (Table IV). Of course it is likely that other sites await discovery, and it is true that until recently no systematic attention was paid to them. Even so, the foundation of the list still includes many sites, like Long Wittenham, Desborough, and Uncleby, which were investigated in the 19th century, and in terms of numbers of individuals it does not look as though we are dealing with more than 10% of Anglo-Saxon burials discovered outside churchyards – probably less. The combined totals of graves excavated from just two minor Late Saxon churchyards, St Helen-on-the-Walls, York, and St Nicholas-in-the-Shambles, London, would outnumber the lot. Quantitatively, therefore, this may be a rather slender body of evidence upon which to base a finished theory.

Thirdly, there is virtually no archaeological evidence to confirm that cemeteries like Winnall II or Polhill were being operated under Christian influence, or that the material culture displayed within them was in any way due to the impact of Christian ideas. Some conversions of truly Pauline rapidity have been envisaged at the very start of the 7th century (eg in connection with developments at Finglesham: Hawkes 1976), and it has been remarked how early the Kentish cemeteries begin to display a greater homogeneity in material culture than pertained in earlier pagan times. However, the notion that Christianity was in a position to propagate a new material culture all over England, at least until the latter part of the pontificate of Theodore, is, perhaps, one we should treat with caution, and certainly in conjunction with other possible explanations. Arnold, for example, has argued that the pattern of grave finds we discern in the 7th century was in some measure the outcome of political and economic trends which had originated in the 6th (Arnold 1980). We cannot beg the question by pointing to objects in some of these cemeteries which bear designs of possible Christian import, such as fish, or the cruciform symbolism of some brooches and pendants. The material will not stand interrogation in these terms. Nor will orientation, unless it is supported by other factors, and least of all an absence of grave-goods.

In our present state of knowledge it would be just as valid to speculate on the persisting *pagan* characteristics of 'Final Phase' cemeteries – to suggest, for example, that they contained folk of lesser status who could or would not be admitted to churchyards, or even to presume that these burial grounds were laid out in perverted parody of the new Christian cemeteries (cf Talbot 1970, 48). Neither possibility is entirely fanciful.

If we look across the Channel to Merovingian Gaul we see the conversion of the aristocracy first, as in England, the transfer of their burials to ecclesiastical sites, as in England, in some cases with an array of grave-goods, while the rank and file of the population remained in

Table IV 'Final Phase' cemeteries: a sample list

This Table summarizes information about examples of so-called 'Final Phase' cemeteries. It will be noted that some of this information comes from early sources of uncertain reliability, while in the cases of a few sites excavated recently full details are not yet available.

The distinguishing characteristics of 'Final Phase' cemeteries were first enumerated by Hyslop (1963), and there has been further discussion since, notably by Meaney & Hawkes (1970) and Hawkes (1973a). However, although the concept of the 'Final Phase' cemetery as a type seems to have won general acceptance, it may be suggested that there are several topics which deserve more attention.

1 Has there been any systematic analysis to demonstrate that the 11-odd distinguishing characteristics of 'Final Phase' cemeteries do in fact occur through most examples?
2 Is there independent evidence from primary English sources to show that the Church wished or attempted to prohibit burial with grave-goods in the 7th century, and hence could be held responsible for a decline in the occurrence of grave-goods in some cemeteries?
3 To what extent are any of the characteristics said to be typical of 'Final Phase' cemeteries foreshadowed by trends in material culture, funerary habits, and cemetery layout which appear in the 6th century?
4 In the 7th century how far is the composition of some cemeteries being modified by external circumstances: eg by the diversion of richer burials to barrows or churches. A few of the barrows present rather *greater* individual concentrations of funerary wealth than have been seen previously; what does this signify?
5 Many (most?) burials in 'Final Phase' cemeteries are unaccompanied by grave-goods. Is it fair to make assumptions about these graves (eg on dating) on the basis of burials that do possess material?

Site	County	No of skeletons encountered*	Reference(s)	Orientation(s) [First letter indicates position of head(s)]	Remarks
Barham Downs	Kent	23	*Medieval Archaeol*, **18** (1974), 179	W–E	Few grave-goods, suggested continuation until late C8. Barrows?
Bedhampton	Hants	89	*Medieval Archaeol*, **21** (1977), 208	Mainly W–E? 2×S–N	Late continuation?
Bishopsbourne	Kent	2 or 3	Meaney 1964, 113	S–N	
Bourton-on-the-Water	Glos	7	Meaney 1964, 93		
Breach Down	Kent	110+	Meaney 1964, 111		Inhumations in barrows; 1 with C8 *sceattas*, another with cross-headed pin. Cemetery suggested as Christian 'at least in part'
Broadstairs i Bradstow	Kent	98?	Hurd 1913; *Medieval Archaeol*, **16** (1972), 156; **18** (1974), 179; **19** (1975), 223; discussion in Hogarth 1973, 119	?	C7 material, structures
ii St Peter's		388	*Medieval Archaeol*, **16** (1972), 156; plan and discussion in Hogarth 1973, fig 4	Mainly NW–SE, but see discussion in Hogarth 1973	C7 material, but most graves unfurnished, structures. Small (?) Christian cemetery nearby (Hogarth 1973, 119)
Broadwell	Glos	2	Donovan & Dunning 1936, esp 165–70		Crouched burials, combs. Doubtful relevance
Burwell	Cambs	140+	Lethbridge 1931	W–E (most); some N–S	52 unfurnished, 12 with knife only. Former church site in vicinity
Camerton	Som	115	*Proc Somerset Archaeol Nat Hist Soc*, **79** (1933), 39–63; further details summarized in Rahtz 1977	W–E (most)	Finds of C4–C7: doubtful relevance
Chadlington	Oxon	25	*VCH Oxon*, **1**, 357	W–E WSW–ENE	Finds sparse
Cowlam (Kemp Howe)	Yorks	6	Mortimer 1906, 336–7	NW–SE (5), W–E (1)	
		12	*Medieval Archaeol*, **13** (1969), 241		In 'narrow graves cut into the side of a round-barrow ditch'. 5 in coffins. Suggested as Christian. Contemporary (?) structure nearby
Crane Down (Jevington)	Sussex	8	Holden *et al* 1969, 126–34	W–E and various	Portion of larger cemetery?
Desborough	Northants	60	*Archaeologia*, **45** (1880), 466–71	W–E SW–NE	2/60 furnished, one with pectoral cross. Site *c* 300 m east of parish church of St Giles
Ducklington	Oxon	2	*Proc Soc Antiq Lond*, 1 ser, **2**, 100	NW–SE	Finds included circular gold pendant bearing cross design; 1 burial of child
		3	*Medieval Archaeol*, **19** (1975), 227	N–S	Comparable group, 2 adults and 1 child, dated to C7. Edge of Roman settlement
Dunstable	Beds		Matthews & Morris 1962, 25–47		
Eccles	Kent		Detsicas 1976; Hawkes 1973b		In Roman villa. Traces of associated timber structure
Farthingdown (Coulsdon)	Surrey	30+	*Surrey Archaeol Collect*, **6** (1874), 109–17 J Morris 1959, 136; Meaney 1964	W–E NE–SW S–N Various	Excavations at various times (1760, 1871, 1939, 1948–9); graves 'under and between low barrows'. Half without grave-goods

Site	County	No of skeletons encountered*	Reference(s)	Orientation(s) [First letter indicates position of head(s)]	Remarks
Finglesham	Kent	243+ (?)	Stebbing 1929; S E Chadwick 1958; Hawkes 1976; discussion also in Hogarth 1973	E–W 2×SN	Begins C6, continuation into C7, including grave with purse-hoard of c 700
Garton Slack	Yorks	60	Mortimer 1906, 247		1 coffin
Holborough	Kent	39	Evison 1956	Roughly W–E	Graves well spaced in cemetery between Roman tumulus and prehistoric barrow; 9 graves with objects
Kingston Down	Kent	308+ (?)	Refs in Meaney 1964, 111	W–E* (most)	Inhumation cemetery including c 263 barrows (arrived at from counts made at different times) and 45 flat graves*. In use from before 600, continuation into C7. On site of earlier cemetery?
Leighton Buzzard II	Beds	68	Hyslop 1963, 161–200	Various but mainly WSW–ENE; 2×S–N	One of the archetypal Final Phase sites, suggested as the (semi-?) Christian successor to Leighton Buzzard I
Long Wittenham	Oxon	10	Proc Soc Antiq Lond, 2 ser, 11 (1862), 133		Mainly (all?) women. Total of 10 includes 2 outliers
Melbourn	Cambs	28	D M Wilson 1956	S–N±10	Full extent of cemetery not explored; 7 children
Milton Regis	Kent		Hawkes & Grove 1963		Finds include sceatta hoard and pectoral cross
Nazeingbury	Essex	180+	Huggins 1978	W–E	Timber buildings; estimated minimum total of c 230
North Leigh	Oxon	8	VCH Oxon, 1, 359; Oxoniensia, 5 (1940)	W–E	
Ocklynge Hill (Eastbourne)	Sussex	100+	Meaney 1964, 252–3; Medieval Archaeol, 15 (1971), 134	W–E	
Polhill	Kent	125	Hawkes 1973a		Earliest burials assigned to first half of C7, latest about 100 years later. Thought to be 'nominally Christian, proto-Christian, or at least only semi-pagan' (1973a, 186)
Shudy Camps	Cambs	158	Lethbridge 1936	NW–SE SW–NE	77 with grave-goods, including 21 with knives only
Standlake Down	Oxon	42	VCH Oxon, 1, 362	W–E	Rumour of c 40 more destroyed in 1820s
Stow-on-the-Wold	Glos	2	Mentioned in Donovan & Dunning 1936, 167, figs 9, 10		Contracted. Finds include iron knife and spiral-headed pin. (For finds of the latter type in relation to Final Phase cemeteries see discussion in Hawkes 1973b)
Uncleby	Yorks	60+	Proc Soc Antiq Lond, 24 (1912), 146–58; Faull 1979	W–E	Burials mainly in prehistoric barrow and in Anglo-Saxon extension, plus later interments beyond outline of barrow, in graves. Those on barrow in spaced rows
Wakerley	Northants	85	Medieval Archaeol, 15 (1971), 132	Roughly W–E	C6 material
Wheatley	Oxon	50+	Leeds 1916, from earlier data	Various	23 with grave-goods, including 7 with knives alone
Winnall II	Hants	45	Meaney & Hawkes 1970	Roughly W–E	Another 'archetype' site (cf Leighton Buzzard), proposed as Christian successor to Winnall I and argued to be in use C7–C8

* Figures in the third column represent rough totals of skeletons (not graves) which have been encountered at the sites in question. Hence in some cases these figures may exceed the totals published for individual excavations.

Fig 17 St Paul-in-the-Bail, Lincoln: hanging bowl within probable graveshaft. (Photo: K Camidge, by courtesy of Lincoln Archaeological Trust)

Fig 18   Breedon-on-the-Hill (Leics): St Mary and St Hardulf. The parish church on the hilltop is the fragment of an Augustinian priory which was founded early in the 12th century on the site of a Mercian minster established c 680. Only the eastern arm of the monastic church was retained for local use after the dissolution, so what is now the western tower was formerly central. The inclusion of St Hardulf in the dedication is of interest, for according to a list of saints' resting places Hardulf was buried at Breedon (Rollason 1978). The sharp profile of the eastern side of the hill has been caused by recent quarrying. The early minster stood within an Iron Age hillfort. Artificial enclosures which were used or re-used by early religious communities on less conspicuous sites may be harder to identify, although recent discoveries at St Ninian Ninekirks, Cumbria (for which see J K St Joseph in Antiquity, **52** (1978), 236–8) and Ruthwell, Dumfries, where the church may have been inserted within an earlier ringwork (C Crowe and G D B Jones, pers comm), confirm the potential of aerial reconnaissance for the study of early monastic topography. (Photo: Mick Sharp, Copyright Reserved)

their former cemeteries, sometimes for a century or more, before they, too, were gradually admitted to churchyards (James 1979). Furnished aristocratic burials were still being made in churches in South Germany in the first half of the 8th century (Stein 1968, 1–2), and attention has been drawn to the occurrence of furnished graves in private churches of this period (1968, 13–18). At home we now have the case of St Paul-in-the-Bail, Lincoln, where an early church contained a large, though empty grave, containing a hanging bowl (Gilmour 1979: Fig 17). Would this be the only object which was originally buried in this grave? We hear of royalty, or bits of them, being buried in the *porticus* of important churches during the 7th century, but it seems that no grave mentioned in a written source has yet been encountered intact and *in situ* under controlled conditions.

Hyslop's assertion that these changes took place 'all over England' is likewise open to question, since her examples are few and the majority are distributed within the east and south of the country. Elsewhere evidence for pre-Christian burial practices is often minimal. In Shropshire and Cheshire, in Cumbria, and over parts of Northumbria, for example, it is not at all clear how the

disposal of the dead was organized between the 5th and 8th centuries. In Shropshire it has been estimated that about 40% of medieval churchyards are circular or oval (Rowley 1972) and hence might be expected to conform to the development outlined by Thomas (1971, 51). Shropshire, however, does not offer the epigraphic and memorial evidence which exists in Wales, and the full significance of circularity in churchyard form has yet to be worked out (O'Sullivan 1980a; 1980b: Fig 19). There are circular churchyards in Wales, for example, which are known to have been newly created in the 12th century: Llanfihangel-y-Traethau (Gwynedd), Bettws Gwerful Goch (Gwynedd), and Llanfair Trelygen (Dyfed) are examples. In Northumbria the 'burial gap' is equally acute. Few post-Roman pre-missionary age burials have been identified in non-English areas (Faull 1977), and over much of the region no burials have been recognized at all at this period. Whether this is because the cemeteries of the era lie masked beneath a proportion of the oldest medieval churchyards (eg perhaps at Bramham (W Yorks), where the churchyard is large and circular: Fig 19), or because cemeteries did not exist at all cannot be decided. Recent area excavations carried out on Roman sites in various parts of Yorkshire have sometimes disclosed a small quota of 'casual' burials (eg at Dalton Parlours, Bessingby), typically in ditches or old corn driers. This practice – really no practice at all – seems to bespeak an off-hand attitude towards the disposal of the dead which could explain why burials hardly ever occur in any kind of concentration.

Returning to the English zone, it is now necessary to consider cases where a medieval churchyard *does* lie in close topographical relation to an earlier cemetery. Writing early in the 1860s, Kemble speculated 'it is very possible that in England the new churchyards were expressly and intentionally placed upon the site of the old cemeteries'. Baldwin Brown disputed this, writing off the few instances he knew about as 'exceptional coincidences', and for three-quarters of a century the idea has been out of fashion. But just as Thomas could note in 1971 that the frequency with which Christian cemeteries in Atlantic and north Britain are often imposed upon pagan burial-grounds was far from generally known (1971, 53), so has this phenomenon been largely overlooked in England.

Bearing in mind that it is not necessary to take up an extreme position on this issue, to insist that *all* churchyards must have originated according to this or that process, we may begin by considering the fact that cemeteries containing burials with grave-goods sometimes occur in the near vicinity of medieval churchyards. Examples include Ecton (Northants), Market Overton (Rutland), and Eggington (Beds). Pagan cemeteries occur very close to churchyards at Sancton (Yorks), Oakington (Cambs), and Steyning and Selmeston (Sus-

sex). A putative pagan cemetery at Oxborough (Norfolk) is adjacent to the site of a former church; the cemetery at Burwell (Cambs) is well away from the present church, but close to a former ecclesiastical site. Reports of Anglo-Saxon burials, with no objects specified, have been made for a number of sites just outside churchyards, including Broughton and Grendon (Northants), Black Bourton (Oxon), and Wing (Bucks). The midlands appear to be richer in such examples than the East Anglian counties, but there are one or two cases where it appears that a medieval churchyard occupies part of the site of a pagan cemetery, although in no instance is it obvious that the churchyard actually came to supersede the earlier burial ground. In Norfolk, for example, the churchyard of St Clement's Chapel, Brundall, overlaps a cremation cemetery. At Earsham late 6th century cremation burials have been encountered within the churchyard. In Suffolk the churchyard of Waldringfield has produced a cremation urn.

The emplacement of churches on or beside barrows has sometimes been noted or suspected. At High Wycombe, for instance, there is a barrow *c* 18m north of the parish church, and there is another in the old churchyard at Taplow Court. The association of the church and a barrow at Coombe, Woodnesborough (Kent), is also of interest. In some cases the existence of churches on prehistoric barrows may have had to do with the presence of secondary, English burials made within them. Fimber (N Yorks) is a case in point.

More numerous are the churchyards which have yielded

Fig 19 Bramham (W Yorks): aerial view of village church showing large oval graveyard and lines of communication. (Photo: R Yarwood, by courtesy of W Yorkshire Archaeological Unit)

Table V 'Pagan' finds from within churches and churchyards

Place	County	Church	Object(s)	Remarks	Reference
Brougham	Cumbria	St Ninian	Cup-mount	Suggested as C8, but possibly later	Baïley 1977
Brundall	Norfolk	St Clement	'Urns', Roman material	Site of destroyed chapel	Meaney 1964, 170–1
Burwell	Cambs	?	Pins, knives	Old church site? (cf Table IV)	Lethbridge 1931
Canterbury	Kent	St Martin	Coins fitted with loops, Roman intaglio, Frankish ornament	Connection with Liudhard?	Grierson 1952–4
Chislet	Kent	St Mary the Virgin			T Tatton-Brown, *pers comm*
Earsham	Norfolk	All Saints	'Urns', said to be Romano-British, but (?) Anglo-Saxon	From barrow NE of site, also occurring partly within churchyard	Meaney 1964, 173
Faversham	Kent	St Mary of Charity	Glass cup		Meaney 1964, 118
Fimber	Yorks	St Mary	Penannular brooch	Anglo-Saxon inhumations secondary in prehistoric barrow, encountered during rebuilding of church	Mortimer 1906, 190–2
Great Addington	Northants	All Saints	Knife	Report mentions six skeletons – hardly surprising, although knife may be valid clue	Meaney 1964, 186
Harrietsham	Kent	St John the Baptist	Crystal ball, bronze radiate brooch, pottery bottle vase		Meaney 1964, 123
High Wycombe	Bucks	All Saints		Barrow *c* 20m N of parish church	Meaney 1964, 59
Hilgay	Norfolk	All Saints	Pot, spearhead, pin	In churchyard	Meaney 1964, 125
Lighthorne	Warws	St Lawrence	Escutcheons (hanging bowl?)	Found on N side of church; possibility of other material	Meaney 1964, 217
Lincoln	Lincs	St Paul	Hanging bowl	From (?) graveshaft on threshold of chancel	Gilmour 1979
Melton	Suffolk	Old St Andrew	Jet annulet		Meaney 1964, 230
Minster in Thanet	Kent	St Mary	Glass vessel	Minster	VCH *Kent*, **1**, 385
Oare	Kent	St Peter			T Tatton-Brown, *pers comm*
Pagham	Sussex	St Thomas à Becket	Pot	Doubtful? Archbishop's estate	*Sussex Notes Queries*, **14** (1954–7), 123–5
Rochester	Kent	St Andrew	Spearhead	Found with burials and other material during works under Gundulph's Tower, adjacent to cathedral (see from 604)	*Medieval Archaeol*, **5** (1961), 309
Skipton	Yorks	Holy Trinity	C7 mounted gold coin		
Soham	Cambs	St Andrew	Cruciform brooch of *c* 550 (other finds?)	Former see	Meaney 1964, 149
Sysonby	Leics	?	Knife, spearhead		Meaney 1964, 149
Taplow	Bucks	?	Barrow burial	In old churchyard	Meaney 1964, 59
Waldringfield	Suffolk	All Saints	Cremation urn (?)		Meaney 1964, 23
Wickhambreaux	Kent	St Andrew	3 pots	Found 1794	*Gentlemen's Mag*, 1794, Pt 1, 501
Wyre Piddle	Worcs	?	2 shield bosses	2 burials in sitting position encountered during lengthening of nave	*Assoc Architect Socs Rep Pap*, **19.2** (1888), esp 427–8
Yeavering	N'blnd			(?) church of (?) 630s–40s within earlier graveyard	Hope-Taylor 1977

Notes to Tables V & VI

These lists contain examples of cases where 'pagan' objects have been found within medieval churches or churchyards (Table V), and supposedly pagan burials have been found in close proximity to medieval churchyards (Table VI). 'Close' has been taken to mean 0·1 mile or less.

Not all the reports inspire confidence, but there are several (eg St Paul-in-the-Bail, Lincoln) which concern finds that have been made under controlled conditions. Finds generally excluded from the lists are items of Scandinavian origin (for these see D M Wilson 1967; Graham-Campbell 1980), and later Anglo-Saxon coins, singletons and hoards, which in some areas occur in churchyards with considerable frequency. Occurrences of *sceattas* in churchyards have been listed elsewhere (Rigold & Metcalf 1977) and are not considered here.

When approaching cases in the second list it should be remembered that churchyards may change in shape, leaving earlier portions outside later boundaries (as at Rivenhall), and that churches may be relocated. Both processes can bequeath a cemetery, now unencumbered, that has come to be described as 'Anglo-Saxon'. Attention is drawn to the number of now-abandoned churches in the lists. Whether the fact that some of these churches were out of register with the later medieval pattern of settlement indicates an early origin, or whether the lack of recent disturbance has simply led to a better survival of evidence are topics that require further investigation.

Table VI · 'Pagan' finds around medieval churchyards

Place	County	Dedication	Object(s)	Remarks	Reference(s)
Ashendon	Bucks	St Mary	Inhumation & saucer brooches		*J Brit Archaeol Assoc*, **5** (1849), 113–16
Belton	Lincs	All Saints	Knives	Rectory garden	Meaney 1964, 152
Black Bourton	Oxon	St Mary	Pottery	Adjacent to churchyard	Meaney 1964, 203
Boughton	Northants	*Old church*	'Saxon burial'	Ruined church nearby	Meaney 1964, 187
Ecton	Northants	*Old Church*	Finds include 2 coins, one of Æthelred	Late – earlier church site?	Meaney 1964, 189
Grendon	Northants	St Mary	'Anglo-Saxon burials' said to be adjacent to church	Doubtful	Meaney 1964, 189
Irchester	Northants	St Katherine	2 saucer brooches	*c* 175 yards from church	Meaney 1964, 190
Kintbury	Berks	St Mary		Anglo-Saxon cemetery said to be in proximity to church	
Mentmore	Bucks	*Old Church*	Spearhead, knife	S of Old Church site	Meaney 1964, 58
Mildenhall	Suffolk	SS Mary & Andrew	Burial and brooch		Meaney 1964, 230–1
Oakington	Cambs	St Andrew	Spears, knives	SW of church	Meaney 1964, 69
Oxborough	Norfolk	St Mary Magdalene (*Old Church*)	Knife & circular brooch	Ruined church hard by	Meaney 1964, 180
Ravensden	Beds	All Saints	Bronze disc & enamel	Vicarage garden	*Antiq J*, **12** (1932), 173–4
Sancton	Yorks	All Saints	Mixed cemetery adjacent to churchyard		Faull 1976
Steyning	Sussex	St Andrew	Pagan cemetery near church	Anglo-Saxon royal estate centre	Bell 1978, 53
Stoke Bruerne	Northants	St Mary	Anglo-Saxon inhumation?	Close to church	
Stone	Bucks	St John Baptist	Saucer brooch	Vicarage garden (adjoins churchyard)	Meaney 1964, 59
Turweston	Bucks	Assumption	Shield boss, knife, spearhead	Adjoins churchyard	Meaney 1964, 196

objects suggestive of burial grounds which, if they were unencumbered, would be regarded as cemeteries of the 6th, 7th, or 8th centuries. Examples include Sysonby (Leics), Great Addington (Northants), Lighthorne (Warwicks), Melton (Suffolk), Soham (Cambs), Skipton (N Yorks), and Harrietsham, Faversham, Minster, possibly Chislet and Oare (Kent). There is, too, the important find of Frankish gold said to be from the churchyard of St Martin, outside Canterbury (Tables V and VI).

The site of the Ladykirk, Ripon, was investigated in 1955 and out of twenty burials yielded some half-dozen skeletons accompanied by bone combs (Miss S Johnson, *pers comm*). Burials described as being of the 10th century were examined at St Mary Bishophill Junior, York, early in the 1960s, and several were accompanied by objects: bracelet, knife, whetstone, strap end, coin. St Mary Bishophill Senior has also produced a burial with a knife, though from outside the later medieval churchyard boundary. Possibly these and some other cases are reflections of Scandinavian custom. Nevertheless, we also find a considerable number of *sceattas* and later coins emanating from churchyards. The most recent check-list (Rigold & Metcalf 1977) contains fifteen examples, excluding others found outside what is now the modern boundary. Some of the sites are familiar: Stone-by-Faversham, Repton, Wharram Percy, Northampton. Others, such as the find from the site of the old church of St John's Ashes, Chedworth (Glos), may fall into a pattern to which attention has already been drawn (above: 52). These canot all be coins which slipped through the trembling fingers of mourners as they paid the soul-scot at the open grave. (The sense of the law, incidentally, suggests that soul-scot had to be paid before the grave was closed.) And in some cases deliberate deposition is indicated, as in the case of the *sceatta* found in a child's grave, under a *porticus* added to the south wall of St Pancras, Canterbury.

The significance of all these examples must, of course, be open to serious question. They have been culled,

more or less indiscriminately, from various sources, usually without benefit of local knowledge. Statistically they are meaningless since they represent only a minute fraction of the total numbers of churchyards and cemeteries concerned. Moreover, churchyards are unusual in that they are regularly subjected to disturbance by hand. Hence any stray artefacts within them are more likely to be found than if, say, they were lying in a field. On the other hand, the constant cycle of burial may have led to the destruction or removal of most artefacts, the discoveries of modern times being (1) only the first to be recorded, and (2) the dregs of a reservoir of material which was once much greater. So whether we are glimpsing aspects of a phenomenon, or merely, as Baldwin Brown argued, dealing with 'exceptional coincidences' (1903, 263), is an issue which only a comprehensive survey might decide.

Assessment must also take account of the possibility that the custom of depositing objects of a personal kind with burials was maintained for a time in Christian graveyards. Biddle (1976a, 69) observes that none of the earliest graves in the cathedral cemetery at Winchester contained grave-goods, but it may be that burials in the vicinity of an important minster were subject to tighter controls than could, or would be applied to graveyards in outlying parts. The occurrence of Viking grave-goods in Christian churchyards in the north of England and the Isle of Man (D M Wilson 1967, 38, 43–4) might be held to reinforce this possibility, although, as Wilson points out, it is the general *absence* of such material which is really the more striking.

It may be of relevance that in several of the cases mentioned above the churches were of some importance before the Conquest. Soham is alleged to have been frequented by St Felix in the 7th century. Pagham was part of an archbishop's estate (Collins 1955). Steyning was originally the centre of a royal estate, and King Æthelwulf was buried there (Bell 1978, 51–2). Leighton Buzzard, too, stood on a royal estate. In her report on the excavations at Chamberlain's Barn, Hyslop noted that the basilican stone-built church at Wing lies within four miles of Leighton Buzzard: 'There is nothing to indicate why Wing should have been chosen as a site for this exceptional building, but it seems reasonable to suppose that Christianity was an established force in the area at the time (ie soon after the middle of the 7th century), and a date in the late 650s remains the most likely for its introduction' (1963, 194). However, the church at Leighton Buzzard itself, less than a mile from Chamberlain's Barn, had a special relation with the chapels which served the outlying hamlets. In this relationship the chapels of ease were closely controlled by the mother church, and Mrs D Owen has noticed that 'the bond between them was more like that between the cathedral and parish churches of such large and ancient towns as Hereford and Worcester, than is anything else normally found in eastern England' (Owen 1978, 11–12).

Conclusion

Despite the uncertainties, five tentative suggestions may now be made about the origins of English graveyards. They all centre on the likelihood that there was no single, coherent process which gave rise to village churchyards. Instead, a multiplicity of factors, each exerting influence according to local conditions, played a part:

1 In some cases the sequence proposed by Hyslop, Meaney, and Hawkes (early pagan cemetery, 'Final Phase' cemetery nearby, Christian graveyard) obtains (?8th century).

2 Where circumstances permitted (eg the character of settlement, quality of land, location of manor house) the 'Final Phase' (or earlier) cemetery could be translated into a churchyard (?8th–9th centuries).

3 As a variant of (2), a graveyard might be created on a nearby site, so that its relationship to the 'Final Phase' cemetery was akin to that between the 'Final Phase' cemetery and its pagan predecessor (8th–9th centuries).

4 Entirely new graveyards were created at a distance from pagan burial sites. These would usually belong to proprietary churches attached to manorial centres (?8th–11th centuries).

5 Developments of the kind outlined in (2) and (3) took place, but were then eclipsed by changes in ecclesiastical geography brought about by shifts in the pattern of settlement, and in particular by alterations in the relative importance of manorial centres, so that they remained 'undeveloped' (?8th–11th centuries).

An issue which deserves more attention than it has received hitherto is the question of whether the distribution of pagan cemeteries is a reflection of the pattern of settlement, or whether it constitutes an independent framework of sites which can be examined in its own right. The sites of hundreds of pagan burial grounds are known, but only a handful of contemporary settlements has been identified.

Perhaps the main point to emerge from this discussion is the exceptional fluidity of burial arrangements in Middle Saxon England. No one explanation fits all the facts because several processes were involved, and could even operate in conjunction. What seems clear is that intensive fieldwork is required in the vicinity of churchyards as a basis for a more informed discussion, and that churchyards should be approached as sites, not merely as collections of graves. We should be on the lookout for early lost churchyards. Some of these, especially in the 8th and 9th centuries, may have been ephemeral, but they could provide stepping stones from the earlier to the later medieval pattern of cemeteries. Above all, the theme of burial should be divided – if it has to be divided at all – not by period but by region. Finally, there is the prospect that the terminology devised by Thomas for cemeteries in the British zone (above: 51) might be applicable, in some cases, in England.

Scope and definitions

This chapter is mainly concerned with the origins and early development of what in the later Middle Ages came to be called parish churches and chapels. Particular emphasis is placed on the study of churches in relation to the history of rural settlement. Whereas urban ecclesiastical geography has received fairly full attention in recent years (eg Brooke 1970; Barley 1977, 459–509), the early church in the countryside has been neglected by archaeologists. In England, apart from the well-known example of Wharram Percy (Hurst 1976; Beresford & Hurst 1976) and a handful of promising recent studies (eg Austin 1976; Wade-Martins 1980;

Drury & Rodwell 1978) (Fig 20), archaeological questions arising from the co-location of church and settlement have hardly been posed. Christopher Taylor, for example, devotes but two pages to churches in his book on medieval fieldwork, and deals only with isolated churches which commemorate deserted villages and churches which occur in striking settings, perhaps for reasons of 'pagan ritual significance' (1974a, 90–3). Rowley, writing of the Shropshire landscape, states that 'the siting of a church or chapel is often of great significance' (1972, 81), but he does not go on to amplify this remark other than by suggesting that a church which occupies a central site in a village may date from the beginnings of the settlement, while a church which

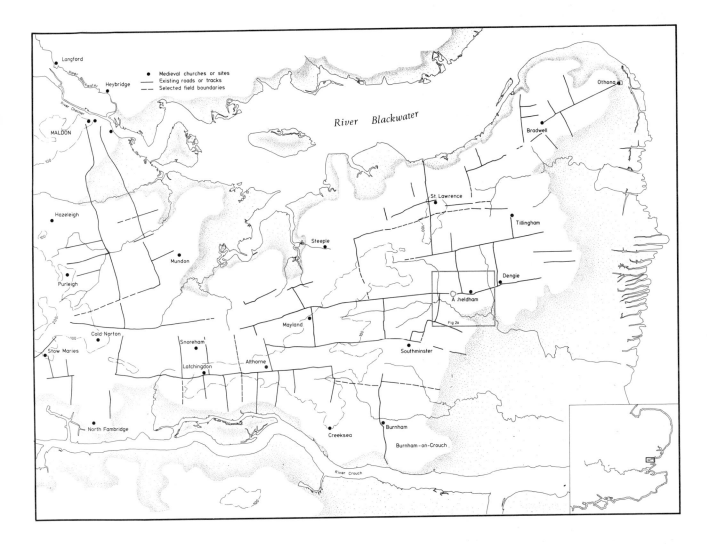

Fig 20   Map showing the Anglo-Saxon and medieval churches of the Dengie Hundred (Essex) in relation to the principal components of a planned rectilinear landscape, now believed to be of Roman date. Only roads and major land boundaries are shown; the field systems also fit within the pattern. Many of the churches have been located on prominent corner plots, at road junctions (eg Dengie, Southminster, Althorne, Latchingdon), while others have been positioned hard against roads (eg Cold Norton, Bradwell, Asheldham). In the last instance the road alignment was adjusted in the Norman period, as the church expanded southwards over the former road-line. St Peter's church at Othona lies at the end of one of the straightest sections of road, over the west gate of the Roman fort. (Map: W J Rodwell)

stands at the edge may be a latecomer. In Wales, by contrast, thoughtful attention has been paid to the location of churches, most notably by Bowen (1954) who devoted a third of his book on the settlements of the Celtic saints to questions of position, site, and form.

Until the time of Henry I there is no single term which is available to describe the churches that are under consideration. A significant minority originated as churches of religious communities, having been transformed into proto-parochial churches at some, usually uncertain, date before the Conquest. This might happen when the estates which sustained a monastery were acquired by laymen, or when political support for a religious community was withdrawn. Former monastic churches are particularly relevant to the theme of this section because they were components of layouts which were settlements in themselves (Rahtz 1973).

'Village church' is a convenient label in most other cases, but it is slightly misleading in so far as it conveys the idea that such churches came into existence as a result of communal action; it also gives accentuation to the supposition that the areas or communities served by churches were usually coincident with villages. Both these beliefs may be correct, in many cases, but to promote them as generalizations, in our present state of knowledge, is more than the evidence will allow.

The term 'proprietary church' is more helpful and accurate, but this, too, has drawbacks since it embraces a wide variety of types and circumstances. In one sense or another all churches were *ecclesiae propriae*. What was looked upon by the community as a *tunkirke* could also be firmly in the hands of an individual, who might be free to grant an hereditary estate in it (eg Whitelock 1930, nos 37, 38). The conception of churches as private property is exemplified with clarity in districts like Norfolk where fragmented ownership was taken to extremes (Page 1915, 85–8).

Diversity is indicated by the classifications of churches given in the law-codes of Edgar, Æthelred, and Cnut, but even in these it appears that the compilers were obliged to simplify. Churches in boroughs with special rights, churches owned by consortia of freemen, churches on bookland, and smaller manorial churches could all be contained under the head of a church with a graveyard, for example (VIII Æthelred, cap 5.i). In the 11th century terminology was in a state of flux: *ecclesia* and *capella* were sometimes employed interchangeably, and the word *monasterium*, though retaining a specialized sense, was sufficiently elastic to describe anything from a cathedral to a new chapel on a private estate.

The Old English diocese was pyramidal in its organization. At the apex stood the head minster or cathedral. Next came minsters of lesser status, often called old minsters or mother churches, which dominated areas roughly equivalent to modern rural deaneries. The old minsters formed the basic framework for the local administration of ecclesiastical affairs. They had their own dependent chapels, but in addition to them numbers of private churches came to be founded by the owners of estates, lay and ecclesiastical. By the late 11th century it was such proprietary churches, together with supplementary *feldcircan*, which comprised the broad base of the structure. Every church had its place in a fiscal and liturgical hierarchy by which, according to its status, it would receive or render payments and dues of various kinds.

The image of a pyramid is schematic, and takes no account of regional variations or the very considerable developments which took place through time. In practice the distinction between one grade of church and another was not always sharp. The concept of the cathedral was not as firm and the structure of the diocese was not as formalized as they were to become after the Norman reorganization of the English Church. A survey made around 1100 mentions the former existence of 'bishoprics' at places like Whitby, Beverley, and Bridport, as well as at places where sees had previously been located (R Morris 1872, 145–6). Where the disruption caused by the Danish invasions had led to the removal of a primary see from one place to another (eg Lindsey and Leicester to Dorchester), it seems nevertheless that elements of the original pattern could linger, the churches retaining some kind of suffragan status. Barlow points out that among words used to describe a bishop's parish, *bisceop* is more widely compounded with *setle*, *seld*, and *stol* than with words expressing jurisdiction, like *dom*, or referring to an area, *scir* (1963, 164). In most areas a basic complement of old minsters was in existence by the middle of the 8th century, but adjustments could follow. In Kent, for instance, a pattern of minsters was probably established in the days of Theodore, but this was badly jarred by Danish attacks in the 9th century, with the result that most of the original capital churches were superseded by others (Douglas 1944, 10–11). In the Danelaw, which seems to have teemed with churches by the time of the Norman Conquest, it has been argued that the disappearance or weakening of religious communities may have helped to create conditions which favoured a more rapid escalation of churchbuilding at parochial level than may have occurred elsewhere (Brooke 1970, 74–7).

The ecclesiastical structure mirrored aspects of secular history. Dioceses ghosted the outlines of vanished kingdoms. Old minsters usually coincided with royal *tūn*, and hence could emerge later on as churches at hundredal centres (Cam 1944). Local churches were an expression of the rank of the thanes by whom they were founded; the parochial organization that crystallized around these churches often made use of the existing divisions of secular land allotment (see below: 71).

The forces which led to the definition of the parochial system lay mainly in a gradual extension and intensification of episcopal control over the network of minsters and smaller churches that has been sketched above (cf Brooke 1970, 72). In course of this the rights of some churches were abridged while those of others were increased. It was, in a sense, a process of equalization, already foreshadowed in the *Leis Willelme*, wherein the four grades of church specified in the laws of Cnut had been simplified to three: *cathedralis ... matrix ecclesia parochialis, capella* (cap 1.i). Much of the impetus for reform was provided by the bishops, but while gaps in the parochial map were still being filled by the creation of new churches in the late 11th and 12th centuries (Lennard 1959, 295–8; Brett 1975, 216–33), the system that emerged was mainly fashioned from a pattern that was already in existence.

If proprietary factors lie behind the origin of the bulk of what later became parish churches, it follows that the study of such buildings is likely to be of special relevance to the wider study of settlement history (eg Phythian-Adams 1978, 36). The fabrics, sites, and surroundings of individual churches offer opportunities for practical research, whereas the homes of the proprietors have usually vanished. The contribution of archaeology deserves emphasis, since it can add extra depth and perspective to a study which hitherto has depended mainly upon information contained in late Old English documents. Where contemporary written evidence is lacking questions of origin and date belong more properly within the province of the archaeologist, who under favourable conditions may be able to determine when a particular church was founded and to describe the stages through which it passed before it comes within range of written records.

Sources and interpretations

The chief written sources of information about secular churches in the Old English period are:

1 *Law-codes of English kings:* These are concerned with the rank of churches, and in particular their economic standing. They provide a useful frame within which to discuss evidence from other sources, but not until the 10th century do they begin to discriminate between one class of church and another (II Edgar, cap 1–3; VIII Æthelred, cap 5.i; I Cnut, cap 3a, 11).

2 *Records of transactions concerning or including churches:* eg in which a church is given to a monastery (eg Hart 1966, 168), is specified in a will (eg Whitelock 1930, no 33, where no less than eleven churches are mentioned), or is conveyed from one hand to another (eg the case of St Mary, Huntingdon, or the two churches which Peter de Valonges bought from Ulwi of Hatfield, mentioned in Domesday Book).

3 *Biographies of saints,* which sometimes contain incidental references to churches or mention visits by bishops to consecrate them (Addleshaw 1970a, 11, with examples).

4 *Surveys of churches* made in connection with reviews of spiritual customs (eg for the distribution of Chrism: Douglas 1944).

5 *Inscriptions* (eg St Gregory, Kirkdale; St Mary Castlegate, York; Odda's Chapel, Deerhurst (Okasha 1971)). The Kirkdale inscription informs that the church was bought as a ruin and reconditioned.

6 *Miscellaneous ecclesiastical writings,* including letters, minutes of synods, penitentials, and canons which contain rulings on the use and proper treatment of churches.

7 *References to churches in chronicles* (eg St Olave at *Galmanho*, York: ASC[D] *sub anno* 1055) or in historical writings (eg *HE*, v.4–5).

8 *Domesday Book.*

9 *Later medieval evidence* (eg pensions, rights of station, or custody of key on saint's day, etc) reflecting the former dependence of one church on another.

The ecclesiastical provisions of the later law-codes have been well explored in recent years (Lennard 1959; Barlow 1963) and it is not necessary to review them in detail here. Until *c* 950 the codes do not mention categories of church. The Kentish laws relating to churches were concerned with compensation, taxation, and expurgation (Æthelbert, cap 1), those of Ine with baptism and the render of church dues (cap 2, 4), and Alfred's with asylum and theft (cap 5–6). The first code to present a hierarchy of churches (II Edgar, cap 1–2) specified that the third part of a thegn's tithes could be paid to his own church if it fulfilled two conditions: first,

the church had to stand on the owner's bookland, and secondly the church had to possess its own graveyard (*legerstow*). The connection with bookland is significant, for it suggests the reason why later parochial territories and the boundaries of many pre-Conquest estates are often to be found in close agreement (Sawyer 1978a, 248). The hierarchy was clarified in VIII Æthelred: 'Not all churches are to be regarded as being of the same temporal status, though in spiritual terms they all possess the same sanctity' (cap 5). Fines for the violation of the protection of churches were fixed according to their civil status: headminsters, churches of medium rank, churches of still lesser status but with graveyards, and country chapels.

Payments for the souls of the dead 'are to be rendered at the places where they are legally due' (I Æthelstan, cap 4). The later law-codes were particular about whether or not a church possessed a graveyard, presumably because this affected the destination of soul-scot. However, there is some doubt as to whether the churches which took soul-scot always coincided with the graveyards containing those who would be liable to pay it. A proviso existed that if a body was buried anywhere other than in the proper area to which it belonged (*rihtscriftscire*), 'payment shall nevertheless be made to the church (*mynstre*) to which the dead man belonged' (V Æthelred, 12.i). The concept of a *rihtscriftscire* for the dead seems to have been used to reinforce the rights of the old minsters, by ensuring that if someone was buried outside the area of his own minster some payment was nevertheless due to his proper parish church, as was the case in the later Middle Ages. However, it is also necessary to explain the presence of graveyards (in some cases attested archaeologically) at some chapels of lesser status which one would not expect to have possessed them. To qualify for burial within a church or beside a minster one had to be a person of rank, and it has been conjectured that the rights of mother churches were only enforced systematically in respect of those whose burial fees were worth having (Lennard 1959, 302, n 1). Barlow has argued that a division of soul-scot would not have harmed the financial position of the old minsters to any great extent, and that in any case a thegn would normally prefer to be buried at the mother church, where the presence of several priests and (possibly) relics would greatly increase the effect of intercessions for his soul (1963, 196). In practice, therefore, there might be two tiers of graveyards: those for the rich and those for the poor. The latter could deliver little revenue to the old minsters and would thus be of only small interest to them for as long as the owners made no attempt to assert rights of their own. If the distinction in the law-codes was fiscal as well as geographical it would be reasonable to envisage a pattern of local graveyards that was at once both older and more extensive than has sometimes been imagined.

The expansion of ecclesiastical provision

It has been argued that the large majority of parish churches in England were founded in the 10th and 11th centuries (Addleshaw 1970a, 13). The increasingly legalistic treatment of churches by the compilers of law-codes in that period might well signify that churches were proliferating at the time, but it could equally, and simultaneously, reflect the growth of an aspiration towards the more efficient regulation of the affairs of those which were already in existence. Until *c* 1050 it is most unusual to glimpse the moment at which a private church was founded, and thereafter it is not always clear whether 'new' churches were really new or the result of rebuilding (eg the case of Lanfranc's church at Harrow: Lennard 1959, 296–7, esp 297, n 3). Likewise, against the probability that the thegns Alsi and Blacheman were the 11th century founders of two churches listed in the *Domesday Monachorum* as *Aelsiescirce* and *Blacemannescirce* (Douglas 1944, 13) must be set the fact that the ownership of estates could change, and place-names with them (Sawyer 1976, 6). Only at the start of the era can references to consecrations be accepted at face value, and even then other factors may have to be taken into account (see below).

Bede tells of the consecration of two churches on the estates of *gesiths*. It is implied that the *gesiths* built the churches (*HE*, v.4–5). Elsewhere Bede mentions the consecration of a church at *Osingadun* by Cuthbert (*d* 687) on an estate belonging to Ælflæd's monastery (Colgrave 1940, 126), and another which stood on a royal estate visited by Aiden (*HE*, iii.17). From the pages of Bede, too, we gather that the building of local churches and baptisteries was a phenomenon which had been gathering momentum up to his own day (*HE*, ii.14; see above: 53). Systematic study of written records will sometimes disclose quite a high total of churches in a given area at an early date. In Worcestershire, for example, it appears that there is literary evidence for some eighteen churches before 757, and for a further eight in the period 757–825 (M Wilson 1969, 23). Nor are these the only signs that local churches were being established before the 10th century. Theodore's *Penitential* stated that it was allowable to build churches 'in various places', according to necessity, and gave instructions as to how they were and were not to be used. The author was evidently worried that materials from churches were being put to profane uses: 'It is forbidden for the wood from a church to be joined to another structure (*opus*) unless it be to another church. . . .' A prohibition on the use of churches as mausolea for pagans, and the ruling *Laicus non debet in aecclesiis recitare, nec Alleluia . . .* contribute to the impression that the author(s) had private churches in mind (Haddan & Stubbs 1869–71, III, 190–1; for reservations, see above: 50).

Private churches were also acknowledged by Egbert, the first archbishop of York (734–66), who in his *Dialogue* insisted that episcopal consent was needed before a priest could serve a church in lay ownership (Haddan & Stubbs 1869–71, III, 403–13). The author of the 9th century poem *De Abbatibus* noted that in his day churches were 'rising everywhere' (A Campbell 1967). This might be dismissed as rhetoric, but no such judgement can be applied to the boast of Herman, Bishop of Ramsbury, made on a visit to Rome in 1050, that England was full of churches. Domesday Book bears him out, for it records over 2600 churches or places served by priests. The real total was a good deal higher, since the Domesday scribes left many churches unrecorded (see below: 68). In summary it may be said that by the 8th century there are definite signs that the proprietary church existed in England, and that thereafter, certain towns apart, the provision of private churches was a matter of sporadic development, probably intensified in the 10th and 11th centuries, but spread across the whole period rather than entirely concentrated in the few decades leading up to the Conquest.

Spiritual matters

A private church was an emblem of thegnly rank and often a source of income to its owner, but its basic functions were of course liturgical in nature, the church building being a centre for the exercise of pastoral care: baptism, mass, confession, burial, intercession. Aspects of these functions have been discussed by other writers (eg H M Taylor 1973a, 52–8; 1978, 1064–5) and tend on the whole to relate more to questions of internal arrangement and use of space rather than to the geographical distribution and positions of the buildings themselves.

By the 11th century a local church could either be the centre of its own pastoral unit, like a parish church in the later sense, or else it could be one component in a network of dependent churches and chapels in direct subjection to a minster or mother church (Brooke 1970, 70; Douglas 1944; Barlow 1963, 179–82, 194). Arrangements of the latter kind can still be observed in some areas well on in the 12th century, as for example at Leominster, which maintained a small force of a priest and three chaplains for pastoral tasks as late as 1186–98, 'on account of the dispersal of the parishes' (Kemp 1968, 510, n 55).

However pastoral work was actually directed, it is clear from the ubiquity of local churches in 11th century England that spiritual needs were often being catered for very much on a neighbourhood basis. Fonts of the Norman and Angevin periods are a commonplace (Bond 1908), and testify to the fact that by the 12th century, at latest, baptism was administered locally. In part this may have been a consequence of the large size and small number of pre-Conquest English dioceses. The rite of initiation which was introduced into England by Augustine in the 7th century was Roman, and hence could only be celebrated in its entirety when a bishop was present to perform the hand-laying and consignation of the forehead that formed the essential conclusion of the ceremony (Fisher 1965, 78). During the early stages of the conversion of the English it seems that initiation in an oratory or other specialized structure was something granted only to royalty or their close associates; members of the general population were initiated at ceremonies of mass baptism conducted in the open air and involving immersion in a river (*HE*, ii.14, 16). However, the Roman rite originated in a country where bishops' parishes were compact, cathedrals were numerous, civic baptisteries were the rule, and access to them was usually straightforward. In its original form the Roman rite was not suited to the sprawling tribal dioceses of Britain, where the fact that distances were great and bishops were few meant that the ideal of initiation at the canonical seasons of Easter and Pentecost was difficult to realize, and virtually impossible when emphasis was transferred from adult to infant baptism (cf Ine, cap 2). So the rite was split. From an early date baptism was delegated to presbyters (*HE*, iii. 22), while confirmation was administered as a separate rite by the bishop, who was supposed to make an annual tour of his diocese for this purpose (Haddan & Stubbs 1869–71, III, 449).

For several centuries ecclesiastical regulations continued to insist that baptism should be administered at the traditional seasons (eg Synod of Chelsea (787), 2; Synod of Winchester (1074), 7), but it is clear from the law-codes, and from the multiplication of baptismal churches, that in practice it was expected that the rite would be performed all the year round, except perhaps in those few districts where a cathedral baptistery and a bishop were near at hand. The disintegration of the rite of initiation into two rites, baptism and confirmation, could help to explain the apparent rarity of baptisteries in pre-Conquest England. Written records provide a solitary example, at Canterbury (H M Taylor 1969c), and archaeology has added only two others, at Potterne (Wilts) (Davey 1964), and Barton-on-Humber (Rodwell & Rodwell 1980), but both integrated with churches.

Pagans and Christians

It is difficult to assess the importance of the legacy of pagan cult sites to early church builders. A fair number of churches stand within or close to prominent earthworks, and such relationships have commonly given rise to speculation about pagan origins. Lost gods have also been invoked to explain the presence of apparently non-Christian features in churchyards, such as the tall monolith at Rudstone (N Yorks) or the small totem-like figure at Braunstone (Leics) (which is probably a displaced corbel). A point worth making here is that churchyards have often acted as collecting places for the keeping of antiquities found elsewhere. The Roman sarcophagus outside the church at Birkin (Humbs), for example, was found some distance away and brought into the churchyard for display. Hence unless the source of a 'pagan' feature is known, it may be unsafe to assume that it had any original connection with the site of the church. Local legends, like the one which records that the church at Dorrington (Lincs) was built of stones removed from a heathen temple, abound but cannot be trusted. Pope Gregory's advice to Mellitus on this matter is well known (*HE*, i.30), but Biddle (1976a, 68) and Olsen (1966) have drawn attention to the problems of relating churches to the sites of nature cults in archaeological terms.

Little is known about the ordinance of Saxon temples. The Northumbrian temple at Goodmanham seems to have consisted of some sort of focal structure within an enclosure, together with outdoor idols and altars. At least, when King Edwin's chief priest set out to desecrate the site, it was said, later, that he was able to approach the enclosure on horseback (*HE*, ii.14). Rædwald, King of East Anglia, hedged his bets by maintaining a dual-purpose shrine, with facilities for pagan and Christian worship (*HE*, ii.15). When the East Saxons relapsed into idolatry *c* 665, Bede reports that they rebuilt ruined temples, suggesting something structural (*HE*, iii.30). However, Bede was writing some years after the events he described, and it would be inadvisable to base conclusions about the characteristics of pagan temples on the strength of Bede's evidence alone. Paganism was not, in any case, a homogeneous phenomenon, but comprised a variety of cults and superstitions which may well have been represented in an equally diverse pattern of cult sites. This was certainly the case in Germany, where the diverse manifestations of paganism encountered by Boniface in his missions to Thuringia, Hesse, and Frisia could be reminiscent of conditions in England a century earlier (Talbot 1970).

Paganism was never extinguished by the Old English Church. The Scandinavian settlements were accompanied by a fresh infusion of pagan beliefs, witnessed not only in fiercely anti-heathen tracts written by men like Wulfstan (Whitelock 1952, 46, n 140, with further references), but also in the ways that makers of crosses

and gravestones mingled elements of the Christian and heroic traditions (Bailey 1980, 101–42). It is hard to tell from the standard warnings offered in law-codes and minutes of synods whether paganism was regarded as a serious danger or merely as an irritation, but as late as the reign of Cnut it was felt necessary to condemn the activities of wizards (II, 4a) and to forbid the worship of 'idols, heathen gods, the sun or moon, fire or flood, springs, and stones or any kind of woodland tree . . .' Officially the Church was uncompromising in its opposition to any kind of heathen pursuit, but in practice it could be more pragmatic, even acquiescent to pagan practices. Fragments of pagan ceremonies are to be found embedded in pre-Conquest Christian rites, and vice versa. In the *Æcer-bot* spell (Storms 1948, no 8), for example, it is taken for granted not only that a mass-priest is available to assist in the ritual, but also that it is feasible for part of it to take place in a church (Hill 1977). Christian texts were built into this elaborate sequence, but the dominant elements are hymns to the sun and earth: survivals from a pagan liturgy? This kind of syncretism could easily arise when standards of latinity were low. The Christian formulas were themselves probably regarded as a kind of magic, and sometimes turn up in places where it is clear that they were not understood by the priests who uttered them (Hohler 1975, 71–4).

There is, however, a risk that we may accord a misplaced emphasis to English paganism. It is easy to slip into a frame of mind which conceives of paganism as being formally 'religious' in anachronistically Christian terms. The theological concepts and liturgical framework to which Christianity has accustomed us were probably entirely novel in 7th century England, when pagan religion may have involved no more than an array of superstitious rituals: a charm against heartburn, a way to fight an infection of crops, or a spell to detain a swarm of bees. Our ideas about temples and cult-sites could, likewise, be partly determined by Christian conditioning, although the example of Yeavering suggests that an English 'temple architecture' may indeed await recognition, and that the possibility of a link between pagan cemeteries and the sites of cult structures has still to be properly explored.

Although study of the location of churches in relation to cult sites is likely to prove complicated, there are certain areas where basic fieldwork might yield results. Wells, for example, were magnets for small Christian shrines and chapels (Butler 1980). The worship of *wæterwyllas* was frowned upon by the Church, but it is not difficult to envisage a process whereby pagan well-cults were adapted and nominally Christianized as a means of perpetuating them in disguised form (Rahtz & Watts 1979, esp 205–8). In several parts of the country well-dressing ceremonies survive to this day (eg in Derbyshire, and until the early years of this century in Bristol). In parts of the north well dedications were often made to St Helen, although for some reason St Anne seems to have been specially favoured as the patron saint for such sites nationally, possibly because she was deemed to be an appropriate dedicatee for chapelries (Forster 1899, I, 99). The origins of wells as cult sites have been discussed by Ross (1967); something of the peculiar resonance of their associations as late as the Tudor period can be perceived from George Peel's strange poem 'A Voice Speaks from the Well' in his play *The Old Wives' Tale*:

Faire maiden white and red,
Combe me smoothe, and stroke my head:
And thou shall have some cockell bread.
Gently dippe, but not too deepe,
For fear thou make the goulden beard to weep.
Faire maide, white and redde,
Combe me smooth, and stroke my head;
And every haire, a sheave shall be,
And every sheave, a golden tree.

It is possible that pagan interest in the orientation of graves (Rahtz 1977, 58; 1978; Hawkes 1976) was transferred to churches. An idea that a new church was normally orientated to sunrise on the day of the patronal festival can be traced back in written records to the 17th century. Some corroboration for an earlier origin for the belief was claimed by Benson (1956, 205–13). Benson's conclusions (eg 'that there are a very large number of churches . . . where the sunrise day preserves the original dedication of the first church on the site' (211)) are perhaps to be received with caution, since in the absence of an accurate plan and definite information about earlier layouts it may not be easy to determine the axis of a structure. Nevertheless, Benson's results for 237 medieval churches and chapels in Oxfordshire do suggest that there is scope for further research. A general correspondence between orientation and dedication, if confirmed, would have fascinating repercussions for ecclesiastical and settlement history.

Churches and Domesday Book

Domesday Book records about 2000 churches and chapels. The existence of roughly 550 other churches and chapels may be inferred from references to priests. (For the criteria used here, see the note which accompanies Table VII.) Domesday is thus the earliest source to survive which provides information about churches on a large scale, and as such the evidence it contains is central to any discussion about churches and settlement. However, the ecclesiastical data given in Domesday Book are manifestly incomplete. The techniques used to record churches varied from one county to another. In some counties, like Cornwall, Devon, and Bedfordshire, the scribes were highly exclusive. In others, notably Norfolk and Suffolk, comparatively few churches seem to have been overlooked. These contrasts are well known, but the irregular manner in which churches were treated in 1086 has long been a cause of puzzlement among scholars. William Page, in his pioneering survey of this subject, made much of what he saw as a contrast between circumstances in the east where 'the organization of the parish church was more fully developed' and the position in the west where he believed a more archaic system of dominant hundredal minsters still prevailed. Page was also driven to account for the absence of references to churches across large parts of England either by the fact – or likelihood – that they were in the hands of religious houses or else because the districts concerned consisted of forest and marshland and so were sparsely settled (1915, 92). The second line of argument no longer seems acceptable as a generalization. Areas can be found into which settlement had not progressed by 1086 (eg the eastern half of Langoe wapentake in Lincolnshire), but where independent information about the distribution of churches is available it may also show that an area was more *densely* settled than Domesday alone suggests. In Kent the lists of churches in the *Domesday Monachorum* and the *Textus Roffensis* contribute nearly 160 place-names

which do not appear in Domesday Book (Darby & Campbell 1962, 495–502). This supplementary detail is particularly significant in the Weald, an area traditionally thought to have been sparsely inhabited before the Conquest, where the ecclesiastical sources reveal the presence of over thirty places with 11th century churches in addition to the eighteen settlements named in Domesday Book (Sawyer 1978a, 136–7). The Kentish churches which were enumerated separately outnumber those recorded in Domesday Book by rather more than 2:1. The contrast may be explained by the fact that the inquiries were undertaken for different reasons, the one being concerned with spiritual, and the other with secular obligations.

Despite the inherent deficiencies of Domesday Book as a guide to the presence, and in some cases the whereabouts of churches, some scholars continue to base their thinking upon an unduly literal acceptance of the data that Domesday contains. Assertions that there were comparatively few churches in certain counties by 1086 are not uncommon, and arguments to the effect that the escalation of local church building was a phenomenon of the 12th century still persist.

A useful way to review the ecclesiastical information in Domesday Book is to rearrange it according to the groups of counties which are thought to have comprised the circuits by which the survey was compiled. It is generally agreed that there were at least seven of these circuits, although in several regions it seems possible that there were more. When the evidence is tabulated (Table VII) a firm correlation emerges between most of the circuits and the methods which were used to present ecclesiastical detail for the counties within them. Thus Circuit A (south-east) has high figures for churches, low figures for churches and priests, and acknowledges chapels as a separate class. In Circuit B (south-west) the low totals of churches are explained by a policy of confining references, in the main, to old minsters. Within Circuit C there appears to be a cleavage between Bedfordshire/Buckinghamshire/Cambridgeshire, each with only a handful of churches and even fewer priests, and Hertfordshire/Middlesex where rather more priests were counted. In Circuit D there is a contrast between Oxfordshire (which resembles Bedfordshire in its treatment of churches) and Leicestershire/Northamptonshire/Warwickshire. Lincolnshire and Yorkshire might be seen as a separate circuit on the basis of their substantially higher figures for churches in comparison with the other four Danelaw counties.

Circuit G is of special interest, partly on account of its exceptionally high total of churches, and also for the contrast between Norfolk/Suffolk and Essex. The *c* 720 churches recorded in Norfolk and Suffolk (27·3% of the DB grand total) need come as no surprise, since it was in these counties that the results of the Inquest came closest to the aspiration expressed in the Anglo-Saxon Chronicle that 'not one ox, nor one cow, nor one pig' should escape enumeration. The returns from Essex, on the other hand, are strikingly lower than those from Norfolk and Suffolk. This contrast is paralleled in other aspects of the Inquest (eg in the figures for markets: Norfolk 3; Suffolk 9; Essex 0) and it may be suggested that a different group of surveyors was responsible.

It is clear from the various characteristics discussed above that the interpretation of the articles of inquiry differed from circuit to circuit. Within individual circuits, however, inner inconsistencies remain. Not all the minsters in Devon were recorded, for example, and the

Table VII Churches and chapels in Domesday Book

This Table shows the numbers of churches and chapels recorded in Domesday Book. The totals are thus not necessarily the same as for numbers of *places* with churches in 1086. Naturally there are no figures for areas which the Inquest did not cover: eg Durham, Northumberland, most of Westmorland and Cumberland, part of the Humberhead region of Yorkshire, Winchester, and London. Unless otherwise stated, figures in the column headed *Priests* refer to numbers of churches thought to be represented by priests; they are not absolute totals of priests. Priests who appear in Domesday Book as landholders in their own right have been excluded from this count. Elsewhere priests, or groups of priests, have been accepted as representing churches, since there is some evidence that at the time of the Inquest the two categories were regarded as being interchangeable (eg Page 1915, 63–4, esp n 1 of 64). It has been assumed that places in receipt of soul- or church-scot possessed churches. Entries marked with asterisks are expanded in brief explanatory notes in the column headed *Remarks*.

In most counties it is difficult to be precise about the numbers of churches recorded in Domesday Book: eg where churches are presented as fractions, or where churches recorded for one county stand in another. Hence all the figures in the Table should be regarded as approximations.

Place-name evidence (eg *lan-*, *kirk-*, and *-minster* elements) has been ignored. If this were to be taken into account, the figures for a number of counties would be substantially higher: eg Yorkshire +17, Cornwall +26. The addition of architectural, archaeological, and sculptural evidence would carry the grand total well beyond 3 000.

Circuit	County	Ch	Chap	Ch+Pr	Pr	Misc	Total	Remarks
A	Berkshire	56	2	7	.		65	
	Hampshire*	117	14	2			133	incl Isle of Wight
	Kent	176	6	4	2*		188	in fact 8 between 2 places
	Surrey	65	3				68	
	Sussex	93	9	4	1		107	
B	Cornwall	7			5*		12	canons
	Devon	7			4*		11	3 priests and 1 canon
	Dorset	12*			4		16	incl 2 at Wareham
	Somerset	14		3	9*		26	incl 6 parochial priests on the lands of Bishop of Wells
	Wiltshire	18		11	3		32	
C	Bedfordshire	4		1*	1*		6	surveyed under Herts
	Buckinghamshire	4					4	
	Cambridgeshire	3			2		5	
	Hertfordshire	4*			49	1 *clericus*	54	incl 2 in Beds
	Middlesex	2*			18		20	incl 1 surveyed under Bucks
D	Leicestershire	6*			42**		48	all at Leicester, **where there was also 1 priest
	Northamptonshire	2		1	59		62	
	Oxfordshire	6*			1	2 *circet*	9	5 in Oxford
	Warwickshire	1*			66		67	at Warwick
E	Cheshire	4		5	14		23	
	Gloucestershire	6		4	44*		54	4 with more than 1 priest
	Herefordshire	1		14*	34		49	at 11 places, 5 of which had 2 priests
	Shropshire	5		21*	29		55	incl 5 at Shrewsbury, + 24 priests between 16 churches at 15 places
	Staffordshire	3*			32**		35	½+½+1. **The figure for priests includes churches represented by canons at Lichfield, Stafford, and Wolverhampton
	Worcestershire	1		4*	56	1 *circet*	62	incl 1 church with 2 priests
F	Derbyshire	1		42*	5		48	incl 4 at Derby
	Huntingdonshire	5*		48			53	incl 2 at Huntingdon
	Nottinghamshire			72	4		76	
	Rutland			8*	7*		15	8 churches with 7 priests at 4 places; 7 priests between 5 places
	Lancashire	13*			2		15	incl 1 surveyed under Cheshire
	Lincolnshire	137		120	2		259	
	Yorkshire ER	8		39	3		50	
	Yorkshire NR	23*		35	4		62	incl 8 at York
	Yorkshire WR	14		52	3	1 *prebendarius*	70	
G	Essex	17*			27*		44	incl 1 church and 7 priests in Colchester
	Norfolk	247*	43**		11		301	incl 11 in Thetford, at least 24 in Norwich, **some or all of which are likely to be subsumed by total for chapels
	Suffolk	416*	2		3		421	incl 11 at Ipswich, 3 at Dunwich
Totals:	35	1498	79	497	546	5	2625	

irregular coverage of churches in Lincolnshire and Yorkshire is not easy to explain. Three groups of factors may be suggested which together help to account for many of the idiosyncracies which have been mentioned so far. It is helpful to introduce these with a reminder that the Domesday Inquest was undertaken with extraordinary rapidity, very possibly within nine months. Hence some errors would be unavoidable, although it is not possible to put a figure on inadvertent omissions of churches.

(1) According to the Anglo-Saxon Chronicle there were two inquests in 1086. King William 'sent his men all over England into every shire and had them find out how many hundred hides there were in the shire, and what land and cattle the king himself had in the country, and what dues he ought to have in twelve months from the shire. Also he had a record made of how much land his archbishops had, and his bishops and his abbots and his earls . . . what or how much everybody had who was occupying land in England . . .' (ASC (E), sa 1085). The production of Domesday thus involved the twining together of *two* strands of inquiry: one into the assets of the king and the other into the circumstances of landholders. This helps to explain why in some counties only a few churches are recorded, and why in others a few churches are recorded but the bulk of the ecclesiastical material is presented in another way (eg through references to priests). The survey of royal rights encompassed royal estates and boroughs. Thus in Bedfordshire the only churches to be recorded were at Bedford itself and for each of the three royal estates of Houghton Regis, Leighton Buzzard, and Luton. In this county churches were completely ignored by the compilers of the inquest into landholding in the shire. In Circuit D almost all the *churches* recorded were urban (six in Leicester, five in Oxford, one in Warwick) and again can be accounted for under the royal side of the inquest; in the same counties, however, returns for churches in the shires were made in the form of priests (except in Oxfordshire where, like Bedfordshire, and presumably for the same reason, rural churches were ignored). The existence of two sets of returns goes far to explain some of the more dramatic contrasts between returns made for different, and sometimes adjacent, counties.

(2) In Circuits like A and F where many but far from all churches were recorded a large proportion of the omissions may be explained by the fact that the compilers in the shires were chiefly interested in places through which payments had to be made. Hence many places, and churches with them, were ignored when their liabilities were subsumed by other entries (Sawyer 1976, 2–4). Here lies a possible reason for the disparity between totals of churches in Circuits F and G and the rather lower figures supplied for certain counties in the west: for 'if the structure of Domesday Book is based on a platform of fiscal lists, it is more likely to include the small holder in the eastern regions where the vill and its freer population seems to be the fiscal entity, and to be less scrupulous about small freeholders in the west where the estate was the responsible unit and where liability is contained within some other Domesday item' (S P J Harvey 1976, 196). The existence of a church could also be concealed when its value was counted in with that of the place in which it stood, or with the other assets of its owner. An aside in the returns for Norfolk explains that 'all the churches on the manors of William de Warenne are valued with the manors' (Darby 1971,

139). This technique may well have been used throughout Yorkshire, where many churches are mentioned but no values are given for any of them. In such circumstances it could scarcely have mattered whether a church was actually referred to or not: a position which seems to be reflected in the arbitrary way in which churches were recorded north of the Humber.

(3) By 1086 there were large portions of England which were covered by hundreds (Cam 1944). In some of these areas the officials of the hundred appear to have formed part of the machinery of the Domesday Inquest (S P J Harvey 1971). Their task involved the integration of information as it pertained on one hand to the territorial framework of local administration, and on the other to the holdings of tenants. These holdings were often widely dispersed, and the reconciliation of the two classes of information would have presented difficulties. However, it has been argued that hidage lists in both hundredal and tenurial form were in existence before 1086 (S P J Harvey 1971, 753–73). The availability of such records would have been of considerable assistance to the compilers, since it would mean that 'only one official writing out and merging of information was necessary to obtain the final form of information by fiefs which also displays a consistent hundredal order' (1971, 772). A processing of data at hundredal level is suggested by the details of churches given for several counties in which a hundredal system obtained. In Cheshire, for instance, the method of description – church, church and priest, or priest – and policy on the inclusion or exclusion of churches vary from one hundred to another, but tend to be consistent within individual hundreds. Where information about churches is forthcoming it usually concerns the dominant churches, or those which were formerly so (P H Sawyer, *pers comm*). Similar patterns of entries can be discerned in Shropshire. In Lincolnshire, which was organized into wapentakes and where churches were recorded more comprehensively than in the west, there is nevertheless some hint of an analogous process. This is visible locally in variations between wapentakes, and more broadly in a contrast – almost as between separate counties – between Lindsey and Kesteven. The list of churches in Lindsey has many gaps, whereas in some of the Kesteven wapentakes it looks as though a complete count of incipient parochial churches was attempted.

In addition to the factors listed above there are several further reasons which might explain why certain churches were omitted from Domesday Book. There would be no need to record a church which was exempt from financial obligations, for example, and still less to refer to one which was not separately endowed, although landless churches are mentioned occasionally: eg at Blythburgh (Suffolk), where two churches without land were attached to the *matrix ecclesia* (VCH *Suffolk* I, 420). In some towns it is noticeable that the churches which were listed were those held by important tenants or else the subject of disputes. This was the pattern in Lincoln and York, where evidence from other sources goes to suggest that more churches existed than were recorded in 1086. In these towns, and possibly in some others, it appears that churches which were not in the hands of identifiable owners were ignored. Whether this means that such churches had been founded by groups of citizens acting on a co-operative basis is a different and open question.

In summary, Domesday Book is a temperamental guide not only to the density and distribution of churches in

1086, but also to parochial organization, since the structure of the Inquest has an inherent tendency to oversharpen contrasts between the patterns of ecclesiastical provision in different areas. The evidence of Domesday is best used in conjunction with information from external sources: art and architectural history, archaeology, and other written records. Where such evidence is available in concentration it often shows that an area was endowed with the greater part of its complement of medieval churches before the end of the 11th century (eg Rodwell & Rodwell 1977, 92). What seems certain is that references to churches in Domesday Book were not made casually, but were conditioned by variations of approach on the part of the compilers, and particularly by the machinery and objectives of the Inquest itself.

Church, hall, and settlement

We have seen that the class structure of Old English society was paralleled by its graduated system of churches: from the episcopal minsters, often originally at or adjacent to foci of royal authority, down through the mother churches at centres of local government, to the rural *ecclesiae propriae*, frequently and suggestively found at a later date in association with manor-houses, mottes, and moated sites, and the clustered 'neighbourhood churches' in towns such as London and Norwich (Brooke 1970, 78–83). Each church in the hierarchy reflected a different level of lordship, or an aspect of the society which founded and used it.

Similar reflections can be seen in areas outside the English zone. In Ireland, for example, the diocese was often co-extensive with the *tuath*, or petty kingdom. The disposition of the early Welsh dioceses seems to have been in broad agreement with basic tribal divisions. In Wales principal churches often stood at places which were twinned with centres of secular authority. It was not unusual for a lord to establish a bond of patronage between his court (*llys*) and a neighbouring ecclesiastical focus. Thus the church at Bangor seems to have been complemented by the princely court at Aber, five miles away, that at Meifod (Powys) with Mathrafal (two miles), and St Asaph with Denbigh (five miles). In the administrative hundred of Aberffraw on the island of Anglesey the royal court was in Aberffraw itself, whereas it has been suggested that the mother church was 'two miles distant in the vill of Eglwys Ail, which was said to be held by the tenure of St Cadwaladr King' (G R J Jones 1976a, 60). New bonds of this kind were still being formed in the 12th century, and can be studied in respect of several Cistercian foundations, most notably in the relationship between Valle Crucis and the nearby *llys* on Dinas Bran (L A S Butler 1977, 62). It is revealing that the Cistercians in Wales were able to capitalize on an older religious tradition, which held some appeal for their own order, in a way which was in contrast 'to the novelty and isolation of similar Cistercian foundations' in Angevin England, 'and in contrast also to the intrusive character of the Benedictine houses in Wales founded by Norman barons in the course of the Conquest' (L A S Butler 1977, 62).

In Wales, Cumbria, and south-west Scotland a correspondence can be seen between the feudal geography of the areas in the 11th and 12th centuries and the oldest known ecclesiastical divisions, those of rural deaneries (G Williams 1962, 16; Barrow 1975). In Cumbria and Scotland 'the deaneries were rather fewer than the

secular divisons, and ... they became fewer still in course of time, whereas secular divisions multiplied. But it can scarcely be denied that in the 12th century there was some close relationship, either of imitation or of independent derivation from a common source' (Barrow 1975, 127).

Relationships of this kind can also be studied on a more local basis. Most of the keeill chapels of the Isle of Man, for example, cannot be dated on architectural grounds alone. However, it has been noticed that the distribution of keeills shows that they were not the cells of hermits or anchorites, but were 'definitely related to areas of rural population'. Specifically, keeills occurred in 'cultivable, and hence inhabited, areas which then (9th–11th centuries), or later came to be known as treen-lands' (Bruce 1966/68, 74 and fig 16). This correspondence between chapels and land-units invites comparison with the 'eyrisland chapels' of Orkney and the scattald chapels of Shetland. In Orkney the relationship between the chapels and eyrislands, or rental districts, was so close that it has been suggested that the pattern was determined by some co-ordinating authority (Cant 1972). However, Dr R Lamb has drawn attention to a 'remarkably consistent coincidence of ... eyrisland chapels with late Iron Age domestic settlements, often on or near the sites of brochs' and sees the churches as developing out of the domestic settlements of the late Iron Age. 'If, as seems likely, the eyrislands/tunships/scattalds are territorial divisions older than the Norse occupation, the coincidence of chapel with eyrisland could have come about without the need for a governing authority.' Lamb develops this argument by suggesting that the introduction of the parochial system in Orkney during the 12th century involved a refocusing of the existing pattern, whereby the most prominent eyrisland chapel in each area – ie that associated with the most influential farmstead – emerged as the parish church (Lamb 1979). This view differs from the 'developed cemetery' sequence put forward by Thomas (1971), although the two are not mutually exclusive. The special interest of the process envisaged by Lamb lies in the presence of a seigneurial factor, showing some similarities with the proprietorial forces which seem to have ruled a substantial part of early parochial development in England.

In 11th century England the possession of a church was looked upon as one of the attributes of thegnly rank, along with a cookhouse, a fortified gatehouse, and five hides of land (Cnut, III, 60.i). Traditional opinion has asserted that a church was normally attached to a thegn's place of residence, or, if he was a man with extensive interests, to his principal seat. Page argued that a reconstruction of the Domesday entries under the holders of 1066 usually showed that where 'a thegn or other lay tenant had many holdings in a county there is frequently the record of a church or a priest at one of them only, and that at the place where the tenant lived. We generally find also that the church or priest was associated in the Domesday entry with the incidents of demesne. ... This will give the reason why in so many instances the churches adjoin the manor house at the present day, and are sometimes a considerable distance from the present village' (Page 1915, 98). Recent studies suggest that the position was not as uniform as Page believed. In the first place it seems that Page was inclined to make 'unwarranted assumptions' about the places of residence of thegns (Lennard 1959, 290–1), and secondly, Domesday Book itself supplies numerous

Table VIII   Broad characteristics of sites of medieval rural churches in the Archdeaconry of Colchester

(*Source:* Rodwell & Rodwell 1977, 94–125)

		Anglo-Saxon fabric	[?] Anglo-Saxon fabric	All churches
A	*Churches standing close to halls*			
	1 Isolated with hall	12	8	68
	2 In village with hall	6	3	15
	3 At village edge with hall	1	2	9
B	*Churches not (now) standing near halls*			
	4 Isolated	3	3	34
	5 Isolated with farm	–	–	1
	6 Isolated with religious house	–	–	1
	7 In village	7	2	60
	8 At village edge	–	–	18
	9 Beside green	–	–	1

instances of thegns with multiple holdings who were also in possession of several churches on lands within one county. The pattern of landholding was, of course, subject to constant alteration, and it cannot be supposed that the ecclesiastical geography which was patchily sketched in Domesday Book was a product of the tenurial structure which existed in 1066. The location of each church would reflect some factor of lordship or social circumstance which prevailed at the moment of its foundation; thereafter it would be the status and condition of the church, rather than its presence, which would be the most sensitive pointer towards subsequent developments.

Where archaeological surveys of churches have taken place it is possible to approach the issues outlined above against the background of an elementary classification of the characteristics of church sites. The rural medieval churches visited by Rodwell in the Archdeaconry of Colchester form a convenient specimen group for this purpose (Table VIII). From analysis it emerges that the largest single category of site type in the Archdeaconry is that of the isolated church and hall (*c* 33%), although all churches coupled with halls (*c* 44%) are slightly outnumbered by those without them. Churches in complete isolation (*c* 16%) and churches in villages (*c* 29%) form the other major types. But an additional calculation, concerned only with churches of definite Saxon origin, reveals that out of a total of 29 churches no less than nineteen are now to be found beside halls, while of a further eighteen churches of possible Saxon character thirteen are hall-related. The value of these figures is, of course, strictly limited: at best they can be no more than a rough guide to the pattern as it exists today, and they do not illuminate the complexities of previous relationships, which themselves may have passed through several transformations. Indeed, one could use the figures to argue that the association is between the church and settlement at the time the church was founded and between the hall and that settlement. If the settlement tended to shift, but church and hall remained stationary, the association between church and hall would be open to misinterpretation. Nevertheless, the nature of the bond between church and hall would seem

to be worth exploration. The special value of the church in relation to the study of settlement lies in its capacity for survival and the tenacity with which it holds to its site. Insulated, until recently (R K Morris (I) 1977), against external pressures by its special spiritual, institutional, and economic position and the high regard in which it has been held by its users, it has been usual for the church to outlive the circumstances of its foundation, and hence to beckon the fieldworker, who may find that the church provides a fixed point in a changing landscape against which to measure settlement growth and mobility (Wade-Martins 1980, 87–8). But the redundant church was no rarity in the Middle Ages, and this in itself may afford additional insights.

Examples

Systematic fieldwork undertaken by Dr P Wade-Martins in the Launditch hundred, Norfolk, has revealed that certain isolated churches in that district stand close to scatters of Middle Saxon pottery. Thus it has been suggested that the church of Longham owes its solitude to the eventual desertion of a pre-Conquest village which was re-established on a new site further to the south. At Mileham it is argued that a Middle Saxon village originally surrounded the church, but that this migrated northwards in the 10th century, later rearranging itself in a linear configuration, thereby leaving the church off to one side (Wade-Martins 1980, 33–9, 41–2).

If it is true that the majority of local churches came into existence as a result of seigneurial initiative, the primary and critical link is likely to have been between church and hall rather than between church and settlement(s). Indeed, the possibility has been raised that thegns who founded churches were imitating the king who had the mother churches at his *villae regales*. The pottery scatters at Longham and Mileham have been interpreted as representing abandoned villages or hamlets; the primary scatter at Longham, at least, might also represent a former manorial centre. Fieldwork elsewhere often produces results which point to this kind of relationship. Thus at Wollaston (Northants) an 18th century enclosure map shows a plan consisting of two separate foci linked by a straight street. Each focus possessed a manor, both of which are mentioned in Domesday Book, and in each case material of early Saxon date has been recovered nearby. Excavations at the parish church, which stands beside the northern Saxon site, have yielded occupation material of Early Saxon date (C C Taylor 1977, 191–2).

The affiliation between church and centre of authority can be studied particularly well in areas where there are, or have been, concentrations of churches. Cases occur in which several churches stand in one settlement (eg Barton-on-Humber), or even in the same churchyard (eg Swaffham Prior and Forncett (Norfolk), Fulbourn (Cambs)). To these may be added the parishes which contain more than one church, or where excavation or historical research has revealed that two or more churches existed in a parish which now contains only one. 'The origin of the double parish in manorial provision is clearly demonstrated by the twin churches of Aldwincle', Northamptonshire (Beresford & St Joseph 1958, 53). In this village there were two manors, each with a church attached. The phenomenon of 'twinning' may have been more common than is usually supposed, since the known examples are recognizable only because they survived long enough to leave tangible traces of the

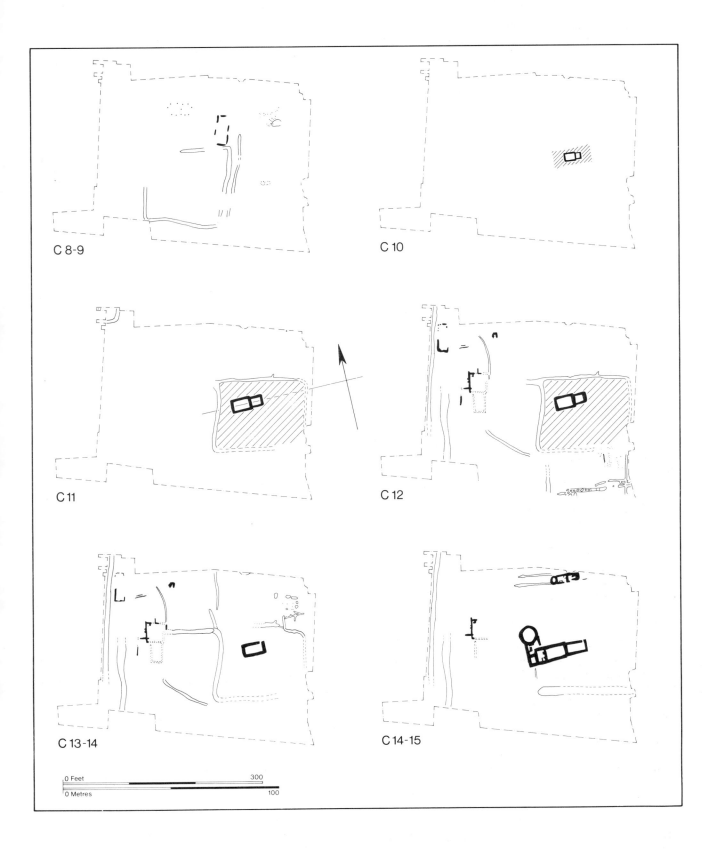

C 8-9

C 10

C 11

C 12

C 13-14

C 14-15

0 Feet   300

0 Metres   100

Fig 21   Raunds (Northants): a pre-Conquest church, its setting and development. 8th to 9th centuries: An enclosure, with traces of timber buildings. 10th century: A single-cell church is built of stone, and soon afterwards this is extended by the addition of a chancel. 11th century: The church is rebuilt and its cemetery is enlarged. The boundary ditches of the churchyard appear to echo the alignment of a pre-existing enclosure, whereas the church itself is more strictly oriented. 12th century: The church continues to be used at least until the middle of the century. To the west, a manor house and ancillary buildings are erected. 13th century: The church is abandoned. However, part of the church is remodelled to provide a stone building of one cell: an early example of the conversion of a redundant church. The manor house is still in use. 14th–15th centuries: The earlier manor is discarded. A new manorial complex is built. This is centred upon the old church site, and it incorporates the 13th century building. 15th century: The manor is abandoned, and the site is eventually given over to pasture. (Source: G Cadman, Raunds – a review (1981)). (Drawing: Dick Raines)

arrangement. When casualties occurred at an earlier date a combination of intensive fieldwork and excavation may be required in order to elucidate the original pattern. Pre-Conquest manorial chapels, in particular, must sometimes have led ephemeral lives, since their fortunes would be subject to the same hazards as the affairs of their owners. Until the rights of a church were defined and strengthened by custom its future might always be in doubt. At Raunds (Northants) excavations have revealed a sequence which seems to be almost an inversion of that at Wollaston: an Anglo-Saxon church and churchyard *below* the east end of a manor house, which was itself abandoned. Raunds possesses another church, which still stands and remains in use. It appears that Raunds was not a nucleated settlement in the early medieval period; more probably it consisted of a number of distinct 'ends' which coalesced to form a single settlement at a later date (Fig 21). The disclosure of an unsuspected pre-Conquest church in close, though not contemporary, relation with a manor site might suggest that early medieval Raunds was comprised of several manorial centres, of which at least two acquired a church (cf Aldwincle) and one of which became redundant as the settlement evolved. Architectural features in the surviving parish church show that this must have co-existed for a time with the lost church. This process seems to be parallel to that which might be suspected to lie behind the foundation of many churches in some towns. Would 10th century Norwich, as a polynuclear settlement, have been much different (except, of course, in scale) from contemporary Raunds (cf Carter 1978; Brooke 1970, 77)? As a final example one may cite Duxford (Cambs), where there were four manors listed in Domesday Book, and down to the 19th century there were three distinct foci to the village. 'Additional evidence for the existence of at least two of these focuses by the early 12th century is the fact that there are two churches in the village, each of 12th century date' (C C Taylor 1977, 190).

The most usual explanation for the occurrence of several churches in close proximity seems to be that the place was subject to divided lordship. Additional churches could, of course, come into being by other conventional means, as daughters of neighbouring parents (Owen 1975; 1976b; 1978). The church of St Mary, Beverley, for example, is often cited as a manifestation of high medieval parochial magnificence, although in terms of status it originated as a chapelry to an altar within Beverley Minster. The large church in the market-place at Barton-on-Humber was also a chapelry, subordinate to the adjacent church of St Peter. Stimuli towards proliferation could also be provided by liturgical factors. The existence of families of churches (eg at Hexham: Bailey 1976; St Augustine's, Canterbury: Saunders 1978) is attested best in the monastic sphere (H M Taylor 1978, 1020–1). Separate structures could be built in honour of individual saints, to act as baptisteries or mausolea, or as stations for processional ritual. There is little to suggest that ordinary secular churches were ever closely arranged for such reasons, but where pairs of churches occur, as at Alvingham (Lincs) or Bywell (Northumberland), the prospect of some kind of monastic background should be kept in mind. Taking this further, one may add that the church archaeologist should always be alert to the possibility of there being a monastic dimension to the history of a church which is now parochial. The example of Brixworth shows the extent to which it was possible for the status of a church to undergo change before the 12th century. In the north,

the demise of many monastic settlements in the 9th century as a result of Scandinavian aggression was not necessarily accompanied by the loss of the churches themselves. Some, like Lastingham, could resurface later on as refounded monastic centres; others, like Hackness, Crayke, and Stonegrave, might be taken over by lay owners for normal 'parochial' purposes; while at a few the life of a community may actually have continued in some attenuated form (Sawyer 1978a, 241; 1978b, 3).

Discussion

The traditional story of medieval settlement tells of a process of outward expansion from a nucleus of ancient sites (Stenton 1971, 285–7). Place-names have been used to track the gradual extension of settlement from favoured into less desirable areas (eg A H Smith 1956b). A corollary of this thesis is that nucleated villages are likely to have resulted from the steady expansion of hamlets or farmsteads, or else to have been deliberately established as single entities (C C Taylor 1977, 189). Some scholars have looked upon the gradual multiplication of daughter churches and chapels within the territories of mother churches as a manifestation of the process of slow growth from an inherently stable pattern of primary centres. Mrs Owen, for example, regards the significance of chapels for the chronology of settlement as being 'self-evident' (1975, 15): in Lincolnshire she argues that 'the oldest and most populous centres formed parishes, while chapels or field churches occur only where settlement is recent, or very sparse' (Owen 1976b, 66).

In recent years a number of scholars have come to question the concept of slow growth. Peter Fowler (1976) has cast doubt upon the received doctrine of the church-town as being, necessarily, the principal focus of pre-Conquest settlement in a parish. Sawyer reminds us that as place-names may change so they are not always trustworthy guides to the chronology of settlement, and has contended that rural resources were almost as fully exploited in the 7th century as they were in the 11th (1976, 1–7). In this view, fluidity rather than stability is seen as being the chief force to shape the settlement pattern. Systematic fieldwork of the kind carried out by Wade-Martins in Norfolk (1975) and Foard in Northamptonshire (1978) and aerial archaeology contribute to the impression that throughout historic times 'much of the pattern of rural settlement was in a constant state of flux' (C C Taylor 1978, 126). Foard's work in the parish of Great Doddington, for instance, has disclosed a scatter of Early and Middle Saxon communities 'more akin to the Iron Age than to the medieval pattern' (1978, 369–70). Elsewhere it has been claimed that a proportion of the 'outlying' farms and hamlets which are customarily interpreted as the product of medieval expansion is in fact the residue of an earlier dispersed pattern (C C Taylor 1974b, 10).

Church archaeology can make a useful contribution to this debate. This lies not in the reinforcement of dogmas, old or new, about the history of settlement, but more in the provision of an order of precedence for the sites themselves, established by survey and investigation, and eventually in the correlation of this framework with the data yielded by fieldwork carried on in the landscape at large. Such results will take time to accumulate. Meanwhile, it seems desirable to formulate a selection of models for testing in the future. For example, not all chapelries can be explained as representing peripheral colonization. Cases occur where several parishes intervene between a church and another church which is, or has been, in subjection to it. Chapelries of this kind can sometimes be accounted for as alienated components of former estates. The relationship between the chapel of South Stainley and the mother church at Aldborough (N Yorks) is a good instance. The two are seven miles apart. The link may be explained by the suggestion that South Stainley was originally a component of a multiple estate with its *caput* at Aldborough; in 1086 South Stainley was in part sokeland of Aldborough (G R J Jones 1976b, 35–7).

Another process which has not received much attention hitherto concerns the 'typical' chapel which serves a hamlet that is now a satellite of a nearby principal centre. If the hamlet to which the chapel belongs is revealed by fieldwork to be a relic of a pattern of settlement which was previously different, the chapel may owe its dependence to the *emergence* of the neighbouring focus as the chief centre of population or authority. In a landscape which was not wholly dominated by nucleated villages the initial status of a church would be bound up with its proprietary circumstances – ie the level of lordship of which it formed an expression – rather than with questions of 'parent villages' or 'daughter settlements', and all that such family metaphors imply in the way of relative chronology. In a proportion of cases, therefore, we might envisage a process which involved an adjustment of the emphasis accorded to an existing church in relation to its neighbours. The position is, of course, complicated by the construction of chapels on virgin sites in the 12th and 13th centuries, because the general absence of written records which deal with such sites before *c* 1250 means that very often the latecomers are indistinguishable from those that were already standing. Even archaeological investigation may not settle all problems, since the provision of a new chapel in, say, the 12th century is not by itself proof that the settlement for which it was intended was young. However, many of the older chapels can be identified by survey work; some of the *ecclesiae* mentioned in 1086 are described in later records as chapels; and here and there documents survive which allow us to glimpse moments of transition. The promotion of the chapel of Allerton Mauleverer (N Yorks) to parochial status is described in a charter of 1109–14 (Farrer 1914, 729–30), and there is the very relevant example of Hanslope (Bucks) where in the 12th century 'a new church took on parochial status and the old one was designated a chapel' (Mason 1976, 19).

Conclusion

In this chapter an attempt has been made to review some of the factors which affected the origins and distribution of churches. Lordship emerges as the chief formative influence, which, though not in itself susceptible to archaeological investigation, is symbolized in various types of site and in characteristic bonds between them. Lordship, moreover, offers a possible line of descent between pagan and Christian sites.

According to Feine the *Eigenkirche* was itself a Germanic pagan concept (1950, 132–5). Its origin lay in 'family assembly for religious services and the cult of ancestral graves' (Barlow 1963, 183). The establishment of local churches by members of the lay nobility might thus be seen at least in part as arising out of pagan custom rather than as a departure from it. In later pre-Conquest England it seems likely that 'the desire of the important

lord to have a special seat within the church he possessed' found direct architectural expression in western towers and galleries (Radford 1961, 173). Before this it has been suggested that some of the earliest private churches were simply rooms set aside in secular halls (Godfrey 1974) (see above: 39). Excavation on a large scale would be necessary to put this idea to the test, and even then the task of identifying a hall-chapel would be difficult indeed. Such chapels, if they existed, would often have been short-lived, and presumably would have been more susceptible to pressures for change than the more durable stone-built churches. This is pure speculation, but the idea that masonry village churches, or even masonry churches on the sites of wooden predecessors, represent the first stage in local ecclesiastical provision is itself an assumption.

The theme may be developed to explain some of the more unusual settings in which churches occur. Churches on hilltops, for example, enjoy a certain mystique which may distract attention from the factors which put them there. At least two classes can be distinguished. First, there are churches of monastic origin (either possible, eg St Michael, Glastonbury; or certain, eg Breedon (Leics)) which owe their lofty sites to the seclusion promised by the summit of a hill. A second class concerns churches which were built on hilltops because these places acquired a political or military importance. Where this status was temporary, as at South Cadbury (and later on at Old Sarum), the need for the church might vanish and the church with it (Alcock 1972). Elsewhere, however, the church could survive, as at Holme-on-Spalding-Moor (Humberside), where the church which is perched on an isolated summit, well apart from the village, is best explained by the fact that the hill was originally occupied by a manorial centre. The elevated sites of some other churches suggest analogous circumstances. Where prehistoric defences existed the presence of a church within them could indicate the re-use of the site at some point before the Conquest over a period long enough for the church to acquire firm rights.

So far churches have been discussed as the products of settlement. It is useful to conclude by glancing at a few of the ways in which churches could play a part in shaping settlement. The dynamic influence exerted by churches on their surroundings is perhaps most noticeable in the towns, as several recent studies go to show (eg Colchester: Rodwell & Rodwell 1977; Canterbury and York: Addyman 1977; Brooks 1977). In certain towns, like London, Lincoln, Norwich, and Winchester, the proliferation of 'tiny box churches' before the Conquest raises questions about the nature of urban life and organization: for example 'whether most of the London churches were built by landlords or single magnates, or by groups of neighbours ...' (Brooke 1977, 470). Study of the locations of such churches, the structure of their parishes in relation to patterns of tenure, and above all their archaeology, will help to clarify the picture. Out in the countryside many questions remain to be answered. In the cases of Longham and Mileham, for example (above: 72; Wade-Martins 1975; 1980), it is not clear whether the churches were primary features in the Middle Saxon villages postulated by Wade-Martins, or whether they were Late Saxon additions to manorial centres which existed before the settlements or outlasted their removal. Likewise, one would like to know the role played by the church or graveyard in cases where the regrouping or coalescence of small units of settlement into one centre is suspected: was this the moment at which the church was often added, perhaps acting as a stabilizing factor and tethering the settlement to its vicinity thereafter? Or was the church or graveyard already there, acting as an attractive force in the process of regrouping?

One example can be given which illustrates the active, formative influence of churches in relation to settlement. This concerns the coincidence of churches and markets. Religious houses and mother churches attracted visitors at times of important festivals. These gatherings provided natural and convenient occasions for exchange, which in time might become regularized as fairs or markets. In some counties the occurrence of markets at ecclesiastical centres or places with dominant churches is evident from Domesday Book. In Bedfordshire markets were recorded at two of the four places credited with churches in 1086 – Leighton Buzzard and Luton – and rendered toll of seven pounds and a hundred shillings, respectively. Of the seven markets recorded in Domesday Book for Somerset five coincide with minsters mentioned in the Inquest (Crewkerne, Frome, Ilchester, Ilminster, and Taunton). In Suffolk most of the markets recorded in 1086 were at places with important churches, such as Blythburgh (minster with two dependent churches), Clare (canons' church), Eye (minster with large endowment), Hoxne (former see), Sudbury, and Thorney (mother churches). In Leicestershire the one market recorded in Domesday was at Melton Mowbray, where there were two priests. At Aylesbury there was a minster and a market yielding toll of ten pounds. In Abingdon we are told of the presence of *x mercatores ante portam ecclesiae manentes*. The correlation continues in Lincolnshire at Louth and Barton-on-Humber, while the other distinguishing feature of Threckingham apart from its market was the presence of two churches. Domesday Book contains an irregular and incomplete record of markets, so it is interesting to find that in some cases the correspondence between important churches and commercial activity is suggested by archaeological evidence, and that in others evidence which does appear in Domesday is reinforced by archaeology. Thus Houghton Regis and Bedford, the two *other* places with churches recorded in the Bedfordshire Domesday, are distinctively rich in finds of Mercian *sceattas*. The same can be said of Dorchester-on-Thames and Abingdon. Smaller finds of these coins have also been made at other places already mentioned, such as Ilchester and Ilminster. It has been argued that the use of this money 'was primarily a consequence of interregional trade' (Metcalf 1977, 102, 92–3, fig 8). The importance of the pre-Conquest church as a stimulus to settlement, as well as an expression of it, is paramount (Sawyer 1981).

Liturgical practice, medieval technology, demography, economic history, and the story of settlement are among the more important subjects upon which the archaeological study of the later medieval church can throw light. Opportunities for the pursuit of some of these themes are reviewed in greater detail below, but they can all be considered within the larger subject of the expansion and decline of ecclesiastical provision in the later Middle Ages.

By about 1250 most medieval parish churches and a substantial number of chapels were already in existence. For the archaeologist, therefore, questions of origins begin to give way to questions about development, adaptation, and, in a few cases, disappearance. In some churches the structural changes made by successive generations are clearly differentiated. In others, later rebuilding to an expanded scale has masked or obliterated what went before. Almost all the surviving parish churches of Norwich, for example, were rebuilt or substantially remodelled in the later 15th and 16th century, with the result that little is known of the earlier building histories of churches in the city. Archaeology can reveal and calibrate earlier development, as well as improve our understanding of those churches in which more of their architectural history is on display, but where yet more remains to be revealed.

Development could involve decline as well as growth. From the 14th century onwards the citizens of towns like Winchester, York, and Lincoln were shedding churches as well as investing, to a greater or lesser extent, in those which were retained. Out in the countryside, too, churches were abandoned, because the communities they formerly served had disappeared, moved away, or entered upon bleak times, or because there were too many churches in close proximity. Figures for the loss of churches before the 15th century are difficult to compile, but it is clear that churches could and did fall redundant throughout the Middle Ages. Where the sites of these lost churches can be identified, investigation may prove to be worthwhile, since the interior will not have been disturbed by later gravedigging, and traces of the ritual layout which existed at the time of closure may still survive. A further, and important, consideration lies in the comparative ease of access to the 'archive' of burials in the graveyard of a lost church (Palliser 1980, 82). The importance of such an archive lies in the fact that it can usually be more closely dated and is more representative of a community at an identifiable stage of its development than is the case with graveyards in use over an extended period.

Decline did not always, or even usually, culminate in the disappearance of a church. More commonly it is manifested in a cessation of architectural growth, or in actual contraction involving the removal or curtailment of parts of the structure. Here, too, archaeology can play its part, by recovering the full evidence of earlier growth and by providing a framework of dates for the periods of expansion and decline.

In general, it is unsafe to extrapolate directly from the history of a church to the history of its users: to assume, for example, that rebuilding on an ample scale in the 15th century signifies that the people responsible were enjoying the fruits of economic growth, or that a church which remained largely unchanged from the 12th century belonged to a stable or latterly impoverished population. Simplistic correlations of this kind may be open to all kinds of objections, not the least of which may be the special sentimental regard in which a church often was, and is, held by its users. Nevertheless, where there is a body of evidence which concerns both the church and its settlement, correlations can be of value as one guide among several to prevailing conditions. This is particularly so in areas where the evidence is sufficiently extensive to permit the study of churches in groups rather than in isolated instances.

The limits of the period

The obvious termini for discussion of the topics that have been outlined above would be the Norman Conquest and the Reformation. For most purposes these termini are logical and convenient. Both mark events which led to important reorganizations of the English Church. Both had signal repercussions for the history of medieval church-building. In each case an upheaval in political affairs was accompanied by a change in artistic thinking and in intellectual mood. The advent of the Normans paved the way for a new architecture and a greatly increased sense of scale in design; the Reformation coincided with the first stirrings of classical revivalism and the beginnings of a gradual submergence of the Gothic tradition.

The acceleration of technical and artistic development in English church architecture after the Conquest is worth remark. It is interesting to ponder that the grandson of a man who participated in the rebuilding of the church at Kirkdale (N Yorks) around 1060 could have witnessed the emergence of English Gothic at a place such as Wells in the 1170s. In saying this, however, it is necessary to remember that our acceptance of the traditional termini comes from an impression created by the revolutionary consequences of Norman and Tudor policies on cathedral and monastic affairs. The effects of these policies on local churches were less dramatic, and it is worthwhile to make a comparison between the two.

The years of the Conqueror, and more particularly those of his successors, William Rufus and Henry I, saw a flurry of changes, involving the relocation of some sees, the reform of existing monastic houses, and the founding of new ones in large numbers. So comprehensive were these revisions that by the end of the 12th century very few pre-Conquest cathedral and monastic churches seem to have escaped complete reconstruction. Old churches were often spared temporarily, while new ones were made ready, as at Winchester, but it is rare to encounter cases in which Anglo-Norman builders accepted pre-Conquest fabric as a starting point for their own work, as seems to have happened at Sherborne (Gibb & Gem 1975) and possibly at Wimborne (RCHM *Dorset* V, 78–83). Dr J H Harvey has maintained that 'so far as the cathedrals are concerned, the Norman Conquest made a clean sweep and art started afresh' (1974, Preface). There was an influential Old English artistic legacy in non-architectural areas, such as textiles, painting, and, in some districts, sculpture, but there is usually a fundamental discontinuity in the building history of the great churches.

Where most of the great churches were concerned the events of the 1530s were of an equally across-the-board nature. Plans were laid for the refoundation of about thirty former monastic churches on a collegiate basis, and for the continuation of some, like Fountains, Waltham, and Bury St Edmunds, as the cathedral churches of new dioceses (Wright 1843, 263). Little in the direction of these reforms was actually accomplished, however, and the usual story was of the suppression of monasteries, friaries, and chantries and the confiscation of their revenues. Where churches did continue, either as cathedrals or as adapted parish churches, the extent of building work which went on in the later 16th, 17th, and 18th centuries has perhaps been underestimated. Nevertheless, for the most part this was work of maintenance, minor adaptation, or the modification of interiors. To generalize, the men of the Middle Ages put the great churches up; those since have been engaged in keeping them up and modifying them to meet changing liturgical needs.

At parish level the story is rather different. Changes there were, but they were neither as far-reaching nor as uniformly overwhelming as those which affected the monastic system. Archaeologically, the Conquest and the Reformation can be seen as events which were often extrinsic to the development of most medieval parish churches. Attention has already been drawn to the great escalation of local church building which seems to have occurred during the 10th and 11th centuries (see above: 66). In some areas the greatest force of this movement may already have been spent by 1100. Where the building boom was still in progress the Normans reinforced a trend which had originated before their arrival.

In the 12th century the Normans engaged in a reorganization of diocesan structure, which included the introduction of administrative subdivisions in the form of archdeaconries and rural deaneries (Brett 1975; Barlow 1979), often, one suspects, by formalizing existing boundaries. Norman lords also brought improved standards of masoncraft to churches on their English estates and promoted certain distinctive types of plan form and sculptural enrichment (Clapham 1934; Zarnecki 1951). But the cultivation of these new ideas did not involve anything near so complete a severance with English tradition as affected the monasteries. Much of the Anglo-Norman work which is a commonplace in English parish churches must reflect the modernization of earlier fabrics or the replacement of old fashioned churches with new ones.

The Reformation, likewise, had marginal consequences for the story of parochial geography. Quite grandiose ideas for reorganization were entertained, or rumoured, in the 16th century, but it seems that these were even less completely worked out than those for new bishoprics, and very little was done to realize them. The Tudor failure to grasp this nettle is in part responsible for the extensive programme of pastoral reorganization which we have witnessed during the last fifteen years (General Synod 1974, 5). Where changes were made they usually occurred piecemeal, and were confined on the whole to areas or towns which now had more churches than they needed (Palliser 1974). Certain towns, notably Norwich

and London, managed to preserve their legacy of churches more or less intact. An interesting point arising from this, which archaeology may help to clarify, is the extent to which late medieval work which has usually been attributed to the decades leading up to the Reformation in fact belongs to the middle or later years of the 16th century. The idea that all parochial building stopped at the Reformation rests on no solid basis of fact (L A S Butler 1974; Simmons 1959). In some areas there may, indeed, have been scope for a limited intensification of parish church modernization in the aftermath of the Dissolution, as monastic works organizations were wound up and stocks of building materials came on the market. It is conceivable that a similar consideration might have affected Anglo-Norman rebuilding of parish churches: materials made available on a large scale for cathedrals and monastic building could have been more readily obtainable for parish use.

In summary, therefore, we may argue that at parish level a degree of continuity in design and fabric was maintained from before the Norman invasion until the Reformation, and sometimes beyond. To support this we may notice that instances of the modest, two-cell square-ended village church or chapel can be cited for every century from the 9th to the 19th.

The development of the later medieval church

In 1801 there were 11 379 parish churches in England and Wales. This figure is unlikely to be much in excess of the late medieval total, for although the extent of new church building in the 17th and 18th centuries has often been underestimated, this must be set against late and post medieval redundancies. In some areas these were high. At least 89 churches fell into disuse in the county of Norfolk during the 16th century. In the 17th century 31 Norfolk churches were abandoned, and 30 more fell redundant in the 18th century (Table IX). The Norfolk figures are unusually high, but abandonments also occurred elsewhere, sometimes in substantial numbers. The reasons behind these losses are not always easy to ascertain. Frequently an explanation can be suggested in the presence of too many churches in close proximity, the active force of the lay rector, or the multiple incumbency, leading to a meagre yield of tithes and bequests, problems which would be exacerbated in times of falling prosperity or a decline in population (Clark & Slack 1972; Dobson 1977). However, these explanations may be simplistic and hardly suffice as generalizations. Where they do apply they invite consideration of the factors which led to the overcrowding in the first place. This brings us back to the opening proposition of the chapter: that ecclesiastical growth was at its most extensive and vital in the period leading up to the 13th century.

The relevance of archaeology to the exploration of this theme can be outlined as follows:

(1) Excavation and study of the standing fabric illuminate the building history of a church in ways which go beyond what can be achieved by the simple inspection of surface features. In cases where a church has been completely rebuilt after the Reformation, as at Allerton Mauleverer (N Yorks) (L A S Butler 1978), or Tong (W Yorks) (Mayes 1980), excavation must play the greater part. However, in both these cases elements of the former churches were echoed or reincorporated in the rebuildings. At Tong, for example, the carpenters who roofed the 18th century church made use of timbers from

Table IX Decline of parochial churches and chapels in Norfolk

This Table gives figures for disused churches in the County of Norfolk, excluding the City of Norwich, where 28 churches remain standing out of a former total of 59. The figure of 230 churches which are disused or have disappeared includes 209 parish churches and 21 parochial chapels. A further 39 chapels of uncertain function have been omitted. The low figures for disappearances in the 12th–15th centuries probably give a correct impression, but the possibility of unrecorded disappearances at this and in earlier periods should be kept in mind. The figures have been derived from an interim note on the survey of ruined churches in Norfolk that has been undertaken by Mr Neil Batcock under the auspices of the Norfolk Archaeological Unit. Full publication of the survey is expected in the *East Anglian Archaeology* series.

	Century when fallen into disuse									
Condition	12	13	14	15	16	17	18	19	20	Totals
Full standing									24	24
Largely standing				3	2	9	8		8	30
Ruined	1			2	22	14	7	2	1	49
Tower only				1	4	2	6	3	1	17
Gone		2	9	17	60	13	7	2		110
Totals	1	2	9	20	89	31	29	15	34	230

a trussed-rafter roof, possibly of early 14th century date (Mayes 1980, 21). If the medieval fabric still stands, structural criticism should provide a more complete picture of its development, and excavation may supply facts about phases now missing or incompletely represented above ground. Recent research at Barton-on-Humber (S Humberside), for example, has added a wealth of new information about the post-Conquest development of the church, including successive expansions made in the 12th and 13th centuries, in addition to clarifying the building history of the Anglo-Saxon church (Figs 22 and 23). The results of investigations carried out at Healing (S Humberside) (Bishop 1978), Asheldham (Essex) (Drury & Rodwell 1978), and Wharram Percy (N Yorks) (Beresford & Hurst 1976; Hurst 1976) provide further recent examples.

(2) Operations carried out as under (1) should at least provide a sequence for the structural development of the church. They may also yield material which suggests dates for the sequence or for episodes within it. Local churches are often deficient in conventional dating evidence such as coins and pottery, although where churches and churchyards have been used for other purposes, like trading, finds can occur in quantity, as at Alton Barnes (Hants) (*Medieval Archaeol*, **23** (1979), 246). Artefacts which are more characteristic of ecclesiastical sites include architectural details, fragments of sculpture, voussoirs, and mouldings, all of which may provide worthwhile if not precise evidence of date, as well as painted wall plaster (*in situ* or as buried debris), fragments of coloured or painted glass, and lead calmes. Precisely dated or datable items, such as epigraphs or foundation inscriptions, are not common. However, the removal of pewing in advance of reordering or measures to combat dampness will sometimes disclose a stretch of medieval floor, which may contain a tombslab, a brass (eg at St Nicholas, Rochester, in 1974 (P Tester, *pers comm*), or at the church of Great Linford (Bucks) in 1980 (R J Williams 1980), both found as a result of watching briefs), or an heraldic tile pavement. Where rebuilding has taken place it is not unusual to find fragments of former roof covering, including ceramic ridge tiles and finials, buried beneath the modern floor. Reused gravestones appear fairly frequently in church walls (eg the selection at Ormesby (Cleveland)) and may provide useful, if not always very exact, *termini post quos* for those parts of the fabric in which they occur.

Mouldings are of critical importance for the church archaeologist, having a value not unlike that of pottery for the phasing of secular sites. Mouldings differ from pottery types, however, in that they are usually specific to an individual, deriving from templates which in turn had been cut to patterns designed by medieval architects (cf J H Harvey 1972; Roberts 1977, 5). Mouldings may thus have a bearing upon questions of authorship in medieval design, as well as upon matters of dating. During the last decade the study of mouldings has been given fresh direction and impetus by the systematic collection and analysis of data (R K Morris II 1978; 1979), and by the application of analytical methods acquired from the 'new archaeology' (Roberts 1977, 10).

The task of discriminating between the significance of variation in moulding forms, for example as between the personal touch of a designer, local tradition, or a period style, is difficult (Roberts 1977, 7), but it may be assisted by the application of quantitative analyses. Dr Roberts's study of mouldings in Hertfordshire churches yielded results which suggest that 'the humblest and least interesting churches' were most characteristic of divisions in local style, whereas 'the finest churches could not be confined within these local styles' (1977, 9). Taken further, with the systematic collection of data across wide areas, it seems likely that here we have a promising tool not only for the dating and attribution of medieval architecture, but also for the investigation of levels and consistency of investment in churches. This in turn may help to refine ideas about the significance of churches in relation to local and regional trends in the medieval economy.

Before leaving mouldings, and architectural detail in general, it is worth pointing out that archaeological investigation may assist in the collection of evidence. Where floor or ground levels have risen, excavation frequently discloses mouldings which have been buried and have suffered less or not at all from erosion or the molestations of 19th century restorers. Architectural fragments also occur fairly often as loose finds, or in positions where they have been reused, thus retaining crisp profiles and sharpness of tooling which may be helpful for comparison with examples surviving in the building or further afield. The excavating archaeologist can thus be a provider as well as a user of this kind of evidence, and provision for the care and qualified

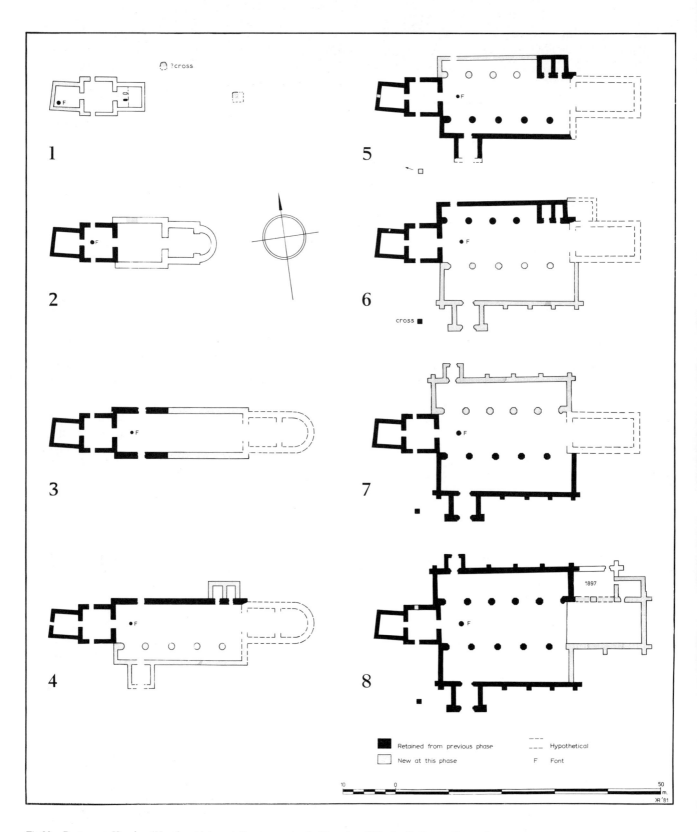

Fig 22   Barton-on-Humber (Humberside): post-Conquest growth. (Drawing: K Rodwell, Crown Copyright Reserved)

Fig 23   Barton-upon-Humber (Humberside): nave of St Peter's church during excavation. The walls of the 10th century chancel can be seen running east from the tower. They are enclosed by walls of a wider nave, leading on to a chancel and apse, all of the 11th century. The arcades of the aisled expansion of the later Middle Ages stand upon earlier substructures. Notice that disturbance by later graves and vaults, though extensive, has not prevented the emergence of a good picture of the development of the church as a result of total internal excavation. (Photo: W J Rodwell, Crown Copyright Reserved)

inspection of this material should always be made. Architectural fragments may, in addition, provide a basis for the reconstruction of the former appearance of parts of the building which are now missing (eg C Wilson 1977; Walsh 1979).

(3) Archaeology can assist in the interpretation of enigmatic features in the standing structure, such as chases or scarred masonry, which in turn may reveal the whereabouts and general character of former screens, galleries, and other fittings. Evidence may also emerge which bears on former patterns of use, including changes in the sites of altars (Colyer 1976), the importance of focal graves or shrines, and the history of baptismal arrangements (Rodwell & Rodwell 1979, 8). The use of archaeology as an instrument to probe patterns of function and liturgical practice is not yet very highly developed in Britain (Biddle 1976a, 70). A great deal of liturgical and social information is available in written records, but as yet there has been no study of the archaeology of liturgy to take advantage of it.

(4) Archaeology is one of the chief means at our disposal for the recovery of facts about medieval building methods. Insights into such matters as systems of scaffolding or even medieval thinking about the behaviour of structures may be afforded by the intensive scrutiny and dissection of church fabrics and substructures (eg Phillips 1975). In recent years scholars have become increasingly attentive to the structural performance as well as the typological characteristics of roofs (Hewett 1977; Heyman 1976). Vaults, until not long ago mainly the province of art- and architectural-historical speculation, are now being considered from the analytical standpoint provided by modern engineering science (Heyman 1966; 1967; 1968). Church archaeology also provides raw materials for the study of other branches of medieval technology, such as tile making, metalworking, bell casting, and the manufacture and use of glass. Data for the investigation of dimensional systems and design methods may also be available (cf Bucher 1968; 1979). Churches are by no means unique providers in these various respects, but their ubiquity as recognizable medieval structures, coupled with the fact that evidence pertaining to many, if not all, of these topics may occur at one site, marks them out as being of particular potential.

Discussion

Although it has been said that the 'fabric of a church is the essential basis for research into its past' (Biddle 1976a, 69), archaeology is not, of course, the only source of information or method of study. From the 13th century the keeping of bishops' registers, sometimes augmented by the records of lesser officials, monastic houses and secular sources (eg inquisitions, disputes, charters, correspondence), provides a considerable amount of information about parish churches, and, to a lesser extent, about their sites and fabrics (L A S Butler 1976; Owen 1976a). The greater churches apart, this evidence is often limited in its value for archaeological purposes, and may do no more than confirm that a particular church existed by a given date. Nevertheless, later medieval diocesan sources and monastic records do provide facts about the status, value, use, and interdependence of churches which are unobtainable on any general basis much before 1200. Information of this kind helps to place the results of archaeological investigation in a sharper historical and social perspective.

The realization that archaeological and historical methods are complementary has bred an interdisciplinary approach to the study of churches which seeks to identify and correlate evidence from written, liturgical, topographical, illustrative, structural, and buried sources. Hitherto this approach has found more support in the committee room than in the field, since its requirement for the co-ordinated participation of scholars in different disciplines is not always easy to realize. Where the approach has best been put into practice it has been aimed mainly at the analysis of important pre-Conquest churches, such as Deerhurst, Brixworth, and Repton. However, some idea of the essentials of the approach as they relate to later medieval churches can be gained from the survey methods which are being promoted by the Working Party on Urban Churches of the CBA's Urban Research Committee (Appendix II).

There are at least four interrelated areas in which the results of such work are needed. The first concerns the history of the church itself. The liturgical development and use of space within churches, for example, are topics about which we have more to learn. The second is the place and significance of the church in medieval society. Important contributions on this theme have been made in recent years (eg Brooke 1970; Owen 1971; J Campbell 1979); significantly, it seems that the only way these can be taken much further is through archaeology, which is the sole source of fresh evidence on any scale. Thirdly, there is the matter of the church as a manifestation of wealth: to what extent is this measurable, and hence of relevance to the economic historian? Fourthly, the graveyard is an important and frequently undervalued source of anthropological data and evidence pertaining to historical demography (see below: 89).

The individual parts of a medieval church are familiar enough: nave, chancel, aisle(s), tower, chantry chapel, sacristy, porch. Some parish churches were transeptal in form. There might also be a crypt, and fairly often a charnel house. At the most elementary level archaeology helps to settle the order and manner in which such components were added, modified, or deleted. For reasons which will be obvious, development can be illuminated most sharply by total excavation, which may lead to the detection of quite a large number of building phases: twelve at Wharram Percy, for example, and no less than eighteen at St Paul-in-the-Bail, Lincoln. Comprehensive investigations of church sites are additionally valuable for the way in which they can trace not only the basic stages of development but also intermediate modifications involving changes of emphasis within individual parts (Biddle 1975a, 312, fig 15, 318–20, fig 16). Equally obviously, total excavation has its drawbacks, since the superstructure, or much of it, is likely to be missing, although, where they exist, topographical drawings, notes made by antiquaries, and possibly even photographs taken before the church was destroyed or replaced may provide some compensation for the absence of an above-ground dimension. Some illustrative evidence was available in the cases of St Mark and St Paul, Lincoln, where the excavators also had to contend with disturbances caused by 18th and 19th century rebuildings.

Some examples

A comparison of the developments of a dozen churches with lives spanning the years under review which have been investigated in recent years raises some interesting issues. The churches concerned (Fig 24) have been

Fig 24 Comparative sketch diagrams to illustrate the developments of twelve medieval parish churches which have been subjected to archaeological investigation. Minor details have sometimes been simplified or omitted. In several cases, knowledge of the layout is incomplete. Key: 1: St Lawrence, Asheldham, Essex (after Drury & Rodwell); 2: St Lawrence, Burnham, Lincs (after Coppack); 3: St Mark, Lincoln (after Gilmour); 4: St Paul, Lincoln (after Colyer & Gilmour); 5: St Bride, London (after Grimes); 6: St Nicholas-in-the-Shambles, London (after Schofield); 7: ? Raunds, Northants (after Boddington & Cadman); 8: St Mary, Rivenhall, Essex (after Rodwell); 9: St Martin, Wharram Percy (after Hurst); 10: St Pancras, Winchester (after Biddle); 11: St Mary, Winchester (after Biddle); 12: St Helen-on-the-Walls, York (after Magilton). (Drawing: Dick Raines)

selected mainly for the reason that they have all been subjected to complete or near-complete excavation. Hence it is revealing to find that all of them were in existence by the end of the 11th century, by which time they consisted either of a single cell, as at St Helen-on-the-Walls, York, or a nave and chancel. Elaborations, like the opposing *porticus* of St Pancras, Winchester, seem uncommon before 1100. However, it should be noted that over half of the churches in question had been modified at least once before the days of Henry I.

The simple layout of nave and chancel, visible in urban churches at London, York, and Lincoln, and also in the countryside at sites like Burnham and Rivenhall, seems to epitomize the intimate 'neighbourhood' church visualized by Brooke (1970, 80–1). Brooke regards these churches, or the urban churches at least, as reflecting a closer and perhaps more vital relationship between a priest and his flock than existed in later centuries (cf Mason 1976), when churches were gradually divided up until in the 14th and 15th centuries the chancels became almost 'impenetrable boxes, the priests, men living in another world' (Brooke 1970, 81). However, close inspection reveals a fair degree of diversity even in these apparently simple early layouts. At St Pancras, Winchester, for example, the early chancel appears as little more than a kind of exaggerated recess at the east end of a long nave (although the evidence, fragmentary at these points, would not preclude a door-like entry to the chancel). By contrast, St Mary in Tanner Street, in the same city, possessed an (added) eastern apse which virtually amounted to an independent chamber, being approached from the nave through a door or arch. At St Mark in Lincoln, likewise, the original division between the nave and chancel was pronounced and doorlike. Initially, the site of the altar at St Mark's seems to have been placed well towards the west end of the chancel (Colyer 1976). If so, then the narrow chancel arch may have been intended as a kind of proscenium to frame the liturgical action which took place just beyond it. The altar within the apse of St Mary Tanner Street seems to have been similarly placed, to judge from the wear pattern on the floor, although this is presumably always the case with an apsidal plan, at least as originally intended. These churches were intimate, certainly, but even at this date it is evident that there was often some kind of demarcation between priest and people. What is not yet clear is whether in the 11th and 12th centuries these differences or 'nuances' of layout can be regarded as representing distinctions between types of ownership (eg lay lord, consortium of parishioners, priest), local or regional custom, the demands of liturgy, or straightforward variations in taste on the part of patrons or groups of church users. When more churches have been fully examined, and the results compared, it may be possible to put these speculations to the test.

From around 1200 there is a definite and not always entirely explicable tendency towards the prolongation of chancels. The 13th century saw the disappearance of many an eastern apse, a process which may have been linked with that of liturgical rearrangement (cf St Mark's, Lincoln), a desire to progress from thatch to tile or lead roof covering, as well as a (slightly later) desire to fit the large new windows which were made possible by the invention of bar tracery. Alterations of this kind provided opportunities to extend as well as to modernize. But it is not clear whether parochial chancel lengthening arose out of a desire to mimic the great eastern arm extensions which were being undertaken by cathedrals and religious houses from the 12th to the 14th centuries, or whether local needs provided the stronger stimulus. Most of the great churches were stretched eastwards for entirely practical reasons: chiefly, the need to provide more spacious surroundings for shrines and feretories, room for processions, and also to accommodate the cult of the Virgin. These considerations can hardly have weighed so heavily at parish level, but factors which might have led to enlargement included the wish to provide independent access to the chancel for the priest, relocation of the altar, desire for an Easter Sepulchre, the installation of sedilia, perhaps coupled with an increase in the number of people assisting with ritual, and dramatic elaborations in liturgy following upon the emergence of a more literate, educated clergy. Pre-Conquest chancels, of which many must have remained until 1200, and Anglo-Norman chancels were generally too small to meet these needs, and this may have provided some incentive for donors to make funds available for enlargements.

The chancels and naves of many churches display different building histories. This can be a reflection of a traditional division of responsibility between the nave, which was maintained by the parishioners, and the chancel, which was the portion of the priest or his patron. This division was not absolute. A wealthy rector could initiate a full rebuilding largely or wholly at his own expense; parishioners sometimes did likewise. But a matter which deserves examination through the study of large samples of churches is whether the chancels of buildings in the hands of lay and ecclesiastical patrons display different patterns of development. Archaeology may in time establish the period (at present apparently in the 12th century) in which the structural histories of parochial naves and chancels began to slip out of phase.

Churches were also expanded by the addition of aisles. Aisles were rare before the Conquest, although it seems that *porticus* could be attached to any grade of church. In the first half of the 12th century aisles, though still uncommon, begin to occur with greater frequency. By the end of that century many parish churches had acquired at least one aisle, and from the 13th century aisles became a normal component of churches large and small. A fairly common phenomenon is the survival of Norman south (sometimes north) doorways in later aisles. The church entrance provided the setting for the preliminary stages of the rites of baptism and matrimony; for this reason it is possible that it claimed a special place in local affections, and hence was often spared when all else around it was subject to renewal.

Various ideas have been put forward to explain the presence and character of aisles. It has been suggested that aisles were added to cater for an expanding population, or that they resulted from a change in the pattern of accommodation within a church, or that the increased importance of preaching in the later Middle Ages required the creation of more spacious interiors.

Communal needs such as these may well lie behind the building of some aisles. The 13th century north aisle of St Pancras, Winchester, for example, was fitted with benches against the north and west walls, and was entered from an adjacent lane by a north door (Biddle 1972, 114; cf Magilton 1980, 21). However, in view of the fact that churches in adjacent parishes of comparable wealth and population sometimes display very different structural histories, some acquiring aisles and others not, it seems unlikely that a primitive pressure on space was the overriding impulse behind aisle formation. A more convincing explanation is to be found in the liturgical function of aisles, which were frequently used for the housing of subsidiary altars, separately endowed and with individual dedications. It is conceivable that the pre-Conquest custom of providing semi-independent adjuncts, *porticus*, alongside the main bodies of churches persisted into the later Middle Ages as a liturgical concept, even though the design solution changed (cf Gilmour 1979, 217). In the north country, for example, aisle chapels were often known locally, and suggestively, as 'quires', conceivably reflecting a contrast between a said mass by a rector and a sung mass by an endowed chantry priest.

In the 14th and 15th centuries, in some cases sooner, as at Wharram Percy, many churches begin to display signs of personal, family, or group interests. These may be manifested in small box-like projections from the main vessel (eg at St Nicholas-in-the-Shambles, London) or in the extension or reorganization of aisles. An aisle could be built in one operation, but it could also result from the extension of a single chapel which acted as a nucleus or from the coalescence of several neighbouring chapels. Sometimes this additive process might culminate in a full rebuilding which rationalized a series of former semi-independent chapels into a single aisle. The part played by gilds in this was often important (T Smith 1870; Westlake 1919). Where gilds flourished they frequently created and endowed chapels for the spiritual security of dead members. Where gilds grew in membership, this could be the stimulus for structural expansion, leading to a new aisle or even, occasionally, a new church. The process of coral-like accretion of chapels is readily responsive to archaeological investigation, both above and below ground. Where towers antedate such rebuilding their east faces may be eloquent of earlier roof lines.

The importance of preaching in the later Middle Ages is reflected in the opening out of church interiors, achieved by the attenuation of supports and simplification of the plan visible in such churches as St Peter Mancroft, Norwich, and the nave of St Mary's, Nottingham, as well as in the buildings of poor parishes, like St Helen-on-the-Walls, York, which in its ultimate form appears as a stark rectangle. The unified interiors of such later medieval churches are, of course, to some extent deceptive in their openness, since most have been deprived of the full array of wooden screen work and embellished fencing which divided off the various subsidiary areas devoted to the needs of family chantries and gild chapels, and the impressive rood screens which provided demarcation between nave and chancel, of which staircases terminating in thin air are now often the only remaining tokens. Nevertheless, the affinities of these designs with the simple layouts pioneered by the friars and the later medieval development of hangar-like church fabrics which overspread liturgical divisions, rather than actually defined them as had been usual in earlier centuries, points to a shift in requirements brought about at least in part by a growing commitment to a preaching function (L A S Butler 1974, 53–6; cf J H Harvey 1978, 67).

A further point worth consideration in connection with aisles concerns the consequences for parish church development of the extent of control over burial which was exercised by religious houses. Where this control was slight, or had earlier been checked or weakened by the intervention of Scandinavians, it appears that restrictions on the establishment of burial grounds next to incipient parish churches were fewer than in those areas where a more traditional relationship between a mother church and its daughters was preserved. All the parish churches recently excavated in York and Lincoln, for example, possessed cemeteries at least as old as the first churches (or, in the case of St Paul-in-the-Bail, Lincoln, the first secular phase). In Winchester, by contrast, the cathedral priory seems to have maintained its monopoly over burial well beyond the Conquest. It was not until later in the Middle Ages that parish churches within the city of Winchester began to acquire rights of their own. With one exception, all the internal burials of St Pancras, Winchester, appeared to belong to the latest phases of the building, and the earliest written reference to a burial there dates from 1503 (Biddle 1975, 319, n 2, fig 16; Dr Derek Keene, *pers comm*). Where a strongly possessive influence of this kind was being exerted by a mother church, this might well have repercussions for the planning development of parish churches in its vicinity.

The church in its setting: change and decay

Archaeological interest in the relationship between church and settlement has hitherto centred mainly on the deserted medieval village and the town. The importance of the isolated or eccentrically positioned church as an indicator of former settlement was stressed by pioneers in this field (Beresford 1954; Hoskins 1955), and has been enlarged upon since (Beresford & Hurst 1971; 1976; Wade-Martins 1975). The value of such churches is seen not only in the fact that they may advertise the whereabouts of vanished communities, but also in the ways that their constructional histories may provide a commentary upon the fortunes of those who built and worshipped in them (Beresford & Hurst 1976). This latter line of inquiry will frequently demand active archaeological investigation if it is to bear fruit, since where a church has outlived its village it has commonly contracted, leaving earlier structural phases absent above ground (as at Wharram Percy), or it has been rebuilt on a smaller scale (as at Goltho (Lincs)). Even where earlier elements do survive, investigation will usually be needed to settle the question of origins.

The importance of churches in relation to the study of urban settlement is now well appreciated (Brooke 1977; J Campbell 1979). Churches loom large in Carter's discussion of the urban origins of Norwich (Carter 1978), for example, and the archaeology of the urban church has clearly contributed a good deal to thinking about the development of other important towns, such as Winchester, York, Lincoln, and London (Brooke & Keir 1975), and to the consideration of suburban growth (Keene 1976). In his comments on the ecclesiastical geography of Colchester, W J Rodwell observed that the 'intra-mural portions of urban parishes are generally quite small in terms of acreage, which makes it easier to assess the physical relationship between church and parish, as well as the propinquity between the parishes themselves' (Rodwell & Rodwell 1977, 24). For the future, there is scope for archaeological research in the lesser towns, such as Stamford (Rogers 1972) and Ilchester (Dunning 1975), which did not acquire such large totals as the regional capitals but nevertheless contained substantial groups of churches in the Middle Ages. Conversely, more consideration could be given to towns which were served by a single church, like Market Harborough and Nantwich, where the churches, although grand structurally, were of chapel status, pointing to an original dependence upon another centre.

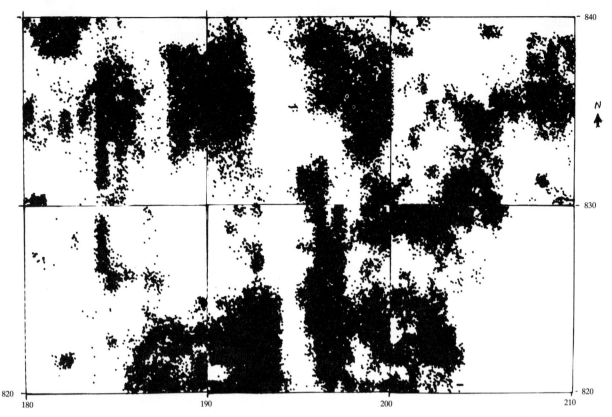

Fig 25   The Hirsel (Berwickshire): (a) plot of resistivity survey of site; (b opposite) graves, features, and structures revealed by excavation (by courtesy of the Universities of Bradford and Durham).

Later in the Middle Ages churches become relevant to the theme of urban decline (Dobson 1977; Palliser 1978), being among the most obvious and lamented, if ambiguous, indicators of trends in the late medieval economy.

Moving back now into the countryside, it is necessary to reiterate that by no means all of the churches which served former *or existing* settlements have survived down to the present day. A good number are now in ruins. Some have been overtaken by coastal erosion, as at Eccles (Norfolk), or buried under sand dunes, as in the case of the Norman church of St Waleric, Alnmouth (Northumberland), where a change in the course of the river Alne severed the church from its settlement. More usual are cases of churches which fell redundant between the Norman and Tudor periods and survive only as sites. Often it is possible to confirm the existence and general whereabouts of a lost church from written records (eg licences, wills, episcopal registers). In some instances such references may be the first clue that a church ever existed. The identification of the Norman borough church of Rhuddlan, formerly in the county of Flint, is a good example (*Medieval Archaeol*, **16** (1972), 178–9): although the existence of a 12th–13th century church was known, the site was lost until it was located by resistivity survey and excavation. A similar process of geophysical survey followed by excavation has led to the identification of the ecclesiastical site at The Hirsel, near Coldstream (Cramp & Douglas-Home 1977–8), previously known only from a small number of rather laconic written references (Figs 25 and 26).

There are also churches for which no records have survived, either because they disappeared at an early date, usually before 1250, as in the cases of Barrow and Raunds, and also at Norwich, where a church demolished to make way for the late 11th century castle has recently been excavated, or because they were of such small value as to escape individual enumeration in general surveys. In cases of this kind only fieldwork, attention to field-names, or the chance discovery of architectural fragments or bones may lead to the recognition of the site. The discovery of a previously unsuspected chapel site at Oversley (Warwicks) during the laying of a pipeline in 1977 is a case in point (Deborah Ford, *pers comm*; short note published in *Birmingham University Bulletin* 1978). Much easier to identify are the sites of churches which were abandoned and replaced by new churches on different sites during the 18th and 19th centuries. Transfers of this kind were quite common (eg Yazor (Herefs), Birdsall (N Yorks), Nocton (Lincs), and sometimes reflect an attempt to rationalize some long-standing anomaly in the relationship between church and settlement.

There are signs that in some parts of England the full extent of lost medieval ecclesiastical provision has been underestimated, or that where a reliable assessment of the scale of the loss has been made, its significance has not been widely appreciated. In just the northern part of the old East Riding of Yorkshire, for example, some 33 deserted church or chapel sites have been identified, and this list is not complete (H G Ramm, *pers comm*).

Scholars have, equally, neglected to give much consideration to the place of the church in settlements which *have* continued down to modern times. The avoidance of this very interesting subject is not as odd as it may seem, since it is now understood that living settlements may contract, grow, combine, and rearrange in ways which make it difficult to attribute long-term stability to any of the components which go to make up a settlement, or a constant relationship between them (C C Taylor 1978).

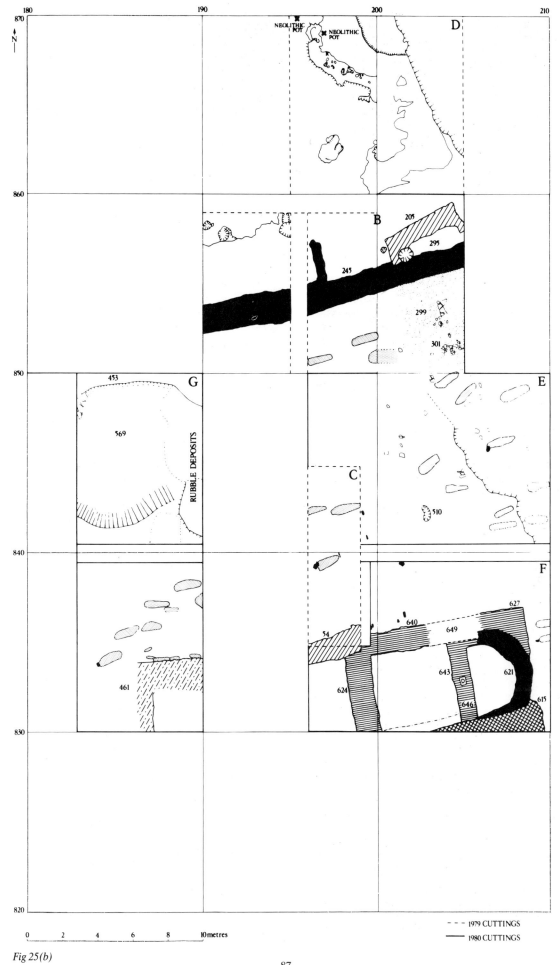

Fig 25(b)

87

Fig 26 The Hirsel: plan of church (by courtesy of the University of Durham)

The shape and site of the modern village, and the place of its church, may bear little or no relation to the arrangements of settlement which pertained when the church was first built. The church, however, is frequently the oldest recognizable building attached to a settlement or occupies the oldest identifiable site. Hence it is of unusual value as providing a fixed point of reference, an historical datum, for the analysis of developments around it. This is a subject which deserves detailed treatment in the near future.

Burials and burial grounds

So far discussion has centred on the church fabric and the site it occupies. Evidence of quite a different sort comes from the churchyard, which contains the remains of all but the wealthiest parishioners. For obvious reasons, access to these remains in conditions suited to scientific study is not usually possible or desirable, except in cases where a church has been abandoned for a long time or where the site of a redundant church is about to be redeveloped and the disturbance of burials is thus inevitable. The propriety and circumstances of churchyard excavations have been considered elsewhere (eg Rodwell & Rodwell 1976; Rahtz 1976b; Phillips 1976) and need not be discussed further here. It is, however, worthwhile to make a brief review of the history of archaeological attitudes to the study of church and churchyard burials, since there are signs that the potential for work in this direction is still not yet fully appreciated.

Throughout the 19th century antiquaries took a more or less academic interest in the tombs and remains of individuals. This was nearly always as a result of the individual's reputation in life (eg in the opening of the tombs of St Cuthbert at Durham, the scholar Ranulph Higden at Chester, and the search for William Rufus at Winchester). Tomb opening was a minor ecclesiastical pastime in the 19th century, especially in the greater churches where groups of clergy sought the remains of their medieval predecessors, often extracting any objects that accompanied them before resealing the tombs. As a result, certain cathedral treasuries are quite well stocked with episcopal rings, the heads of croziers, and other mortuary items. Perfunctory notes on the physical anthropology and palaeopathology of the individuals were sometimes made on these occasions, but, in general, curiosity rather than scientific interest seems to have been the ruling motive. This tradition seems to have been maintained almost to the present day, a recent manifestation being in the slightly bizarre exploits of the Thomas More Society at Canterbury in 1978 in pursuit of the skull of their patron (Tatton-Brown 1981).

Interest in the remains of nameless, common folk has not been so strong. Since the Middle Ages builders and their employers have had few scruples about disturbing or destroying such remains in the path of works necessary to repair or modify churches. Latterly there have been attempts by archaeologists to record skeletal remains in advance of minor works in churchyards, but as these have tended to yield but a tiny minority of burials out of large populations (eg P R Wilson 1979), the results have seldom seemed to justify the effort involved. Indeed, there now exists in some quarters a certain resistance to the concept of churchyard investigations, at least on a small scale, arising from the conviction that such projects are poor in their yield of data. In the last twenty-five years there have been very few excavations of churchyards which have provided statistically useful samples of burials.

This position is now beginning to change. In part this is due to the fact that some 19th century churches on medieval sites have been declared redundant under the Pastoral Measure 1968, demolished, and the sites made available for study in advance of redevelopment (eg St Mark, Lincoln). At the same time there has been some concentration on the sites and surroundings of lost medieval churches which fell redundant in the 16th century, such as St Helen-on-the-Walls, York, and St Nicholas-in-the-Shambles, London. These sites are particularly important, since they have not been disrupted by subsequent burial or the insertion of large, destructive vaults (Fig 27).

Results from St Helen-on-the-Walls have now been published, and are plausibly claimed as the largest single excavated medieval churchyard group in England (Dawes & Magilton 1980). The St Helen's material is important for several reasons. First, the size of the sample (at least 1041 individuals) imparts a fair degree of reliability to statistically based conclusions drawn from it. This in turn marks the sample out as being of prime value for purposes of comparison with other groups (Dawes & Magilton 1980, 66–82). Secondly, the sample places the assessment of physique, health, and life-expectancy of medieval residents in the parish upon a secure footing. This is all the more important for the reasons summarized by Palliser in his comments on the results, namely that they must represent 'a high proportion of the entire population of the parish over five or six centuries, and what is more a relatively poor parish which is not well documented' (1980, 82). Some of the social and historical implications of these results are unusually interesting: for example, the fact that beyond the age of 35 men outnumbered women (1980, 63–6, table 14), and the 'marked change in skull type between Saxon and medieval graveyard groups' which emerges from comparisons between the St Helen's population and other (smaller) samples (Beresford & Hurst 1971, 135; Brothwell 1972, 82; Palliser 1980, 82) and from within the St Helen's population itself (Dawes & Magilton 1980, 66–81). Progress in the explanation of some of these topics may be expected when more large graveyard groups have been published to an adequate standard.

Graveyard groups do not, of course, provide facts about all aspects of population history. The consequences of infectious diseases and epidemics cannot normally be established from skeletal evidence, although methods of maximizing the potential of burial evidence do exist, for example through sampling for parasite eggs in burials encountered in suitable conditions, which would, it is claimed, 'provide a wealth of information on the history of infectious diseases and would give a better understanding of standards of health in the past' (A K G Jones 1979, 3). The full potential of environmental church archaeology, like that of the archaeology of liturgy, has yet to be realized.

Large numbers of redundant medieval churchyards exist throughout Britain. Hitherto there has been a tendency to investigate only those which belong to churches which are assessed as being of intrinsic importance, sometimes in circumstances which have led to the subordination of the study of burials in the interests of facilitating the study of structures (eg Kjølbye-Biddle 1975). Hence churchyard archaeology has been a by-product of (often

(a)

(b)

Fig 27   Derby Cathedral: the Cavendish vault: (a) original vault, constructed c 1605; (b) the 'new vault', built as an overflow chamber c 1810. (Photos: S Pentelow)

urban) structurally orientated church archaeology, rather than an enterprise to be undertaken for independent academic reasons. The materials for such an enterprise nevertheless exist, and deserve a much more full and concerted exploitation than they have received in the past. This may well require a greater emphasis upon investigations undertaken for reasons of pure research, rather than the more breathless rescue operations which do not always allow the painstaking recording, sampling, and post-excavation facilities which are now seen to be essential for a full recovery and analysis of the data. The importance of sites abandoned at an early date may be stressed once more. The remains of infants, for example, usually account for no more than a very small percentage of burials, despite the fact that infant mortality in the Middle Ages was extremely high (Hatcher 1977). The paucity of such remains has usually been attributed to their extreme fragility, and consequent susceptibility to disturbance, destruction, and dispersal, or the effects of adverse soil conditions, although there have been speculations about the possibility of there having been special areas set aside for the reception of young children. However, the example of Raunds, a church which underwent only very limited expansion and was out of use by c 1200, shows that infant burials occurred very frequently along the base of exterior walls: a phenomenon which would have been completely obscured in the case of a church which underwent successive rebuildings (A Boddington, *pers comm*).

Before leaving the subject of churchyards, it is worth pausing to consider the character of the medieval 'yardscape'. While a good deal is now known about the appearance of graveyards in the late Saxon period and in the 12th century, it is a curious fact that rather less information is available for the period c 1200–1600. Monuments, of course, abound in some regions (L A S Butler 1964), but they are seldom encountered *in situ*, and tend to relate more to the church itself than to the churchyard. A few medieval monuments do survive out of doors. The 14th century chest tomb at Loversall (S Yorks) is a famous example, and another survives not far away at Maltby. In both cases the tomb-chest is capped by a decorated slab. At Thornton Steward (N Yorks) there are two rough sarcophagi beside the south-west corner of the nave, each covered by a decorated slab. In one case the slab is broken and part of another has been substituted. But it would seem that here we have evidence of a custom of burial in a coffin which stood proud of the churchyard turf, and that decorated slabs could be used to cap outdoor monuments. The custom of burial with a slab, head, and low footstone certainly persisted into the later Middle Ages, for examples are sometimes encountered *in situ* during excavations for drains or cables in churchyards, as recently at St Andrew, Great Linford (Bucks) (R J Williams 1980, 18–19). It is, indeed, during such 'minor works' that fresh examples are likely to come to attention, and in the course of which many must already have been lost.

The opportunity to excavate an entire medieval churchyard will be enhanced in value if it proves possible to extend the area of study beyond the present limits of the site. Apart from the possible presence of ancillary structures within the churchyard, like bell-cages or dwellings (Drury & Rodwell 1978), it frequently happens that the present churchyard boundaries are not the earliest, but are preceded by lines of enclosure which may extend within or beyond the latest perimeter. Apart from this, it is highly desirable to form a picture of the environment of the church (paths, trackways, boundaries, structures, etc), as has been done in the cases of Raunds and Wharram Percy, and to establish stratigraphic relationships between different phases of the churchyard and adjacent features.

Conclusion

Enough has been said to show that the archaeological study of the medieval church is of acute relevance to many aspects of medieval history. However, a distinction needs to be kept between the actual practice of archaeology, which is a kind of technology, and the uses to which the evidence it produces can be put. Archaeology reveals and records physical data: it responds only to that which is tangible. Hence if a full use of archaeology is to be made, its limitations must always be kept in view.

The basic contribution of church archaeology is that it provides a framework of patterns and chronologies for activities on sites which we know from other sources were held in special regard by the community at large. It enables us to measure, compare, and relate the effort which went into the development of these sites and leads us to consider the investment behind it. Much of this information is unobtainable from other sources. It is, however, difficult, and often hazardous, to extrapolate from the physical circumstances of sites and their settings to religious, social, and economic questions, which are usually assumed to be within the province of the historian. Archaeologists must, nevertheless, attempt to equip themselves to ask such questions of their evidence, for their own ways of thinking can lead to insights not available to specialists in other disciplines.

The archaeology of those churches and chapels erected after the Reformation in Britain is less problematical than at earlier periods but does still present a number of difficulties. The major alterations to churches followed in the wake of the Gothic Revival inspired by the Oxford Movement. A general desire to remove all 'pagan' architectural forms and to replace all impediments to a Catholic Christian ritual brought about the destruction of most insertions in the fabric and fittings introduced between 1550 and 1820. It also resulted in the 'correction' of architectural detail added in the period 1820 to 1850.

The alterations of the late 19th century took many forms. At the one extreme was the total destruction and replacement of an entire fabric, often without preliminary record; at the other extreme was the minor tinkering to obtain the desired and 'authentic' result. In some cases the post-medieval sequence within a totally destroyed church will only be recovered by archaeological means. In the majority of cases where Victorian restoration has been severe, the ritual changes of the three centuries between *c* 1550 and *c* 1850, which are a very real part of the building's history and use, need a combination of approaches to understand them. For this period few architectural plans survive other than those by the major architects (Wren, Hawksmoor, Paine) until the work of the Ecclesiastical Commissioners for New Churches (1818 Commission). There is a similar dearth of material recording internal alterations and fittings, and this information is just as likely to be found among the family papers of benefactors as among the records of the Consistory Court or among the Faculties approved by the Chancellor of the Diocese. There were few topographical artists recording work of their own time; the cultivation of interest in Roman and Druidic antiquities, and, after Horace Walpole, of medieval antiquities ensured that many new works went unrecorded, particularly if these were in remote locations. After the great enthusiasm for sweeping away the 'pagan' building of the 17th and 18th centuries gathered momentum, the normal record of the previous building was perfunctory apart from its monumental inscriptions and heraldry. It was seldom recorded in illustration.

It is convenient to divide the period under consideration into three phases. The first is the search for a Puritan religious expression *c* 1540–1660, the second is the emphasis upon preaching and comfort for the listeners *c* 1660–1820, and the third is a gradual return to a ritualistic approach with a greater degree of experiment in plan and architecture *c* 1820–50.

During the first phase there were two major problems: the first was how to deal with the overlarge cathedrals and abbeys and with unwanted chantries, and the second how to bring the Protestant message to the urban population. In those abbeys, normally Benedictine and Augustinian, that were retained for public worship the usual solution was to remove the eastern arms and erect a plain wall in the western crossing arch. In a few cases it was another part of the monastery that was retained for use, and sometimes a more drastic solution was for the fabric to be divided into western and eastern churches

(as at Aberdeen, Glasgow, and Exeter). In most cases these solutions have been reversed by late 19th century reformers and the blocking walls removed, sometimes with no evidence now surviving about their precise position. The problem of the superfluous chantries could be solved by their total removal when such a course of action would not impair the safety of the fabric, but generally they were purified by the plastering up of unwanted piscinae, the whitewashing over of unnecessary texts and imagery, and the reglazing of particularly seditious motifs and inscriptions. The wholesale appropriation of religious chantries to secular use for family worship and burial retained the fabric at the expense of the fittings. In Wales and Scotland, where chantries were fewer, the secular appropriation in the chancel often led to the building of a burial chapel or 'aisle' leading off the chancel. In Wales this addition may have been swept away in Victorian restoration, as at Llanfor near Bala; in Scotland the 'aisle' remains roofed and repaired where the medieval church has been abandoned. A more serious aspect of the destruction of chantries, together with the confiscation of their endowments, was the neglect of individual field chapels, which had relied upon gifts of land and offerings at altars to provide the maintenance of their priests. For these a slow process of decay was set in train unless a later benefactor provided generously for the provision of services and the repair of the fabric. The Visitation inquiries in the mid 18th century show how rare it was for any specific financial provision to exist for repair of the fabric.

The gradual expansion of the towns beyond their medieval defences brought extensive suburban growth, particularly at London, Bristol, Norwich, and Exeter. These suburbs were usually within a city centre parish whose church could not be expanded by the addition of an aisle. Instead new churches were built, as at Exeter St Davids 1541, London St Paul, Covent Garden 1637, and Plymouth Charles Church 1646. The desire of the Protestant reformers to bring their message to the urban population either led to former medicant churches being converted to this purpose (Coventry Grey Friars) or a new church being built as at Denbigh in North Wales (Butler 1974) or at Burntisland, a small burgh in Fife. In England appeals for money to assist in building (known as 'briefs') were widely circulated; they are sometimes the principal source of information about a building campaign, though the desirability for and the extent of the necessary repairs may be much exaggerated. The characteristic of these early experiments is the mobility of their furniture. Unlike pre-Reformation churches the communion table, pulpit, and font could be moved according to the dictates of the predominant doctrine. Hence it is often difficult to determine by archaeological means where these fittings stood.

During the period 1660–1820 the main plan form adopted was rectangular, usually aisled in the town churches. The altar was placed against the east wall and railed off from the pews. The pulpit was placed against a long wall, usually against the north wall or in aisled churches against a pillar in the north arcade. The font might be free-standing near the west end, or wall-mounted near a west or south door, or else be capable of being moved into a position near the pulpit. The gradual filling of the church with pews made the alleys within the building permanent in their position. These alleys were increasingly used for burial, though in rural churches burial was often beneath the family pew where the living members of the same family knelt in worship. Paving in rural churches was restricted to the sanctuary.

Where buildings of this date and nature have been totally replaced, the archaeologist must obtain by excavation as much information as possible about the former plan and internal arrangements. Where churches of this period have been altered to conform with late Victorian ideas of religious propriety, the architectural historian can discover the original appearance by mentally discarding all later additions, usually Gothic windows and doors, an added sanctuary, an inserted chancel arch, and a new organ chamber with choir vestry.

In rural churches where the alterations were not so drastic, it is often possible to detect some of the changes through a careful examination of the fabric. The presence of a free-standing altar may be deduced from a blocked door in the east wall; the former position of the pulpit may be reconstructed from alterations to windows in the north wall to give more light to a preacher in a two- or three-decker structure. The former existence of a western balcony may be determined from a blocked doorway close to the west end, often approached by an external flight of stairs, from windows newly built in the late 18th century or heightened to light the balcony or even from the Victorian replacement of timber wind-braces in a medieval roof to repair the aperture formerly occupied by a dormer window. The survival of the medieval rood beam against the western wall may indicate that the medieval screen remained in position until the mid 18th century when it was transferred to the west and cannibalized to form a balcony or singers' loft; the Victorian restoration will have rejected all the Georgian material, leaving the medieval rood beam intact and recovering a few *disjecta membra* of the screen for use in the new choir stalls. Such survival and conservatism is more often found in Wales and the Marches than in eastern England.

The support of documentary sources, principally faculties, visitations, and briefs, will help to create a general picture of the changes in progress from 1640 to 1820 and may allow the individual buildings to be reconstructed in some detail, especially if churchwardens' accounts survive and if Victorian reconstruction was late in the century and well recorded by architects' plans, engravings, and photographs.

The final phase of church building from 1820 to 1850 is sufficiently distinct to require separate notice. It is a period distinguished by experiment in plan form and by an eclecticism in architectural style. There is far less uniformity in internal arrangement though an auditory church was still desirable; the speculative ventures of proprietary chapels added to the variety of internal seating plans. In archaeological terms this is a less rewarding period, largely because the opportunities for new discoveries and fresh contributions are fewer. The urban churches in the inner ring of suburbs are often well recorded because they were financially dependent upon the Ecclesiastical Commissioners or on the Incorporated Church Building Society. The rural churches might still be experiencing the pressure to expand private seating provision in the face of Nonconformist rivalry. However, this was a period when many churches were erected hastily and cheaply by landowners with a Christian conscience. It was these 'unworthy' buildings that were enlarged out of all recognition in the Oxford Movement.

In the foreseeable future the contribution of archaeology will be of restricted use in the post-medieval period and will find its greatest achievements in the structures of Late Roman, post-Roman, and medieval centuries.

An attempt has been made to summarize all significant recorded church archaeological work. Sites in Ireland are not included, but it is hoped that the list is reasonably complete for England, Scotland, and Wales. Apart from sites which have been omitted as a result of oversights on the part of the compilers, there are some others, assessed (subjectively) as being of only marginal ecclesiastical significance, which have been deliberately excluded. Gravestone recordings have not been counted. Potentially Christian Anglo-Saxon or British cemeteries (eg Leighton Buzzard II, Cannington) have not been included unless there is evidence to indicate the presence of a Christian structure (eg Nazeingbury), or to show that the site was under ecclesiastical management.

Notes
Details are listed under twelve main heads, as follows:

1   *Place-name*

2   *County*
Both pre- and post-reorganization (1974) counties are cited, depending upon the usage specified when the work was carried out

3   *National Grid Reference*

4   *Dedication(s)* (if known)

5   *Status*
Coding:

Abb	abbey
C	chapel
Cat	cathedral
Cem	cemetery
Col	college
Fri	friary
Gr	grange
Hos	hospital
PC	parish church (or pre-Conquest equivalent)
Pre	preceptory
Pri	priory
VC	vicars choral
( ) denotes former status	

6   *Order* (if relevant)
Coding:

Aug	Augustinian
Aus	Austin
Ben	Benedictine
Car	Carthusian
Cis	Cistercian
Clu	Cluniac
Crm	Carmelite
Dom	Dominican
Fra	Franciscan
Fon	Fontevrault
Gil	Gilbertine
KH	Knights Hospitaller
KT	Knights Templar
Obs	Observantine
Pre	Premonstratensian
Tir	Tironian
Tri	Trinitarian
N	nuns
( ) denotes former users	

7   *Site condition*
Coding:

CiU	church in use
Ru	ruin
Str	structures (often incorporated in later buildings)
R	redundant (Pastoral Measure 1968 or equivalent)
S	site

In many cases it will be found that two or more of these codings are used in conjunction: eg where excavation has occurred on the site of a demolished portion of a church, but where part of that church remains in use, or is in a markedly different condition.

8   *Director(s) and responsible organization(s)*

9   *Year(s) of investigation(s)*
Where two years are cited, these normally mark the limits of the work, which may have been intermittent. Where a year is followed by a dash but no concluding date is given, it is believed that the project is still in progress.

10   *Style of investigation*
Coding:

E	excavation
FS	fabric study
Ob	observation of works carried out by another agency
S	survey

11   *Summary*

12   *Reference(s)*
Where an interim or final report is known, details are summarized or reference is made to the main bibliography. Where no report has yet appeared, or where the compilers have failed to notice such an appearance, attention is drawn to a conveniently accessible summary, such as in the annual listings carried by *Medieval Archaeology*. In instances of this latter kind reference is normally made only to the most recent notice, on the assumption that this can be used as a starting point for tracing earlier entries. In order to save space, standard CBA bibliographical contractions have sometimes been abandoned in favour of shorter forms. References other than those which are given in a self-explanatory form have been abbreviated as follows:

AA	Aerial Archaeology
Arch J	Archaeological Journal
Arch Camb	Archaeologia Cambrensis
Arch Cant	Archaeologia Cantiana
Antiq J	Antiquaries Journal
BAR	British Archaeological Reports
Beds AJ	Bedfordshire Archaeological Journal
BCBACC	Bulletin of the CBA Churches Committee
Berks AJ	Berkshire Archaeological Journal
BNFAS	
BNJ	British Numismatic Journal
DAJ	Derbyshire Archaeological Journal
EAH	Essex Archaeology and History
Herts Archaeol	Hertfordshire Archaeology
JBAA	Journal of the British Archaeological Association
J Northants Mus	Journal of the Northampton Museum and Art Gallery
KAR	Kent Archaeological Review
LHA	Lincolnshire History and Archaeology
Med Arch	Medieval Archaeology
MKJAH	Milton Keynes Journal of Archaeology and History
Oxon	Oxoniensia
PDAS	Proceedings of the Devon Archaeological Society
PDNHAS	Proceedings of the Dorset Natural History and Archaeological Society
PHFCAS	Proceedings of the Hampshire Field Club and Archaeological Society
PIOMNHAS	Proceedings of the Isle of Man Natural History and Antiquarian Society
Post Med Arch	Post-Medieval Archaeology
Proc Cambs AS	Proceedings of the Cambridge Antiquarian Society
PSANHS	Proceedings of the Somerset Archaeological and Natural History Society
PSAS	Proceedings of the Society of Antiquaries of Scotland
PSIAH	Proceedings of the Suffolk Institute of Archaeology and History
Publ Thoresby Soc	Publications of the Thoresby Society
Rec Bucks	Records of Buckinghamshire
RPNAS	Reports and Papers of the Northamptonshire Antiquarian Society
Surrey AC	Surrey Archaeological Collections
Sussex AC	Sussex Archaeological Collections

TAMS	Transactions of the Ancient Monuments Society	
TBGAS	Transactions of the Bristol and Gloucestershire Archaeological Society	
TB(W)AS	Transactions of the Birmingham and Warwickshire Archaeological Society	
TCHS	Transactions of the Caernarvonshire Historical Society	
TCWAAS	Transactions of the Cumberland and Westmorland Antiquarian and Archaeological Society	
TDA	Transactions of the Devon Association	
TDGNHAS	Transactions of the Dumfriesshire and Galloway Natural History and Antiquarian Society	

TLAHS	Transactions of the Leicestershire Archaeological and Historical Society
TLMAS	Transactions of the London and Middlesex Archaeological Society
T Radnors Soc	Transactions of the Radnorshire Society
TSSAHS	Transactions of the South Staffordshire Archaeological and Historical Society
TTS	Transactions of the Thoroton Society of Nottinghamshire
TWNFC	Transactions of the Woolhope Naturalists' Field Club, Herefordshire
WAM	Wiltshire Archaeological and Natural History Magazine
YAJ	Yorkshire Archaeological Journal

Key:

(1)	**Place-name**	(7)	**Condition of site**
(2)	**County**	(8)	**Director/under auspices of**
(3)	**NGR**	(9)	**Year(s)**
(4)	**Dedication**	(10)	**Type(s) of study**
(5)	**Status**	(11)	**Remarks**
(6)	**Order (if relevant)**	(12)	**Reference(s)**

(1)	(2)	(3)	(4)	(5)	(6)	(7)	(8)	(9)	(10)	(11)	(12)
Aberdaron	Gwynedd (Caerns)	SH139253	St Mary	PC		Ru	D B Hague W J Ellis	1955	FS	Church abandoned C19, sea erosion	*Arch Camb*, **105** (1956), 154–5
Abererch	Gwynedd (Caerns)	SH396365	St Cawrdraf	PC		CiU	D B Hague	1955	FS	C14 west door and graveslab	*Arch Camb*, **105** (1956), 155
Abbotsbury	Dorset	SY577852	St Peter	Abb	Ben	S	C P Green	1971	E	of part of nave	*Med Arch*, **16** (1972), 173
Abercorn	W Lothian	NT078792		PC (Mon)		CiU	A C Thomas Univ Edinburgh	1963	E	of parts of monastic site of *Aebbercurnig*, now parish church and kirkyard. C7 structures, discussion of early, Irish-derived layout	*Med Arch*, **9** (1965), 177–8
Aberdeen	Aberdeens	NK961064	St Nicholas	PC		CiU	J Hunter/DoE (Scot) Soc Ant Scot	1974	E	of N transept and part of former crossing	*PSAS*, **105** (1972–4), 236–47
Abingdon	Berks	SU499969	St Mary (SS Peter & Paul)	Abb	Ben	Str	J M Fletcher G Lambrick	1968	FS	of domestic building	*Med Arch*, **13** (1969), 243
Aismunderby	N Yorks	SE304683		C?		S	C V Bellamy	1964	E	on 'Chapel Garths' site of DMV; rectangular building on E–W orientation	Med Arch, 9 (1965), 187–8
Aldridge	Staffs	SK057009	St Mary Virgin	PC		CiU	J Gould	1975	Ob	in advance of addition of new vestry	*TSSAHS*, **18** (1977), 47–52
Allerton Mauleverer	N Yorks	SE416579	St Martin	PC (Pri)	(Ben)	R	L A S Butler/ Redundant Churches Fund	1976	E	of chancel prior to repair. C12 apse and ?C14 modifications; elucidation of standing structure, mainly of c 1745. Church in possession of small priory from C12	*YAJ*, **50** (1978), 177–88
Alton Barnes	Wilts	SU109621	St Mary	PC		CiU	N P Thompson	1971–72	E	exposing A/S remains of N wall	*WAM*, **68** (1973), 71–8
		SU107620					H Ross/C J Gingell/Devizes Museum & DoE	1978	E	outside W end of church; much C11–12 pottery	*Med Arch*, **23** (1979), 246
Anglesey	Cambs	TL529624	St Mary	Pri	Aug	Str/S	P G M Dickinson	1963	S	of standing remains (now in domestic use) and plan of church, disclosed by air reconnaissance	*Med Arch*, **8** (1964), 241
Angmering	Sussex	TQ068044	St Nicholas	PC		S	O Bedwin/Sussex Arch Fld Unit	1974	E	disclosing late A/S church with apsidal chancel and subsequent modifications	*Med Arch*, **19** (1975), 238
Annan	Dumfriess	NY186712	St Bridget	C		S		1969	E	Foundations	*Med Arch*, **14** (1970), 174
Appleby Magna	Leics	SK315098	St Michael & All Angels	PC		CiU	D Parsons/Leics DAC	1975	E	prior to external drainage	*TLAHS*, **50** (1974–5), 41–5
Ardnadam	Argyll	NS163791		C		S	Cowal Archaeol Soc	1964 1973	E	of stone cell; grave markers	*Med Arch*, **9** (1965), 188; **18** (1974), 186
Ardwall Isle	Kirkcudbr	NX573496		C		S	A C Thomas/Univ Edinburgh	1964–65	E	?C5 Christian cemetery & shrine; subsequent timber oratory, stone chapel	Thomas 1967
Argyll	Argyll	NS163791		C		S		1967	E	of chapel site; C8 pottery, position of altar, evidence of cruck construction	*Med Arch*, **12** (1968), 163
Arundel	Sussex	TQ019071		Hos		S/Ru	J Evans/Worthing Museum/MPBW	1965	E	to elucidate remains of Maison Dieu Hosp.; recovery of N and W ranges, incl chapel	*Med Arch*, **10** (1966), 181
			St Nicholas	PC (Col)		CiU	Diocesan Archaeological Consultant	1976	Ob	Recording during removal of organ loft	
Asheldham	Essex	TL979013	St Lawrence	PC		R	W J Rodwell P Drury	1975–76	E	revealing C12 plan with apsidal sanctuary and towered chancel; pre-Conquest timber church; C7 occupation. Discussion of church in historic landscape	Drury & Rodwell 1978
Ashtead	Surrey	TQ193581	St Giles	PC		CiU	R Reece	1963	E	in churchyard, which is within Roman site	*Surrey AC*, **63** (1966), 173–4

(1)	(2)	(3)	(4)	(5)	(6)	(7)	(8)	(9)	(10)	(11)	(12)
Astley	Warwicks	SP311995	St Mary	PC/Coll		CiU/S	H E Brown	1961–64	E	of transept of former collegiate church	*Med Arch*, **9** (1965), 185 cf *TBAS*, **71** (1953), 59–62
Aston	Warwicks	SP082899	SS Peter & Paul	PC		CiU	M M Archibald		Ob	Find of C13–14 coins	*BNJ*, **31** (1962), 164–5
Aylesbury	Bucks	SP818129	St Mary	PC		CiU	B Durham		FS	evidence of late A/S fabric	*Rec Bucks*, **20.4** (1978)
Bangor	Caernarvons (Gwynedd)	SH580723		Mon		S	L Alcock/ Cambrian Archaeol Ass	1964	E	of supposed site of early Christian religious community; likely that site lies beneath cathedral	*Med Arch*, **9** (1965), 178
Bargham	Sussex	TQ066089		PC		S	A Barr-Hamilton		E	revealing two-cell A/S church with subsequent medieval enlargements	*Sussex AC*, **99** (1961), 38–65
Barking	Essex	TQ440840	SS Mary & Ethelburga	Abb	Ben N	S	W Essex Archaeol Group	1971	E	in vicinity of frater	*Med Arch*, **16** (1972), 173
Barnack	Cambs (Northants)	TF079051	St John Baptist	PC		CiU	D Parsons	1977	FS	of tower	*Med Arch*, **22** (1978), 142
Barrow on Humber	Humberside (Lincs)	TA074218	?			S	Humberside Archaeol Unit	1976–77	E	revealing foundations of pre-Conquest church and associated cemetery	*Med Arch*, **22** (1978), 147; final report forthcoming
Barry	Glamorgan	ST105669	St Nicholas	PC		CiU		1965	Ob	of cable laying in churchyard: structure, evidence of occupation	*Med Arch*, **10** (1966), 189
Barry Island	Glamorgan	ST119666	St Baruch	C		S	J K Knight/MPBW	1968	E	Re-excavation and planning of medieval pilgrimage chapel. Associated priest's house	*Trans Cardiff Natur Soc*, **99**, 28–65
Barton upon Humber	Humberside	TA035219	St Peter	PC		R	W J Rodwell/DoE	1978–	E FS	Total excavation of interior of tower, W annex and nave: building sequence running from C10 (tower & annex) to late medieval; pre-C10 burials, structures and wells, all contained within large oval earthwork. Project continues	*Med Arch*, **23** (1979), 239 *BCBACC*, **13** (1980), 6–9
Bath	Somerset	ST751646	SS Peter & Paul	Abb	Ben	S	J Greene/Bath Excav Cttee DoE	1971	E	Precinct wall	*Med Arch*, **16** (1972), 175
									E	to recover part of layout of medieval S transept	
							T O'Leary Bath Archaeol Trust	1979	E	of part of NE area of Anglo-Norman eastern arm, revealing a periapsidal east end; cemetery	
Bath	Somerset	ST 7564	St James	PC		S	W J Wedlake		E	of church and discussion of its setting	*PSANHS*, **110** (1966), 85–107
Battle	Sussex	TQ 747155		Abb	Ben	S	J N Hare/DoE	1978–9	E	Chapter-house, reredorter	*Med Arch*, **23** (1979), 253; **24** (1980), 240–2
Bawsey	Norfolk	TF663208		PC		Ru		1960	Ob	Discovery of A/S gravestone	*Med Arch*, **5** (1961), 309
Bayfield	Norfolk	TG049405	St Margaret	PC		Ru	D R Howlett	1956	Ob	Finding of setting for font in nave of ruined church	*Med Arch*, **1** (1957), 155
Bayham	Sussex	TQ650365	B V Mary	Abb	Pre	Ru	S E Rigold	1965	Ob	Roofing materials, window- and vessel-glass found in deposit of debris on shell of vault	*Med Arch*, **10** (1966), 181–2
Beckery (Glastonbury)	Somerset	ST485384	St Bridget	C		S	P A Rahtz/Chalice Well Trust	1967–68	E	of multi-phase chapel site; A/S cemetery	Rahtz & Hirst 1974
Bedford	Beds	TL069495	St Paul	Pri	Aug	S	W Annan D Baker	1971	E	of earthwork near C12 priory	*Med Arch*, **16** (1972), 171
Bedford	Beds	TL052494	St Mary	PC		CiU	T P Smith	1971	FS	disclosing evidence of pre-Conquest fabric	*Beds AJ*, **9** (1975)
Beverley	Humberside (E Yorks)	TA038394		Fri	Dom	S	K A MacMahon MPBW	1960–63	E	of friary site	*Med Arch*, **8** (1964), 245
Beverley	Humberside (E Yorks)	TA 038392		VC		S	P Armstrong/ Humbs Archaeol Unit	1979–81	E	of Vicars Choral complex S of Minster graveyard	*BCBACC*, **14** (1981), 12–13
Bicester	Oxon	SP584221	St Eadburg	Pri	Aug	S	D Hinton	1968	Ob	yielding facts on C12–C17 building history; use made of written sources	*Oxon*, **33** (1969), 22–52
Bidlington	Sussex	TQ178103	St Mary Magdalene	PC		S	G D Lewis	1963	E	of churchyard	*Sussex AC*, **102** (1964), 1–8
Binderton	Sussex	SU 850108		PC?		S	F Aldsworth	1976	S	locating lost Domesday church	*Sussex AC*, **117** (1979), 121–4
Binham	Norfolk	TF982400	St Mary	Pri*	Ben	S & CiU	J K Knight/MPBW	1961	E	of S and W ranges of monastic layout * (nave of church remains in parochial use)	*Med Arch*, **9** (1965), 181
Bleddfa	Radnors	SO207684	St Mary Magdalene	PC		S	L A S Butler/ Radnors Soc	1961	E	of mound in churchyard revealed collapsed tower	*T Radnors Soc*, **32** (1962), 7–9
Blore Ray	Staffs	SK138494	St Bartholomew	PC		CiU	J Gould	1975	Ob	of contractor's excavation	*SSAHST*, **17** (1977), 89–90
Bolton, Fangfoss	Yorks	SE775522		C		S	G Coppack/DoE	1973	E	Chapel of C11 origin, 3 phases	*YAJ*, **50** (1978), 93–150
Bonhunt	Essex	TL511335	St Helen	C		R	B Hooper	1967 1968	E	in vicinity of C12 chapel now used as barn; burials, occupation material, incl C5 pottery	*Med Arch*, **13** (1969), 250
Bordesley	Worcs	SP035697	St Mary	Abb	Cis	S	P Rahtz *et al*	1966–	E S	of church and conventual buildings; survey of site	*BAR*, **23** (1976)
Bosham	Sussex	SU804039	Holy Trinity	PC		CiU	M Hare	1971	FS	concentrating on A/S work in tower	*Med Arch*, **16** (1972), 163
Boston	Lincs	TF330438		Fri	Fra	S	A E Musty/DoE/ Lincs Arch Res Cttee/Ass of Lincs Life	1973	E		*Med Arch*, **18** (1974), 191
Boxley Abbey	Kent	TQ761587	St Mary Virgin	Abb	Cis	S	P J Tester		E	disclosing C12 plan	*Arch Cant*, **88** (1973), 129–58
Bradford-on-Avon	Avon	ST824609	St Laurence	C		CiU	H M Taylor		FS	Full survey and discussion of fabric	*Arch J*, **130** (1973), 141–71
Bradwell	Bucks	SP827396	St Mary	Pri	Ben	S Str	C N Gowing/Bucks County Museum D C Mynard/ Milton Keynes Devel Corp	1968 1972–73	E E Ob	Structures and excavation of chapel	*Med Arch*, **13** (1969), 243–4 *MKJAH* (1974), 31–66
Brattleby	Lincs	SK947807	St Cuthbert	PC		CiU		1972	Ob	of A/S cross shaft in churchyard	*Med Arch*, **17** (1973), 145

(1)	(2)	(3)	(4)	(5)	(6)	(7)	(8)	(9)	(10)	(11)	(12)
Breedon on the Hill	Leics	SK406234	St Mary	PC (Pri) (mon)	(Aug)	CiU	R Abbott	1959	Ob	during restoration, with finds of A/S sculpture	*TLAHS*, **39** (1963–4), 20–3
							A Dornier	1975	E	in part of churchyard extension; pre-Conquest finds and kitchen block of former priory	Dornier 1977b
Brentingby	Leics	SK785187	St Mary	C		R	P Liddle *et al*	1972–73	E Ob	Complex structural history, Norman onwards	*TLAHS*, **54** (1978–9), 1–13
Bricett	Suffolk	TM036507	St Leonard	PC (Pri)	(Aug)	CiU S	P G M Dickinson	1963	Ob	of clearance located NW transeptal tower, with evidence for apsidal chapel	*Med Arch*, **8** (1964), 244
Bristol	Avon	ST583726	St Augustine	Cath (Abb)	(Aug)	CiU/S	C Godman	1960	E	of part of conventual layout	*Med Arch*, **5** (1961), 312–13
		ST587733		Fri	Fra	S	M W Ponsford	1970 1973	E	of church, parts of conventual layout, cemetery	M Ponsford, *The Grey Friars in Bristol*
		ST585725	St Mary le Port	PC		Ru	P A Rahtz/ MPBW/Bristol City Museum	1962	E	full excavation of bombed church	*Med Arch*, **8** (1964), 249, 251
Bristol		ST591731	St Peter	PC		CiU	D P Dawson R G Jackson	1970	FS E	disclosed plaster bearing C16, C13, and C12 designs yielded evidence of kilns, and an earlier undated stone structure	*TBGAS*, **91** (1972), 159–67
Bristol		ST586732	St Bartholomew	Hosp		Str	R Price/Bristol City Museum/ Bristol CC/DoE	1977	E FS	revealing much of layout; C12–C14 evidence	*Med Arch*, **23** (1979), 248
Bristol		ST573774		Col		S Str	M Ponsford/ Bristol City Museum/MPBW	1970	E	of C15 range of Westbury College	*Med Arch*, **15** (1971), 138
Brixworth	Northants	SP748712	All Saints	PC		CiU	E D C Jackson E G M Fletcher D N Hall	1958 1971	E E	to re-examine compartments in N aisle in advance of pipe-laying at NW corner of nave	*JBAA*, **24** (1961), 1–15 *JBAA*, **130** (1977), 123–32
		SP746712					P Everson/ Brixworth Archaeol Research Cttee	1972	E	in vicarage garden: part of monastic site?	*JBAA*, **130** (1977), 55–122
							D Parsons *et al*/ BARC	1976–	FS	including drawing of elevations, petrological study of building materials, analysis	Parsons 1977 *Med Arch*, **23** (1979), 241–2
Broadfield	Herts	TL325312		PC		S	P A Rahtz E C Klingelhofer MPBW	1965	E	of DMV, including church and cemetery	*BAR*, **2** (1974)
Brough of Birsay	Orkney	HY239285		?		S	C D Morris/ University of Durham/SDD		E	of possible episcopal complex, incl church and cemetery	*Med Arch*, **22** (1978), 153–4
Brough of Deerness	Orkney	HY596087		C		S	C D Morris/ University of Durham/SDD	1975–77	E	of chapel and enclosure	*Med Arch*, **22** (1978), 155
Bullingham	Herefords	SO511371	St Peter	PC		Ru	R Shoesmith	1968	Ob	Prompted by summary clearance of Old Church site and reduction of walls	*TWNFC*, **40** (1970), 71–4
Burgh Castle	Suffolk	TG474045		?		S	C Green	1960–61	E	within Saxon shore fort revealing huts, cemetery, structures	*Med Arch*, **6–7** (1962–3), 311 Discussion in Cramp 1976a, 212–15
Burnham	S Humberside (Lincs)	TA058172	St Lawrence	C		S	G Coppack R Williams/DoE	1977	E	of church of DMV established early C10 and abandoned in C16	*BCBAAC*, **8** (1978), 5–6
Burry Holms	Glamorgan (W Glam)	SS400925		Pri		Ru/S	D B Hague	1965–69	E	of dependant priory, early C8–14	*RCAHM Glamorgan* I.iii, 14
Burton on Trent	Derbys	SK2522		Abb	Ben		C O'Brien		E		*TSSAHS*, **19** (1977)
Bury St Edmunds	Suffolk	TL857642	St Edmund	Abb	Ben	Ru	MPBW	1957–66	E	during consolidation disclosed plan of presbytery and eastern apse	*PSIAH*, **31** (1969), 256–62
Cadbury	Somerset	ST6225		?		S	L Alcock		E	of post-Roman complex within hillfort revealed traces of possible cruciform church	Alcock 1972, 198–200
Camborne	Cornwall	SW658382	St Ia	C		S	A C Thomas N D Thomas	1962–63	E	Chapel of *c* 1000 located and excavated	*Med Arch*, **8** (1964), 231
Cambridge	Cambs	TL446581		Fri	Crm	S	P V Addyman M Biddle	1959	E	Excavation for new building at Queen's College revealed clunch footings and burials	*Proc Cambs AS*, **58** (1965), 74–137
Cambridge		TL450584		Fri	Fra	S	P Salway	1959	E	on site of friary church of 1267	*Med Arch*, **4** (1960), 139
Campsea Ash	Suffolk	TM318545	B V Mary	Pri	Aug N	Ru	D Sherlock	1970	E	in S aisle of choir	*PSIAH*, **32** (1971), 121–39
Canons Ashby	Northants	SP578505	B V Mary	Pri	Aug	Ru/CiU	S J Taylor/MPBW	1969	E	claustral buildings	*Northants Archaeol*, **9** (1974)
Canterbury	Kent	TR148579		Fri	Dom	S	L Millard/ Canterbury Archaeol Soc/ MPBW	1970	E	confirming S wall of chapter-house and N wall of church	*Med Arch*, **15** (1971), 139
Canterbury	Kent	TR148579	Christ Church	Cat (Pri)	(Ben)	CiU	Canterbury Archaeol Soc	1973	Ob	of trench dug for dean and chapter revealed part of Roman or A/S buildings	*Med Arch*, **18** (1974), 179
							Canterbury Archaeol Trust	1979–80	E	at exterior of St Gabriel's chapel: Roman building	*BCBACC*, **12** (1980), 18–19
Canterbury		TR146577		Fri	Fra	S	Canterbury Archaeol Soc	1972–73	E	on site of Greyfriars	*Med Arch*, **18** (1974), 191
Canterbury		TR147580	St Peter	PC		CiU	T P Smith		FS	Saxo-Norman work in tower, *c* 1075–1115	*Arch Cant*, **86** (1971), 99–108
Canterbury		TR154579	St Augustine	Abb	Ben	S Ru	A D Saunders MPBW/DoE	1955–58	E	clarifying pre-Conquest layout, including western chapel with western apse, and SW tower	Saunders 1978
Canterbury							H M Woods/DoE	–1977	E		*Med Arch*, **22** (1978), 158–9
Canterbury		TR155777	St Pancras	?		Ru	F Jenkins/DoE	1973–75	E	leading to revised phasing for A/S church	*Canterbury Archaeol*, (1976), 4–5 cf Thomas 1980
Canterbury		TR143583	St Dunstan	PC		CiU	Canterbury Archaeol Trust		E	of Roper Chantry	Tatton-Brown 1980
Canterbury		TR158577	St Martin	PC		CiU	Canterbury Archaeol Trust	1978	FS	recording elevations of church	

(1)	(2)	(3)	(4)	(5)	(6)	(7)	(8)	(9)	(10)	(11)	(12)
Canterbury		TR150590		Pri	Aug	S	F Jenkins	1958	Ob	of structure during building of Post office	*Med Arch*, **3** (1959), 305
Canterbury		TR148576	St Mary Bredin	PC		S	Canterbury Archaeol Trust	1980–	E	of St Mary Bredin – in progress	
Canterbury		TR151582	St Mary Northgate	PC		CiU	Canterbury Archaeol Trust	1977	E FS	Church built against Roman city wall	*Curr Archaeol*, **62** (1978), 80–1
Capel Erbach	Carmarthen	SN530147		C		Ru	G R Jones W H Morris		E	of medieval well chapel	*Carmarthen Antiq*, **7** (1971), 48–57
Capel Newydd	Caernarvon	SH286309		C		Ru	D B Hague	1956	FS	Independent chapel of 1770	*Arch Camb*, **105** (1956), 142–4
Carlisle	Cumbria	NY400558		Fri	Dom	S	M McCarthy/DoE/ Carlisle City C	1977	E	Cemetery of Blackfriars?	*Med Arch*, **22** (1978), 156
Carlton	Beds	SP952548	St Mary	PC		CiU	M J Hare		FS	A/S two-cell structure	*Beds AJ*, **6** (1971), 33–40
Carno	Montgoms	SN962966		Hosp		S	W G Putnam	1964	E	supposed Roman fort re-used in Middle Ages, perhaps by Knights Hospitallers of St John	*Montgomery Collect*, **62.2** (1972), 195–201
Castle Acre	Norfolk	TF814148	St Mary SS Peter & Paul	Pri	Clu	Ru	J K Knight/MPBW	1964	E	of apses of Anglo-Norman chapter-house; C14 rebuilding	*Med Arch*, **9** (1965), 181
Castletown	Isle of Man	SC263674	St Mary	C		CiU	A M Cubbon		E	south aisle of medieval chapel	*PIOMNHAS*, **7.3** (1968–70), 307–42
Castor	Northants	TL125985	St Kyneburga	PC*		CiU	C Green	1958	E	in churchyard extension revealed Roman building	
							G B Dannell J P Wild/Nene Valley Res Cttee/ Middle Nene Archaeol Group	1970–71	E	in churchyard extension yielded Middle Saxon pottery, possible structure	*Med Arch*, **16** (1972), 158 cf *BNFAS* (1971), 13–19 Wild 1978, 59–69
Caterham	Surrey	TQ337554	St Lawrence	PC		CiU	M Saaler/Bourne Society	1968	E	around church	*Med Arch*, **13** (1969), 251
Cefn (Capel Ffynnon Fair)	Denbighs	SJ029711	St Mary	C		Ru	C F Wright		E	and clearance of chapel and well	*TAMS*, **15** (1967–68), 59–82
Cheddar	Somerset	ST457532		?		S	P A Rahtz/MPBW	1960–62	E	Saxon and medieval palace and chapel	*BAR*, **65** (1979)
Cheddar		ST460527	St Andrew	PC		CiU	P A Rahtz	1965	E	in vicarage garden near church; post-Roman structures; possible minster complex	*PSANHS*, **110** (1966), 52–84
Chelmsford	Essex	TL709065		Fri	Dom	S	E Sellers/MPBW/ Chelmsford Exc Cttee	1969–73	E	of parts of Dominican friary layout	*Med Arch*, **18** (1974), 188–9 *Curr Archaeol*, **41** (1973), 176
							P Drury	1973	E	reredorter	*EAH*, **6** (1974), 40–81
Chepstow St Kynemark's	Monmouths	ST526942	St John the Baptist	Pri	Aug	S	L A S Butler/ MPBW	1962–65	E	of Augustinian layout; church not located; cemetery	*Monmouth Antiq*, **2.i** (1965), 33–41
Chepstow		ST536939	St Mary	Pri	Ben	CiU	R Shoesmith/DoE	1973–74	E	of conventual buildings to S of church	*Med Arch*, **19** (1975), 237
Chester	Cheshire	SJ403659	St Mary	Pri	Ben N	S	S N McNamee/ Grosvenor Mus	1964	E	revealing chapel and cloisters	*Med Arch*, **9** (1965), 179
Chester		ST402601		Fri	Dom	S	T J Strickland/ Chester City C/ DoE	1977	E	revealing nave and N aisle of church	*Med Arch*, **23** (1979), 249
Chichester	W Sussex	SZ860048	Holy Trinity	Cat		CiU	M Rule	1966–68	E	showing radial apse of ambulatory and ?pre-Norman graves	
Chichester				Fri	Dom	S	Chichester Excavation Soc	1975	E	Cemetery of Blackfriars	*Med Arch*, **20** (1976), 180
Chichester			St Andrew	PC		R	F Aldsworth/ Chichester Excavations Cttee	1975–76	E	in advance of alteration	
Christchurch	Hants	SZ161924	Christ Church	PC (Pri)	(Aug)	CiU	M Ridley/ Bournemouth Archaeol Soc	1968	E	near church. Finds	*Med Arch*, **13** (1969), 244–6
Christchurch	Hants	SZ144952		C		S	M Ridley/ Bournemouth Archaeol Soc	1967–69	E	Sequence of chapels from C11–16	*Med Arch*, **14** (1970), 168
Cirencester	Gloucs	SP022023	St John Evangelist	Hosp		S	R Leech/ CRAAGS	1976	E	Infirmary hall of hospital	*Med Arch*, **21** (1977), 223–4
Cirencester		SP023023	St Mary	Abb	Aug	S Ru	J S Wacher A D McWhirr/ Cirencester Excav Cttee	1964–66	E	on site of C12 abbey; pre-Conquest church with burials	Brown & McWhirr 1966; 1967; P D C Brown 1976
Clapham	Beds	TL035525	St Thomas	PC		CiU	M J Hare	1971	FS	makes case for Saxo-Norman tower	*Beds AJ*, **8** (1973)
Clare	Suffolk	TL770450		Pri	Aug	S	P G M Dickinson	1963	Ob	of clearance and laying out of site as lawn	*Med Arch*, **8** (1964), 244
Clopton	Cambs	TL302488		PC		S	J Alexander	1961–64	E	of church and churchyard	*Med Arch*, **9** (1965), 184, 208
Colchester	Essex	TL995245		?		S	P J Crummy/ Colchester Excav Cttee	1972	E	of lost A/S church in grounds of St John's Abbey; church lies within area of Late Roman cemetery	*Med Arch*, **17** (1973), 139–40 Crummy 1980
Colchester		TL998252	St Nicholas	PC		S	M R Hull/ Colchester Mus	1956	Ob	after demolition of church identified Roman building	Hull 1960
Colchester		TL998248	St Giles	PC		R	Colchester Archaeol Unit	1975	E	in nave of church, suggesting C12 origin	*Med Arch*, **20** (1976), 181
Coldingham	Berwicks	NT904659		Pri	Ben	CiU Ru	H Clarke/ Edinburgh Univ	1967	E	of part of conventual layout	*Med Arch*, **12** (1968), 171–3
Coulsdon	Surrey	TQ313582	St John Evangelist	PC		CiU	L Ketteringham/ Bourne Soc Archaeol Group	1975	E		*Surrey AC*, **71** (1977), 101–10
Coventry	Warwicks	SP336792	St Mary	Cat Pri	Ben	S	P Woodfield B Hobley	1960–67	E	revealing parts of cathedral priory layout	*TBAS*, **84** (1967–70), 45–139
Coventry		SP345783		Pri	Car	S	B Hobley/MPBW/ Coventry City Mus	1968	E	part of Charterhouse layout	*Med Arch*, **13** (1969), 248
Coventry		SP340787		Fri	Crm	S	C Woodfield/ Coventry City Mus		E	Church and N of cloister	
Crail	Fife	NO613079		PC		CiU	R B K Stevenson	1962–63	Ob	during restoration revealed details suggesting C13 date for part of tower; jar found just below tower floor	*Med Arch*, **8** (1964), 250
Creake, North	Norfolk	TF856395	St Mary de Pratis	Abb	Aug	Ru	MPBW	1957	E		*Med Arch*, **2** (1958), 191
Croxden	Staffs	SK067397	St Mary	Abb	Cis	Ru	MPBW	1956	E		*Med Arch*, **2** (1958), 191
Croyde	Devon	SS442390	St Helen	C		Ru	J M Crowley	1952	E	of ruined chapel	*TDA*, **86** (1954), 166–72
Cuddington	Surrey	TQ228631		PC		S	M Biddle/MPBW/ Nonsuch Palace Excav Cttee	1959	E	revealed church underlying Tudor palace layout; extensive graveyard	*Med Arch*, **4** (1960), 143–5

(1)	(2)	(3)	(4)	(5)	(6)	(7)	(8)	(9)	(10)	(11)	(12)
Dartington	Devon	SX797627	St Mary	PC		Ru	A Hamlin	1968	E	Site of former parish church	*Med Arch*, **13** (1969), 250
Dean	Cumberland	NY068256	St Oswald	PC		CiU	J Hughes		Ob		*TCWAAS*, **70** (1970), 289–90
Deerhurst	Gloucs	SO871300	St Mary	PC (Pri)	(Ben)	CiU	P A Rahtz/ Birmingham Univ	1971–73	E	of ruined apsidal east end	*CBA Res Rep*, **15** (1976)
							L A S Butler	1974–80	E	Research project focused on	L A S Butler *et al* 1975
							P A Rahtz		FS	fabric and site of A/S	
							H M Taylor		S	monastic church (now PC); limited excavation; research into written sources	*Deerhurst Studies I* (1977)
Denbigh	Denbighs	SJ054658				Ru	L A S Butler		FS	and discussion of Lord Leicester's church	Butler 1974, 40–62
Denny	Cambs	TL494685		Abb	Ben KT Fra(N)	Ru		1968–75	E		*Arch J*, **137** (1980), 138–279
Derby		SK3536	St Alkmund	PC		R	C A R Radford	1967–68	E	prior to demolition. C9 origin	*DAJ*, **96** (1976), 26–61
Dover	Kent		St Edmund	C			P A Rahtz	1968	E		*KAR*, **21** (1970), 3–7
							B Philp	1978	E		
Dover		TR318414	St Martin	Col		S	B J Philp Kent Archaeol Rescue Unit	1973–74	E	Nave and part of transept of collegiate church of St Martin le Grand	*Med Arch*, **20** (1976), 182
		TR318413					B J Philp Kent Archaeol Rescue Unit	1978	E	Graves and timber buildings of pre-Conquest ?monastic site	*Med Arch*, **23** (1979), 240
Dunstable	Beds			Fri	Dom	S	Manshead Soc			Cemetery, structures	
Durham	Co. Durham	NZ273429	SS Mary & Cuthbert (Pri)	Cat	(Ben)	CiU	RCHM	1961	Ob	of repairs to frater	*Med Arch*, **6–7** (1962–3), 313–15
Earls Barton	Northants	SP852637	All Saints	PC		CiU	M Andovy/ Northants County Council/ DoE	1979	E	in angle between tower and S aisle	*Med Arch*, **24** (1980), 229
Edinburgh				PC		R	N M McQ Holmes	1974	E	within Tron Kirk	*Post Med Arch*, **9** (1975), 137–63
Elstow	Beds	TL049474		Abb	Ben N	S	D Baker Beds Archaeol Soc	1965–71	E	Nunnery of *c* 1078. Pre-existing cemetery. Excavation disclosed chapter-house, conventual buildings	*Med Arch*, **16** (1972), 171–2; *Beds AJ*, **6** (1971), 55–64
Eriswell	Suffolk	TL721807		PC?		S Str	Lady Briscoe		Ob	Parchmark revealing outline of chancel and W tower of lost church; E part of nave survives as secular building	*Med Arch*, **8** (1964), 250
Escomb	Durham	NZ189301	St John Evangelist	PC		CiU	M Pocock H Wheeler	1968	E	elucidating two flanking *porticus*, W chamber	*JBAA*, **34** (1971), 11–29
							B Gill	1979	E	of churchyard boundary	*Med Arch*, **24** (1980), 244–5
Ewen	Gloucs	SU004975		PC?		S	R Reece	1970	E	Site of (?) dismantled medieval church; stone structures, Roman, post-Roman, and C12–13 pottery; nothing later than 1300	*Med Arch*, **15** (1971), 144
Ewenny	Glamorgan	SS912778		Pri	Ben	CiU	MPBW	1956	Ob	of removal of C19 buttresses, unblocking of arch leading to transept chapel	*Med Arch*, **1** (1957), 154
Exeter	Devon	SX922922		Fri	Fra	S	A Hamlin *et al*/ Exeter Univ/ Exeter Archaeol Field Unit	1973	E	? E end of friary church	*Med Arch*, **18** (1974), 188
Exeter		SX902925	St Mary Major	PC		S	P T Bidwell/Exeter Archaeol Field Unit	1971–77	E	in cathedral close revealing (a) C5–C7 burials; (b) cemetery of presumed C7 monastery; (c) Late Saxon minster (site of C11 see); medieval parish church, rebuilt in 1864 and demolished in 1971	Bidwell 1978; 1979
Exeter	Devon	SX917925	St Nicholas	Pri	Ben	S	M G Griffiths	1971	E	on site of church	*Med Arch*, **16** (1972), 173
Eynsham	Oxon	SP434091		Abb	Ben	S	M Gray	1971	E	to determine E limit of abbey revealed pre-Conquest cemetery E of parish church	*Oxon*, **43** (1979), 100–22
Faversham	Kent	TR020617		Abb	Clu	S	B Philp/MPBW	1965	E	recovering plan of church	Philp 1968
Felixstowe	See under Walton, Suffolk										
Fleet Marston	Bucks	SP779159	St Mary	PC		R	M Farley	1975	E	within church; origin of *c* 1200 suggested	*Med Arch*, **20** (1976), 180
Frocester	Gloucs	SO771033	St Peter	PC		S	H S Gracie	1958	E	on site of demolished C19 church on site of (?) A/S minster; Roman building and post-Roman graves below	*TBGAS*, **82** (1963), 148–67
Furness	Cumbria	SD223715		Abb	Cis	Ru	J C Dickinson/ MPBW		Ob	Report on clearance of site	*TCWAAS*, **67** (1967), 51–80
Garendon	Leics	SK502199		Abb	Cis	S	B C J Williams/ Loughborough & District Archaeol Soc	1968	E		*Med Arch*, **13** (1969), 246 *Citeaux*
Gedgrave	Suffolk	TM405486		C		S		1969	Ob	of disturbance of (?) chapel site for foundation of new barn	*Med Arch*, **14** (1970), 174
Glasgow	Lanarks	NS603656	St Mungo	Cat		CiU	G Hay/MPBW	1965	Ob	of stonework under effigy of Bishop Wishart	*Med Arch*, **11** (1967), 282–3
Glasgow		NS597653		Fri	Obs	S	E Talbot	1969	E	of enclosure and church of C15	*Med Arch*, **14** (1970), 171
Glastonbury	Somerset	ST500387		Abb	Ben	Ru	C A R Radford	1954–64	E	of parts of early layout; C12 church	Radford 1968
Glastonbury		ST501389					P Ellis R Leech/ CRAAGS	1978	E	monastic precinct boundary	*Med Arch*, **23** (1979), 242–3
Glastonbury Beckery: see under Beckery											
Glastonbury Tor	Somerset	ST513386	St Michael	C		Ru S	P A Rahtz/Chalice Well Trust	1964–66	E	disclosing post-Roman occupation, medieval church sequence	*Arch J*, **127** (1970), 1–81
Glencairn	Dumfries	NX809905	St Cuthbert	PC		Ru		1969	E		*Med Arch*, **14** (1970), 174
Glentworth	Lincs	SK945881	St Michael	PC		CiU		1972	Ob	of clearance revealed A/S graveslab in W tower	*Med Arch*, **17** (1973), 145
Gloucester	Gloucs	SO832185	St Michael	PC		R	M D Cra'ster	1956	E	Site of demolished church	*TBGAS*, **80** (1961), 59–74

(1)	(2)	(3)	(4)	(5)	(6)	(7)	(8)	(9)	(10)	(11)	(12)
Gloucester		SO8218	Holy Trinity	PC		S	Gloucester Mus	1959	Ob	of gas main trench; traces of church demolished in 1698? Norman font	Med Arch, 4 (1960), 143
Gloucester		SO831183		Fri	Fra	S	D C Mynard/ MPBW	1967	E	disclosing plan	Med Arch, 12 (1968), 166
Gloucester		SO830184		Fri	Dom	S Str	C J Gray/DoE	1978	E	in transept	Med Arch, 23 (1979), 250–2
							P J Brown/DoE	1975	E	nave and S aisle	Med Arch, 20 (1976), 177
							J Blair J M Fletcher O Rackham	1974	FS	of roofs of church and conventual buildings	Med Arch, 22 (1978), 105–22
Gloucester		SO831188	SS Peter & Paul	Cat (Abb)	(Ben)	CiU	C Heighway	1976	Ob FS	during disturbance of N transept wall; C14 tile floor, wall painting	Med Arch, 21 (1977), 225
Gloucester		SO830190	St Oswald	Pri	Aug	Ru	C Heighway R Bryant/ Gloucester City Excav Unit	1975–	E FS	elucidating pre-Norman to C19 building sequence	Antiq J, 58 (1978), 103–32
Gloucester		SO829189	St Mary de Lode	PC		CiU	R Bryant/ Gloucester City Excav Unit	1978 1979	E	Roman building succeeded by C5–6 timber structure enclosing burials; later A/S and medieval development of church	BCBACC, 13 (1980), 15–18
Godstow	Oxon	SP483092	SS Mary & John Baptist	Abb	Ben N	S Str	R E Linnington/ Oxford Univ Archaeol Soc	1960	E	N of existing buildings revealed C12 structures	Med Arch, 5 (1961), 313
Grace Dieu	Leics	SK435184		Pri	Aug	S	E J Miller/ Loughborough & District Archaeol Soc	1968	E	Priory converted to manor house	Med Arch, 13 (1969), 246
Grafton Regis	Northants	SP752467	SS Mary & Michael?	Pri	Aug	S	C Mahany/MPBW	1964–65	E	(?) Priory or hermitage; eccles. layout and domestic buildings	Med Arch, 10 (1966), 202–4 cf G Parker, Northants Past Present (1981–2), 247–52
Great Linford	Bucks	SP852423	St Andrew	PC		CiU	R J Williams/ Milton Keynes Dev Corp	1979–80	Ob E	Medieval monument, tile pavement, brass, pre-1100 structure	BCBACC, 13 (1980), 18–22
Great Paxton	Hunts	TL210642	Holy Trinity	PC		CiU	P G M Dickinson/ Hunts Local History Soc	1970–71	FS E	and excavation of site of N transept	Med Arch, 16 (1972), 156
Great Yarmouth	Norfolk	TG527068		Fri	Dom	S	C G Rye	1970	E		Med Arch, 15 (1971), 139
Greensted-juxta-Ongar	Essex	TL540030	St Andrew	PC		CiU	H Christie A R Dufty B Hope-Taylor O Olsen	1960	E	in chancel	Christie et al 1979
Grosmont	Monmouths	SO405243	St Nicholas	PC		CiU	C R Currie	1971	FS	of roof of disused nave	Med Arch, 16 (1972), 179
Grove	See under Leighton Buzzard										
Guildford	Surrey	SU994495		Fri	Dom	S	F W Holling/ Guildford Mus	1973–74	E	revealing foundations	Poulton & Alexander 1979
Guildford		SU996493	St Mary	PC		CiU	F W Holling	1966–67	Ob	of foundations during restoration	Surrey AC, 64 (1967), 165–8
Guildford		SU994493	St Nicholas	PC		CiU	Guildford Group	1977	E	adjacent to C15 chantry chapel	Surrey Archaeol Bulletin
Hadstock	Essex	TL559447	St Botolph	PC		CiU	W J Rodwell/DoE Soc of Antiqs/ Essex Archaeol Soc	1973–	E FS	demonstrating longer building history than previously thought; 'Late Saxon' details in secondary positions; study of standing fabric	Antiq J, 56 (1976), 55–71
Hailes	Gloucs	SP050300		Abb	Cis	Ru	P J Brown et al/ DoE	1971–77	E	during consolidation of remains	Med Arch, 22 (1978), 157
Halesowen	Worcs	SO975828	B V Mary	Abb	Pre	Ru	C J Bond	1970	E	guest house, earthwork round abbey	Worcs Archaeol Newsletter, 5 (1970), 10
Haltemprice	Yorks	TA050332	St Mary Virgin & Holy Cross	Pri	Aug	S		1959	Ob	of angle of building uncovered by owners of site	Med Arch, 4 (1960), 140
Hamble	Hants	SU482067	St Andrew	PC (Pri)	(Tir)	CiU	M Hughes		E		PHFCAS, 37 (1981), 23–39
Harlowbury	Essex	TL478119		C		CiU	C A Hewett H M Taylor		FS	suggesting that Norman features were inserted into pre-existing fabric; late-A/S roof?	Med Arch, 23 (1979), 223–5
Hartley	Kent	TQ602663		C		S	J E L Caiger	1967	S	of earthworks and (?) chapel	Arch Cant, 82 (1967), 285
Harwell	Berks	SU493890	St Matthew	PC		CiU	J M Fletcher P S Spoker	1962	E	Stone coffins, mortuary chalice	Berks AJ, 61 (1963–4), 37–9
Hastings	Sussex	TQ815094	Holy Trinity	Pri	Aug	S	D Martin/Hastings Area Archaeol Group	1972	E	C12 priory	Hastings Area Archaeol Pap, 2 (1973)
Haughmond	Salop	SJ542152	St John	Abb	Aug	S	R Robertson-Mackay/MPBW	1958	E	Infirmary hall, kitchen	Med Arch, 3 (1959), 305
							J J West/DoE	1975	E		Med Arch, 20 (1976), 179–80
Haverholme	Lincs	TF109493		Pri	Gil	S	M U Jones/MPBW	1963–64	E	buildings, variety of finds	Med Arch, 9 (1965), 181
Healing	Humbs (Lincs)	TA214102	SS Peter & Paul	PC		CiU	H Bishop/DoE	1975	E	of C13 S aisle, possible A/S foundation on S side of chancel; unidentified metal vessel	LAH, 13 (1978), 25–32
Hereford	Herefords	SO513405		Fri	Dom	S	L A S Butler/ MPBW	1958	E		TWNFC, 36.3 (1960), 334–42
Hereford		SO514396	St Guthlac	PC		S	F G Heys J F L Norwood	1960	E	C12 church; earlier burials	TWNFC, 36 (1960), 343–57
							R Shoesmith	1965–76	E		Shoesmith 1980
Herne	Kent	TR182658		C			B Philp H Gough		E	Saxo-Norman apsidal chancel	KAR, 44 (1979)
Hexham	Northumb	NY935640	St Andrew	PC (Pri)	(Aug)	CiU	R N Bailey D O'Sullivan	1978	E	over crypt	Archaeol Aeliana, 5, ser 7 (1979), 144–57
Heysham	Lancs	SD411617	St Patrick	C		Ru	T Potter R D Andrews	1977	E	demonstrating that preceding chapel was shorter than present structure	BCBACC, 8 (1978), 2
Higham	Kent	TQ717742	B V Mary	Pri	Ben N	S	P J Tester/Kent Archaeol Soc	1966	E	Site of small church and claustral range explored	Arch Cant, 82 (1967), 143–61
Hinchingbrooke	Hunts	TL228715	St James	Pri	Ben N	S	P G M Dickinson	1965–67	E		Med Arch, 12 (1968), 166–7

(1)	(2)	(3)	(4)	(5)	(6)	(7)	(8)	(9)	(10)	(11)	(12)
Hinton	Somerset	ST778592	St Mary Virgin	Pri	Car	S Ru	P Fletcher	1950–58	E	Church and priory; chapter-house standing as manor house	PSANHS, 103 (1958–9), 76–80
Hirsel, The	Berwicks	NT831407				S	R J Cramp/SDD/ Univ Durham/ Douglas & Angus Estates	1979–	S E	Church, cemetery, early settlement	PSAS, 109 (1977–8), 223–32
Holton-le-Clay	Humbs (Lincs)	TA286028	St Peter	PC		CiU	F Heath; J Sills	1973–; 1975	E E	outside nave and tower, investigation of churchyard boundary	BCBACC, 2 (1975); Report in LAH imminent
Horsham St Faith	Norfolk	TG216152	St Mary Virgin	Pri	Ben	S	D Sherlock/ MPBW	1970	E	Farmhouse occupying frater range	Norfolk Archaeol, 36 (1976), 202–23
Huish	Wilts	SU145637	St Nicholas	PC		CiU	N P Thompson	1966	E	C13 church and adjacent chapel; C15 paving; beneath rebuilding of 1785	WAM, 62 (1967), 51–66
Hulton	Staffs	SU905493		Abb	Cis	S	D Leake	1961–	E		Med Arch, 11 (1967), 276
							J Newey/Stoke-on-Trent Mus Archaeol Soc	1964–66			
						Str		1974–76	E	in chancel	Med Arch, 21 (1977), 227
							S J Greaves	1979	E	in transept	Med Arch, 24 (1980), 240
Huntingdon	Hunts	TL236714		C		S	B K Davison/ MPBW	1967	E	Roman villa, Christian cemetery, late A/S church, C12 defences	Med Arch, 12 (1968), 175
Icklingham	Suffolk	TL783719				S	S West		E	Late Roman inhumation cemetery on earlier (?) religious site; associated buildings, incl probable church and baptistry	East Anglian Archaeol, 3 (1976), 63–125
Iken	Suffolk	TM412567	St Botolph	PC		Ru	S West	1978	FS E	A/S sculpture, pre-Norman graves and structural evidence. Candidate for Icanho	Med Arch, 23 (1979), 245–6
Ingrave	Essex	TQ622930	St Nicholas	PC		S	C R Couchman		E	on site of old church	EAH, 9 (1977)
Iona	Argyll	NM287245		Abb	Ben	S	A C Thomas/Univ Edinburgh	1956–59	E	Earthwork of monastery under present abbey; church of c 1200, earlier structures	Med Arch, 21 (1977), 228
							M Redknap	1976	E	Site of 'St Columba's Shrine'	PSAS, 108 (1976–7), 228–53
								1964–74	E	Burials, vallum, later economic buildings	Univ London Inst Archaeol Occas Publ, 5 (1981)
Ipswich	Suffolk			Fri	Dom	S	K Wade J Blatchley	1976	E	Corner of chapter-house, (?) Sacristy; clarification of earlier observations	PSIAH, 34 (1977), 25–34
Ipswich		TM161442		Fri	Fra	S	K Wade S Dunmore Ipswich Archaeol Soc	1974	E	Precinct wall	Med Arch, 19 (1975), 236
Irthlingborough	Northants	SP951703	All Saints	PC		S	G Brown/MPBW	1965	E	after levelling of site. Total excavation	RPNAS, 65.1 (1964–6), 2–18
Island of Tean	Cornwall	NG910165	St Theona	C		Ru	B Wailes J V S Megaw	1956	E	Chapel partly overlying series of Christian graves	Med Arch, 1 (1957), 147
Islay	Argyll	NS007772		C			H Millar/Glasgow Archaeol Soc	1964	E	Castle chapel	Med Arch, 9 (1965), 188
Islay		NR330605		C		S	N Logan	1960	E	Site of (?) chapel, burial ground	Med Arch, 5 (1961), 318
		NR227552		C		S	B R S Megaw	1960	E	Early chapel, burial ground, oval enclosure	Med Arch, 5 (1961), 318
Ixworth	Suffolk	TL931703	B V Mary	Pri	Aug	S	P G M Dickinson	1962–63	E	Church, prior's house, dorter, refectory	Med Arch, 8 (1964), 244
Jarrow	Tyne & Wear (Durham)	NZ337653	St Paul	Pri	Ben	CiU	R Cramp/Univ Durham C D Morris	1963–76	E	Layout of C7–C8 monastic community	Cramp 1969 Cramp 1976b Med Arch, 21 (1977), 214, 227–8
Kelso	Roxburgh	NT729338		Abb	Tir	S	C J Tabraham/ DoE	1971 1974–76	E	Transept, nave, domestic buildings	Med Arch, 21 (1977), 228
Kenley	Surrey	TQ321594		PC		S	M Saaler	1966	E	Foundations of (?) church, burials	Med Arch, 11 (1967), 283
Kennington	Kent	TR033437		C		S	P Keeling/Ashford Archaeol Soc	1976	E	Rectangular building on reputed site of Conningbrook chapel	Med Arch, 20 (1976), 182
Kersey	Suffolk	TL999445		Hos		S	P G M Dickinson	1958–62	E	Plan of church, early wooden buildings, prior's house	Med Arch, 8 (1964), 244
Keynsham	Avon (Somerset)	ST656696	B V Mary SS Peter & Paul	Abb	Aug	S	E Greenfield/ MPBW	1956	E	Footings and evidence of cemetery near parish church of St John	Grinsell 1956 Greenfield 1960
		ST656688					B Lowe A Vince/Folk House Archaeol Club	1964– 1969–70	Ob E		Med Arch, 15 (1971), 140 Summary of recent work in Leech 1975
Kilwinning	Ayrshire	NS304433		Pri	?Ben	S	MPBW	1961	E	Clearance and excavation of C12 church	Med Arch, 6–7 (1962–3), 318
Kings Langley	Bucks	TL064024		Fri	Dom	S	R Fisher	1956	E	Foundations on (?) site of church	Herts Archaeol, 3 (1973), 31–72
Kingston upon Hull	Humbs (Yorks E R)	TA100284		Fri	Aus	S	J B Whitwell/ Humbs Archaeol Unit	1976	E		Med Arch, 21 (1977), 225
Kirkhill	Northumb	NT975008		C		S	R Miket	1972	E	recovering plan of chapel site; Bronze Age cremation burials within area of medieval churchyard	Archaeol Aeliana, 5, ser 2 (1972), 153–87
Kirkmahoe	Dumfries	NX989818	St Blane	C		S		1969	Ob	Site of chapel	Med Arch, 14 (1970), 174
Kirkstall	W Yorks	SE259361	St Mary	Abb	Cis	Ru		1950–64		Abbot's house, kitchen, infirmary	Publ Thoresby Soc, 48 (1961); 51 (1967)
							J Thorpe/Leeds City C/W Yorks Archaeol Unit	1978–79	E	Clearance of guesthouse	
Latchingdon	Essex	TQ888987	St Michael	PC		R	C Couchman/ Essex County C	1976	E	Excavation in advance of conversion of redundant church	Med Arch, 21 (1977), 230
Leeds	Kent	TQ823530	SS Mary & Nicholas	Pri	Aug	S	P J Tester/Kent Archaeol Soc	1973–75	E	Outline of priory, cloister range	Arch Cant, 93 (1977), 33–46; 94 (1978), 75–98

(1)	(2)	(3)	(4)	(5)	(6)	(7)	(8)	(9)	(10)	(11)	(12)
Leicester	Leics	SK585044		C Hos			T C Pearce/Leeds Mus	1973	E	Chapel of Wygeston's hospital	Post Med Arch, 8 (1974)
Leicester		SK580044		Fri	Aug	S	J Mellor & T C Pearce/Leics Mus	1973–75	E	Cloister ranges	CBA Res Rep, 35 (1981)
Leighton Buzzard (Grove)	Beds	SP923227		Pri	Ben (Font)	S Ru	E Baker/Beds County C/DoE	1973–78	E	of priory site; underlying A/S occupation	Med Arch, 23 (1979), 248
Lenton	Notts		Holy Trinity	Pri	Clu	S		1962–64	E		TTS, 70 (1966)
Leominster	Herefs	SO497593		C		CiU	J W Tonkin	1971	S	of Forbury chapel; C15 roof	TWNHFC, 40.ii (1972)
Levisham	N Yorks	SE832901	St Mary	PC		R	R A Hall/DoE/ Univ Bradford	1976	E FS	prior to conversion	
Lewes	Sussex	TQ414094	St Pancras	Pri	Clu	S Ru	R Lewis	1972–	E		Med Arch, 17 (1973), 156
Lichfield	Staffs	SK092092	SS Mary and Chad	Cat		CiU S	J Gould	1975	E	of conduit in cathedral close	Med Arch, 20 (1976), 183
Lichfield		SK124095	St Michael	PC		CiU	J Gould	1974	S	of hilltop graveyard around church	TSSAHS, 16 (1974–5)
							P R Wilson/ Birmingham Univ Field Unit	1978	E	in advance of extension	Med Arch, 23 (1979), 259
Liddesdale	Roxburghs	NY537914		C		Ru	R E Scott	1958	E	of chapel	Med Arch, 3 (1959), 307
Lilleshall	Salop	SJ737143	B V Mary	Abb	Aug	S	J K Knight/MPBW	1961	E	foundations of church	Med Arch, 6–7 (1962–3), 316–17
Lincoln	Lincs	SK974708	St Mark	PC		R S	C Colyer M Jones B Gilmour/Lincoln Archaeol Trust	1976	E	Total excavation of C11 church with later enlargements; earlier burial ground; Roman strip buildings below	BCBACC, (1976), 5–9 Med Arch, 21 (1977), 210
Lincoln		SK975719	St Paul	PC		S	C Colyer B Gilmour/Lincoln Archaeol Trust	1975 1978–79	E	on site of C19 rebuilding, demolished under faculty. Sequence of medieval and post-medieval churches preceded by apsidal church, standing within forum of upper *colonia*	Gilmour 1979
Little Dalton	Norfolk	NY089747				Ru		1968	Ob	Clearance and consolidation of C15 church	Med Arch, 13 (1969), 251
Little Holland	Essex	TM209167		PC		S	K Walker	1960 1972–73	E		EAH, 5 (1973), 234–5
Little Somborne	Hants	SU382325	All Saints	C		R	M Biddle/ Redundant Churches Fund/ Sawyer Partners	1975–76	E FS	Excavation and recording of fabric of A/S chapel	Med Arch, 20 (1976), 182 BCBACC, 2 (1975), 17
Little Woolstone	Bucks	SP875393	Holy Trinity	PC		R	R Croft/Milton Keynes Dev Corp	1980	E	Pre-conquest–C19 building sequence	BCBACC, 13 (1980), 22–3
Little Wymondley	Herts	TL219280	St Mary	Pri	Aug	Str		1973	FS	Church nave incorporating in later farmhouse	Med Arch, 18 (1974), 191
Llandegai	Caernarvons	SH593711		C		S	C Houlder	1967	E	of (?) early chapel site	Current Archaeol, 5 (1967), 116–19
Llanfair Green	Monmouths	SO391192		Gr	Cis	S		1969		Clearance of W end of church of grange	Med Arch, 14 (1970), 175
Llanfeithin	Glam (E Glam)	ST051712		Gr	Cis	S		1969		Renovations to house revealed 5 E–W burials preceding C12 monastery	Med Arch, 14 (1970), 165
Llangar	Merioneth	SH064425		PC		R	R Shoesmith/DoE	1973	E	prior to structural repairs by DoE, and survey of graveyard	Arch Camb, 129 (1980), 64–132
Llansilin	Denbighs	SJ209279	St Silin	PC		CiU	C A R Radford		FS	Structural criticism of medieval church	Arch Camb, 115 (1966), 128–33
Llantony	Gwent	SO289279	St Silin	Pri	Aug	Ru	D H Evans/Univ Cardiff/DoE	1978	E	transept	Monmouthshire Antiq, 4 (1980), 5–43
Lochmaben	Dumfries	NY081825	St Magdalene					1969	E	of churchyard and walls	Med Arch, 14 (1970), 175
LONDON Bermondsey		TQ335794	St Saviour	Pri	Clu	S	D Corbett/ MPBW/R&MLRC	1956	E		
							W F Grimes	1963	E	of Cluniac church	Grimes 1968, 210–17
City		TQ324815	St Alban Wood St	PC		S	W F Grimes/ R&MLRC	1962	E	Saxon or early Norman chancel, nave; later aisles	Grimes 1968, 203–9
		TQ316811	St Bride	PC		CiU	W F Grimes/ R&MLRC		E	Roman buildings and A/S church; Norman and later medieval church	Grimes 1968, 173–99
		TQ320813	Christ Church	PC			T Johnson	1973	E	East end of Wren church overlying C14 Greyfriars	TLMAS, 25 (1974), 220–34
				Fri	Fra		P Herbert/Dept Urban Archaeol	1976	Ob	Greyfriars church of 1307	Med Arch, 22 (1978), 159
		TQ327813	St Margaret Lothbury	PC		CiU	Dept Urban Archaeol	1977	Ob	C15 work (extension of chancel over Walbrook)	Med Arch, 22 (1978), 165
		TQ324812	St Mary le Bow	PC		CiU	Guildhall Mus	1959	Ob	of restoration revealed C11 staircase from crypt	Med Arch, 4 (1960), 143
		TQ325815	St Michael Bassishaw	PC		S	P Marsden/City of London Excav Group	1965	E	of church, pre-1196	TLMAS, 22.1 (1968), 1–17
		TQ323810	St Mildred Bread St	PC		S	P Marsden T Dyson M Rhodes	1973–74	E	Fragmentary medieval foundations	TLMAS, 26 (1975), 171–208
		TQ328811	St Nicholas Acon	PC		S	P Marsden/ Guildhall Mus	1964	Ob/E	revealing foundations of pre-1084 church during clearance of burials	TLMAS, 22.1 (1968), 1–17
		TQ320813	St Nicholas Shambles	PC		S	A Thompson/Dept Urban Archaeol	1975–78	E	of church demolished 1547–52; A/S origins and cemetery	Med Arch, 22 (1978), 165–6
		TQ325811	St Pancras	PC		S	P Marsden/ Guildhall Mus	1964	Ob/E	of foundations during removal of burials	TLMAS, 22.1 (1968), 1–17
		TQ327809	St Swithun	PC		S	R&MLRC	1961	E	Mainly C15 outline	Grimes 1968, 199–203
		TQ334812	Holy Trinity	Pri	Aug	S	J Schofield/Dept Urban Archaeol	1979	E	W range of cloister, C12	
Southwark		TQ327803	St Mary Overey	Cat (Pri) (PC)	(Aug)	CiU	G Dawson/Surrey Archaeol Soc	1969	E	of chapter house and N transept	Research Vol Surrey Archaeol Soc, 3 (1976), 37–58
							H Sheldon	1977	E	of burial vault below presbytery; Roman sculpture	Britannia, 9 (1978), 453–4; 10 (1979), 354
Long Sutton	Lincs	TF432229	St Mary	PC		CiU	J T Smith	1968	FS	of C13 timber spire	Med Arch, 13 (1969), 251
Lullington	Sussex	TQ528031		PC		S	A Barr-Hamilton	1965–66	E	recovering plan	Sussex AC, 108 (1970), 1–22
Lundy Island	Devon	SS137442		C		S	K Gardner/Lundy Field Soc	1961–63	E	of early chapel	Med Arch, 8 (1964), 231, 249

(1)	(2)	(3)	(4)	(5)	(6)	(7)	(8)	(9)	(10)	(11)	(12)
Lydd	Kent	TR043209	All Saints	PC		CiU	E D C Jackson E G M Fletcher	1966	E	in church and churchyard; basilican building; conceivably Roman	*JBAA*, **31** (1968), 19–26
Mackney Court Farm	Berks	SU580899		Cem		S	G Pike		E	Medieval cemetery	*Berks AJ*, **61** (1963–4), 40–7
Maenan	Caernarvons	SH789657	St Mary	Abb	Cis	S	L A S Butler/ MPBW	1963–68	E		*TCHS*, **30** (1963), 28–37 *Arch Camb*, **129** (1980), 37–63
Maesyronen	Radnors	SO187412		C		CiU	D B Hague	1956	FS	Early (1697) nonconformist chapel	*Arch Camb*, **105** (1956), 144–7
Mamble	Herefs & Worcs	SO688716	St John Baptist	PC		CiU	A G Taylor C R J Currie	1976	FS	of timber bell tower	*Med Arch*, **21** (1977), 230
Manningtree	Essex	TM108318	St Michael	PC		S	W J Rodwell	1974	E	of demolished church	Rodwell & Rodwell 1977, 23
Marstow	Herefs	SO554192				S	N P Bridgewater/ Archenfield Archaeol Group	1964	E	revealing plan of medieval church	*Med Arch*, **9** (1965), 185
Mendham	Suffolk	TM261818		Abb	Clu	S			S	Plan revealed by air photography	*Med Arch*, **23** (1979), 252–3
Merston	Kent	TQ704722		PC		S	A F Allen	1956	E	Church site of DMV	*Arch Cant*, **71** (1957), 198–205
Merther Uny, Wendrow	Cornwall	SW703294	St Uny	C		Ru	Cornwall Archaeol Soc/Univ Leicester	1968	E	of ovoid enclosure around standing cross and remains of chapel	*Med Arch*, **13** (1969), 230
Merton	Surrey	TQ265696	St Mary	Pri	Aug	S	J S McCracken/SW London Archaeol Unit/DoE/Borough of Merton	1978	E	Chapter-house	*Med Arch*, **23** (1979), 252
Michelham	Sussex	TQ558094		Pri	Aug	S	M Baldwin Sussex Archaeol Soc	1959 1964 1971	E	plan of church	*Sussex AC*, **105** (1967), 1–12
Milton	Dorset	ST799024	St Mary V St Michael	Abb	Ben	CiU S	E Gee	1956	E	to determine part of church plan	*PDNHAS*, **78** (1956), 87
Mistley	Essex	TM129310	St Mary	PC		Ru	J S Appleby	1961	E	Unpublished. Circumstances summarized in Rodwell & Rodwell 1977, 114
Monks Kirkby	Warwicks	SP436832	St Edith	PC	(Ben)	CiU	S M Wright/ Warwicks Museum	1979	E		*Med Arch*, **24** (1980), 242
Monkwearmouth	Tyne & Wear (Durham)	NZ403577	St Peter	Abb	Ben	CiU S	R Cramp/Durham Univ	1959–71	E	of monastic layout	Cramp 1969 *Med Arch*, **16** (1972), 150–2
Monmouth	Monmouths	SO510130		Pri	Ben	S		1969	E	prior to development	*Med Arch*, **14** (1970), 170
Mount Grace	Yorks	SE450985	Assumption of V Mary St Nicholas	Pri	Car	Ru	A D Saunders/ MPBW L Keen	1957–61 1976–	E	Cells, cloister, and church More cells	*Med Arch*, **6–7** (1962–3), 317
Much Wenlock	Salop	SJ625001	SS Michael & Milburga	Pri	Clu	S	P J Brown/DoE C A R Radford	1976	E		*Med Arch*, **21** (1977), 227
Nazeingbury	Essex	TL387066		Cem		S	P J Huggins/ Waltham Abbey Hist Soc	1976	E	Middle Saxon cemetery in corner of RB field; possible timber churches	Huggins 1978
Neath	Glam	SS737974	Holy Trinity	Abb	Cis	Ru	MPBW	1956	Ob	Material found in clearance of extrados of vault	*Med Arch*, **1** (1956), 154 *BNJ*, **28** (1956), 294, 555
Netley	Hants	SU455096	St Mary V	Abb	Cis	Ru	A M Burchard/ Hants C Mus Service	1974	S	of medieval conduit	*Med Arch*, **19** (1974), 234
Newark	Notts	SK799539	St Mary Magdalen	PC		CiU		1976 1977	FS Ob	of screen of disturbance in crossing	*TTS*, **81** (1977), 84
Newcastle Upon Tyne		NZ252642		Fri	Aug	S	B Harbottle/Soc Antiq Newcastle/ MPBW	1970–71	E	Church of friary	*Med Arch*, **16** (1972), 175
Newcastle Upon Tyne		NZ244643		Fri	Dom	S	B Harbottle	1973–74	E	to define limits of church	*Med Arch*, **19** (1975), 236–7
Newcastle Upon Tyne		NZ249638		Fri	Crm	S	B Harbottle/ MPBW	1965–67	E		*Archaeol Aeliana*, **46**, 4 ser (1968), 163–223
Newham	London	TQ392834		Abb	Cis	S	P Wilkinson/ Passmore Edwards Mus	1976	E	Line of moat of abbey of Stratford Langthorne	*Med Arch*, **21** (1977), 227
Newminster Abbey	Northumb	NZ189858		Abb	Cis	S	B Harbottle	1961–63			
							P Salway		E	Church, sacristy, library; C13 infirmary and abbot's lodge	*Archaeol Aeliana*, **42**, 4 ser (1964), 85–171 *Med Arch*, **10** (1966), 181
Newton in the Willows	Northants	SP884833	St Leonard	PC		Str	D N Hall	1969			
							J B Hastings		E	of nave of church	*J Northants Mus*, **7** (1970), 16–36 *Med Arch*, **16** (1972), 178
Northampton		SP750603	St Peter	PC		CiU S	J Williams/ Northampton Dev Corp	1975–76	E	of part of Middle Saxon church to E of present building	*Northampton Devel Corp Archaeol Monograph*, **2** (1979) J H Williams 1979
Northampton		SP756609		Fri	Crm	S	M McCarthy/ Northampton Dev Corp/DoE	1974	E		*Med Arch*, **19** (1975), 236
Northampton		SP747606		C		S	J Alexander/ MPBW	1962	E	Norman church and chapel	*Med Arch*, **8** (1964), 250
Northampton		SP755607		Fri	Fra	S	J Williams/ Northampton Dev Corp/DoE	1972	E	Founded 1230s, later expansion	*Northants Archaeol*, **13** (1978), 96–160
Northampton		SP751615	St Andrew	Pri	Clu	S	D C Mynard/ MPBW/Northampton Dev Corp	1970	E	Burials	*Med Arch*, **15** (1971), 140
North Elmham	Norfolk	TF988217		Cat		Ru	S E Rigold/MPBW	1954–56	E	A/S cathedral	*Med Arch*, **6–7** (1962–3), 67–108
North Elmham Park	Norfolk	TF987251		Cem		S	P Wade-Martins	1967–72	E	Cemetery and settlement	*East Anglian Archaeol*, **10** (1980)
North Rona	Ross & Cromarty	HW809323	St Ronan	C		Ru	Univ Glasgow	1958–59	S	of chapel; oratory, early altar, oval enclosure	*Med Arch*, **4** (1960), 138
North Stoke	Lincs	SK916286	St Andrew			S	D Kaye	1969–70	E	of church; clarification of plan, early medieval pottery	*Med Arch*, **15** (1971), 144

(1)	(2)	(3)	(4)	(5)	(6)	(7)	(8)	(9)	(10)	(11)	(12)
Norton Priory	Cheshire	SJ548831	St Mary	Pri	Aug	Ru S Str	J P Greene/ Runcorn Dev Corp	1971–	E FS S	Excavation, conservation, and display of priory site	Notices annually in *Med Arch Curr Archaeol*, **43** (1974), 246–50
Norwich	Norfolk	TG235083		Fri	Aug	S	T H Clough R B Woodings/E Anglia Archaeol Soc	1968	E	prior to redevelopment	*Med Arch*, **13** (1969), 247
		TG231088		Fri	Dom	Str		1970	E	for new seating in St Andrew's Hall revealed earlier Blackfriars buildings	*Med Arch*, **15** (1971), 139–40
		TG231089					J Roberts/Norwich Survey	1974	E	Claustral range	*Med Arch*, **19** (1975), 236
		TG225088	St Benedict	PC		S	J Roberts/Norwich Survey	1972	E	Late C11 church, subsequent expansion	*Norfolk Archaeol*, **35**.4 (1973), 443–68
		TG234085	St John Evangelist	Cem		S	B Green/Norwich Castle Mus	1964	E	Burials of churchyard found	*Med Arch*, **9** (1965), 185–7
		TG233085		PC		S	B Ayers/ Norfolk Archaeol Unit	1979	E	Church demolished in late C11 to make way for castle during conversion	*BCBACC*, **15** (1981), 13–16
		TG233093	St James	PC		R			E Ob		
Offchurch	Warwicks	SP358657	St Gregory	PC		CiU	F Radcliffe/Bishop Bright School Archaeol Soc	1974	E	Finds from trenches	*Med Arch*, **19** (1975), 238
Old Buckenham	Norfolk	TM073913	St Andrew	PC		Str	Norwich Castle Mus	1968	Ob	of foundations for new barn in churchyard	*Med Arch*, **13** (1969), 251
Old Erringham	Sussex	TQ205077		C		S	E W Holden	1957	E	Chancel of two cell church within ringwork	*Sussex AC*, **118** (1980), 257–97
Old Warden	Beds	TL121439		Abb	Cis	S	G T Rudd/Beds Archaeol Soc	1961	E		*Med Arch*, **6–7** (1962–3), 313
							E Baker/Beds County C/DoE	1974	E	Re-excavation of tile pavement	*Med Arch*, **19** (1975), 233
Old Yeavering	Northumb	NT925305				S	B Hope-Taylor/ MPBW	1952–61	E	A/S township, royal centre, cemetery, church; pagan background to site	Hope-Taylor 1977
Ormesby	Cleveland (N Yorks)	NZ531167	St Cuthbert	PC		CiU	M Brown/ Cleveland County C	1976	E	prior to insertion of new floor	*BCBACC*, **5** (1976), 9–11
Oversley	Warwicks	??090560		C?		S			Ob E	Burials from site of vanished chapel encountered during laying of pipeline	
Oxford		SP511059		Fri	Crm	S	T G Hassall Oxford Excav Cttee	1969–75	E		*Med Arch*, **20** (1976), 179
		SP512058		Fri	Dom	S	J W Banks/Oxford Excav Cttee	1961	E		*Oxon*, **41** (1976), 168–231
							T G Hassall/ Oxford Excav Cttee	1969–75	E		
		SP512059		Fri	Fra	S	T G Hassall/ Oxford Excav Cttee	1968–69	E	Mid-C13–C15 phases of church	*Oxon*, **35** (1970), 5–18; **36** (1971), 1–14; **37** (1972), 137–49
								1975	E	Cloister	*Med Arch*, **20** (1976), 148
		SP514002	All Saints	PC		R	T G Hassall B Durham/Oxford Excav Cttee	1973–74	E	Origins of church, building sequence	*Med Arch*, **19** (1975), 238
		SP515060	St Frideswide	Cat	(Aug)	CiU	T G Hassall/ Oxford Excav Cttee/DoE	1972	E	Charcoal burials at W end of church	*Med Arch*, **17** (1973), 148
Pagham	Sussex	SZ884975	St Thomas Martyr	PC		CiU	D J Freke/Sussex Archaeol Field Unit	1976	E	in nave and transept revealed A/S and C11 structures; C10 sculptures	*Sussex AC*, **118** (1980), 231–44
Peel	Isle of Man	SC242845	St German	Cat		Ru	C A R Radford/ Royal Archaeol Inst/IoM Nat Hist & Antiq Soc	1962	E		
		SC242845	St Patrick			Ru	C A R Radford Royal Archaeol Inst/IoM Nat Hist & Antiq Soc	1962–63	E		
Pennant Melangell	Montgomery	SJ023265	St Melangell	PC		CiU	C A R Radford & W J Hemp			C12 shrine	*Arch Camb*, **108** (1959), 81–113
Penrith	Cumberland	NY518301		Fri	Aus	S	B Harbottle/Soc Antiq Newcastle/ MPBW	1970	E		*Med Arch*, **15** (1971), 137–8
Peterborough	Northants	TL193984	St Peter	Cat (Abb)	(Ben)	CiU	A Challands	1971	Ob	of (?) C11 corner tower	*Med Arch*, **16** (1972), 175
Pevensey	Sussex	TQ651068	St Mary	C		S	Archaeol Div Ordnance Survey	1961	E		*Med Arch*, **6–7** (1962–3), 320
Pleshey	Essex	TL666144		C		S	P A Rahtz/Essex Archaeol Soc	1959–63	E	Castle chapel	*BAR*, **42** (1977) (F Williams)
Plympton	Devon	SX562538	SS Peter & Paul	Pri	Aug	S	V B Ledger	1958–59	E		*Med Arch*, **4** (1960), 139
Polesworth	Warwicks	SK262024	St Editha	PC (Abb)	(Ben) N	CiU S	H C Mytum/DoE/ Warwicks Mus	1976	E	Boundary	*TBWAS*, **89** (1978–9), 79–90
Polsloe	Devon	SX941938	St Katherine	Pri	Ben N	S	J P Allan/Exeter Mus	1978	E	Conventual buildings and part of church	*Med Arch*, **23** (1979), 250–1
Pontefract	Yorks	SE463226	St John Evangelist	Pri	Clu	S	C V Bellamy	1958–72	E		*Publ Thoresby Soc*, **49** (1962–4)
		SE458221	St Richard	Fri	Dom	S	K Wilson	1962–66	E		*Med Arch*, **11** (1967), 281
Portchester	Hants	SU625029		PC (Pri)	(Aug)	CiU	B Cunliffe		E		D Baker & A Berg in Cunliffe 1977, 97–120
Potterne	Wilts	ST996586				S	N Davey	1962–63	E	of pre-Conquest timber church and baptistry	*WAM*, **59** (1964), 116–23
Quenington	Gloucs	SP147039		Pre	KH	S	R Reece	1971	E	preceptory of *c* 1200	*Med Arch*, **16** (1972), 173–5
Ramsey	Hunts	TL296874	SS Mary & Benedict	Abb	Ben	CiU S	P G M Dickinson	1968	S		*Med Arch*, **13** (1969), 246
Raunds	Northants	TL000731		PC?		S	A Boddington/ Northants County C Archaeol Unit	1977–80	E	A/S church and cemetery under manor house of C13. Surrounding traces of Middle Saxon settlement and land use	*Raunds 1979*
Ravensden	Beds	TL078544	All Saints	PC		CiU	D N Hall J B Hutchings G J Dring	1969	E	C12 plan, site of font?	*Beds Archaeol*, **6** (1971), 41–53
Reading	Berks	SU720736 SU719735		Abb	Ben	S	C F Slade	1971–3 1976	E	(?) stables	*Med Arch*, **21** (1977), 223

(1)	(2)	(3)	(4)	(5)	(6)	(7)	(8)	(9)	(10)	(11)	(12)
Reading (*cont.*)									E	Cloister area	*Berks AJ*, **66** (1971–2), 65–116; **68** (1975–6), 29–70
Reculver	Kent	TR227695				Ru	B J Philp/Reculver Excav Group/ MPBW	1969	E		*Med Arch*, **14** (1970), 161
Repton	Derbys	SK303272	St Wystan	PC		CiU	M Biddle B Kjølbye-Biddle H M Taylor	1974–	E FS S	around chancel/crypt; analysis of fabric; survey of locality	*BCBACC Repton Parish Mag*, **25**, 9 (Sept 1975) *Repton Studies* **I** (1977) *Repton Studies* **II** (1979)
Rhuddlan	Flints	SJ026778		PC		S	H Miles/DoE	1971	E	Location of Norman borough church	*Med Arch*, **16** (1972), 178–9
Rhynd	Perths	NO142218		Pri	Cis N	S	M Stewart/ Archaeol & Hist Section of Perths Soc	1969–70	E		*Med Arch*, **15** (1971), 142
Richmond (Barnes)	London	TQ220765	St Mary	PC		CiU	J S McCracken/SW London Archaeol Unit	1978–	FS E	after fire damage	*Med Arch*, **23** (1979), 257
Rievaulx	Yorks	SE577850		Abb	Cis	Ru	M W Thompson/ MPBW	1957–60	E	of conventual buildings	*Med Arch*, **5** (1961), 314
Ripon	Yorks	SE315712				S	A Baggs	1955	E	of site of Ladykirk; pre-Conquest burials with combs	
Ripon	Yorks	SE314712	SS Peter & Wilfrid	Cat		CiU	R Hall/York Archaeol Trust/ DoE	1975	E	of C7 crypt during alterations	*YAJ*, **49** (1977), 59–64
Rivenhall	Essex	TL828178	St Mary & All Saints	PC		CiU	W J Rodwell/Essex Archaeol Soc/DoE	1972–73	E FS	at exterior of church; underlying Roman buildings; earlier timber church off to side; Middle Saxon cemetery found in churchyard extension	*Antiq J*, **53** (1973), 219–31
Rochester	Kent	TQ744684	St Andrew	Cat		CiU		1960	Ob	of A/S graves revealed during installation of heating	*Med Arch*, **5** (1961), 309
							C A R Radford		Ob	of pre-Conquest wall encountered during excavation in transept	*Annual Rep Friends Rochester Cathedral* (1969), 13–16
Romsey	Hants	SU351213	SS Mary & Elfleda	PC (Abb)	(Ben) N	CiU S	K Stubbs/Romsey Archaeol Res Cttee	1973–	E FS	of site of Lady Chapel	*Gesta*, **14** (1975), 27–40
Ruddington (Flawford)	Notts	SK563332	St Peter	PC		S	H M James/ Ruddington & Dis Local Hist Soc	1967–	E	of church site and underlying Roman buildings	*Med Arch*, **21** (1977), 211–12
Rufford	Notts	SK645647		Abb	Cis	S	MPBW	1957	E		*Med Arch*, **9** (1965), 161–3
Rumburgh	Suffolk	TM346819	St Michael	Pri	Ben	CiU/S	P G M Dickinson	1962–63		Planning of site	*Med Arch*, **8** (1964), 244–5
Runston	Monmouths	ST497916		PC		Ru	MPBW	1956	Ob	Uncovering of tower foundation during consolidation of Norman DMV church	*Med Arch*, **1** (1957), 156
Rushden	Northants	SP957665	St Mary	PC		CiU	D N Hall	1970	FS	Reappraisal of structural history; new evidence observed during restoration	*Northants Past & Present*, **5** (1974), 71–5
Rushen	Isle of Man	SC277703		Abb	Cis	Ru S	L A S Butler/Manx Mus & Nat Trust	1978	E	Elucidation of layout	*Med Arch*, **23** (1979), and *Guide*
Ruthwell	Dumfries	NY101684				S	C Crowe/Univ Manchester/Mous-wald Trust/ Dumfries Mus	1980	E	in glebe field to study ring ditch encircling churchyard, revealed by air photography in 1978 (G D B Jones)	*TDGNHAS* forthcoming
Salisbury	Wilts	SU147296		Fri	Fra	S	C N Moore/ Salisbury Mus	1966	E	during clearance of buildings of site of friary	*Med Arch*, **11** (1967), 280; **13** (1969), 248
Sands of Forvie	Aberdeens	NK022265				Ru	W Kirk	1958–60	E	of medieval church from sand	*Med Arch*, **5** (1961), 318
Sandwich	Kent	TR329579		Fri	Crm	Ru	A C Hogarth/ Chatham House Grammar School	1972	S		*Med Arch*, **17** (1973), 155
Sandwich (Ham)	Kent	TR326548		C		R	B Philp/Kent Archaeol Rescue Unit	1977	S	of church and graveyard prior to conversion	*Med Arch*, **22** (1978), 165
St Albans	Herts	TL136074	St Michael	PC			I E Anthony	1966	E		*Herts Archaeol*, **2** (1971)
St Albans		TL145067	St Alban	Cat (Abb)	(Ben)	CiU S	V R Christophers/ MPBW	1968	E		*Med Arch*, **13** (1969), 246
							M Biddle/Dean & Chapter	1978	E	of chapter-house	*Expedition*, **22** (2) (1980), 17–32
St Andrews	Fife	NO514166	St Andrew	Cat		CiU	N Bogdan/DoE	1976	E	of St Rule's tower prior to reconstruction work	*Med Arch*, **21** (1977), 229
							St Mary's cemetery			Erosion by sea	
St David's	Pembs	SM734273	St Patrick	C		S		1969	Ob	of exposure of burial ground by visitor erosion	*Med Arch*, **14** (1970), 175
St Dogmael's	Pembs	SN163488	St Mary V	Abb	Tir	Ru	MPBW	1956	E	of buildings in W range, following earlier clearance in 1950–1	*Arch Camb*, **102** (1951), 115–16 HMSO Guide (1962)
St German's	Cornwall	SX359577	St German	PC (Pri) (Cat)	(Aug)	CiU S	C A R Radford		FS		*J Royal Inst Cornwall*, ns **7**.(3) (1975–6), 190–6
St Helen's	Isle of Scilly	SV902169		C		S	H E O'Neil		E	of hermitage	*Arch J*, **121** (1964), 40–69
St Neots	Hunts	TL182263	St Neot	Pri	Ben	S	C F Tebbutt	1958–64	E	of C13 priory revealed early C11 church	*Proc Cambs AS*, (1966), 33–74
St Ninian's Isle	Shetland	HU367207		C		S	A C O'Dell	1955–59	E	of medieval church, pagan burials below	A Small *et al* 1973
St Tudwal's Island	Caernarvons	SH342259		Pri	Aug	S	D B Hague/ RCAHM	1959–63	E		*Med Arch*, **8** (1964), 246–8
Scarborough	Yorks	TA047891	St Mary	PC (Abb)	(Cis)	CiU	R A Varley/ Scarborough Mus	1970	E	during restoration revealed foundations of C12 church	*Med Arch*, **15** (1971), 144–5
Seacourt	Oxon	SP482073		PC		S	M Biddle		E	of church and DMV	*Oxon*, **26/27** (1961/2), 70–201
Selborne	Hants	SU755345	B V Mary	Pri	Aug	S	G E C Knapp	1956–71	E	Foundations of chapter-house and church	*Med Arch*, **16** (1972), 175
Shap	Westmor	NY548152	St Mary Magdalene	Abb	Pre	S	R Lowther/MPBW	1956–57	E	of nave and S aisle of presbytery	
Shenstone	Staffs	SK109043		PC		Ru	D & J Gould	1973	E FS	on site of Old Church; A/S stone church	*SSAHST*, **15** (1973–4), 43–9

(1)	(2)	(3)	(4)	(5)	(6)	(7)	(8)	(9)	(10)	(11)	(12)
Sherborne	Dorset	ST638164	All Hallows	PC		S	J H P Gibb	1964–65 1968	E	mostly concerned with C14 parish church at W end of abbey	PDAS, **93** (1971), 197–210
			St Mary	PC (Abb) (Cat)	(Ben)	CiU	J H P Gibb R D H Gem L Keen D W Thackray/ DoE	1974–	FS E	of monastic offices	Arch J, **132** (1975), 71–110 Med Arch, **19** (1975), 233–4
Shotesham St Mary	Norfolk	TM247990	St Botolph	PC		S	K Wade D Smith	1965	Ob	of plough damage to former churchyard; A/S pottery	Med Arch, **10** (1966), 186
Shouldham	Norfolk	TF684086		PC		S		1970	Ob	of water-pipe trench across field E of church site yielded finds from A/S & medieval burials	Med Arch, **15** (1971), 129–30
Silchester	Hants	SU639625				S	I A Richmond	1961	E	Re-excavation of Roman church	Frere 1975
Singleton	Sussex	SU878130	St John Evangelist	PC		CiU	M Hare	1971	FS	of tower: A/S fabric noted	Med Arch, **16** (1972), 163
Sompting	Sussex	TQ162057	St Mary	PC		CiU	E Holden	1969	Ob	of restoration	Med Arch, **14** (1970), 174
							C Ainsworth/ Worthing Archaeol Group C Hewett H M Taylor	1976	E FS	prior to reflooring in south chapel of A/S timber work in Rhenish helm	Anglo-Saxon Engl, **8** (1978), 205–30
Sopwell	Herts	TL150064	St Mary	Pri	Ben N	S	E A Johnson O J Weaver/St Albans & Herts Architect & Archaeol Soc	1962–66	E		
South Elmham	Suffolk	TM307826		PC		Ru	N Smedley E Owles	1963–64	E	of Old Minster	PSIAH, **32**.1 (1970), 1–16
South Witham	Lincs	SK920205		Pre C	KT	S	P Mayes/MPBW	1965–68	E	of small preceptory	Report imminent
Southampton	Hants	SU427121		C		S S	Univ Southampton/MPBW	1969	E E	C8 cemetery and (?) timber chapel Cemetery and (?) church	Med Arch, **14** (1970), 157
Southampton				Fri	Fra	S	F A Aberg	1960–67	E		Platt & Coleman-Smith 1975
Southend-on-Sea	Essex	TQ876873	St Mary	Pri	Clu	S	Prittlewell Priory Mus	1965–67	E		Med Arch, **12** (1968), 164
Stafford	Staffs		St Bertelin	PC		CiU	A Oswald		E		Oswald 1956
Stafford		SJ228951	St Thomas	Pri	Aug	S	County Planning and Dev Officer	1965	E	Burials	Med Arch, **10** (1966), 181
Stainburn	N Yorks	SE248486	St Mary	C		R	R K Morris/RCF/ DoE/Univ Leeds	1977	E FS	in advance of repairs	BCBACC, **10** (1979), 9–15
Stamford	Lincs	TF300070	St John	PC		CiU	Stamford & Rutland Nat Hist Soc	1966	S	of area adjoining church; (?) earlier church	Med Arch, **11** (1967), 283
Stamford		TF039074	St Leonard	Pri	Ben	S	C Mahany/ Stamford Excav Cttee	1967–70	E		Med Arch, **15** (1971), 139
Stillingfleet	Yorks	SE594410	St Helen	PC		CiU	P V Addyman I Goodall et al	1974–75	FS	of C12 door and ironwork	Archaeologia, **106** (1979), 75–105
Stoke Orchard	Gloucs	SO917282	St James	PC		R	R Leech/ CRAAGS	1977	E	revealing three phases	Med Arch, **22** (1978), 164
Stone-by-Faversham	Kent	TQ991613	Our Lady	C		Ru	E Fletcher E D C Jackson G W Meates	1967–68	E	Pre-Conquest church incorporating Roman (?) mausoleum	Antiq J, **49** (1969), 273–94; **57** (1977), 67–72
Strata Florida	Cardigans	SN747658	St Mary	Abb	Cis	Ru	MPBW	1966	Ob	Report that path-laying W of church has revealed foundations	Med Arch, **11** (1967), 281 See New Guide
Strood	Kent	TQ737693		Hos		S	A C Harrison/Kent Archaeol Soc/ MPBW	1966	E	Plan of hospital with hall and chapel	Med Arch, **11** (1967), 274
Sudbury	Suffolk	TM389578		Fri	Dom	S	T Howlett	1969	E		Med Arch, **14** (1970), 170
Swaffham	Norfolk	TF805108	St Guthlac	PC		S		1959	Ob	of ploughing on former graveyard	Med Arch, **4** (1960), 143
Tamworth	Staffs	SK209050		C		Str	J Gould	1968	E	around Spital Chapel	TSSAHS, **10** (1968–9), 23–31
Tamworth		SK207041	St Editha	PC		CiU	R Meeson/ Tamworth Excav Cttee	1978	E S	A/S burials; structures; survey of site	BCBACC Med Arch, **23** (1979), 245
Temple Ewell	Kent	TR286455		Pre	KT	S	F L Page	1965–67	E		Med Arch, **12** (1968), 167–8
Tenby	Pembs	SN004134	St Mary	PC		CiU	G Thomas	1965	S		Arch Camb, **115** (1966), 134–65
Thelsford	Warwicks	SP271583	St John Baptist	Fri	Tri	S	M Gray/MPBW	1966–72	E		Med Arch, **17** (1973), 156 W Midlands Archaeol News Sheet, **15** (1972)
Thetford	Norfolk	TL865831	Holy Sepulchre	Pri	Aug	S	J Hare/MPBW	1969	E		Norfolk Archaeol, **37** (1979), 190–200
		TL868835	St Mary V	Pri	Clu	S	MPBW	1956	E	C13 farmery divided into hall and chapel; C15 alterations	Med Arch, **1** (1957), 153 See New Guide
							R Wilcox	1973	E	Further excavation	Med Arch, **18** (1974), 192
		TL869825	St Edmund	PC		S	G Knocker	1957	E	of late-Saxon foundations for church	Med Arch, **2** (1958), 188
		TL864830	St Martin	PC		S	G Knocker	1957–59	E	Middle Saxon graves; C11 church	Norfolk Archaeol, **34**.2 (1967), 119–86
		TL870823	St Michael	PC		S	B K Davison R Mackey/MPBW	1969–70	E	Plan	Med Arch, **15** (1971), 130–1
		TL839874	?			S	R R Clarke/ Norfolk Res Cttee	1961–63	E	of (?) church 90' long; redundant by C14	Med Arch, **8** (1964), 249
Thorney	Cambs			PC (Abb)	(Ben)	CiU S	D Mackreth	1978	Ob	of contractor's work near church	
Thornholme	Humbs (Lincs)	SE966126		Pri	Aug	S	G Coppack/DoE	1976–78		outer precinct	Med Arch, **22** (1978), 157–9
Thornton	Leics	SK468076	St Peter	PC		CiU	D Parsons/DAC	1975	E	Font base and bell pit	Med Arch, **20** (1976), 182
Throckmorton	Worcs	SO981499		PC		CiU	J Roberts	1978	Ob	during works for new floor	
Thurleigh	Beds	TL052585	St Peter	PC		CiU	D N Hall	1971	E	during restoration	Beds AJ, **14** (1980)
Tilty	Essex	TL601267		Abb	Cis	S	P G M Dickinson	1962–63	S	Plan	Med Arch, **8** (1964), 241
Tintern	Monmouths	SO533001		Abb	Cis	Ru	J K Knight/MPBW	1969–71	E	church, cloisters, guesthouse	Med Arch, **16** (1972), 176–7
Titchfield	Hants	SU541058	St Peter	PC		CiU	M Hare	1975	FS	elucidating 'Old Minster'	PHFCAS, **32** (1976), 5–48
Tong	W Yorks	SE219306		PC (C)		CiU	W Yorks County C Archaeol Unit	1979	E FS	Total excavation of interior	BCBACC, **12** (1980)

(1)	(2)	(3)	(4)	(5)	(6)	(7)	(8)	(9)	(10)	(11)	(12)
Torbryan	Devon	SX817674	C? Herm?				F E Zeuner		E	Building of c 1350–1450 at cave entrance	TDA, **92** (1960), 311–30
Tower Hill (London)		TQ337807	St Mary	Abb		S	B K Davison	1972	E	to locate site of C14 abbey of St Mary Graces of Eastminster	Med Arch, **17** (1973), 155
Trowbridge	Wilts	ST856579	?	PC		S	Wilts County Council	1977	E	A/S church, abandoned C13	Med Arch, **22** (1978), 169
Tynemouth	Northumb	NZ374695		Pri		S	G Jobey/MPBW	1963	E	revealed Iron Age, Roman, post-Roman timber buildings; post-Conquest monastic structures	Archaeol Aeliana, ser 4, **45**, (**1967**), 33–104
Tynron	Dumfries	NX754951		C		S		1969	S	of site of chapel	Med Arch, **14** (1970), 175
Uchelolau	Glam	ST096700		PC		S	H J Thomas G Davies	1964–66	E	of small church, part of DMV	Morganwg, **10** (1966), 63–6; **11** (1967), 82–3
Upleatham	Yorks	NZ632195	St Andrew	C		CiU	S J Knight	1970–71	E	to recover plan of deleted part of church	CBA Res Report, **13** (1976), 40–1
Upper Beeding	Sussex	TQ139112	St Peter	Pri	Ben	Ru	D Kaye	1966	E		Med Arch, **11** (1967), 276
Vale Royal	Cheshire	SJ638699		Abb	Cis	S	H M Colvin A J Taylor/ Grosvenor Mus	1958	E		Med Arch, **3** (1959), 302–3 Antiq J, **42** (1962), 183–207
Valle Crucis	Denbighs	SJ205442		Abb	Cis	Ru	MPBW	1956	Ob	of adjustment of level in presbytery	
							L A S Butler	1970–71	E	Cloister W and S ranges	Arch Camb, **125** (1976), 80–126
Wakefield	W Yorks	SE333208		Cat (PC)		CiU	P Mayes W Yorks Archaeol Unit	1974 1980	E E	in nave N of N aisle	Med Arch, **19** (1975), 230, 238
Walsingham	Norfolk	TF935367		Pri	Aug	S Str	C Green A B Whittingham	1961	E FS	Review of past studies excavation of Chapel of Our Lady, survey of site	Arch J, **125** (1968), 255–90
Waltham	Essex	TD382007	Holy Cross	PC (Abb)	(Aug)	CiU S	P J Huggins/ Waltham Abbey Hist Soc	1967–76	E	of claustral area; pre-C12 cemetery	Trans Essex Archaeol Soc, **3**, ser 2 (1970), 216–66 Essex Archaeol Hist, **4** (1972), 30–127
										SE transept	Med Arch, **21** (1977), 207, 233, 243 EAH, **5** (1973), 127–84; **10** (1978), 127–73
Walton	Bucks	SP885369	St Michael	PC		R	D C Mynard	1976	Ob	within precinct during reflooring	Archaeol in Milton Keynes, (1976), 91
Walton	Suffolk	TM297358		Pri	Ben	S	S E West/Suffolk County C	1971	E	Unusual plan	PSIAH, **33** (1974), 131–52
Warwick	Warwicks	SP283651		Col		S	H C Mytum/ Warwick Mus/ DoE	1975	E	of College Gardens showing position of C16 college of vicars choral attached to St Mary's Church	
Warwick		SP283653	St Sepulchre	Pri	Aug	S	W J Ford/Warwick Mus/DoE	1971	E	of early C12 priory	Med Arch, **16** (1972), 175–6
Waterbeach	Cambs	TL499649	Piety of SS Mary & Clare	Abb	Fra N	S	M Cra'ster/MPBW	1962–63	E	of house of minoresses	Proc Cambs AS, **59** (1966), 75–94
Watten	Caithness	ND233524		C		Ru	E Talbot/Univ Aberdeen	1975	E	of Clow Chapel	Med Arch, **20** (1976), 183–4
Wells	Somerset	ST551459	St Andrew	Cat		CiU	W J Rodwell/ CRAAGS/DoE	1978–80	E FS	of medieval lady chapel, underlying A/S minster. Detailed recording of W front	Rodwell 1979 Med Arch, **23** (1979), 255–7
Wendling	Norfolk	TF938128	B V Mary	Abb	Pre	S	RCHM/R M Butler	1957	S	of earthworks over monastic buildings	Norfolk Archaeol, **32**, 226
West Bergholt	Essex	TL953280	St Mary	PC		R	R Turner/Essex County C/DoE	1978	E FS	Discovery of C11 work leading to redating of parts of fabric	Med Arch, **23** (1979), 257
West Dean (Chilgrove)	Sussex	SU834157	St Margaret	C		S	F G Aldsworth/ Chichester Excavation Committee/Sussex Archaeol Soc	1976	S E	to locate exact site of chapel	Sussex AC, **117** (1979), 110–17
West Dereham	Norfolk	TF662004	St Mary	Abb	Pre	S	D Edwards/ Norfolk Archaeol Unit	1976	S	Plan revealed by air photography	Med Arch, **21** (1977), 227, pl XVIIB
West Malling	Kent	TQ685575	St Mary	Abb	Ben N	CiU S	M Biddle/MPBW	1961	E	to reconsider eastern termination	Med Arch, **6–7** (1962–3), 316
Westminster	London	TQ300795	St Peter	Abb	(Ben)	CiU	G Black/Inner London Archaeol Unit/DoE	1975–76	Ob	of building works revealed domestic building	Med Arch, **21** (1977), 228
West Thurrock	Essex	TQ593772	St Clement	PC		CiU	B Milton/ Essex County Council/ DoE	1979	E	Clarification of unusual C11 plan	Med Arch, **24** (1980), 220
Wharram-le-Street	N Yorks	SE864660	St Mary	PC		CiU	RCHM		FS	Photographic survey of tower prior to works	
Wharram Percy	N Yorks	SE858642	St Martin	PC		R Ru	J G Hurst et al/ Medieval Village Research Group		E FS	revealing A/S predecessors; study of churchyard and boundaries	Hurst 1976 Beresford & Hurst 1976 Med Arch, **23** (1979), 259–60
Whithorn	Wigtowns	NX444404	St Martin	Pri			MPBW		E		TDGNHAS, **34** (1957), 131–94 Med Arch, **6–7** (1962–3), 318
							C Tabraham/ SDD	1972, 1975	E		TDGNHAS, **54** (1979), 29–38
Whitwick	Leics	SK435162	St John Baptist	PC		CiU	D Parsons/DAC	1975	Ob	during reflooring; former arcade	Med Arch, **20** (1976), 182–3
Winchester	Hants	SU476295		C		S	Winchester Excav Cttee	1970–71	E	of early Norman castle chapel; rectangular nave and stilted apse	Antiq J, **55** (1975), 106–9
		SU476299	St Anastasius	PC		S	Winchester City Rescue Archaeologist	1972	E	of N wall of C13 church	Med Arch, **17** (1973), 157
		SU484295	St Mary in Tanner St	PC		S	M Biddle/ Winchester Excav Cttee	1965–71	E	Complete excavation of church C10–C16, of late medieval burial within it, of earlier building incorporated in church, and of underlying cemetery of C7–8	Antiq J, **55** (1975), 312–15

(1)	(2)	(3)	(4)	(5)	(6)	(7)	(8)	(9)	(10)	(11)	(12)
Winchester (cont.)		SU482293	St Maurice	PC		S	J C McCulloch/ Winchester Archaeol Soc/M Biddle	1959–70	E	of church of C10, Norman rebuilding, additions of C12, C14, cemetery of c 900	Antiq J, 50 (1970), 277–326; Med Arch, 15 (1971), 142–3
		SU48382956	St Pancras	PC		S	M Biddle/ Winchester Excav Cttee	1968–71	E	Complete excavation of church (?) C9–C16, of two (?) earlier burials, and of C14–C16 burials within church	Antiq J, 55 (1975), 318–20
		SU48062953	St Peter-in-the-Fleshambles	PC		S	Winchester Archaeol Soc/ MPBW	1956	E	Late C11 church	Cunliffe 1964
		SU48192932	New Minster	Mon		S	Winchester Excav Cttee	1961–70 int	E	Partial excavation of church, fuller investigation of monastic buildings C10–C12	Antiq J, 52 (1972), 115–25
		SU482293	St Michael (?)	C		S	Winchester Excav Cttee	1961	E	Oval chapel of C11 in New Minster precinct	Archaeol J, 119 (1962), 160–5
		SU29774793	St Mary in Brudene St	PC? C?		S			E	Church or chapel of C12–C15	Cunliffe 1964, corrected in Winchester Studies I
				C		S	Winchester Excav Cttee		E	of chapel of C11, part of pre-C12 episcopal palace	Antiq J, 55 (1975), 327
		SU482293	St Peter	Cat		S	M Biddle B Kjølbye-Biddle/ Winchester Excav Cttee	1962–9	E	Old Minster, founded C7, mightily enlarged C10 Cathedral cemetery	Antiq J, 50 (1970), 277–326; World Archaeol, 7 (1) (1975), 87–108
		SU484292	SS Mary & Edburga	Abb	Ben N	S	K Qualmann	1973	E	prior to development in area of Nunnaminster	Med Arch, 18 (1974), 178, 200
Wing	Bucks	SP881226	All Saints	PC		CiU	E D C Jackson E G M Fletcher		E	Apse and nave of A/S church	JBAA, 25 (1962), 1–20
Witham	Somerset	ST758417	SS Mary & John	Pri	Car	S	P Barlow R D Reid/Wells Archaeol Soc	1966–69	E		Med Arch, 14 (1970), 170
Wix	Essex	TM165292		PC		CiU S	B Blake/ Colchester & Essex Mus	1961	E	Part of demolished monastic church	TEAS, 1 (1962), 105–10
Woodford	Essex			PC		CiU	F R Clark/W Essex Archaeol Group	1971	E	Grave-slab after fire	Litten 1971
Woodhorn	Northumb	NZ301888	St Mary	PC		R	B Harbottle	1974	E	within nave	Archaeol Aeliana, 3, ser 5 (1975), 117–20
Woodkirk	Yorks	SE272250	St Mary	PC (Pri)	(Aug)	CiU S	C V Bellamy	1964	E	on N side of church	Med Arch, 9 (1965), 183
Wooton Wawen	W Midlands	SP153633	St Peter	PC (Pri)	(Ben)	CiU S	H Barnie/W Midlands Rescue Archaeol Cttee	1974	E	within churchyard	Med Arch, 19 (1975), 235–6
Worcester	Worcs	SO849545	St Mary	Cat (Pri)	(Ben)	CiU	H Clarke/MPBW	1970–71	E	Refectory undercroft, college green, W front	see Carver (ed) 1980, 127–35
							Staff and pupils of King's School, Worcester, for dean and chapter	1975	E	SE transept	see Carver (ed) 1980, 143–52
							J Sawle	1979	Ob	in precinct	
							P A Barker	1980	E	before rebuilding after	
Yateley	Hants	SU818609		PC		CiU	D Hinton F Gale	1980	E FS	damage by fire	BCBACC, 13 (1980), 23–4
Yeavering	See Old Yeavering										
York		SE602514	St Mary Bishophill Senior	PC		S	RCHM MPBW	1964	E	after demolition; A/S church on site of Roman building	YAJ, 48 (1976), 35–68
		SE600515	St Mary Bishophill Junior	PC		CiU	York Archaeol Trust	1980	FS	Recording of A/S tower	BCBACC, 15 (1981), 20–1
		SE604507	All Saints Pavement	PC		CiU	York Archaeol Trust	1976	Ob	of floor levels and walls during underpinning	Med Arch, 21 (1977), 216
		SE606521	St Helen-on-the-Walls	PC		S	York Archaeol Trust/York Excav Group	1973–74	E	Total excavation of church, and greater part of cemetery. Underlying Roman building and single Roman burial. Study of 1 000+ individuals from cemetery	Magilton 1980 Dawes & Magilton 1980
		SE607516	St Mary Castlegate	PC		R	York Archaeol Trust	1975	Ob	during conversion; pre-Conquest sculpture	BCBACC, 3 (1976), 11–14
		SE603502	St Clement	Pri	Ben N	S	S Donaghy/York Archaeol Trust	1976	E	of part of nunnery; earlier burials, possible pre-Conquest church in vicinity	Med Arch, 21 (1977), 228, 249
		SE604497	St Oswald, Fulford	PC		R	P A Rahtz/Univ York	1980	E	disclosing A/S predecessor	BCBACC, 13 (1980), 12–15
		SE604522	St Mary-ad-Valvas	PC		S	D Phillips/York Minster Advisory Cttee	1967–72	Ob	and limited excavation of church beyond E end of Minster	Med Arch, 12 (1968), 174
		SE603522	St Peter	Cat		CiU	D Phillips/York Minster Advisory Cttee	1967–73	E FS	during restoration. Excavations in transept, E & W ends of nave, E arm, at various points round exterior. Buildings of Roman legionary fortress below	Hope-Taylor 1971 Phillips 1975 Phillips 1976
Zennor	Cornwall	SW434383		C		S	V Russell P A S Pool	1964	E	of Chapel Jane	Cornish Archaeol, 7 (1968), 43–60

Introduction

Churches are among the most numerous of our surviving monuments and even where the structure above ground has long since disappeared, its archaeological remains are often readily identifiable and will provide a full account of its history. More than any other type of building a church reflects the fortunes and aspirations of the community as a whole. Nowhere is this more so than in towns, where the variety, intensity, and self-consciousness of urban life is reflected in an equally diverse pattern of churches. The study of town churches is a fundamental aspect of the study of town life, and will illuminate both its origins and its distinguishing characteristics.

This diversity and the rapid changes in the fortunes of urban communities intensify the problems of studying churches in towns, particularly those which served a parish or similarly restricted area or social group. It is probable that a higher proportion of medieval urban than of rural churches has disappeared, leaving no more than minimal traces on the documentary or archaeological record. To an even greater degree than with rural churches, the written evidence for the early years, or even centuries, of the life of a town church is entirely lacking, and this history will have to be written solely from the archaeological or structural evidence. Where an urban church survives, the concentration of wealth in the town has often resulted in a sequence of enlargements and rebuildings which have obliterated the architectural evidence for the early stages of its development much more thoroughly than for its rural counterpart. In dealing with urban churches it is therefore particularly necessary to combine the approaches of the archaeologist with those of the documentary and architectural historians.

The first requirement of this study is to identify the body of material on which it is to be based, that is, the individual churches themselves. Given the state of the surviving evidence this is no easy task, and beyond this there are many important questions concerning pre-Reformation churches, and in particular parish churches, which remain unanswered. When, why, and by whom were the churches founded? When did they prosper and when decay? Did a church have a special significance for its particular neighbourhood or community within the town? How did the parochial system in towns evolve and how was it regulated? What were the reasons for the major differences in parochial provision between one town and another? How were these developments reflected in the structural evolution of the church and the architectural setting for worship? Archaeological and architectural evidence is capable of providing an answer even to questions which have been posed as a result of documentary researches. Above all we lack the detailed organization of evidence without which adequate comparisons between individual churches and towns will be impossible. Only when such comparisons have been made will there emerge any generally applicable answers to these questions.

The working party has devised a form of record which is intended to provide a structure for information on pre-Reformation urban churches in Great Britain, and to stimulate and co-ordinate lines of enquiry. Many of the formal headings in the record relate only to parish churches, the most numerous group, but it is proposed that the survey should cover all churches in towns in this period and should attempt to evaluate the part which each type of church played in urban life. At present questions relating to the church in medieval towns seem most urgently in need of concerted effort, but it is hoped that eventually the survey will be extended to cover all places of worship in towns down to modern times.

A survey of this type has a particular value at present when, as a result of redundancy and urban redevelopment, an unusually large number of church structures are threatened with destruction or extensive remodelling. The final section of the survey is therefore devoted to an assessment of the foreseeable opportunities for investigating the physical remains of the church, both above and below ground, and of the potential value of such investigation for understanding the history of the church and its site.

The records of the survey

In almost every case an enquiry into the history of an individual church will require detailed investigation of original source material, written and otherwise. Full accounts of these investigations will be bulky and so it is proposed that the record of the survey be maintained at two levels: (1) a detailed file of information with full references to sources, discussion of alternative interpretations where necessary, and a bibliography; (2) a record form (Fig 28) which will present this information in as clear and condensed a manner as possible under a consistent series of headings. These record forms will be widely consulted, and will be the basis on which comparisons between individual churches and towns will be made.

The headings of the record form represent the main lines of enquiry adopted by the working party and are discussed more fully later in this note. Obviously not everyone will always be able to deal with all aspects of the enquiry: church historians may be unwilling to contribute an architectural analysis, and archaeologists may be diffident in offering an interpretation of parochial rights. Nevertheless, every attempt should be made to view the history and development of the church as a coherent whole, and any aspect which has not been dealt with on the record form should be clearly indicated. The record form should be seen not as a check-list or questionnaire but as a reasoned summary of all aspects of the church's development. Topics entered mainly under one heading may have an important bearing on topics discussed elsewhere, and so the investigator should not hesitate to insert cross-references where appropriate.

It is important that the records of the survey should be accessible. In order to assist in this it is suggested that completed forms be sent to the CBA Research Officer at the Department of Archaeology, The University, Leeds LS2 9JT, where they will be copied and filed and the originals returned to the compiler(s). The records of any church that has been surveyed may be inspected on request, or copies made available.

The record form

There follows an outline of the topics to be considered under each heading of the record form. In some cases this simply amounts to a check-list. Elsewhere it is not possible to do more than suggest general areas of enquiry, or some particular (and perhaps at first sight, unlikely) points worthy of consideration. It is perhaps in these areas that new insights are most likely to emerge.

For a record of this type to be of value the information it contains must be accurate and reliable. Respondents are therefore enjoined to include only information of which they have certain knowledge, and clearly to distinguish from this both speculation and inference. Where a section cannot be filled in, please indicate one of the following reasons:

- a absolute lack of information
- b respondent unable to deal with this topic
- c section not applicable to this church

A *Identification*

NB: Use a separate record sheet for each successor church on a different site; where a dedication has changed it would be advisable to make out the first part of the record form for each dedication with a reference to the form dealing with the full history of the church on that site.

3 Provide annotated extract from OS plan, eg at 1:1 250 for exact and approximate site and at 1:2 500 where general area only is known. In 3(c) indicate quality of knowledge of the location of the church by ticking one of the three degrees suggested.
4 What are the grounds for counting it as an urban church, and at what dates was it included in the urban area?
5 eg parish church, friary church, charnel chapel, etc.
6 This section is principally concerned with the present nature of the site and should include information necessary for estimating the degree of preservation of remains, the degree of permanence of the present use, and the likely availability of the site for future investigation. The subsections should cover the following topics:
    a note if the church is still standing and in use. If the former but not the latter, note briefly how the structure has been used since it was last a place of worship. If neither, give brief outline of what has happened to the site since the church was demolished.
    b eg burial ground, house and garden, house with cellar, car park, plot about to be rebuilt.
    c state if still a place of worship. If not, has the site any legal protection (Ancient Monuments and/or Town and Country

CBA Urban Churches Record Form

Name and address of respondent	Date of compilation

A: IDENTIFICATION

1	(a) Town	(b) Civil Parish 1894 & Historic County before 1974	(c) Present local Authority
2 Name of church	(a) Modern or predominant name	(b) Other names (and dates)	
3 Location	(a) Grid reference	(b) Street or area	(c) Knowledge of site Exact Approximate General
4	Urban Status		
5	Function		
6 Nature of site	(a) Outline history	(b) Present physical character	
	(c) Present legal status/ownership	(d) Listing Grade (MHLG/DoE)	
7 Diocese	(a) Present	(b) Former (and dates)	
8 Ordinary			
9 Outline chron-ology	(a) Origin and earliest evidence		
	(b) Earliest documentary evidence		
	(c) Earliest visible structural evidence		
	(d) Date of disappearance		

B: ORIGIN AND OUTLINE HISTORY

1 Patron

2 Dedic-ation	(a) Significance of main dedication	(b) Other cults, including side altars

3 Origin

4 History of church

2 Parish Officers

3 Parish property

H: GUILDS AND FRATERNITIES

J: CHANTRIES, OBITS, AND LIGHTS

K: OTHER LITURGICAL EVIDENCE

L: VALUE

1 Sources of revenue

2 Valuations

M: POTENTIAL FOR FUTURE INVESTIGATION

Fig 28 Urban Churches Record Form.

C: THE STRUCTURE

1 Nature of evidence

2 Outline development of structure

	(a) Bearing(s)	(b) Significance
3 Orient- ation		

4 Altars, side chapels, images

5 Other furnishings and fittings

6 Burials within church

7 Building materials

8 Medieval masons, carpenters etc; post-medieval architects

D: SITE AND SETTING

1 General significance

2 Relationships to immediate surroundings; access to church

3 Church yard/burial ground

4 Clergy House

E: CLERGY

1 Status of incumbent

2 Numbers of priests and clerks

3 Special characteristics of clergy

F: PAROCHIAL STATUS

1 Contemporary terminology

2 Baptism

3 Burial

4 Relationship to superior churches

5 Dependant chapels

6 Associations with other churches

7 Tithes

G: THE PARISH

	(a) Earliest evidence for parish boundaries
1 Parish Boundar- ies	(b) Significant features
	(c) Amalgamations, divisions, and other alterations
	(d) Size

Planning Acts) and (if possible) who owns it?

d   *NB:* Many churches have been listed as of architectural or historical merit under the terms of the Town and Country Planning Act, even though the protection afforded by the act may not apply to them.

8   *NB:* Was it exempt from the jurisdiction of the archdeacon?

9   Brief notes only required, sufficient to identify the period in which the church flourished and the type of evidence available.

B   *Origin and outline history*

1   Give an account of the descent of the patronage, including reasonable inferences.

2   Relationship to local cults, relics, and events. Do you know of or suspect any other associations (eg St Nicholas and fish markets); is there a local 'family' of such dedications? These points could be relevant to B.1 and F.4 and 5. Under *b* no more than a list of dedications (with dates) is required, plus comment on special significance of cults if any. Details of chapels etc should appear in C.4, to which reference should be made if necessary.

4   Include: first specific documentary evidence; possible earlier references; account of founder and foundation if known; DB evidence if relevant; earliest structural or archaeological evidence (in the case of a parish church this will often considerably antedate the written record). This may turn out to be the most important part of the form for a consideration of the origins of town churches; it is certainly the most difficult for which to suggest categories of information. Points to consider should probably include: evidence for the use of the site before the church was founded; whether any part of the church structure previously had a different function; relationship to earlier cemeteries or pre-urban settlements; association with a neighbouring house or property; whether the lord of the surrounding land subsequently possessed the advowson.

5   Outline the general development of the church: estimate periods of prosperity, decay, disuse, revival. Is the church still in use? If not, what happened to the structure and when, and what was the subsequent history of the site? Was the church merged with that of another parish or transferred to another site? If the latter, refer to a separate record form.

C   *Structure*

1   Not a bibliography (which should appear in the bulkier file) but an indication of the evidence available for an account of the structural development. If the church has been demolished do any architectural features survive, even on another site?

2   This can only be an outline. Full discussion should be confined to the file of detailed evidence, which should contain copies of all such plans, elevations, sections, etc as it is possible to obtain or make. If possible, this section of the form should include an analytical plan of the church or a sequence of plans. It should be emphasized that all the remaining headings in section C of the record form will contain topics relevant to the general development of the church structure, and it would perhaps be advisable to complete C.2 after these other topics have been considered. C.2 should provide a rapid and clear introduction to the overall structural development of the church and is therefore placed before the sections dealing with more detailed aspects of the structure.

3   Compass bearing of main and subordinate axes. What determined the orientation(s)?

4   Cross-refer to B.2.

5   eg paintings, tiles, screens, pews, walls: summarize existence of objects (with dates); comment on significance if possible.
4 and 5: include reference to any fittings which may have been removed elsewhere.

6   Cross-refer to D.3. Include comment on the state of the evidence: eg have gravestones been removed from their original positions? Indicate date of earlier and latest burials; count or estimate numbers; note existence and position of vaults.

7   Enumerate materials and date at which they were used. Are any particularly characteristic of any period? Are there any re-used materials, eg Roman, medieval architectural fragments indicating the existence of an earlier church on the site. Is there any evidence for the history of building techniques, eg carpentry details, masonry tooling?

8   Did any notable craftsmen work on the church? Any named medieval craftsman? It may be necessary to refer to a list of post-medieval architects contained in the bulkier file.

D   *Site and setting*

1   Hill-top, market-place, next to or over town gate, within cemetery or precinct of another church. Did the site give the church any special advantages or disadvantages?

2   Relationship to street, surrounding houses, or other buildings. Access. Any changes in the setting?

3   Where was the cemetery, if any? Give contemporary term if known. Did the church yard contain any special structural or topographical features, eg crosses, lock-ups, wells? Do the burials have any special characteristics, including their orientation? Date of earliest and latest burials? Is the total number of burials known? Comment on the state of the evidence.

4   Where did the incumbent live? What was the relationship of the clergy-house to the church? Cross-refer to D.3 if appropriate.

E   *Clergy*

1   *NB:* Was the church ever held in plurality as a stage to unification?

2   ie any evidence for the numbers of priests, clerks, etc at different dates?

3   Do they belong to any particular group at any period, eg ecclesiastical or royal officials, relatives of the patron or a local property owner, are they graduates, Augustinian canons, etc?

F   *Parochial status*

1   What terms were used to describe the church? What is their significance in their context? When are there references to the parish?

2 and 3   Use architectural or archaeological evidence if available. The account of burial should simply deal with features diagnostic of parochial status; it should, however, include an estimate of whether burial at the church was a usual or an infrequent practice.

4 and 5   Include all evidence of pensions, station, and other rights. Were there any changes in the relationship?

6   eg Was it held in plurality?

7   Any evidence for their payment and how they were assessed?

G   *The parish*

1.a   eg maps, location of properties, taxation lists, and surveys.

1.b   Do they follow or respect any topographical or tenurial feature? Has anything else conditioned the shape of the parish? Are there detached portions, and is their significance known?

1.d   Acreage, number of houses, households, or communicants?

3   Cross-refer to D.3 and 4.

H, J, and K   *Guilds, chantries, and 'other liturgical evidence'*

These headings are largely self-explanatory. K should include a note of special liturgical practices (eg stations, processions, drama) associated with the church.

L   *Value*

1   Include what you know of the church's sources of revenue apart from tithes (cf F.7) and parish property (cf G.3).

2   *NB:* Late medieval valuations tend to follow those of the Pope Nicholas taxation.

M   *Potential for further investigation*

Give an appraisal of the archaeological potential of the church, and list any outstanding problems which archaeological investigation might be expected to solve. If the church is threatened with redundancy or major restoration, give details.

Bibliography

Addleshaw, G W O, 1970a *The beginnings of the parochial system*, St Anthony's Hall Pub **3**, 3 edn

——, 1970b *The development of the parochial system from Charlemagne (768–814) to Urban II (1088–1099)*, St Anthony's Hall Pub **6**, 2 edn

Addleshaw, G W O, & Etchells, F, 1948 *The architectural setting of Anglican worship: an inquiry into the arrangements for public worship in the Church of England from the Reformation to the present day*

Addyman, P V, 1973 The potential of church excavation, in Jesson 1973, 19–22

——, 1977 York and Canterbury as ecclesiastical centres, in Barley 1977, 499–509

Addyman, P V, & Morris, R K (eds), 1976 *The archaeological study of churches*, Counc Brit Archaeol Res Rep, **13**

Alcock, L A, 1963 *Dinas Powys: an Iron Age, Dark Age and early medieval settlement in Glamorgan*

——, 1970 Was there an Irish Sea culture-province in the Dark Ages?, in *The Irish Sea Province in archaeology and history* (ed D Moore), 55–65

——, 1971 *Arthur's Britain: history and archaeology AD 367–634*

——, 1972 *'By South Cadbury is that Camelot. . . .' Excavations at Cadbury Castle 1966–70*

Allcroft, H, 1928 The Circle and the Cross: Appendix D, Archbishop Cuthbert and the churchyards, *Archaeol J*, **35**, 147–8

Ambrose, T, 1979 *Gods and goddesses of Roman Ancaster*, Lincolnshire Mus Info Sheet (Archaeol Ser), **8**

Andrews, R D, 1978 St Patrick's Chapel, Heysham, Lancs, *Bull Counc Brit Archaeol Churches Committee*, **8**, 2

Applebaum, S, 1972 Roman Britain, in Finberg 1972, 5–267

Arnold, C J, 1977 Early Saxon settlement patterns in southern England, *J Hist Geogr*, **3**, 309–15

——, 1980 Wealth and social structure: a matter of life and death, in *Anglo-Saxon cemeteries 1979: the fourth Anglo-Saxon symposium at Oxford* (eds P A Rahtz, T Dickinson, & L Watts), Brit Archaeol Rep, **82**, 81–142

Atkinson, R J C, 1960 *Archaeology, history and science; an inaugural lecture*, Cardiff

Austin, D, 1976 Fieldwork and excavation at Hart, Co Durham, *Archaeol Aeliana*, 5 ser, **4**, 69–132

Bailey, R N, 1976 The Anglo-Saxon church at Hexham, *ibid*, **4**, 47–67

——, 1977 A cup-mount from Brougham, Cumbria, *Medieval Archaeol*, **21**, 176–80

——, 1980 *Viking Age sculpture in northern England*

Bailey, R N, & O'Sullivan, D, 1979 Excavations over St Wilfrid's Crypt at Hexham, 1978, *Archaeol Aeliana*, 5 ser, **7**, 145–57

Baker, N, 1980 Churches, parishes and early medieval topography, in Carver 1980, 31–8

——, 1980b The urban churches of Worcester, in Carver 1980, 115–24

Baldwin Brown, G, 1903 *The arts in early England*, **1**

Barker, K, 1980 The early Christian topography of Sherborne, *Antiquity*, **54**, 229–31

Barker, P A, 1969 The origins of Worcester: an interim survey, *Trans Worcestershire Archaeol Soc*, 3 ser, **2**, 1–116

——, 1977 *Techniques of archaeological excavation*

——, 1979 The latest occupation of the site of the baths basilica at Wroxeter, in Casey 1979, 175–81

Barley, M W (ed), 1976 *The plans and topography of medieval towns in England and Wales*, Counc Brit Archaeol Res Rep, **14**

—— (ed), 1977 *European towns: their archaeology and early history*

Barley, M W, & Hanson, R P C (eds), 1968 *Christianity in Britain, 300–700*

Barlow, F, 1963 *The English Church 1000–1066: a constitutional history*

——, 1979 *The English Church 1066–1154*

Barrow, G W S, 1973 *The Kingdom of the Scots; government, church and society from the eleventh to the fourteenth century*

——, 1975 The pattern of lordship and feudal settlement in Cumbria, *J Medieval Hist*, **1**, 117–38

Beckerlegge, J J, 1953 Ancient memorial inscription on a stone at Hayle, *Old Cornwall*, **5**, 173–8

Bede, *Historia Ecclesiastica Gentis Anglorum*, ed C Plummer, *Venerabilis Baedae Opera Historica*, 2 vols (1896). *Bede's Ecclesiastical history of the English people*, eds B Colgrave & R A B Mynors (1969)

Bedwin, O, 1975 The excavation of the church of St Nicholas, Angmering, 1974, *Sussex Archaeol Collect*, **113**, 16–34

Bell, M, 1978 Saxon settlements and buildings in Sussex, in Brandon 1978, 36–53

Benson, H, 1956 Church orientations and patronal festivals, *Antiq J*, **36**, 205–13

Beresford, M W, 1954 *The lost villages of England*, 4 imp

——, 1967 *New towns in the Middle Ages*

Beresford, M W, & Hurst, J G (eds), 1971 *Deserted medieval villages*

——, & ——, 1976 Wharram Percy: a case study in microtopography, in Sawyer 1976, 114–44

Beresford, M W, & St Joseph, J K S, 1958 *Medieval England: an aerial survey*

Bidder, H F, & Westlake, H, 1930 Excavations at Merton Priory, *Surrey Archaeol Collect*, **38**, 49–66

Biddle, M, 1964 Excavations at Winchester, 1962–3, 2nd interim report, *Antiq J*, **44**, 188–219

——, 1965 Excavations at Winchester, 1964, 3rd interim report, *ibid*, **45**, 230–64

——, 1966 Excavations at Winchester, 1965, 4th interim report, *ibid*, **46**, 308–32

——, 1967 Excavations at Winchester, 5th interim report, *ibid*, **47**, 251–79

——, 1968 Excavations at Winchester, 6th interim report, *ibid*, **48**, 250–84

——, 1969 Excavations at Winchester, 1968, 7th interim report, *ibid*, **49**, 295–329

——, 1970 Excavations at Winchester, 1969, 8th interim report, *ibid*, **50**, 277–326

——, 1972 Excavations at Winchester, 1970, 9th interim report, *ibid*, **52**, 93–131

——, 1975a Excavations at Winchester, 1971, 10th and final interim report, *ibid*, **55**, 96–126, 295–337

——, 1975b *Felix Urbs Winthonia*: Winchester in the age of monastic reform, in Parsons 1975, 123–40

——, 1976a The archaeology of the church: a widening horizon, in Addyman & Morris 1976, 65–71

——, 1976b Towns, in D M Wilson 1976, 99–150

—— (ed), 1976c *Winchester studies 1: Winchester in the early Middle Ages: an edition and discussion of the Winton Domesday*

Biddle, M, & Hudson, D M, 1973 *The future of London's past: a survey of the archaeological implications of planning and development in the nation's capital*

Biddle, M, & Kjølbye-Biddle, B, 1969 Metres, areas and robbing, *World Archaeol*, **1**, 208–19

Biddle, M, Lambrick, H T, & Myres, J N L, 1968 The early history of Abingdon, Berkshire, and its Abbey, *Medieval Archaeol*, **12**, 26–69

Bidwell, P T, 1978 The Cathedral Close, Exeter, *Bull Counc Brit Archaeol Churches Committee*, **8**, 8–11

Bidwell, P T, *et al*, 1979 *The legionary bath-house and basilica and forum at Exeter, with a summary account of the legionary fortress*, Exeter Archaeol Rep, **1**

Bieler, L, 1952 *Libri Epistolarum Sancti Patricii Episcopi*, 2 vols

——, 1968 The Christianization of the insular Celts during the sub-Roman period and its repercussions on the Continent, *Celtica*, **8**, 112–25

Bilson, J, 1911 The plan of the first cathedral church at Lincoln, *Archaeologia*, **62**, 543–64

Binding, G, 1975 Quellen, Brunnen und Reliquiengräber in Kirchen, *Zeitschrift für Archäologie des Mittelalters*, **3**, 37–56

Binford, L R, 1972 *An archaeological perspective*

Birch, W de G, 1885–99 *Cartularium Saxonicum*, 3 vols

Bishop, H, 1978 Excavations at the church of SS Peter and Paul, Healing, South Humberside, *Lincolnshire Hist Archaeol*, **13**, 25–32

Blomqvist, R, & Mårtensson, A W, 1963 Thulegrävningen 1961, *Archeologica Lundensia*, **2**

Boden, J M, & Whitwell, J B W, 1979 Barrow-on-Humber, *Lincolnshire Hist Archaeol*, **14**, 66–7

Bond, F, 1905 *Gothic architecture in England*

——, 1908 *Fonts and font covers*

——, 1914 *Dedications and patron saints of English churches: ecclesiastical symbolism, saints and their emblems*

Bonney, D J, 1966 Pagan Saxon burials and boundaries in Wiltshire, *Wiltshire Archaeol Natur Hist Mag*, **64**, 56–64

——, 1972 Early boundaries in Wessex, in *Archaeology and the landscape* (ed P J Fowler), 168–86

Boon, G C, 1976   The Shrine of the Head, Caerwent, in Boon & Lewis 1976, 163–75

Boon, G C, & Lewis, J M (eds), 1976   *Welsh antiquity: essays mainly on prehistoric topics presented to H N Savory upon his retirement as Keeper of Archaeology*

Bowen, E G, 1954   *The settlements of the Celtic saints in Wales*

——, 1969   *Saints, seaways and settlements in the Celtic lands*

Brandon, P (ed), 1978   *The South Saxons*

Brereton, C, 1865   St Mary's Parish Church, Beverley, *Assoc Architect Socs Rep Pap*, **8**, 91–110

Brett, M, 1975   *The English Church under Henry I*

Bridges, 1960   *Report of the Archbishops' Commission on Redundant Churches 1958–60*

Briggs, C S, 1979   Ysbyty Cynfyn churchyard wall, *Archaeol Cambrensis*, **128**, 138–46

Brooke, C N L, 1970   The missionary at home: The church in the towns, 1000–1250, *Stud Church Hist*, **6**, 59–83

——, 1977   The medieval town as an ecclesiastical centre: general survey, in Barley 1977, 459–73

Brooke, C N L, & Keir, G, 1975   *London 800–1216: the shaping of a city*

Brooks, N P, 1977   The ecclesiastical topography of early medieval Canterbury, in Barley 1977, 487–96

Brothwell, D, 1972   British palaeodemography and earlier British populations, *World Archaeol*, **4**, 75–87

Brown, M, 1978   St Cuthbert, Ormesby, *Bull Counc Brit Archaeol Churches Committee*, **5**, 9–11

Brown, P D C, 1971   The church at Richborough, *Britannia*, **2**, 225–31

——, 1976   Archaeological evidence for the Anglo-Saxon period, in *Studies in the archaeology and history of Cirencester* (ed A D McWhirr), 19–45

Brown, P D C, & McWhirr, A D, 1966   Cirencester 1965, *Antiq J*, **46**, 240–54

——, & ——, 1967   Cirencester 1966, *ibid*, **47**, 185–97

Bruce, J R, 1966/68   *Keeills and burial grounds in the sheadig of Rushen*, Manx Archaeol Survey, Sixth Report

Bryant, R, 1980   Excavations at the church of St Mary de Lode, Gloucester, *Bull Counc Brit Archaeol Churches Committee*, **13**, 15–18

Bucher, F, 1968   Design in Gothic architecture – a preliminary reassessment, *J Soc Architect Hist*, **27**, 49–71

—— (ed), 1979   *Architector: the lodge books and sketch books of medieval architects*, **1**

Buckley, D G (ed), 1980   *Archaeology in Essex to AD 1500*, Counc Brit Archaeol Res Rep, **34**

Bu'lock, J D, 1956   Early Christian memorial formulae, *Archaeol Cambrensis*, **105**, 133–41

Burgess, F, 1963   *English churchyard memorials*

Burrow, I, 1973 (1974)   Tintagel – some problems, *Scot Archaeol Forum*, **5**, 99–103

——, 1979   Roman material from hillforts, in Casey 1979, 212–29

Bury, J B, 1905   *The life of St Patrick and his place in history*

Butler, L A S, 1964   Minor medieval monumental sculpture in the East Midlands, *Archaeol J*, **121**, 111–53

——, 1974   Leicester's Church, Denbigh: an experiment in Puritan worship, *J Brit Archaeol Ass*, 3 ser, **37**, 40–62

——, 1976   Documentary evidence and the church fabric, in Addyman & Morris 1976, 18–21

——, 1977   Continuity of settlement in Wales in the central Middle Ages, in Laing 1977, 61–6

——, 1978   St Martin's Church, Allerton Mauleverer, *Yorkshire Archaeol J*, **50**, 177–88

——, 1979   The 'Monastic City' in Wales: myth or reality?, *Bull Board Celtic Stud*, **28**, 458–67

——, 1980   The churchyard in eastern England, AD 900–1100: some lines of development, in *Anglo-Saxon cemeteries 1979: the fourth Anglo-Saxon Symposium at Oxford* (eds P A Rahtz, T Dickinson, & L Watts), 383–9

Butler, L A S, Rahtz, P A, & Taylor, H M, 1975   Deerhurst 1971–1974: the Society's research project on the archaeology of the English church, *Antiq J*, **55**, 346–65

Butler, R M (ed), 1971   *Soldier and civilian in Roman Yorkshire*

Cam, H, 1944   *Liberties and communities in medieval England*

Cambridge, E, 1979   C C Hodges and the nave of Hexham Abbey, *Archaeol Aeliana*, 5 ser, **7**, 159–68

Cameron, K, 1968   Eccles in English place-names, in Barley & Hanson 1968, 87–92

Campbell, A (ed & trans), 1967   *Æthelwulf, De Abbatibus*

Campbell, J, 1979   The church in Anglo-Saxon towns, *Stud Church Hist*, **16**, 119–35

Cant, R G, 1972   The church in Orkney and Shetland and its relations with Norway and Scotland in the Middle Ages, *Northern Scot*, **1**, 1–18

Capes, W W (ed), 1909   *The Register of Richard de Swinfield, 1283–1327*, Cantilupe Soc

Carter, A, 1978   The Anglo-Saxon origins of Norwich: the problems and approaches, *Anglo-Saxon Engl*, **7**, 175–204

Carver, M O H, 1978   Book review: Historic churches – a wasting asset, *Bull Counc Brit Archaeol Churches Committee*, **8**, 10–12

—— (ed), 1980   Medieval Worcester: an archaeological framework. Reports, surveys, texts, essays, *Trans Worcestershire Archaeol Soc*, 3 ser, **7**

Casey, P J (ed), 1979   *The end of Roman Britain*, Brit Archaeol Rep, **71**

Cathedrals 1972, 1973   *Architectural history of some English cathedrals. A collection in two parts of papers delivered during the years 1842–1863 by the Rev Robert Willis, MA, FRS*, 2 vols

Chadwick, O, 1959   The evidence of dedications in the early history of the Welsh church, in *Studies in early British history* (ed N K Chadwick), 173–88

Chadwick, S E, 1958   The Anglo-Saxon cemetery at Finglesham, Kent: a reconsideration, *Medieval Archaeol*, **2**, 1–71

Charles-Edwards, T M, 1976   Boundaries in Irish law, in Sawyer 1976, 83–90

Cherry, B, 1976   Ecclesiastical architecture, in D M Wilson 1976, 151–200

Christie, H, Olsen, O, & Taylor, H M, 1979   The wooden church of St Andrew at Greensted, Essex, *Antiq J*, **59**, 92–112

Clapham, A W, 1930   *English Romanesque architecture before the Conquest*

——, 1934   *English Romanesque architecture after the Conquest*

Clark, P, & Slack, P, 1972   *Crisis and order in English towns 1500–1700*

Colgrave, B (ed), 1927   *The Life of Bishop Wilfrid by Eddius Stephanus*

—— (ed & trans), 1940   *Two Lives of St Cuthbert*

Colgrave, B, & Mynors, R A B, 1969   see Bede

Collingwood, R G, & Wright, R P, 1965   *The Roman inscriptions of Britain:* **1**, *Inscriptions on stone*

Collingwood, W, G, 1927   *Northumbrian crosses of the pre-Norman age*

Collins, A H, 1955   Saxon cinerary urn from Pagham churchyard, *Sussex Notes Queries*, **14**, 123–5

Colyer, C, 1976   Excavations at St Mark, Lincoln, *Bull Counc Brit Archaeol Churches Committee*, **5**, 5–9

Coppack, G, 1978   St Lawrence, Burnham, South Humberside, *Bull Counc Brit Archaeol Churches Committee*, **8**, 5–6

Corder, P (ed), 1961   *The Roman town and villa at Great Casterton, Rutland. Third report for the years 1954–1958*, Univ Nottingham

Corney, A, et al, 1967 (1969)   A prehistoric and Anglo-Saxon burial ground, Ports Down, *Proc Hampshire Fld Club Archaeol Soc*, **24**, 20–41

Cramp, R J, 1969   Excavations at the Saxon monastic sites of Wearmouth and Jarrow, County Durham: an interim report, *Medieval Archaeol*, **13**, 21–66

——, 1973   Anglo-Saxon monasteries of the north, *Scot Archaeol Forum*, **5**, 114–24

——, 1976a   Monastic sites, in D M Wilson 1976, 200–53

——, 1976b   St Paul's Church, Jarrow, in Addyman & Morris 1976, 28–35

——, 1977   The Brixworth Archaeological Research Committee, *J Brit Archaeol Ass*, **130**, 52–4

Cramp, R J, & Douglas-Home, C, 1977–8   New discoveries at The Hirsel, Coldstream, Berwickshire, *Proc Soc Antiq Scot*, **109**, 223–32

Cra'ster, M D, 1961   St Michael's, Gloucester, *Trans Bristol Gloucestershire Archaeol Soc*, **80**, 59–74

Cronne, H A, & Davis, R H C (ed), 1968   *Regesta Regum Anglo-Normannorum*, **3**

Crummy, P J, 1974   *Colchester: recent excavations and research*, Colchester Excavation Committee

——, 1980   The temples of Roman Colchester, in Rodwell 1980, 243–83

Cunliffe, B W, 1964   *Winchester excavations 1949–1960*

——, 1977   *Excavations at Portchester Castle*, **3**, *Medieval, the outer bailey and its defences*, Rep Res Comm Soc Antiq London, **34**

Darby, H C, 1971   *The Domesday geography of eastern England*, 3 edn

Darby, H C, & Campbell, E M J (eds), 1962   *The Domesday geography of south-east England*

Darlington, R R, 1968   *Cartulary of Worcester Cathedral Priory*, Pipe Roll Soc

Davey, N, 1964   A pre-Conquest church and baptistery at Potterne, Wilts, *Wiltshire Archaeol Natur Hist Mag*, **59**, 116–23

Davidson, H R E, & Webster, L, 1967   The Anglo-Saxon burial at Coombe (Woodnesborough) Kent, *Medieval Archaeol*, **11**, 1–41

Davies, J G, 1962   *The architectural setting of baptism*

——, 1964   Baptismal architecture, in Lockett 1964, 1–12

Davies, W, 1973   Liber Landavensis: its construction and credibility, *Engl Hist Rev*, **88**, 335–51

——, 1978   *An early Welsh microcosm: studies in the Llandaff charters*, Roy Hist Soc Stud Hist, **9**

——, 1979a   *The Llandaff charters*

——, 1979b   Roman settlements and post-Roman estates in south-east Wales, in Casey 1979, 153–73

Davies, W H, 1968   The Church in Wales, in Barley & Hanson 1968, 131–50

Dawes, J D, & Magilton, J R, 1980   *The cemetery of St Helen-on-the-Walls, Aldwark, The archaeology of York,* **12**/1, Counc Brit Archaeol

Detsicas, A P, 1976   Excavations at Eccles, 1975, *Archaeol Cantiana,* **92**, 157–63

Dobson, R B, 1976   The historical documentation of monastic sites (to 1500), in *Working Party on the archaeology of monastic sites: a compilation of papers* (Counc Brit Archaeol), 9–13

——, 1977   Urban decline in late medieval England, *Trans Roy Hist Soc,* 5 ser, **27**, 1–22

Donovan, H E, & Dunning, G C, 1936   Iron Age pottery and Saxon burials at Foxcote Manor, Andoversford, Gloucestershire, *Trans Bristol Gloucestershire Archaeol Soc,* **58**, 167

Dornier, A (ed), 1977a   *Mercian studies*

——, 1977b   The Anglo-Saxon monastery at Breedon-on-the-Hill, Leicestershire, in Dornier 1977a, 155–68

Douglas, D C (ed), 1944   *The Domesday Monachorum of Christchurch, Canterbury*

Down, A, 1971   *Chichester excavations,* **1**

——, 1974   *Chichester excavations,* **2**

Drury, P J, & Rodwell, W J, 1978   Investigations at Asheldham, Essex. An interim report on the church and the historic landscape, *Antiq J,* **58**, 133–51

Dryden, H, 1878   Records of restoration of churches, *Assoc Architect Socs Rep Pap,* **14**, 244–59

Dunning, R W, 1975   Ilchester: a study in continuity, *Somerset Archaeol Natur Hist Soc,* **119**, 44–50

Dymond, D P, 1968   The Suffolk landscape, in *East Anglian studies* (ed L Munby), 17–47

Eagles, B N, 1979   *The Anglo-Saxon settlement of Humberside,* Brit Archaeol Rep, **68**, 2 vols

Ekwall, E, 1922   *The place-names of Lancashire*

Evans, K J, 1974   Excavations on a Romano-British site, Wiggonholt, 1964, *Sussex Archaeol Collect,* **112**, 97–151

Everson, P, 1977   Excavations in the vicarage garden at Brixworth, 1972, *J Brit Archaeol Ass,* **130**, 55–122

Evison, V I, 1956   An Anglo-Saxon cemetery at Holborough, Kent, *Archaeol Cantiana,* **70**, 84–141

——, 1963   Sugar-loaf shield-bosses, *Antiq J,* **43**, 38–96

Fairweather, F H, 1926   Some additions to the plan of the Benedictine Priory Church of St Mary, Blyth, Notts, *ibid,* **6**, 36–42

Farrar, R A H, 1962 (1963)   Some Roman *tesserae* under the nave of Wimborne Minster, *Proc Dorset Natur Hist Archaeol Soc,* **84**, 106–9

Farrer, W (ed), 1914   *Early Yorkshire charters,* **1**

Faull, M L, 1976   The location and relationship of the Sancton Anglo-Saxon cemeteries, *Antiq J,* **56**, 227–33

——, 1977   British survival in Anglo-Saxon Northumbria, in Laing 1977, 1–55

——, 1979   *British survival in Anglo-Saxon Yorkshire,* unpub PhD thesis, Univ Leeds (publication forthcoming)

——, 1981   The pre-Conquest ecclesiastical pattern, in *West Yorkshire: an archaeological survey to AD 1500* (eds M L Faull and S A Moorhouse), 210–23

Faull, M L, & Smith, R T, 1980   Phosphate analysis and three possible dark age ecclesiastical sites in Yorkshire, *Landscape Hist,* **2**, 26–43

Fawtier, R (ed), 1912   *La vie de Saint Samson*

Fehring, G P, 1972   *Unterregenbach,* 3 vols

Fehring, G P, *et al,* 1970   Arbeiten der archäologie des mittelalters in Baden-Württemberg, *Nachriten Blatt der Denkmalpflege in Baden-Württemberg,* **13**, 65–114

Feine, H E, 1950   *Kirkliche Rechtsgeschichte,* **1**, *Die Katholische Kirche*

Fenn, R W D, 1968   The character of early Christianity in Radnorshire, *Trans Radnorshire Soc,* **37**, 7–16

Finberg, H P R, 1961   *The early charters of the West Midlands*

—— (ed), 1972   *The agrarian history of England and Wales,* **1**(ii)

Fisher, J D C, 1965   *Christian initiation: baptism in the medieval west. A study in the disintegration of the primitive rite of initiation,* Alcuin Club Collect, **47**

Fletcher, E, & Meates, G W, 1969   The ruined church of Stone-by-Faversham, *Antiq J,* **49**, 273–94

——, & ——, 1977   The ruined church of Stone-by-Faversham: second report, *ibid,* **57**, 67–72

Foard, G, 1978   Systematic fieldwalking and the investigation of Saxon settlement in Northamptonshire, *World Archaeol,* **9**, 357–74

Folk, R L, & Valastro, S, 1976   Successful technique for dating of lime mortar by carbon-14, *J Fld Archaeol,* **3**, 203–8

Forster, F Arnold, 1899   *Studies in church dedications,* 3 vols

Fowler, J T, 1888   Notes on All Saints', Winterton, *Assoc Architect Socs Rep Pap,* **19**, 2, 363–75

Fowler, P J, 1976   Agriculture and rural settlement, in D M Wilson 1976, 23–48

Frend, W H C, 1955   Religion in Roman Britain in the fourth century, *J Brit Archaeol Ass,* 3 ser, **18**, 1–18

——, 1968   The Christianization of Roman Britain, in Barley & Hanson 1968, 37–50

Frere, S S, 1961   Some Romano-British sculptures from Ancaster and Wilsford, Lincolnshire, *Antiq J,* **41**, 229–31

——, 1975   The Silchester Church: the excavation by Sir Ian Richmond in 1961, *Archaeologia,* **105**, 277–302

Fulford, M, & Sellwood, B, 1980   The Silchester ogham stone: a reconsideration, *Antiquity,* **54**, 95–9

Galbraith, V H, 1961   *The making of Domesday Book*

Gelling, M, 1961   Place-names and Anglo-Saxon paganism, *Univ Birmingham Hist J,* **8**, 7–25

——, 1977   Latin loan words in Old English place-names, *Anglo-Saxon Engl,* **6**, 1–13

General Synod 1974   *Report of the Bishop of Sheffield's Working Group on redeployment of the clergy*

Gibb, J H, & Gem, R D H, 1975   The Anglo-Saxon cathedral at Sherborne, *Archaeol J,* **132**, 71–110

Gilbert, E, 1964   The Church of St Mary and St Eadburg, Lyminge, *Archaeol Cantiana,* **79**, 143–8

Gildas   *Gildae De Excidio Britanniae,* ed H Williams (1899–1901), Cymmrodorion Record Ser, **3**. *Gildas: The ruin of Britain and other works,* ed & trans M Winterbottom (1978)

Gilmour, B, 1979   The Anglo-Saxon church at St Paul-in-the-Bail, Lincoln, *Medieval Archaeol,* **23**, 214–18

Godfrey, J, 1974   The emergence of the village church in Anglo-Saxon England, in Rowley 1974, 131–8

Gould, J, 1973   Letocetum, Christianity and Lichfield, *Trans S Staffordshire Archaeol Hist Soc,* **13**, 30–1

——, 1976   *Lichfield: archaeology and development*

——, 1977   Saxon *cathedra* or 17th-century niche in Lichfield Cathedral?, *Trans S Staffordshire Archaeol Hist Soc,* **18**, 69–72

Gould, J, & Gould, D, 1973–4   Excavation on the site of the old church at Shenstone, Staffs, and the identification of Saxon stonework there, *ibid,* **15**, 44–9

Gracie, H S, 1963   St Peter's Church, Frocester, *Trans Bristol Gloucestershire Archaeol Soc,* **82**, 148–67

Graham-Campbell, J, 1980   The Scandinavian Viking-age burials of England – some problems of interpretation, in *Anglo-Saxon cemeteries 1979* (eds P A Rahtz, T Dickinson, & L Watts), 379–82

Gransden, A, 1980   Antiquarian studies in fifteenth-century England, *Antiq J,* **60**, 75–97

Green, C J S, 1977   The significance of plaster burials for the recognition of Christian cemeteries, in Reece 1977, 46–53

——, 1979   *Poundbury. A summary of recent excavations at Poundbury, Dorchester*

Greenfield, E, 1960   Keynsham Abbey, Somerset, *Somerset Archaeol Natur Hist,* **104**, 130–1

——, 1970   Henley Wood, *Archaeol Rev,* **5**, 28

Grierson, P, 1952–4   The Canterbury (St Martin's) hoard of Frankish and Anglo-Saxon coin-ornaments, *Brit Numis J,* **27**, 39–51

Grimes, W F, 1968   *The excavation of Roman and medieval London*

Grinsell, L V, 1956   Human remains from Keynsham Abbey cemetery, *Notes Queries Somerset Dorset,* **27**, 118–19

Guy, C J, 1978   A Roman lead tank from Burwell, Cambridgeshire, *Proc Cambridge Antiq Soc,* **68**, 1–4

Haddan, A W, & Stubbs, W (eds), 1869–71   *Councils and ecclesiastical documents relating to Great Britain and Ireland,* 3 vols

Hall, R, 1977   Rescue excavations in the crypt of Ripon Cathedral, *Yorkshire Archaeol J,* **49**, 59–63

Hanson, R P C, 1968   Summary and prospect, in Barley & Hanson 1968, 207–13

Harbottle, B, 1975   An excavation in the nave of Woodhorn Church, Northumberland, *Archaeol Aeliana,* 5 ser, **3**, 117–20

Hare, M J, 1976   The Anglo-Saxon Church of St Peter, Titchfield, *Proc Hampshire Fld Club Archaeol Soc,* **32**, 5–48

Harrison, K, 1960   The pre-Conquest churches of York: with an appendix on eighth-century Northumbrian annals, *Yorkshire Archaeol J,* **40**, 232–49

——, 1973   The Synod of Whitby and the beginning of the Christian era in England, *ibid,* **45**, 108–14

——, 1976   *The framework of Anglo-Saxon history to AD 900*

Hart, C R, 1966   *The early charters of eastern England*

Harvey, J H (ed & trans), 1969   *William Worcestre: Itineraries*

——, 1972   *The mediaeval architect*

——, 1974   *Cathedrals of England and Wales*

——, 1978   *The perpendicular style 1330–1485*

Harvey, S P J, 1971   Domesday Book and its predecessors, *Engl Hist Rev,* **86**, 753–73

——, 1976   Evidence for settlement study: Domesday Book, in Sawyer 1976, 195–9

Hatcher, J, 1977   *Plague, population and the English economy 1348–1530*

Hawkes, S C, 1973a   The dating and social significance of the burials in the Polhill cemetery, in Philp 1973, 186–201

Hawkes, S C, 1973b   Finds from the Anglo-Saxon cemetery at Eccles, Kent, *Antiq J*, **53**, 281–6

——, 1976   Orientation at Finglesham: sunrise dating of death and burial in an Anglo-Saxon cemetery in east Kent, *Archaeol Cantiana*, **92**, 33–51

Hawkes, S C, & Grove, L R A, 1963   Finds from a seventh century cemetery at Milton Regis, *ibid*, **78**, 22–38

HE   see under Bede

Heighway, C M (ed), 1972   *The erosion of history: archaeology and planning in towns*, Counc Brit Archaeol

Hewett, C A, 1977   Understanding standing buildings, *World Archaeol*, **9**, 174–84

Heyman, J, 1966   The stone skeleton, *Internat J Solids Structures*, **2**, 249–79

——, 1967   Spires and fan vaults, *ibid*, **3**, 243–57

——, 1967–8   Beauvais Cathedral, *Trans Newcomen Soc*, **40**, 15–32

——, 1968   On the rubber vaults of the Middle Ages, and other matters, *Gazette des Beaux-Arts*, 177–88

——, 1976   An apsidal timber roof at Westminster, *Gesta*, **15**, 53–60

Hill, T D, 1977   The *aecerbot* charm and its Christian user, *Anglo-Saxon Engl*, **6**, 213–21

Hirst, S, 1976   *Recording on excavations.* **1**, *the written record*

Hogarth, A C, 1973   Structural features in Anglo-Saxon graves, *Archaeol J*, **130**, 104–19

Hohler, C E, 1975   Some service books of the later Saxon church, in Parsons 1975, 60–83

Holden, E W, Evison, V I, & Ratcliffe-Densham, H B A, 1969   The Anglo-Saxon burials at Crane Down, Jevington, Sussex, *Sussex Archaeol Collect*, **107**, 126–34

Hood, A B E (ed & trans), 1978   *St Patrick: his writings and Muirchu's Life*

Hope-Taylor, B, 1971   *Under York Minster: archaeological discoveries 1966–71*

——, 1977   *Yeavering: an Anglo-British centre of early Northumbria*

Hoskins, W G, 1955   *The making of the English landscape*

Huggins, P J, 1978   Excavation of Belgic and Romano-British farm with Middle Saxon cemetery and churches at Nazeingbury, Essex, 1975–6, *Essex Archaeol Hist*, **10**, 29–117

Hugot, L, 1968   *Kornelimünster*, Beihefte der Bonner Jahrbücher, **26**

Hull, M R, 1960   The St Nicholas Church site, Colchester, *Trans Essex Archaeol Soc*, **25**, 301–28

Hunter, J, 1972–4   The Church of St Nicholas, Aberdeen, *Proc Soc Antiq Scot*, **105**, 236–47

Hurd, H, 1913   *Some notes on recent archaeological discoveries at Broadstairs*

Hurst, J G, 1976   Wharram Percy: St Martin's Church, in Addyman & Morris 1976, 36–9

Hyslop, M, 1963   Two Anglo-Saxon cemeteries at Chamberlain's Barn, Leighton Buzzard, Bedfordshire, *Archaeol J*, **120**, 161–200

Jackson, E D C, & Fletcher, E, 1968   Excavations at the Lydd Basilica, *J Brit Archaeol Ass*, 3 ser, **31**, 19–26

Jackson, K H, 1953   *Language and history in early Britain*

James, E, 1979   Cemeteries and the problem of Frankish settlement in Gaul, in *Names, words and graves: early medieval settlement* (ed P H Sawyer), 55–89

Janssen, W, 1976   Some major aspects of Frankish and medieval settlement in the Rhineland, in Sawyer 1976, 41–60

Jenkins, F, 1965   St Martin's Church at Canterbury; a survey of the earliest structural features, *Medieval Archaeol*, **9**, 11–15

——, 1976   Preliminary report on the excavations at the Church of St Pancras at Canterbury, *Canterbury Archaeol 1975–76*, 4–5

Jesson, M, 1973   *The archaeology of churches: a report from the Churches Committee of the CBA presented to the conference on the archaeology of churches, held at Norwich on April 13–15, 1973*

Jobey, G, 1967   Excavations at Tynemouth Priory and Castle, *Archaeol Aeliana*, 4 ser, **45**, 33–104

Johnston, D E (ed), 1977   *The Saxon Shore*, Counc Brit Archaeol Res Rep, **18**

Jones, A K G, 1979   Parasite eggs and church archaeology, *Bull Counc Brit Archaeol Churches Committee*, **11**, 2–3

Jones, C W, 1934   The Victorian and Dionysiac paschal tables in the west, *Speculum*, **9**, 408–21

—— (ed), 1943   *Bedae Opera de Temporibus*

Jones, G R J, 1976a   Historical geography and our landed heritage, *Leeds Univ Rev*, **19**, 53–78

——, 1976b   Multiple estates and early settlement, in Sawyer 1976, 15–40

Jones, J, 1976   *How to record graveyards*, Counc Brit Archaeol (2 edn 1979)

Jones, W T, 1980   Early Saxon cemeteries in Essex, in Buckley 1980, 87–95

Keene, D J, 1976   Suburban growth, in Barley 1976, 71–82

Kemp, B R, 1968   The monastic dean of Leominster, *Engl Hist Rev*, **83**, 505–15

Kjølbye-Biddle, B, 1975   A cathedral cemetery: problems in excavation and interpretation, *World Archaeol*, **7**, 87–108

Knight, J K, *et al*, 1977 (1978)   New finds of early Christian monuments, *Archaeol Cambrensis*, **126**, 60–73

Kreusch, F, 1963   *Beobachtungen an der Westanlage der Klosterkirche zu Corvey*, Beihefte der Bonner Jahrbücher, **9**

——, 1967   Kirche, atrium und portikus der Aachener Pfalz, in *Karl der Grosser* (W Braunfels), **3**, 463–533

Laing, L (ed), 1977   *Studies in Celtic survival*, Brit Archaeol Rep, **37**

Lamb, R, 1979   *Church archaeology in Orkney and Shetland*, unpub memorandum, circulated by the author

Lang, J T, 1978   Anglo-Scandinavian sculpture in Yorkshire, in *Viking age York and the north* (ed R A Hall), Counc Brit Archaeol Res Rep, **27**, 11–20

Leech, R, 1975   *Small medieval towns in Avon: archaeology and planning*, Committee Rescue Archaeol Avon Gloucestershire Somerset, Survey No **1**

——, 1980   Religion and burials in South Somerset and North Dorset, in Rodwell 1980, 329–66

Leeds, E T, 1916   An Anglo-Saxon cemetery at Wheatley, Oxfordshire, *Proc Soc Antiq London*, **22**, 48–65

Lennard, R, 1959   *Rural England 1086–1135. A study of social and agrarian conditions*

Lethbridge, T C, 1931   *Recent excavations in Anglo-Saxon cemeteries in Cambridgeshire and Suffolk*, Cambridge Antiq Soc Quarto Publ, n ser, **3**

——, 1936   *A cemetery at Shudy Camps, Cambridgeshire*, Cambridge Antiq Soc Quarto Publ, n ser, **5**

Levison, W, 1941   St Alban and St Albans, *Antiquity*, **15**, 337–59

——, 1946   *England and the continent in the eighth century*

Lewis, J M, 1976a   A survey of the Early Christian monuments of Dyfed, west of the Taf, in Boon & Lewis 1976, 177–92

——, 1976b   Field archaeology in Wales, AD 400–1100: some priorities and prospects, *Archaeol in Wales* (Counc Brit Archaeol Gp 2), 13–16

Lewis, J M, & Knight, B, 1973   Early Christian burials at Llanvithyn House, Glamorgan, *Archaeol Cambrensis*, **122**, 147–53

Lewis, M J T, 1966   *Temples in Roman Britain*

Litten, J W, 1971   A village church in the metropolis, *Essex Countryside*, **19**, 34–6, 50–1

Liversedge, J, 1959   A new hoard of Romano-British pewter from Icklingham, *Proc Cambridge Antiq Soc*, **52**, 6–10

Livett, G M, 1889   Foundations of the Saxon cathedral church at Rochester, *Archaeol Cantiana*, **18**, 261–78

Lockett, W E A (ed), 1964   *The modern architectural setting of the liturgy. Papers read at a conference held at Liverpool, September 1962*

Loyn, H R, & Percival, J, 1975   *The reign of Charlemagne: documents on Carolingian government and administration*

Macalister, R A S (ed), 1945–9   *Corpus Inscriptionum Insularum Celticarum*, 2 vols

Magilton, J R, 1980   *The church of St Helen-on-the-Walls, Aldwark, The archaeology of York*, **10**/1, Counc Brit Archaeol

Mann, J C, 1961   The administration of Roman Britain, *Antiquity*, **35**, 316–20

Markus, R A, 1974   *Christianity in the Roman world*

Marsden, P, Dyson, A, & Rhodes, M, 1975   Excavations on the site of St Mildred's Church, Bread Street, 1973–4, *Trans London Middlesex Archaeol Soc*, **26**, 171–208

Martin, E A, 1978   St Botolph and Hadstock: a reply, *Antiq J*, **58**, 153–9

Mason, E, 1976   The role of the English parishioner 1100–1500, *J Ecclesiastical Hist*, **27**, 17–29

Matthews, C L, & Morris, J, 1962   The Anglos-Saxon cemetery at Marina Drive, Dunstable, *Bedfordshire Archaeol J*, **1**, 25–47

Mayes, P, 1980   St James, Tong, West Yorkshire, *Bull Counc Brit Archaeol Churches Committee*, **12**, 20–1

Meaney, A L, 1964   *A gazetteer of early Anglo-Saxon burial sites*

Meaney, A L, & Hawkes, S C, 1970   *Two Anglo-Saxon cemeteries at Winnall*, Soc Medieval Archaeol Monogr Ser, **4**

Meates, G W, 1955   *Lullingstone Roman villa*

——, 1979   *The Roman villa at Lullingstone, Kent:* **1**, *the site*, Kent Archaeol Soc Monogr Ser, **1**

Metcalf, D M, 1977   Monetary affairs in Mercia in the time of Æthelbald, in Dornier 1977a, 87–106

Miles, H, 1971–2   Excavations at Rhuddlan, 1969–71: interim report, *Flintshire Archaeol Soc Publ*, **25**

Miller, M, 1979   *The saints of Gwynedd*

Mohrmann, C, 1961   *The Latin of St Patrick*

Moorman, F W, 1910   *The place-names of the West Riding of Yorkshire*

Moosbrugger-Len, R, 1956   Gräber frühmittelalterlicher kirchenstifter?, *Jahrbuch der schweizerischen Gesellschaft für Urgeschichte*, **45**

Morris, C, 1976   Pre-Conquest sculpture of the Tees Valley, *Medieval Archaeol*, **20**, 140–6

Morris, J, 1959   Anglo-Saxon Surrey, *Surrey Archaeol Collect*, **56**, 132–58

——, 1966   The dates of the Celtic saints, *J Theological Stud*, n ser, **17**, 342–91

——, 1968   The date of St Alban, *Hertfordshire Archaeol*, **1**, 1–8

——, 1973   *The age of Arthur*

—— (ed & trans), 1980   *Nennius: British history and the Welsh annals*

Morris, R, 1872   *An Old English Miscellany*, Early Engl Text Soc, o ser, **49**

Morris, R K (I), 1976   Kirk Hammerton Church: the tower and the fabric, *Archaeol J*, **133**, 95–103

—— (I), 1977   Redundant churches and the historic landscape, in *Planning and the historic environment*, **2** (eds R T Rowley & M Breakell), 94–119

—— (I), 1978   *Churches and archaeology: archaeological work in and around Anglican churches in use*

Morris, R K (I), & Roxan, J, 1980   Churches on Roman buildings, in Rodwell 1980, 175–209

Morris, R K (II), 1978   The development of later Gothic mouldings in England *c* 1250–1400, Part I, *J Soc Architect Hist Great Brit*, **21**, 18–57

—— (II), 1979   The development of later Gothic mouldings in England, *c* 1250–1400, Part II, *ibid*, **22**, 1–48

Mortimer, J R, 1906   *Forty years' researches in the British and Saxon burial mounds of East Yorkshire*

Myres, J N L, 1969   *Anglo-Saxon pottery and the settlement of England*

Nash-Williams, V E, 1930   Further excavations at Caerwent, Monmouthshire 1923–25, *Archaeologia*, **80**, 229–88

——, 1950   *The early Christian monuments of Wales*

——, 1953   The Forum-and-Basilica and public baths of the Roman town of *Venta Silurum* at Caerwent in Monmouthshire, *Bull Board Celtic Stud*, **15**, 159–67

O'Connell, D J, 1936   Easter cycles in the early Irish Church, *J Roy Soc Antiq Ir*, **66**, 67–106

OED   *The Oxford English Dictionary* (reprint 1970)

Okasha, E, 1971   *Handlist of Anglo-Saxon non-runic inscriptions*

Olsen, O, 1966   *Hørg, Hov og Kirke*

O'Neil, H E, 1960   Saxon burials on the Fosse Way at Bourton-on-the-Water, Glos, *Proc Cotteswold Natur Fld Club*, **33**, 166–9

O'Sullivan, D, 1980a   Curvilinear churchyards in Cumbria, *Bull Counc Brit Archaeol Churches Committee*, **13**, 3–5

——, 1980b   A reassessment of the early Christian archaeology of Cumbria, unpublished MPhil thesis, Univ Durham

O'Sullivan, T D, 1978   *The De Excidio of Gildas: its authenticity and date*

Oswald, A, 1956   *The Church of St Berthelin at Stafford and its cross*

Owen, D, 1971   *Church and society in medieval Lincolnshire*

——, 1975   Medieval chapels in Lincolnshire, *Lincolnshire Hist Archaeol*, **10**, 15–22

——, 1976a   Documentary sources for the building history of churches in the Middle Ages, in Addyman & Morris 1976, 21–5

——, 1976b   Chapelries and rural settlement: an examination of some of the Kesteven evidence, in Sawyer 1976, 66–71

——, 1978   Bedfordshire chapelries: an essay in rural settlement history, in *Worthington George Smith and other studies presented to Joyce Godber*, Bedfordshire Hist Rec Soc, **57**, 9–20

Page, W, 1915   Some remarks on the churches of the Domesday Survey, *Archaeologia*, **66**, 61–102

Painter, K S, 1969   The Lullingstone wall-plaster; an aspect of Christianity in Roman Britain, *Brit Mus Quart*, **33**, 131–50

——, 1971   Villas and Christianity in Roman Britain, in *Prehistoric and Roman studies* (ed G de G Sieveking), 156–75

——, 1975   A 4th-century Christian silver treasure found at Water Newton, England, in 1975, *Riv Archaeol Cristiana*, **51**, 333–45

——, 1976   The design of the Roman mosaic at Hinton St Mary, *Antiq J*, **56**, 49–54

——, 1977   *The Water Newton early Christian silver*

Palliser, D M, 1974   The unions of parishes at York, 1547–1586, *Yorkshire Archaeol J*, **46**, 87–102

——, 1978   A crisis in English towns? The case of York, 1460–1640, *Northern Hist*, **14**, 108–25

——, 1980   Historical assessment, in *The cemetery of St Helen-on-the-Walls, Aldwark* (J D Dawes & J R Magilton), *The archaeology of York*, **12**/1, 82–3

Parsons, D (ed), 1975   *Tenth-century studies: essays in commemoration of the millennium of the Council of Winchester and Regularis Concordia*

——, 1977   Brixworth and its monastery church, in Dornier 1977a, 173–90

——, 1979a   Past history and present research at All Saints' Church, Brixworth, *Northamptonshire Past Present*, **6**, 61–71

——, 1979b   St Mary, Ketton, and some other Rutland churches, *Archaeol J*, **136**, 118–24

——, 1980a   Brixworth and the Boniface connexion, *Northamptonshire Past Present*, **6**, 179–83

——, 1980b   A dated timber fragment from Brixworth Church, Northamptonshire, *J Brit Archaeol Ass*, **133**, 30–6

Pearce, S, 1978   *The Kingdom of Dumnonia: studies in history and tradition of south-western Britain AD 350–750*

Peers, C R, 1927   Reculver: its Saxon church and cross, *Archaeologia*, **77**, 241–56

——, 1931   Recent discoveries in the minsters of Ripon and York, *Antiq J*, **11**, 113–22

Peers, C R, & Clapham, A W, 1927   St Augustine's Abbey church, Canterbury, before the Norman Conquest, *Archaeologia*, **77**, 201–18

Peers, C R, & Radford, C A R, 1943   The Saxon monastery of Whitby, *ibid*, **89**, 27–88

Pepperdene, M, 1958   Bede's *Historia Ecclesiastica*: a new perspective, *Celtica*, **4**, 253–62

Percival, J, 1976   *The Roman villa*

Petch, D F, 1962   A Roman inscription, Ancaster, *Lincolnshire Architect Archaeol Soc Rep Pap*, **9**, 97–9

Phillips, A D, 1975   Excavations at York Minster 1967–73, *Friends of York Minster Annu Rep*, **46**, 19–27

——, 1976   Excavation techniques in church archaeology, in Addyman & Morris 1976, 54–9

Philp, B J, 1968   *Excavations at Faversham 1965*

—— (ed), 1973   *Excavations in west Kent 1960–1970*

Phythian-Adams, C, 1977   Rutland reconsidered, in Dornier 1977a, 63–84

——, 1978   *Continuity, fields and fission: the making of a midland parish*, Univ Leicester Dep English Local Hist Occas Pap, 3 ser, **4**

Platt, C, & Coleman-Smith, R, 1975   *Excavations in medieval Southampton 1953–1969*

Pocock, M, & Wheeler, H, 1971   Excavations at Escomb church, County Durham, *J Brit Archaeol Ass*, 3 ser, **34**, 11–29

Poole, R L, 1934   *Studies in chronology and history*

Poulton, R, & Alexander, M, 1979   *Guildford's Dominican Friary: recent excavations*

Prigg, H, 1901   *Icklingham papers*

Radford, C A R, 1935a   Tintagel; the castle and Celtic monastery – interim report, *Antiq J*, **15**, 401–19

——, 1935b   *Tintagel Castle*, HMSO

——, 1942   Tintagel in history and legend, *J Roy Inst Cornwall*, **86**, 25–41

——, 1957   Excavations at Whithorn (final report), *Trans Dumfriesshire Galloway Natur Hist Antiq Soc*, **34**, 131–94

——, 1961   The church of St Mary, Stoke D'Abernon, Surrey, *Archaeol J*, **118**, 165–74

——, 1961–62   The church in Somerset down to 1100, *Somerset Archaeol Natur Hist*, **106**, 28–45

——, 1962   The Celtic monastery in Britain, *Archaeol Cambrensis*, **111**, 1–24

——, 1967   The early church in Strathclyde and Galloway, *Medieval Archaeol*, **11**, 105–26

——, 1968   Glastonbury Abbey, in *The quest for Arthur's Britain* (ed G Ashe), 119–38

——, 1969   Rochester Cathedral: a new fragment of pre-Conquest wall, *Annu Rep Friends Rochester Cathedral*, 13–16

——, 1971   Christian origins in Britain, *Medieval Archaeol*, **15**, 1–12

——, 1975   The early Christian inscriptions of Dumnonia, *Inst Cornish Stud for Cornwall Archaeol Soc*

Radford, C A R, & Swanton, M J, 1975   *Arthurian sites in the west*

Rahtz, P A, 1966   Cheddar Vicarage, *Somerset Archaeol Natur Hist*, **110**, 52–84

——, 1971   Excavations on Glastonbury Tor, Somerset, 1964–66, *Archaeol J*, **127**, 1–81

——, 1973   Monasteries as settlements, *Scot Archaeol Forum*, **5**, 125–35

——, 1976a   *Excavations at St Mary's Church, Deerhurst, 1971–73*, Counc Brit Archaeol Res Rep, **15**

——, 1976b   The archaeology of the churchyard, in Addyman & Morris 1976, 41–5

——, 1976c   Research directions at Deerhurst, in *ibid*, 60–3

——, 1977   Late Roman cemeteries and beyond, in Reece 1977, 53–64

——, 1978   Grave orientation, *Archaeol J*, **135**, 1–14

Rahtz, P A, & Fowler, P J, 1972   Somerset AD 400–700, in *Archaeology and the landscape* (ed P J Fowler), 187–217

Rahtz, P A, & Hirst, S, 1974   *Beckery Chapel, Glastonbury 1967–8*

Rahtz, P A, & Watts, L, 1979   The end of Roman temples in the west of Britain, in Casey 1979, 183–210

Ramm, H G, 1971   The end of Roman York, in R M Butler 1971, 179–99

——, 1976   Excavations in the church of St Mary Bishophill Senior, York, *Yorkshire Archaeol J*, **48**, 35–68

Reece, R (ed), 1977   *Burial in the Roman world*, Counc Brit Archaeol Res Rep, **22**

Reynolds, N, 1976   The structure of Anglo-Saxon graves, *Antiquity*, **50**, 140–4
RIB   see Collingwood & Wright 1965
Rickard, G, & Hannan, A, 1978   St Mary's Church, Staverton, Northants: survey of churchyard, *Northamptonshire Archaeol*, **13**, 171–5
Rigold, S E, 1960–1   The two primary series of sceattas, *Brit Numis J*, **30**, 6–53
——, 1961   The supposed see of Dunwich, *J Brit Archaeol Ass*, 3 ser, **24**, 55–9
——, 1962–3   The Anglian Cathedral of North Elmham, Norfolk, *Medieval Archaeol*, **6–7**, 67–108
——, 1968   The 'Double Minsters' of Kent and their analogies, *J Brit Archaeol Ass*, **31**, 27–37
——, 1972   Roman Folkestone reconsidered, *Archaeol Cantiana*, **87**, 31–42
——, 1974   Further evidence about the site of 'Dommoc', *J Brit Archaeol Ass*, 3 ser, **37**, 97–102
——, 1977   *Litus Romanum* – the Shore forts as mission stations, in Johnston 1977, 70–5
——, 1978   The principal series of English sceattas, *Brit Numis J*, **47**, 21–30
Rigold, S E, & Metcalf, D M, 1977   A check-list of English finds of sceattas, *ibid*, **46**, 31–52
Rigold, S E, & Webster, L E, 1970   Three Anglo-Saxon disc brooches, *Archaeol Cantiana*, **85**, 1–18
Rivet, A F L (ed), 1969   *The Roman villa in Britain*
Roberts, E, 1977   Moulding analysis and architectural research: the late Middle Ages, *J Soc Architect Hist Great Brit*, **20**, 5–13
Rodwell, K A, & Rodwell, W J, 1976   The investigation of churches in use: a problem in rescue archaeology, in Addyman & Morris 1976, 45–54
Rodwell, W J, 1973   Excavations at Rivenhall Church, Essex, *Antiq J*, **53**, 219–31
——, 1975   Archaeology and the church, *Antiquity*, **49**, 33–42
——, 1976   The archaeological investigation of Hadstock Church, Essex, *Antiq J*, **56**, 55–71
——, 1979   *Wells Cathedral: excavations and discoveries*
—— (ed), 1980   *Temples, churches and religion in Roman Britain*, Brit Archaeol Rep, **77**, 2 vols
Rodwell, W J, & Rodwell, K, 1977   *Historic churches – a wasting asset*, Counc Brit Archaeol Res Rep, **19**
——, & ——, 1980   St Peter, Barton-on-Humber, *Bull Counc Brit Archaeol Churches Committee*, **13**, 6–9
Rogers, A, 1972   Parish boundaries and urban history: two case studies, *J Brit Archaeol Ass*, 3 ser, **35**, 46–64
Rollason, D W, 1978   Lists of saints' resting-places in Anglo-Saxon England, *Anglo-Saxon Engl*, **7**, 61–94
Ross, A, 1967   *Pagan Celtic Britain: studies in iconography and tradition*
——, 1968   Shafts, pits, wells – sanctuaries of the Belgic Britons?, in *Studies in ancient Europe* (eds J M Coles & D Simpson), 255–85
Rowe, G, 1877   Remarks on some monumental stones found at Brompton, Northallerton, Yorkshire, *Assoc Architect Socs Rep Pap*, **14**(1), 61–5
Rowley, R T, 1972   *The Shropshire landscape*
—— (ed), 1974   *Anglo-Saxon settlement and the landscape: papers presented to a Symposium, Oxford 1973*, Brit Archaeol Rep, **6**
St John Hope, W, 1914–15   Recent discoveries in the abbey church of Saint Augustine, *Archaeologia*, **66**, 201–18, 377–400
Saunders, A D, 1978   Excavations in the Church of St Augustine's Abbey, Canterbury, 1955–58, *Medieval Archaeol*, **22**, 25–63
Sawyer, P H, 1968   *Anglo-Saxon charters: an annotated list and bibliography*
——, 1974   Anglo-Saxon settlement: the documentary evidence, in Rowley 1974, 108–19
—— (ed), 1976   *Medieval settlement: continuity and change*
——, 1978a   *From Roman Britain to Norman England*
——, 1978b   Some sources for the history of Viking Northumbria, in *Viking age York and the north* (ed R A Hall), Counc Brit Archaeol Res Rep, **27**, 3–7
——, 1981   Fairs and markets in early medieval England, in *Danish medieval history: new currents* (eds N Skyum-Nielsen & N Lund), 153–68, Copenhagen
Schwarz, E, 1905   Christliche und jüdische Ostertafeln, *Abhandlungen der Königl. Gesellschaft zu Göttingen, Phil.-Hist. Klasse*, **8**(6)
Shoesmith, R, 1980   *Hereford City Excavations 1: Excavations at Castle Green*, Counc Brit Archaeol Res Rep, **36**
Simmons, J, 1959   Brooke Church, Rutland, with notes on Elizabethan church-building, *Trans Leicestershire Archaeol Hist Soc*, **35**, 36–55
Small, A, Thomas, C, & Wilson, D M, *et al*, 1973   *St Ninian's Isle and its treasure*, 2 vols
Smith, A H, 1956a   *English place-name elements*, Engl Place-Name Soc, **25–6**
——, 1956b   Place-names and the Anglo-Saxon settlement, *Proc Brit Acad*, **42**, 67–88

Smith, D J, 1969   The mosaic pavements, in Rivet 1969, 71–126
——, 1978   Regional aspects of the winged corridor villa in Britain, in Todd 1978, 117–48
Smith, L T (ed), 1907   *The itinerary of John Leland in or about the years 1534–43*
Smith, T, 1870   *English gilds*, Early English Text Soc, o ser, **40**
Stanley, A R, 1870   Observations on the Roman sarcophagus lately discovered at Westminster, *Archaeol J*, **27**, 103–9
Stebbing, W P D, 1929   The Jutish cemetery near Finglesham, Kent, *Archaeol Cantiana*, **41**, 115–26
Stein, F, 1968   Pre-Carolingian graves in South Germany, *J Brit Archaeol Ass*, 3 ser, **31**, 1–18
Stenton, F M, 1971   *Anglo-Saxon England*, 3 edn
Storms, G, 1948   *Anglo-Saxon magic*
Talbot, C H, 1970   St Boniface and the German mission, *Stud Church Hist*, **6**, 45–58
Tatton-Brown, T, 1978   Canterbury Cathedral, *Bull Counc Brit Archaeol Churches Committee*, **9**, 6–7
——, 1980   The Roper Chantry in St Dunstan's Church, Canterbury, *Antiq J*, **60**, 227–46
Taylor, C C, 1970   *The making of the English landscape: Dorset*
——, 1974a   *Fieldwork in medieval archaeology*
——, 1974b   The Anglo-Saxon countryside, in Rowley 1974, 5–15
——, 1977   Polyfocal settlement and the English village, *Medieval Archaeol*, **21**, 189–93
——, 1978   Aspects of village mobility in medieval and later times, in *The effect of man on the landscape: the Lowland Zone* (eds S Limbrey & J G Evans), Counc Brit Archaeol Res Rep, **21**, 126–34
Taylor, H M, 1968   Reculver reconsidered, *Archaeol J*, **125**, 291–6
——, 1969a   The special role of Kentish churches in the development of pre-Norman (Anglo-Saxon) architecture, *ibid*, **126**, 192–8
——, 1969b   Lyminge Churches, *ibid*, **126**, 257–60
——, 1969c   The Anglo-Saxon Cathedral Church at Canterbury, *ibid*, **126**, 101–30
——, 1972   Structural criticism: a plea for more systematic study of Anglo-Saxon buildings, *Anglo-Saxon Engl*, **1**, 259–72
——, 1973a   Archaeological investigation of churches in Great Britain, *Antiq J*, **53**, 13–15
——, 1973b   The position of the altar in early Anglo-Saxon churches, *ibid*, **53**, 52–8
——, 1974   Archaeological study of churches, *Theology*, January 1974, 7–14
——, 1975   Tenth-century church building in England and on the continent, in Parsons 1975, 141–68
——, 1976   The foundations of architectural history, in Addyman & Morris 1976, 3–9
——, 1977a   *Repton studies 1: the Anglo-Saxon crypt 1974–76*
——, 1977b   *Deerhurst studies 1: the Anglo-Saxon fabric 1971–76*
——, 1978   *Anglo-Saxon architecture*, **3**
——, 1979   *Repton studies 2: the Anglo-Saxon crypt and church*
Taylor, H M, & Taylor, J, 1965   *Anglo-Saxon architecture*, 2 vols
Thomas, A C, 1967   An early Christian cemetery and chapel on Ardwall Isle, Kirkcudbrightshire, *Medieval Archaeol*, **11**, 127–88
——, 1968   The evidence from north Britain, in Barley & Hanson 1968, 93–122
——, 1971   *The early Christian archaeology of north Britain*
——, 1976   Imported late-Roman Mediterranean pottery in Ireland and western Britain: chronologies and implications, *Proc Roy Ir Acad*, **76**, 245–56
——, 1979   Saint Patrick and fifth-century Britain: an historical model explored, in Casey 1979, 81–101
——, 1980   Churches in late Roman Britain, in Rodwell 1980, 129–64
——, 1981   *Christianity in Roman Britain, to AD 500*
Thomas, A C, Fowler, P J, & Gardner, K, 1969   Lundy, 1969, *Curr Archaeol*, **16**, 138–42
Thompson, E A, 1977   Britain AD 406–410, *Britannia*, **8**, 303–18
Todd, M (ed), 1978   *Studies in the Romano-British villa*
Toynbee, J M C, 1953   Christianity in Roman Britain, *J Brit Archaeol Ass*, 3 ser, **16**, 1–24
——, 1964   The Christian Roman mosaic at Hinton St Mary, Dorset, *Proc Dorset Natur Hist Archaeol Soc*, **85**, 1–10
——, 1968   Pagan motifs and practices in Christian art and ritual in Roman Britain, in Barley & Hanson 1968, 177–92
——, 1971   *Death and burial in the Roman world*
Wacher, J, 1975   *The towns of Roman Britain*
——, 1978   *Roman Britain*
Wade, K, 1980   A settlement site at Wicken Bonhunt, in Buckley 1980, 96–102
Wade-Martins, P, 1975   The origins of rural settlement in East Anglia, in *Recent work in rural archaeology* (ed P J Fowler), 137–57
——, 1980a   *Village sites in the Launditch Hundred*, E Anglian Archaeol Rep, **10**
——, 1980b   *Excavations in North Elmham Park*, E Anglian Archaeol Rep, **9**, 2 vols
Wade-Martins, P, & Morris, R K, 1976   Diocesan archaeological consultants: steps towards a plan for church archaeology in England, in Addyman & Morris 1976, 10–14

Walsh, D A, 1979   A rebuilt cloister at Bordesley Abbey, *J Brit Archaeol Ass*, **132**, 42–9

Walters, B, & Phillips, B, 1979   *Archaeological excavations in Littlecote Park, Wiltshire, 1978: first interim report 1979*

Ward, G, 1932   The list of Saxon churches in the Textus Roffensis, *Archaeol Cantiana*, **44**, 39–59

——, 1933   The lists of Saxon churches in the Domesday Monachorum and White Book of St Augustine, *ibid*, **45**, 60–89

Webster, G, 1969   The future of villa studies, in Rivet 1969, 217–49

Welch, M, 1978   Early Anglo-Saxon Sussex: from *civitas* to shire, in Brandon 1978, 13–35

West, S, & Plouviez, J, 1976   The Roman site at Icklingham, *E Anglian Archaeol*, **3**, 63–126

Westlake, H F, 1919   *Parish gilds of medieval England*

Wheeler, R E M, & Wheeler, T V, 1936   *Verulamium: a Belgic and two Roman cities*

White, H L, 1977   *Monuments and their inscriptions: a practical guide*

Whitelock, D (ed), 1930   *Anglo-Saxon wills*

—— (ed), 1952   *Wulfstan: Sermo Lupi ad Anglos*, 2 edn

—— (ed), 1955   *English historical documents c 500–1042*

——, 1972   The pre-Viking age church in East Anglia, *Anglo-Saxon Engl*, **1**, 1–22

Whitwell, J B, 1964   Torso of life-sized statue ... Ancaster, *Lincolnshire Architect Archaeol Soc Rep Pap*, **11**, 6–8

——, 1970   *Roman Lincolnshire*

Wild, J P, 1978   Villas in the lower Nene Valley, in Todd 1978, 59–69

Williams, G, 1962   *The Welsh Church from Conquest to Reformation*

Williams, H, 1899–1901   see Gildas

Williams, J H, 1979   *St Peter's Street Northampton: excavations 1973–6*, Northampton Devel Corp Archaeol Monogr, **2**

Williams, R J, 1980   Milton Keynes: St Andrew, Great Linford, *Bull Counc Brit Archaeol Churches Committee*, **13**, 18–22

Willis, R, 1842   *Report of a survey of the dilapidated portions of Hereford Cathedral in the year 1841*

——, 1845   *The architectural history of Canterbury Cathedral*

——, 1846   *The architectural history of Winchester Cathedral*

——, 1848   *The architectural history of York Cathedral*

——, 1861a   *The architectural history of Chichester Cathedral*

——, 1861b   On foundations of early buildings, recently discovered in Lichfield Cathedral, *Archaeol J*, **18**, 1–24

——, 1862–3   The crypt and chapter-house of Worcester Cathedral, *Trans Roy Inst Brit Architects*, 1 ser, **13**, 213–25

——, 1863   The architectural history of the cathedral and monastery at Worcester, *Archaeol J*, **20**, 83–133, 254–72, 301–18

Wilson, C, 1977   *The shrines of St William of York*

Wilson, D M, 1956   The initial excavation of an Anglo-Saxon cemetery at Melbourn, Cambridgeshire, *Proc Cambridge Antiq Soc*, **49**, 29–41

——, 1967   The Vikings' relationship with Christianity in northern England, *J Brit Archaeol Ass*, 3 ser, **30**, 37–46

—— (ed), 1976   *The archaeology of Anglo-Saxon England*

Wilson, D R, 1968   An early Christian cemetery at Ancaster, in Barley & Hanson 1968, 196–9

Wilson, M, 1969   The Hwicce, in P A Barker 1969, 20–5

Wilson, P A, 1966   Romano-British and Welsh Christianity: continuity or discontinuity? *Welsh Hist Rev*, **3**, 5–21, 103–20

——, 1978   Eaglesfield: the place, the name, the burials, *Trans Cumberland Westmorland Antiq Archaeol Soc*, **78**, 47–54

Wilson, P R, 1979   Lichfield, St Michael's church and St Mary's church, *Bull Counc Brit Archaeol Churches Committee*, **11**, 6–7

Winterbottom, M, 1978   see Gildas

Wood, I N, 1979a   *Avitus of Viennes: religion and culture in the Auvergne and the Rhone valley 470–530*, unpublished PhD thesis, Univ Oxford

——, 1979b   Early Merovingian devotion in town and country, *Stud Church Hist*, **16**, 61–76

——, forthcoming   The end of Roman Britain: continental evidence and parallels

Wright, R P, & Jackson, K H, 1968   A late inscription from Wroxeter, *Antiq J*, **48**, 296–300

Wright, T (ed), 1843   *Letters relating to the suppression of the monasteries*, Camden Soc, **26**

Wuilleumier, P, Déniau, J, Formige, J, & Albrand, E-L, 1947   *Le Cloître de Saint-André-le-Bas*

Yates, W N, 1973a   The 'Age of the Saints' in Carmarthenshire: a study of church dedications, *Carmarthenshire Antiq*, **9**, 53–81

——, 1973b   The distribution and proportion of Celtic and non-Celtic church dedications in Wales, *J Hist Soc Church Wales*, **23**, 5–17

Zarnecki, G, 1951   *English Romanesque sculpture 1066–1140*